Discovering Orson Welles

The publisher gratefully acknowledges the generous support of Edmund and Jeannie Kaufman as members of the Literati Circle of University of California Press.

Discovering Orson Welles

Jonathan Rosenbaum

UNIVERSITY OF CALIFORNIA PRESS

BERKELEY   LOS ANGELES   LONDON

University of California Press, one of the most distinguished university presses in the United States, enriches lives around the world by advancing scholarship in the humanities, social sciences, and natural sciences. Its activities are supported by the UC Press Foundation and by philanthropic contributions from individuals and institutions. For more information, visit www.ucpress.edu.

University of California Press
Berkeley and Los Angeles, California

University of California Press, Ltd.
London, England

Library of Congress Cataloging-in-Publication Data
Rosenbaum, Jonathan.
  Discovering Orson Welles / Jonathan Rosenbaum.
    p. cm.
  Includes bibliographical references and index.
  ISBN 978-0-520-24738-3 (cloth : alk. paper)
  ISBN 978-0-520-25123-6 (pbk. : alk. paper)
    1. Welles, Orson, 1915–1985—Criticism and interpretation.   I. Title.
PN1998.3.W45R67   2007
791.43023'3092—dc22   2006021749

Manufactured in the United States of America
16   15   14   13   12   11   10   09   08   07
10   9   8   7   6   5   4   3   2   1

This book is printed on New Leaf EcoBook 50, a 100% recycled fiber of which 50% is de-inked post-consumer waste, processed chlorine-free. EcoBook 50 is acid-free and meets the minimum requirements of ANSI/ASTM D5634-01 *(Permanence of Paper).*♾

To my fellow Wellesians—
above all, the long-termers: Bill, Catherine, Ciro, Esteve,
François, Gary, Jim, Joe, and Oja—and especially to the
fond memory of Gary—the most selfless and generous of all
Welles facilitators, who made the last third of the Welles
filmography possible, and who died just as this book was going
to press

Contents

Acknowledgments

The author's thanks go to those who have suggested or encouraged a book of this kind—including, among others, Frank Brady, Ronald Gottesman, Clinton Heydin, James Naremore, and Yuval Taylor—and to those who have facilitated its writing and assembly, including Piet Adriaanse, Jr., Michael Anderegg, Geoff Andrew, Catherine Benamou, Janet Bergstrom, Jean-Pierre Berthomé, Gheraro Casale, Issa Clubb, Peggy Daub, Abb Dickson, Stefan Drössler, Bernard Eisenschitz, Chris Feder, Robert Fischer, Mary Francis, Ciro Giorgini, Gary Graver, Carlos F. Heredero, Oja Kodar, Bill Krohn, Joseph McBride, José Maria Prado, Marco Müller, James Naremore, Kalicia Pivirotto, Esteve Riambau, Hans Schmid, François Thomas, Peter Tonguette, Frank Uhle, Leslie Weisman, Bart Whaley, other employees of the Filmmuseum München, the Filmoteca Españole, and the Special Collections Library, University of Michigan, Ann Arbor, Michigan, and editors who assisted me on the original publications of these articles, including those at A Cappella Press, *Chicago Reader, Cineaste, Cinematograph,* Criterion, *Film Comment, Film Quarterly, Persistence of Vision, Premiere,* Santa Teresa Press, *Sight and Sound, Time Out* (London), and *Trafic.*

Introduction

The process-oriented methods that permitted at least four Welles features
and a number of short works to be left unfinished are easier to understand
than they would be if we adopted the mental habits of producers, which is
exactly what more and more critics today seem to be doing; but that is no
comfort to those of us eager to understand, and eager as critics always are to
have the last word, which we are not about to have with this filmmaker. At
least our direction, as always, is laid out for us: as long as one frame of film
by the greatest filmmaker of the modern era is moldering in vaults, our work
is not done. It is the last challenge, and the biggest joke, of an oeuvre that has
always had more designs on us than we could ever have on it.

Bill Krohn's cautionary words in *Cahiers du cinéma*'s special *"hors série"*
Orson Welles issue in 1986 offer a useful motto for the present collection
of essays, whose own title, *Discovering Orson Welles,* suggests an ongoing
process that necessarily rules out completion and closure—the two mythical absolutes that Welles enthusiasts and scholars seem to hunger for the
most. Accepting this ground rule is a prerequisite for understanding both
the form and content of what follows: a chronological and historically
minded ordering of still-evolving research, and one that considers the
very notion of a "definitive" view of Welles an ideological and practical
roadblock, a casualty of what might be called the ever-popular Rosebud
Syndrome. Consequently, I can't pretend to any sort of completeness
even in relation to the 13 features released during Welles's lifetime; there

1

are no extended treatments here of THE MAGNIFICENT AMBERSONS, THE STRANGER, THE LADY FROM SHANGHAI, MACBETH, CHIMES AT MIDNIGHT, or THE IMMORTAL STORY, and, disproportionately, there are several devoted to TOUCH OF EVIL and F FOR FAKE. Well over half of the pieces are either book reviews or discussions of works by Welles that are not usually considered part of his canon: unrealized screenplays, unfinished works, or, in a few cases, films such as THE FOUNTAIN OF YOUTH and FILMING OTHELLO that have eluded canonization simply because they aren't readily available.

The unwieldiness and unruliness of the Welles oeuvre as certain parts become uncovered (or remain obstinately lost or unseeable) have confounded many biographers and critics, some of whom have opted for ignoring the existence of this extra material—or even, in the case of David Thomson, explicitly expressing their hopes that it will go away. Yet the first question many nonspecialists ask me is when, if ever, they are going to be able to see THE OTHER SIDE OF THE WIND, DON QUIXOTE, or THE DEEP. No less characteristically, even on those occasions when I'm able to answer their queries at least partially or provisionally, their eyes often start to glaze over before I can get halfway through my explanation.

This is of course emblematic of what it sometimes means to chart the labyrinths of Welles research, which most journalists understandably (if lamentably) prefer to circumvent or leap over. Nonetheless, I sympathize with the desire to have these conundrums sorted out in bite-size form— expressed most recently by one of the first readers of this book, who asked me to be considerate of nonspecialists and start off with (a) the state of the "unseen/unknown Welles" legacy today, and (b) the state of Welles studies today.

The way I've responded to this request is to write a version of (a) that includes "known" as well as "unknown" Welles films and place this in an appendix (where such information can more easily be consulted rather than read as a narrative) while incorporating a very modest version of (b) in this introduction. I hasten to add that portions of this material can already be found elsewhere in the book, but I recognize that up-to-date overviews are also helpful.

I also want to stress, however, that most of this book is specifically designed to follow the labyrinths, and to give some impression of what it means to follow them. Therefore, readers who choose to read the 26 essays, reviews, or (in three cases) fragments collected here while skipping the connecting commentaries between most of them will encounter a fair number of errors, misconceptions, and mistaken paths, and will moreover be missing a particular narrative and unfolding argument that are only partially inscribed in the texts themselves. (In a few cases, the commentaries are even longer than the pieces they introduce.) It would be grossly oversimplifying matters to call this narrative and argument the only ones that are being offered here, but one could still maintain that a proper understanding of them serves as a useful prerequisite to grasping most of the others.

From the beginning, Welles scholarship has been undermined by the seductiveness of diverse kinds of journalistic shortcuts, the perceived need to fill in blank spaces in order to offer a coherent picture of the career and oeuvre. Versions of the same impulse have played substantial roles in re-editing, reshooting, remixing, abbreviating, simplifying, streamlining, misrepresenting, or otherwise short-changing the films themselves, almost always with the claim of making them more accessible or marketable. As a filmmaker who delighted for most of his career in the very process of continuous revision, either allowing or being allowed to arrive at a definitive form for one of his features only a few times, Welles challenges commodification like few other directors. But this hasn't prevented critics, journalists, biographers, and scholars as well as producers from attempting to halt that flow of metamorphosis and to freeze the forms and meanings into something comprehensible and finite. I'm just as guilty of this effort as some of my colleagues, though the 33 years of carrying out the effort represented in this collection have also persuaded me that it can remain a legitimate activity only if one agrees to keep certain conclusions tentative and certain options open.

A common way of explaining this problem is to blame much of it on Welles's own flair for invention and spin. If one adds to this the taste for theatrical hyperbole that creeps into many of the earliest journalistic accounts as well as press releases of Welles, one has basically defined the slippery slope of the earliest and most primitive phase of writing about him, as well as the tendency ever since to counter these exaggerations with heavy doses of skepticism. As a partisan, I'm often inclined to view this scoffing mainly as a lazy and expedient solution for his less friendly biographers, betraying a certain impatience that comes from their frustration at hammering on doors that remain locked. But I also have to acknowledge that biographical certainties regarding Welles are often difficult to come by—especially if one considers the amount of misinformation that still carries a great deal of currency among nonspecialists.

Without claiming for a moment that Welles always told the truth, I think most accounts of him as a compulsive liar tend to be both exaggerated and self-serving. Sometimes the distortions aren't his at all but those of his colleagues, employees, and/or commentators. I include myself in this company, and one reason for letting many of my own errors stand while calling attention to them is to show, at least in some cases, how I managed to arrive at them.

So rather than systematically revise or correct these pieces (apart from the odd typo, a few minor cosmetic adjustments, and restoring some passages that were cut prior to their original publications), I've elected to reprint them in something close to their original forms—as part of a record of my evolving and still-fallible research into Welles's work and career, pointing out various limitations, problems, and fresh information that I've subsequently become aware of as the book proceeds. By necessity, and in keeping with much of my other writing, part of the recent commentary is autobiographical in nature, tracing certain steps in both my development as a writer and critic and my personal as well as professional engagements with the Welles legacy, including some of Welles's collaborators and employees.

One of the drawbacks of this approach is a lot of repetition; even the above quotation from Bill Krohn can be found elsewhere in this book (see chapter 14), and other evidences of a recycling journalist will recur on a regular basis. (Most flagrantly, this can be seen in all the ways I've managed to spin out my only meeting with Welles, lasting scarcely more than an hour, over the course of this entire book, all the way from the second article to the last.) I apologize for this irritation, which is bound to become especially vexing for anyone who reads the book straight through. But I see no way of avoiding it without meddling with the status of these texts as part of an overall historical progression. I'm interested in charting the evolution of my understanding of Welles conceptually and factually as well as rhetorically and critically, including the ways I've refined and developed certain elements, repeated some others, and dropped still others en route. The reason for this interest is in part a desire to clarify how my positions have taken shape over time, and in part a more general (and, I believe, Wellesian) desire to view "discovery" as an overall and ongoing activity more than as a terminal goal.

Although most of my writing on Welles is reprinted here, I've excluded the passages written for *This Is Orson Welles* (2nd ed., New York: Da Capo, 1998)—a compendium of interviews, documents, and career summary by Welles and Peter Bogdanovich that I edited and annotated—as well as some other contextual material, including my response to an essay by Robin Bates in *Cinema Journal* and my introduction to a shortened version of Welles's memo to Universal Pictures about the re-editing of TOUCH OF EVIL.[1] Some of the material found in those texts, however, has been recast in new material written for this volume, and I have generally also tried to summarize here the most recent findings of Welles scholarship as well as my most recent critical conclusions—with full awareness that many of these "up to date" entries are likely to be superseded by further discoveries and assessments.

■

As indicated above, the earliest books about Welles tend to be either promotional (as typified by Roy Alexander Fowler's in 1946 and Peter Noble's in 1956) or efforts to undercut that promotional tendency (as in the books on Welles by Charles Higham published in 1970 and 1985), so that the pattern of usually being either partisan or adversarial is firmly established from the outset. In chapter 20, while arguing from the vantage point of a partisan, I try to theorize about some of the motivations for the adversarial positions. But over the next few paragraphs, I think it's more important to interrupt the partisan rhetoric that informs the remainder of this book and, while attempting to be more distanced from the issues involved, emphasize that these dialectical positions often tend to give impetus to one another.

To complicate matters in the history of Welles studies, sometimes the same writer has taken different positions towards Welles on separate occasions. The clearest instance of this is Pauline Kael, who went from a passionate defense of Welles as an inspired independent in CHIMES AT MIDNIGHT ("Orson Welles: There Ain't No Way," *The New Republic,* June 24, 1967) to an attack on him as a credit thief (while acknowledging both his charm as an actor and his flamboyance as a director) regarding CITIZEN KANE ("Raising KANE," *The New Yorker,* February 20 and 27, 1971).

Significantly, both these essays are reprinted in Kael's final collection, *For Keeps* (New York: Dutton, 1994), which omits her no less celebrated attack on Andrew Sarris and his "auteur theory" ("Circles and Squares: Joys and Sarris," *Film Quarterly,* Spring 1963). The juxtaposition of these decisions is pertinent because "Raising KANE" was Kael's final and most extended polemical foray against auteur theory—motivated by a clear desire to topple Sarris's exaltation of the director, especially the American director, as the ultimate criterion of value—and to do so within a mainstream context in which most readers wouldn't even be aware of this secondary agenda.[2]

Kael's essay was also designed to be read as an entertaining, anecdotal account of the making of CITIZEN KANE that restored glory to its neglected and principal screenwriter, and she deliberately skewed her research by speaking only to John Houseman about the script's authorship and ignoring everyone else, including Welles—who maintained in *This Is Orson Welles,* published over two decades later, that Houseman himself deserved some credit as a "junior writer" on the script who "made some very important contributions" (2nd ed., New York: Da Capo, p. 55). Kael's reasoning appears to have been that because Welles was viewed as the ultimate auteur and thus the veritable linchpin of auteur theory, any argument that proved he wasn't really the author of his most celebrated film could serve to topple that theory. And, to be fair, it was certainly true that Welles had tended to minimize the major role of Mankiewicz in writing the script—a fact that had already been noted by even such a partisan and pro-Welles critic as Joseph McBride (as well as by Houseman himself—who was generally if erroneously perceived by most readers at the time, including myself, as pro-Welles).

Kael, in any case, isn't the only critic to have become relatively adversarial towards Welles after having been more supportive. (Simon Callow, by contrast, can be said to have moved from a more adversarial position in the first volume of his projected three-volume biography, *Orson Welles: The Road to Xanadu*, to a more supportive position in the second, *Orson Welles: Hello Americans*—at least insofar as one can credit him with either position in an enterprise that strives overall for balance.) While it would be inaccurate to call Robert L. Carringer's *The Making of* CITIZEN KANE (Berkeley: University of California Press, 1985) a partisan study in relation to Welles, it's hard to avoid the conclusion that his lengthy "Oedipus in Indianapolis" in THE MAGNIFICENT AMBERSONS: *A Reconstruction* is adversarial, at least in the sense that all the "questionable judgments and rash actions" in Carringer's account of AMBERSONS are assigned to Welles, while the judgments and actions of the RKO executives are generally taken to be beyond dispute. But it also should be noted that, despite Carringer's contention that Kael's account of the authorship of the KANE script is "a flagrant misrepresentation," given all the contrary evidence in the Mercury files and elsewhere, he also concludes in both his Welles books that Welles's artistic success was predicated on the quality of his collaborators—high in the case of KANE and not high enough in the case of AMBERSONS. Thus it could be argued that his position towards Welles in both books is inflected by a view of Hollywood cinema as a collaborative, industrial art, in contradistinction to Sarris's auteurism.

By the same token, the more partisan, pro-Welles books—including André Bazin's *Orson Welles: A Critical View*, James Naremore's *The Magic World of Orson Welles*, Barbara Leaming's and Frank Brady's biographies, all three of Joseph McBride's books about Welles (the most recent of which, *What Ever Happened to Orson Welles?*, I've read only in manuscript), and Welles and Peter Bogdanovich's *This Is Orson Welles*—are inflected with auteurist biases (as is David Thomson's almost entirely adversarial *Rosebud*, just to confound the overly neat divisions that I've been sketching). Much the same could be said of all the most recent Welles books I've consulted in some form as this book goes to press, including *What Ever Happened to Orson Welles?*, *Hello Americans*, Jean-Pierre Berthomé and François Thomas's *Welles au travail* (Paris: Cahiers du cinéma, 2006), the still-unpublished but invaluable volumes of Todd Tarbox and Bart Whaley that are cited below, and even Catherine L. Benamou's more academic and postauteurist *IT'S ALL TRUE: Orson Welles's Pan-American Odyssey* (Berkeley: University of California Press, 2007), scheduled to appear shortly before this volume.

■

There are many booby-traps lying in wait for all Welles researchers, and many of them can be traced back in one way or another to Welles's theatricality—not necessarily or invariably his own theatrical spin on certain events in his life and career (although this obviously plays a role), but in many cases the theatricality with which he is viewed by others. Oja Kodar, his companion, muse, and collaborator, recalls him coming home one day and reporting his dismay that Joseph Cotten, one of his oldest and dearest friends, had admitted to him that he'd been telling some tale about him to others that he knew was untrue because it "made such a good story"—and the fact that I'm using quotation marks here based on hearsay is a perfect, if relatively innocuous, illustration of what I mean. In terms of historical accuracy, there are far too many "good stories" when it comes to Welles—one reason among many others why the prospect of writing another Welles biography has never appealed to me.

A more telling example of this problem can be seen in the historical treatment of Isaac Woodard Jr., which to my mind represents a key, neglected moment in Welles's career, if not in his film career. The lack of an obvious connection to Welles's film career is part of the point I wish to make: with the exception of a few notable books, such as Michael Anderegg's *Orson Welles, Shakespeare, and Popular Culture* (New York: Columbia University Press, 1999), Catherine L. Benamou's *IT'S ALL TRUE: Orson Welles's Pan-American Odyssey,* Simon Callow's *Orson Welles,* vol. 2: *Hello Americans* (New York: Viking, 2006), Youssef Ishaghpour's *Orson Welles Cinéaste, Une Caméra Visible* (Paris: Éditions de la Différence, 2001), James Naremore's *The Magic World of Orson Welles* (2nd ed., Dallas: Southern Methodist University Press, 1989), and Bart Whaley's lamentably unpublished *Orson Welles: The Man Who Was Magic* (2005), most ambitious Welles studies have been unresponsive to the wider aspects of culture apart from film that Welles himself was engaged with throughout his life—that is to say, they're more parochial than Welles himself was. For this reason, while researching Welles's career for *This Is Orson Welles*, which I did without the resources of the Internet, I found that I could often make significant discoveries by checking the indexes of some books that had no apparent relation to film. Even Welles's FBI file was helpful in pinpointing many of his leftist activities during the 30s—so much so that I was sorely tempted to include J. Edgar Hoover on the acknowledgments page. By tracing the representations and misrepresentations of the Woodard incident through some of the standard texts on Welles, I think a few points about Welles research in general can be made.

On February 12, 1946, Woodard, a black veteran who had served for 15 months in the South Pacific and earned one battle star, received his honorable discharge. Hours later, on his way home, he got into an altercation with a white bus driver in South Carolina about the time allotted for a rest stop. At the next stop, the driver summoned two police officers, one of whom proceeded to beat Woodard so brutally with a blackjack that he was blinded in both his eyes.

Over five months later, Welles appeared on his weekly 15-minute radio show, *Orson Welles Commentaries*—the last extended radio show that he had originating in the U.S.—and read an affidavit from the NAACP signed by Woodard that described the incident, including Woodard's subsequent arrest and fine. He then gave an impassioned speech promising to root out the officer responsible for the blinding that's probably the most powerful piece of political and social rhetoric I've ever heard him utter—impressive both as a piece of writing and as a performance. I've played a recording of this broadcast on many occasions as part of presentations of some of Welles's important lesser-known activities, always to great effect. (Other works I've presented in such programs have included such earlier radio shows as *His Honor the Mayor* and *Huckleberry Finn* and such later short films as THE FOUNTAIN OF YOUTH and his nine-minute F FOR FAKE trailer.)

The speech initially prompted a flood of letters (both pro and con) that can still be read in the Lilly Library's Welles collection in Bloomington, Indiana. Woodard became the major focus of the show over the following month, and his case more generally became a *cause célèbre.* An additional controversy was sparked because Welles initially misidentified the town where the incident occurred as Aiken rather than Batesburg, leading to threatened lawsuits and angry demonstrations in Aiken, where Welles's current film as a star, TOMORROW IS FOREVER, was boycotted in protest. A New York benefit for Woodard, held in Lewisohn Stadium—where Milton Berle, contralto Carol Brice, Woody Guthrie (who'd composed a song about Woodard for the occasion), Billie Holiday, Cab Calloway, Joe Louis, and Paul Robeson were among the featured celebrities—was attended by some 20,000 people. The officer responsible for the blinding, Lynwood Schull, was eventually uncovered and brought to trial, but an all-white jury acquitted him, a decision greeted in the courtroom with cheers.

As nearly as I can determine, the above is more or less what happened. But turn to the Welles biographies of Barbara Leaming and Charles Higham (both reviewed in chapter 9), which contain the first and lengthiest accounts of the Woodard story I've come across, and one reads nothing about the acquittal (which occurred, I should stress, after Welles's radio show was terminated by its sponsor). The impression left in both books is that justice was served; Higham even reports that "Shull was sentenced to one year in prison," and I repeated this error in *This Is Orson Welles,* suggesting that the reader go to Leaming's book for more details, and also misspelling Woodard's last name as "Woodward" in the bargain. (I already knew that "Woodard" is the correct spelling, so I'm baffled at how this error crept into both editions of the book—to be discovered by me only when I sat down to write this.)[3] And Whaley's 656-page manuscript, which spells the name correctly, repeats Higham's and my error about the one-year sentence.[4] Judging by their indexes, there are no references to Woodard in the Welles books of Frank Brady (reviewed in chapter 12), David Thomson (reviewed in chapter 20), or Peter Conrad, or in *The Encyclopedia of Orson Welles;* and there are only passing references in Naremore's *The Magic World of Orson Welles* and Paul Heyer's recent *The Medium and the Magician: Orson Welles, The Radio Years, 1934–1952,* both of which also misspell the name. Heyer, I should add, is less impressed by Welles's speech than me: "One hears in his voice a strident and dramatic tone—ham in the service of justice—that must have alienated some listeners, despite the merits of his argument."[5] Bret Wood's 1990 *Orson Welles: A Bio-Bibliography,* reviewed in chapter 13, spells the name correctly and accurately summarizes the first broadcast, but doesn't touch on the story's outcome. In fact, it's only in Callow's recent *Hello Americans* that the full story finally receives its due.

How, then, did I already know that Shull was acquitted before reading Callow? From Welles himself, in another unpublished text—bolstered by the logical conclusion, which I should have reached while reading Leaming and Higham, that *any* jury in South Carolina in 1946 would surely have been all white, and that the odds of an all-white jury convicting a white police officer of such a crime in that period would have been slim. So I'd argue that the stirring theatricality of Welles's broadcasts at the time, just before his show was canceled (and before a final verdict was reached), helped to predispose me to perpetuate this misinformation.

The unpublished text is a fascinating draft of a book by Todd Tarbox, grandson of Welles's boarding-school teacher and mentor Roger Hill, called *Standing in a Hammock* and subsequently retitled *Orson Welles and Roger Hill: A Friendship in Four Acts.* Towards the end of their lives, Hill and Welles recorded many of their conversations, on the phone and in person, with the idea of eventually turning them into a book; the audiotapes were willed to Tarbox, who transcribed and edited them and supplemented them with other materials from his grandfather and various other sources. The two pages of the 272-page manuscript that are devoted to Woodard, which also include excerpts from Welles's speech, conclude as follows:

Roger: Was justice served?
Orson: Sadly, no. Though the Department of Justice took the case to trial, and after fifteen minutes of deliberation, an all-white jury acquitted the cop. I'll never forget a line from the defense attorney's closing argument to the jury, "If you rule against my client, then let South Carolina secede again."[6]

I've subsequently learned, from more recent research, that deliberations lasted twenty-five minutes and that the D.A.'s line was "If siding against federal government prosecution meant the state should secede from the Union as it did in 1860, then it should do so again"—neither of which discredits Hill's memory of Welles's account as a responsible paraphrase of the proceedings. So I find his conclusion to the story far more authoritative than most of those I've encountered in print in books about him, and the fact that Tarbox hasn't yet succeeded in finding a publisher doesn't—and shouldn't—invalidate what his book has to say and offer. On the other hand, if I'd Googled Woodard on the Internet, without reference to Welles, as I was unable to do while researching *This Is Orson Welles,* I would have quickly discovered the entire story. (At the Welles conference held at the Locarno film festival in 2005, I saw Robert Fisher and Richard France's fascinating 30-minute promo for a projected 75-minute documentary on the subject, CITIZEN OF AMERICA: ORSON WELLES AND THE BALLAD OF ISAAC WOODARD, that promises to be close to definitive—even though, paradoxically, and for strictly cinematic reasons, it can't incorporate the original broadcast.)

Similarly, it should be noted that some of the most valuable resources for Welles researchers have relatively low profiles, especially for American readers; one recent example is Stefan Drössler's trilingual collection *The Unknown Orson Welles* (Belleville/Filmmuseum München, 2004), which grew out of the Munich Film Archives' recent restoration work and two Welles conferences held under their auspices. This contains, among other things, the first appearance in English of Bill Krohn's 1982 interview with Welles—perhaps the last lengthy one of substance that he gave in English—and a compilation of Drössler's own interviews with Kodar between 2000 and 2002. It also includes the most complete accounts I've read of DON QUIXOTE and THE DREAMERS, by Esteve Riambau and Peter Tonguette, respectively.[7]

By the same token, the fact that so many of Welles's unfinished or fugitive works remain unavailable to the general public shouldn't diminish (*or* enhance, for that matter) their intrinsic worth. Unless one assumes, as certain academics and journalists do, that the film industry is almost always right, there is no necessary correlation between commercial availability and artistic value. Furthermore, the fact that Welles kept much of his work beyond the usual commercial margins has often led to the neglect of this work. (An embarrassing key example of this would be my own unwitting, absent-minded exclusion of CHIMES AT MIDNIGHT in the list of 1000 favorite films appended to my most recent collection, *Essential Cinema.*)[8] But consumption habits die hard, and even some of the works dealt with or alluded to in this book that *are* available—such as AROUND THE WORLD WITH ORSON WELLES and THE DOMINICI AFFAIR (on DVDs), or the unfilmed screenplays of THE BIG BRASS RING and THE CRADLE WILL ROCK (both out of print, but readily accessible for anyone willing to look for them)—are routinely treated as if they weren't (that is, mainly excluded from the Welles canon, and commonly regarded as beyond-the-pale esoterica). Multiregional DVD players can be purchased for a pittance at outlets such as Radio Shack, and, at the moment I'm writing this, acceptable DVDs of THE TRIAL and CHIMES AT MIDNIGHT and a less acceptable DVD of THE IMMORTAL STORY (including both the English and French versions, but not, alas, the final cuts in either case) can be ordered respectively from France, Spain, and Italy without spending an inordinate amount of money. There's also an essential three-disc box set devoted to Welles's MACBETH that has just been issued in France, including both Welles cuts and the 1940 Mercury production of the play recorded for 78 RPM records (as well as a newsreel record of the last few minutes of the 1936 *Voodoo Macbeth* staged in Harlem). But many viewers are still too mired in conventional patterns of consumption to consider such possibilities thinkable, much less viable.

As an example of the kind of negative obfuscation Welles's life and career are almost routinely subjected to in the mainstream—especially in the trade press, whose values have dominated the mainstream press in recent years—let me quote from the beginning of a review in *Variety* of a one-act play about Welles that premiered in 2000, one of the countless Wellesian spinoffs that seem to crop up nowadays on a regular basis:

> Misspent genius has its own prodigiousness, and there's no better emblem of that quality than the life of Orson Welles. Beginning his public career at 23 with a famous radio hoax, *War of the Worlds* [*sic*], which launched the country into waves of extraterrestrial hysteria, and going on to make one indelible film, CITIZEN KANE, as well as minor masterpieces and half-remembered turkeys, Welles lived far beyond his golden moment to see his reputation and fortunes decline. At the end of his life, he was the voice of Paul Masson wine and the last slender resource of latenight TV hosts whose more desirable guests bagged at the final hour. Overfed and overexposed, Welles died a wash-up.[. . .]9

Without even speculating on what "minor masterpieces" and "half-remembered turkeys" the reviewer has in mind—or to what degree such works as CHIMES AT MIDNIGHT or F FOR FAKE (not to mention DON QUIXOTE or THE OTHER SIDE OF THE WIND) might have contributed to Welles's alleged "overexposure"—I think the main point to be made about this characteristic invective is that its basis is ideological rather than reflective of any desire for information about what Welles was up to during his later years.[10] In this respect, it resembles the myths underlying various contemporary statements about the love of "the French" for Jerry Lewis (a phenomenon whose limited factual basis is by now about three decades out of date) and "the uncut GREED" (perceived as a single and fixed entity rather than as a series of versions). This suggests that a refutation of such myths becomes possible only when a minimal amount of curiosity about their factual basis can be said to exist.

■

A final note on the styling of film titles in this book. As in my previous books published by University of California Press (*Moving Places: A Life at the Movies, Placing Movies: The Practice of Film Criticism,* and *Movies as Politics*), all film titles, including the titles of unrealized film projects and screenplays, are printed in roman in small capital letters, while the titles of books, plays, and radio and TV shows are capitalized more conventionally and are in italics. If this procedure tends to privilege actual and theoretical film texts over other kinds of texts, this is a bias that, for better and for worse, tends to inform most contemporary studies of Welles.

J. R.

December 2006

Notes

1. *Cinema Journal* 26, no. 4 (summer 1987): 60–64; Introduction, "Memo à la Universal," translated by Julien Deleuze, *Trafic,* no. 4 (Autumn 1992): 39–41; "Memo to Universal," *Film Quarterly* 46, no. 1 (Fall 1992): i–xx. I've also omitted a second 1992 article about the refurbished OTHELLO, "Improving Mr. Welles," that appeared in the October 1992 *Sight and Sound* and doesn't add much of substance to "OTHELLO Goes Hollywood," as well as liner notes for the Voyager laserdiscs of both the unrefurbished OTHELLO and CONFIDENTIAL REPORT. Similarly, I've omitted a brief piece about the re-edited TOUCH OF EVIL written for the January 2002 issue of *American Movie Classics Magazine,* a piece about an expanded version of GREED that contains many references to Welles ("Fables of the Reconstruction: The Four-Hour GREED," reprinted in my collec-

tion *Essential Cinema: On the Necessity of Film Canons* [Baltimore and London: Johns Hopkins University Press, 2004], 3–12); a recent article, "Orson Welles at 90," that appeared in the special "auteur" issue of *Stop Smiling*, no. 23 (2005): 54–59; and "The Corinth Version: The Elusive MR. ARKADIN," my liner notes included in Criterion's MR. ARKADIN DVD box set (released in April 2006).

2. Some friends of Kael have suggested to me that her decision to omit "Circles and Squares" from *For Keeps* was motivated by a desire not to cause further grief to Sarris, who had already suffered a great deal from her invective and its wide impact. Although she may have been aware of both the grief that "Raising KANE" had caused Welles and the misleading factual basis of some of her arguments, Welles had been dead for almost a decade when *For Keeps* was published, perhaps reducing her sense of potential injury; and her reluctance to correct or acknowledge factual errors when she republished her pieces was unfortunately a constant throughout her professional career.

3. See *Orson Welles* by Barbara Leaming (New York: Viking Penguin, 1985), 402–404; *Orson Welles: The Rise and Fall of an American Genius* by Charles Higham (New York: St. Martin's Press, 1985), 233–234, 238; and *This Is Orson Welles* by Orson Welles and Peter Bogdanovich, edited by Jonathan Rosenbaum, 2nd ed. (New York: Da Capo, 1998), 398, 399, 417.

4. As explained by its editor, Susan Aykroyd, the "special limited printing 'not for sale' Magician's Edition" of Whaley's book, which I've seen only on CD, has remained unpublished to date due to his understandable unwillingness to cut it by half (the suggestion of the only publisher to date that has proposed bringing it out) before other Welles scholars have had a chance to evaluate it with its full documentation. (Postscript: Just as I was about to return the page proofs of this book in December 2006, a magician friend, Allan Zola Kranzck, emailed me the spectacular news that Whaley's book has now become available online in PDF form at www.lybrary.com/orson-welles-magic-p-400 .html, for $30.)

5. Lanham, MD: Rowman & Littlefield, 2005, 192.

6. My thanks to Tarbox for granting me permission to quote this passage.

7. Peter Prescott Tonguette—the most vigorous and painstaking of the younger Welles scholars, who has specialized in such late, unfinished projects as THE DREAMERS and THE MAGIC SHOW—has a book that promises to be invaluable: *Orson Welles Remembered: Interviews with His Actors, Editors, Cinematographers and Magicians*, scheduled for publication by McFarland & Company in 2007.

8. *Essential Cinema: On the Necessity of Film Canons* (Baltimore: Johns Hopkins University Press, 2004).

9. Review by Pamela Renner of stage production, *War of the Worlds*, posted on October 6, 2000, and accessed at www.variety.com.

10. According to my friend Robert Koehler, at a Preservation Festival held at UCLA in August 2006, Joseph McBride discussed the popular American notion that "Welles was his own worst enemy" and then added, "I think that his biggest enemy was capitalism."

1

I Missed It at the Movies

Objections to "Raising KANE"

The first item in this collection—written in late 1971 as an article for Film
Comment *but run as a book review—is one of the first pieces of film criticism I
ever published. It also proved to be one of the most consequential for me personally. Among its probable consequences was the blocking of any possible friendship with Pauline Kael—a writer I had admired and learned from, in spite of the
objections stated here, and whose own early polemical forays in* I Lost It at the
Movies *undoubtedly exerted some influence on my own, as my title suggests. (I
was surprised to hear from friends of hers much later that this article had such a
negative effect on her; I had wrongly and perhaps naïvely assumed that because
she had been so adroit at such polemical forays herself, in a spirit of fair play, she
would have been more tolerant of one waged against her own writing.) Another
possible (and more important) consequence was getting invited to lunch by
Orson Welles in Paris a few months later, after writing him a letter asking a few
questions about his first feature film project—the subject of chapter 2.*

*I don't know if Welles ever read my attack on "Raising KANE," and Kael's ar-
ticle never came up during our lunch. In my letter I alluded to having just published such an attack, which might have bolstered his good will if he hadn't already been aware of it. In late June 2006—during a brief visit to the newly
acquired "Everybody's Orson Welles" collections at the University of Michigan
(see my introduction to chapter 17) to select some images for the cover design of
this book—I was delighted to discover that the voluminous Welles papers previously held by Oja Kodar contained a copy of my attack on "Raising KANE." But*

I have no way of knowing whether Welles acquired this before or after our meeting. It seems likelier that he acquired it afterwards—not only because he never mentioned it, but also because my first paragraph contains a phrase that might well have dissuaded him from reading any further: "[Kael's] basic contention, that the script of [CITIZEN] KANE is almost solely the work of Herman J. Mankiewicz, seems well-supported and convincing."

I posted my letter on a Saturday afternoon and, having little hope of it being answered, went ahead and finished a draft of my HEART OF DARKNESS article by staying up Sunday night until around seven in the morning. Two hours later my phone rang, and the voice at the other end said something like, "I'm an assistant of Orson Welles, and Mr. Welles was wondering if you could have lunch with him today at noon." Less than three hours later, I found myself walking a few blocks south of my rue Mazarine flat to La Méditerranée, the seafood restaurant across from the Odéon theater where I was asked to meet Welles. Fearful of bungling such a rare opportunity out of nervousness compounded by sleep deprivation, I decided not to bring along a tape recorder, restricting myself to a notebook. Welles arrived at his reserved table only five or ten minutes late and immediately apologized for his tardiness. When I began by expressing my amazement at his invitation, he cordially explained it was because he didn't have time to answer my letter.

My belief that Welles didn't have much to do with the writing of CITIZEN KANE was based almost entirely on my conviction that John Houseman, whose Run-Through *I had recently read, was a reliable source of information about Welles—a belief sorely tested by Welles himself during our lunch when I brought up Houseman's remarks in that book about the HEART OF DARKNESS project. Welles insisted that Houseman was in no position to have known much about the project because he hadn't even been around during any of the story conferences. Then he went on to say (I'm paraphrasing from memory), "He's the worst possible enemy anyone can possibly have, because he gives the impression to others"—meaning me in this case—"of being sympathetic." "That's really a pity," I replied, "because his discussion of the Mercury radio shows is probably the most detailed account of them that's appeared anywhere in print." There was a long, smoldering silence at this point—the only moment during our meeting when Welles betrayed any anger—after which he said quietly, with a touch of both sorrow and sarcasm, "So be it."*

The subsequent publication of "The KANE Mutiny," signed by Peter Bog-danovich, in Esquire *(October 1972) raised further doubts in my mind about Houseman's reliability, especially on the issue of Welles's work on the* KANE *script. These were finally confirmed by the scholarship of Robert L. Carringer on the subject—above all in an essay, "The Scripts of* CITIZEN KANE," *published in* Critical Inquiry 5 *(1978). This remains the definitive and conclusive word on the issue of the script's authorship—even more than Carringer's book on the mak-ing of* KANE—*yet it would appear that few Welles scholars are aware of it; none of the Welles biographies in English even cites it. I suspect this could partially be because the biographers wrongly concluded that the same facts were available in Carringer's book; some of them are, but many of them aren't. In any case, Car-ringer's essential article was finally reprinted—first in Ronald Gottesman's ex-cellent (albeit pricey) hardcover collection* Perspectives on CITIZEN KANE *(New York: G. K. Hall & Co., 1996)—where it appears immediately after "I Missed It at the Movies"—and then, more recently, in James Naremore's* CITIZEN KANE: A Casebook *(New York: Oxford University Press, 2004).*

For the Gottesman collection, I incorporated into the present article some brief passages that had originally been cut by Film Comment's *editors—deletions that I protested and quoted in a letter published in their Summer 1972 issue, and which I have restored again here. I have two other regrets about this piece apart from my bungling of the script's authorship, both of them much less serious. One is my contention that there is only one scene in* KANE *with the " 'News on the March' people" (for some reason, I wasn't counting the final scene in the Kane mansion). The other is my penchant at this stage in my writing for italicizing various words and phrases for emphasis—a habit probably influenced by film the-orist Noël Burch—that would be impossible for me to sustain today at the* Chi-cago Reader, *where I have been writing since 1987, given my editors' complete lack of tolerance for this practice.*

Finally, a postscript relating to my allusion to André Bazin's 1950 mono-graph on Welles: One likely consequence of this allusion was receiving an offer from a Harper & Row editor in 1974, shortly after I moved to London, to trans-late a book of Bazin's called Orson Welles—*an assignment and experience I'll have more to say about later (see chapter 7). For now, I'd only like to clear up the common misconception that the book I wound up translating was the same book I'm alluding to here. Despite the claim of François Truffaut in his foreword to*

Orson Welles: A Critical View *(New York: Harper & Row, 1978), the book I translated was not a "revised and expanded edition" of Bazin's 1950 book but a later and inferior study, written towards the end of his life. As of 2006, I'm sorry to say that the 1950 book by Bazin—his first, incidentally—remains unavailable in English. And as for the "embarrassing factual errors" that I allude to, I can recall only one of these today: attributing the cinematography of* THE MAGNIFI-CENT AMBERSONS *to Gregg Toland.*

■

> The conceptions are basically *kitsch* . . . popular melodrama—
> Freud plus scandal, a comic strip about Hearst.

Although these words are used by Pauline Kael to describe CITIZEN KANE, in a long essay introducing the film's script, they might apply with greater rigor to her own introduction. Directly after the above quote, she makes it clear that KANE is *"kitsch* redeemed," and this applies to her essay as well: backed by impressive research, loaded with entertaining nuggets of gossip and social history, and written with a great deal of dash and wit, "Raising KANE" is a work that has much to redeem it. As a bedside anecdote collection, it is easily the equal of *The Minutes of the Last Meeting* and Robert Lewis Taylor's biography of W. C. Fields, and much of what she has to say about Hollywood is shrewd and quotable (e.g., "The movie industry is always frightened, and is always proudest of films that celebrate courage.") Her basic contention, that the script of KANE is almost solely the work of Herman J. Mankiewicz, seems well-supported and convincing—although hardly earth-shaking for anyone who was reading Penelope Houston's interview with John Houseman in *Sight and Sound* nine years ago (Autumn 1962). But as criticism, "Raising KANE" is mainly a conspicuous failure—a depressing performance from a supposedly major film critic—in which the object under examination repeatedly disappears before our eyes. Contrary to her own apparent aims and efforts, Kael succeeds more in burying KANE than in praising it, and perpetrates a number of questionable critical methods in the process. The following remarks will attempt to show how and why.

First, a word about *The* CITIZEN KANE *Book* itself, which appears to be a

fair reflection of Kael's tastes and procedures. In many ways, it epito-
mizes the mixed blessing that the proliferating movie book industry has
generally become: one is offered too much, yet not enough, and usually
too late. Thirty years after the release of CITIZEN KANE, the script is finally
made available, and it is packaged to serve as a coffee table ornament—
virtually out of the reach of most students until (or unless) it comes out as
an expensive paperback, and illustrated with perhaps the ugliest frame
enlargements ever to be seen in a film book of any kind.[1] One is grateful
for much of the additional material—notes on the shooting script by Gary
Carey, Mankiewicz's credits, an index to Kael's essay, and above all, the
film's cutting continuity—and a bit chagrined that (1) no production stills
are included, (2) Carey's notes are somewhat skimpy, and (3) apart from
THE MAGNIFICENT AMBERSONS, FALSTAFF, and MR. ARKADIN, no other titles
directed by Welles are even mentioned (and the last, inexplicably, is listed
only under its British title, CONFIDENTIAL REPORT).

When Kael began carving her reputation in the early Sixties, she was
chiefly known for the vigorous sarcasm of her ad hominem attacks
against other critics. Now that she writes for a vastly wider audience in
The New Yorker (where "Raising KANE" first appeared), the sarcasm is still
there, but generally the only figures attacked by name are celebrities—
like Orson Welles; the critics are roasted anonymously. This may be due
to professional courtesy, or to the likelier assumption that *New Yorker*
readers don't bother with film books by other writers, but it makes for an
occasional fuzziness. Thus we have to figure out on our own that "the latest incense-burning book on Josef von Sternberg" is Herman G. Weinberg's; and that when she ridicules "conventional schoolbook explanations for [KANE's] greatness," such as "articles . . . that call it a tragedy in
fugal form and articles that explain that the hero of CITIZEN KANE is time,"
she is referring not to several articles but to one—specifically, an essay by
Joseph McBride in *Persistence of Vision*.[2] The opening sentence of
McBride's piece reads, "CITIZEN KANE is a tragedy in fugal form; thus it is
also the denial of tragedy," and three paragraphs later is the suggestion
that "time itself is the hero of CITIZEN KANE." Yet taken as a whole,
McBride's brief essay, whatever it may lack in stylistic felicities, may contain more valuable insights about the film than Kael's 70-odd double-
columned pages. While it shows more interest in KANE as a film than as

the setting and occasion for clashing egos and intrigues, it still manages to cover much of the same ground that *The* CITIZEN KANE *Book* traverses three years later—detailed, intelligent comparisons of the shooting script with the film (the first time this was ever done, to my knowledge), an examination of the movie's relationship to Hearst, and a full acknowledgement (amplified by a quotation from the Houseman interview) that "Welles does play down Mankiewicz's contribution." And if we turn directly to Kael's own account of KANE published in *Kiss Kiss Bang Bang* the same year, we find not only "conventional school book explanations" that are vacuous indeed (Kane is "a Faust who sells out to the devil in himself"), but also the assumption that KANE is "a one man show . . . staged by twenty-five-year-old writer-director-star Orson Welles."

For all its theoretical limitations and embarrassing factual errors, the best criticism of CITIZEN KANE is still probably found in André Bazin's small, out-of-print, and untranslated book on Welles (*Orson Welles*, Paris: P.-A. Chavane, 1950). It is one sign of Kael's limitations that she once wrote in a book review about Bazin's essays being "brain-crushingly difficult"—in English translation. A brain *that* easily crushed is somewhat less than well equipped to deal with intellectual subjects, as her early remarks on Eisenstein and Resnais (among others) seem to indicate. IVAN THE TERRIBLE, for her, is "so lacking in human dimensions that we may stare at it in a kind of outrage. True, every frame in it looks great . . . but as a movie, it's static, grandiose, and frequently ludicrous, with elaborately angled, over-composed photography, and overwrought, eyeball-rolling performers slipping in and out of the walls. . . . Though no doubt the extraordinarily sophisticated Eisenstein intended all this to be a nonrealistic stylization, it's still a heavy dose of décor for all except true addicts" *(Kiss Kiss Bang Bang)*. And LAST YEAR AT MARIENBAD is "a 'classier' version of those Forties you-can-call-it-supernatural-if-you-want-to movies like FLESH AND FANTASY—only now it's called 'Jungian' " *(I Lost It at the Movies)*. Basic to both these reactions is a refusal or inability to respond to self-proclaiming art on its own terms, an impulse to cut the work down to size—or chop it up into bite-size tidbits—before even attempting to assimilate it. At her rare best, as in her sensitive review of MCCABE AND MRS. MILLER last year, Kael can grapple with a film as an organic unity; more frequently, it becomes splintered and distributed into ungainly heaps of pros and cons, shards of loose matter that are usually dropped unless they can yield up generalities or wisecracks, until all that remains visible is the wreckage. Many films, of course, *are* wreckage, and few critics are better than Kael in explaining how certain ones go over the cliff—the complex (or simple) mentality that often lies just behind banality or incoherence. But confronting the depth of KANE, she can hail it only as a *"shallow* masterpiece."

Small wonder, then, that so much of the film confuses or eludes her. First she tries to "explain" as much of the film as she can by relating it to the biographies, public personalities, and (presumed) psychologies of Welles, Mankiewicz, and Hearst ("Freud plus scandal"). And when some parts of the film don't seem to match her "real-life" drama, she connects them anyway: "There's the scene of Welles eating in the newspaper office, which was obviously caught by the camera crew, and which, to be 'a good sport,' he had to use." But what's so obvious or even plausible about this fantasy when we find the eating scene already detailed in the script?

Kael is at her weakest when she confronts the film's formal devices. The use of a partially invisible reporter as a narrative device, for instance—training our attention on what he sees and hears rather than on what he is—clearly confuses her. After criticizing William Alland in a wholly functional performance for being "a vacuum as Thompson, the reporter," she goes on to note that "the faceless idea doesn't really come across. You probably don't get the intention behind it in KANE unless you start thinking about the unusual feebleness of the scenes with the 'News on the March' people and the fact that though Thompson is a principal in the movie in terms of how much he appears, there isn't a shred of characterization in his lines or performance; he is such a shadowy presence that you may even have a hard time remembering whether you ever saw his face. . . ."

Quite aside from the speculation she sets up about "the scenes with the 'News on the March' people" (isn't there only one?), it is distressing—and unfortunately, not uncharacteristic—to see her treating one of the film's most ingenious and *successful* strategies as a liability. Where, indeed, can one find the "unusual feebleness" in the brilliant projection-room sequence—a model of measured exposition, a beautiful choreography of darting sounds and images, dovetailing voices and lights—except in her misreading of it? Kael's use of the second person here, like her resort to first person plural on other occasions, is ultimately as political and rhetorical as it is anti-analytical: one is invited to a party where only one narrow set of tastes prevails.

> It's hard to make clear to people who didn't live through the transition [from silent to sound films] how sickly and unpleasant many of those "artistic" silent pictures were—how you wanted to scrape off all that mist and sentiment.

It's hard indeed if you (Kael) fail to cite even one film as evidence—does she mean SUNRISE or THE DOCKS OF NEW YORK (lots of mist and sentiment in each), or is her knife pointed in another direction?—but not so hard if you (Kael) don't mind bolstering the prejudices of your lay audience: *they'd* probably like to scrape off "all that silent 'poetry' " too, and producers at the time with similar biases often did it for them.

Kael finds a similar difficulty in taking KANE straight:

> The mystery . . . is largely fake, and the Gothic-thriller atmosphere and the Rosebud gimmickry (though fun) are such obvious penny-dreadful popular theatrics that they're not so very different from the fake mysteries that Hearst's *American Weekly* used to whip up—the haunted castles and the curses fulfilled.

Within such a climate of appreciation, even her highest tributes come across as backhanded compliments or exercises in condescension, as in her reversions to nostalgia. Having established why none of us should take KANE very seriously, she grows rhapsodic: "Now the movie sums up and preserves a period, and the youthful iconoclasm is preserved in all its freshness—even the freshness of its callowness."

But if Kael can be dreamy about the past, she also records her misgivings about film as "the nocturnal voyage into the unconscious" (Buñuel's phrase): "Most of the dream theory of film, which takes the audience for passive dreamers, doesn't apply to the way one responded to silent comedies—which, when they were good, kept the audience in a heightened state of consciousness." But does a dreamer *invariably* relate to his own dream—much less someone else's—passively? And are "dreams" and "a heightened state of consciousness" really antithetical?

Much of the beauty of CITIZEN KANE, and Welles's style in general, is a function of kinetic seizures, lyrical transports, and intuitive responses. To see KANE merely as the "culmination" of Thirties comedy or "a collection of blackout sketches" or a series of gibes against Hearst is to miss most of what is frightening and wonderful and awesome about it. When the camera draws back from the child surrounded by snow through a dark window frame to the mother's face in close-up, one *feels* a free domain being closed in, a destiny being circumscribed, well before either the plot or one's powers of analysis can conceptualize it. As Susan Alexander concludes her all-night monologue, and the camera soars up through the skylight over her fading words ("Come around and tell me the story of your life sometime"), the extraordinary elation of that movement is too sudden and too complex to be written off as superficial bravura: a levity that comes from staying up all night and greeting the dawn, the satisfaction of sailing over a narrative juncture, the end of a confession, a gesture of friendship, the reversal of an earlier downward movement, a sense of dramatic completion, a gay exhaustion, and more, it is as dense and immediate as a burst of great poetry. At its zenith, this marvelous art—which is Welles's and Welles's alone—can sketch the graceful curve of an entire era; in the grand ball of THE MAGNIFICENT AMBERSONS, perhaps the greatest achievement in his career, a track and dissolve through the mansion's front door, while a fleeting wisp of garment flutters past, whirls us into a magical continuum where the past, present and future of a family and community pirouette and glide past our vision—the voices and faces and histories and personal styles flowing by so quickly that we can never hope to keep up with them.

What has Kael to say about AMBERSONS? It's "a work of feeling and imagination and of obvious effort . . . but Welles isn't in it [as an actor], and it's too bland. It feels empty, uninhabited." It's nice of her, anyway, to give him an A for effort.

Throughout "Raising KANE," a great show is made of clearing up popular misconceptions about Welles. Yet within my own experience, the most popular misconception is not that Welles wrote CITIZEN KANE (although that's popular enough), but that he "made" or "directed" THE THIRD MAN. And the worst that can be said about Kael's comments is that they don't even say enough about his style as a director to distinguish it from Carol Reed's. So intent is she on documenting Welles's vanity that the films wind up seeming secondary, trails of refuse strewn in the wake of the Great Welles Myth, and many of his finest achievements are denied him.

Seeing KANE again recently, she reports that "most of the newspaper-office scenes looked as clumsily staged as ever" (no reasons or explanations given). With a sweep of her hand, she consigns the rich complexity of THE LADY FROM SHANGHAI and TOUCH OF EVIL to oblivion: "His later thrillers are portentous without having anything to portend, sensational in a void, entertaining thrillers, often, but *mere* thrillers." (Like James Bond?) A page later, noting "the presence in KANE of so many elements and interests that are unrelated to Welles's other work," she takes care of those elements and interests by adding, parenthetically, that "mundane activities and social content are not his forte." I'm still puzzling over what she could mean by "mundane activities," in KANE or elsewhere, but if interesting social content is absent from *any* of Welles's later movies (including the Shakespeare adaptations), I must have been seeing different films.

A case *could* be made, I think, that the influence of Mankiewicz and Toland on KANE carries over somewhat into Welles's later work, for better and for worse: MR. ARKADIN, in particular, suggests this, both in the clumsiness of its KANE-derived plot and the beauty of its deep-focus photography. But in her zealous efforts to carry on her crusade against Welles's reputation as an auteur, Kael seems to find more unity in Mankiewicz's career as a producer than in Welles's as a director. And despite her lengthy absorption in the battle of wills between Mankiewicz, Welles, and Hearst, all she can find to say about the following quotation, from one of Mankiewicz's letters, is that it "suggests [Mankiewicz's] admiration, despite everything, for both Hearst and Welles."

> With the fair-mindedness that I have always recognized as my outstanding
> trait, I said to Orson that, despite this and that, Mr. Hearst was, in many

ways, a great man. He was, and is, said Orson, a horse's ass, no more nor less, who has been wrong, without exception, on everything he's ever touched.

Here, in a nutshell, we have a definition of contrasting sensibilities that is almost paradigmatic: Welles (almost) at the beginning of his career, Mankiewicz (almost) at the end of his own. Considering this quote, it's hard to agree with Kael when she writes of Mankiewicz that he "wrote a big movie that is untarnished by sentimentality," that is "unsanctimonious" and "without scenes of piety, masochism, or remorse, without 'truths.' " KANE, on the contrary, has all of these things, and never more so than when it entertains and encourages the idea that Kane is "a great man," and worships raw power in the process of condemning it. It is a singular irony that the aspect of KANE that Kael writes about best—Welles's charm as an actor—is precisely the factor that makes the script's corruptions, obeisance to wealth and power (and accompanying self-hatred), palatable. But when similar sentimental apologies for megalomania occur in ARKADIN and TOUCH OF EVIL, they carry no sense of conviction whatever. One suspects, finally, that KANE's uniqueness in Welles's work largely rests upon the fact that it views corruption from a corrupted viewpoint (Mankiewicz's contribution), while the other films view corruption from a vantage point of innocence. By abandoning the "charismatic demagogue" and "likeable bastard"—the sort of archetypal figure that commercial Hollywood thrives on, in figures as diverse as Hud and Patton—Welles gave up most of his audience; but it could be argued, I think, that he gained a certain integrity in the process.

The overwhelming emotion conveyed by KANE in its final moments is an almost cosmic sense of waste: an empire and a life that have turned into junk, and are going up in smoke. If we compare this smoke to the smoke that rises at the end of THE TRIAL, we may get some measure of the experience, intelligence, and feeling that Mankiewicz brought to CITIZEN KANE. Yet thankful as one may be to Kael for finally giving him his due, one wishes that some of the despair and terror of KANE's ending had found its way into her tribute. Perhaps if, as Kael claims, KANE "isn't a work of special depth or a work of subtle beauty," the ending may be just another joke in what she calls "almost a Gothic comedy"—the final black-out gag. But for some reason, I didn't feel like laughing.

Notes

1. As evidence, I can cite the examples on pages 104, 234–35, and 276 as exhibits A, B, and C. Most of the others are nearly as bad. It is also regrettable that the stills illustrate the script rather than the cutting continuity, a strategy that gives the former no chance to exist on its own (although it may subliminally—and unfairly—reinforce the notion that the film is more Mankiewicz's than Welles's). A bizarre consequence is that some of the images shown, like the fa-mous cockatoo, *mis*represent the script. And for the record, the shot shown on pages 116–17 is out of sequence, misplaced by some 93 pages.
2. An anthology edited by McBride and published by the Wisconsin Film Society Press in 1968. In the same collection is an article on THE MAGNIFICENT AMBER-SONS, also by McBride, which is probably the most useful account of the film that has yet been written. It includes a rather complete description of the orig-inal 135-minute version that far surpasses the inadequate summary given in Charles Higham's *The Films of Orson Welles.*

—*Film Comment*, Spring 1972

2

The Voice and the Eye

A Commentary on the HEART OF DARKNESS Script

The following article was inspired by my having been lent Welles's first film script by the late Cuban-born film critic Carlos Clarens while we were both living in Paris. This was supplemented eventually by my meeting with Welles, and initially by research in the library at that city's American Center and correspondence with Richard Wilson, a longtime Welles assistant and associate who was probably unique among Welles's close collaborators in his scholarly meticulousness (as evidenced in his superb rebuttal to an article by Charles Higham about IT'S ALL TRUE, *appropriately entitled "It's Not* Quite *All True," in the Autumn 1970 issue of* Sight and Sound—*an essay that lamentably had no sequels).*

As a former graduate student at the State University of New York at Stony Brook in English and American Literature (1966–69) who had dropped out shortly before moving to Paris, I was still somewhat under the sway of my academic training when I wrote this piece, which partially accounts for its literary orientation. (In fact, Jonah Raskin, whose essay on HEART OF DARKNESS *is cited in endnote 6, had been one of my Stony Brook teachers.) I regret the awkward use of asterisks to indicate in some cases which of my facts came directly from Welles, a likely consequence of the last-minute additions and revisions occasioned by our meeting. And I regret even more the extremely sketchy way that I describe the script's historical significance in relation to both race and imperialism—a subject that James Naremore deals with quite thoroughly and persuasively in his* More Than Night: Film Noir in Its Contexts *(University of California Press, 1998)—although there's also a discussion of* HEART OF DARKNESS *in his in-*

28

valuable The Magic World of Orson Welles *(2nd ed. [Dallas: Southern Methodist University Press, 1989]). It's emblematic of my own lack of historical grounding that, as I pointed out much later in my notes to Welles and Peter Bog-danovich's* This Is Orson Welles *(2nd ed. [New York: Da Capo, 1998], p. 512), I didn't know what to make of Welles's passing reference to Otto Skorzeny as one of the models for his Kurtz—one of the cryptic details in our conversation that later made me wish I'd brought a tape recorder (even though I ultimately concluded that, given the dates of Skorzeny's exploits as an SS officer, Welles must have been thinking at the time of another Nazi figure. Indeed, as I eventually discovered from Spanish film scholar Esteve Riambau in 2005, Skorzeny was approached as a potential investor in* MR. ARKADIN *in the 1950s, which is no doubt why the name was still floating around in Welles's head).*

Although I've never been able to confirm it, this article may have had a direct or indirect impact on the development of APOCALYPSE NOW *in the early 70s. The film certainly shows a great deal of Welles's influence—a topic I've explored elsewhere (see "Vietnam, the Theme Park [*HEARTS OF DARKNESS: A FILMMAKER'S APOCALYPSE*]" in my collection* Movies as Politics*).*

About twenty-five years after this article was written, I sent a copy of it to Walter Murch (who, incidentally, worked on APOCALYPSE NOW*) as one of several materials, along with some Welles radio shows, to use as "stylistic reference points" for the new sound-mix he was planning for the opening shot of* TOUCH OF EVIL*, based on indications by Welles in a studio memo (see chapter 21)—with specific reference to the "snatches of sound and music, the beginning of life of the city at night" in Manhattan quoted early on.*

■

Last July, a week before the completion of this article, I had the unexpected privilege of meeting Welles for lunch in Paris, where he was busy editing a new film entitled HOAX, which has something to do with the Clifford Irving / Howard Hughes scandal. ("Not a documentary," Welles assured me, but "a new kind of film"—although he didn't elaborate.) As other commentators have observed, the search for the truth about any Welles project is an endless trip through a labyrinth; possibly no other living director has been the subject of so many conflicting accounts, in large matters as well as small ones. To indicate my sources, all the information given to me by Welles is either stated explicitly or indicated by an aster-isk. Unless otherwise noted, the remaining facts about the HEART OF DARKNESS project come from either Richard Wilson or the script itself. (The interpretations, needless to say, are all my own.) Wilson, who was with Welles in Hollywood for most of this period, has generously sup-plied me with material from the early Welles-Mercury files. I am also in-debted to Carlos Clarens for lending me his copy of the script.

I: The Voice

> I became aware that that was exactly what I had been looking forward to—a talk with Kurtz. . . . The man presented himself as a voice. . . . The point was in his being a gifted creature, and that of all his gifts the one that stood out pre-eminently, that carried with it a sense of real pres-ence, was his ability to talk, his words. . . .
> —Marlow in Conrad's *Heart of Darkness*

Appropriately, Orson Welles's first Hollywood project begins as a primal initiation [see the appendix to this chapter]: his voice in darkness, fol-lowed by an iris opening out into a birdcage. With a master magician's in-stinct, he leads us directly from estrangement to entrapment—carrying us in the space of seconds from radio into cinema.

The "revised estimating script," from which the introduction is taken, runs to 184 pages and is dated November 30, 1939. Although no author is listed on the title page, it is clear from the existing evidence that it was written and adapted by Welles alone.[1] The previous November, shortly after his Halloween eve broadcast of *The War of the Worlds,* Welles had pre-sented *Heart of Darkness* on *Mercury Theatre on the Air* as the ninth and next to last program in the series (*War of the Worlds* was the seventh); like the earlier adaptation, it was scripted by Howard Koch,[2] with the probable editorial assistance of John Houseman. According to Welles, the radio ver-sion—in which he played both Marlow *and* Kurtz—was weak, and except for the parts that came from Conrad, its influence on the screenplay was minimal. Without the availability of Koch's script, this cannot be verified.

The central drama of *Heart of Darkness* revolves around the myth of vir-tually unlimited power, achieved by Kurtz, an ivory agent, in the depths of the Congo, where he becomes a god to the natives. The story is narrated by Marlow, a skipper hired by the ivory company, and the plot mainly consists of his long journey down the river towards Kurtz. As with the central character of *The Great Gatsby,* our total sense of Kurtz comes to us filtered through the narrator's consciousness; he looms in the story as a mysterious figure of rumor and conjecture, and his meaning becomes the sum of everything that Marlow sees and experiences on his way into the jungle. In Conrad's novella, the actual appearance of Kurtz is somewhat anticlimactic, and is handled rather elliptically; in Welles's script, it becomes the dramatic climax that all the preceding action builds up to.

Welles said that he originally planned to play only the part of Marlow, hoping he could find someone else for the part of Kurtz. By the time the final estimating script had been written, however, he had decided to take on both parts. As a penetration into the mystery of a powerful, legendary man, HEART OF DARKNESS clearly prefigures CITIZEN KANE; exploring the tension between Marlow and Kurtz, Welles was obviously interested in expressing the same sort of ambivalence about power and position that informs his later films. To make this concern more personal and immediate, he updated Conrad's story to the present, made Marlow into an American, and explicitly linked Kurtz's despotism to the tyranny that was currently sweeping over Europe. As Marlow, he would figure primarily as Narrative Voice and unseen hero, glimpsed only occasionally as a reflection or, between episodes, back on his boat in the New York harbor, telling the story. As Kurtz, he would also remain offscreen for most of the film, but then make a grand demonic appearance at the climax.

Welles deliberately pointed up the *doppelgänger* aspect of this dual role by frequently drawing attention to the physical resemblance between Marlow and Kurtz in the dialogue; expanding the part of Kurtz's unnamed fiancée into a full-fledged heroine named Elsa,[3] he even created a love triangle of sorts. Thus, broadly speaking, the multiple equations proposed by the introduction, whereby I = eye = camera = screen = spectator, are extended still further in the script proper so that spectator = Marlow = Kurtz = Welles = dictator—a notion that is at once so abstract and so audacious that, coupled with a million-dollar budget, an 82-day shooting schedule *and* the outbreak of World War II, it is hardly surprising that

RKO shelved the project. Welles told me he later learned the primary resistance came not from George Schaefer—the president of RKO, who'd brought him to Hollywood—but the other studio heads.

The roots of the script can be traced through much of Welles's theater and radio work in the late Thirties. In 1936, he had already conjured up a sinister atmosphere of jungle tribalism in his "voodoo" stage production of *Macbeth*, set in Haiti with an all-Negro cast. The following year, he played the title role in his staging of *Dr. Faustus*—a character who quite likely contributed to his conception of Kurtz—and then played Brutus in his modern-dress *Julius Caesar*, which was particularly noted at the time for its contemporary political parallels (fascist-style uniforms and salutes, "Nuremberg lighting," etc.). But the importance of his radio work was probably even more decisive. The first Mercury radio series, *First Person Singular*, broadcast eight programs in the summer of 1938 and introduced a narrative technique that was, at the time, completely new to the medium. *Newsweek* ran a brief story about the show on the day that it premiered (July 11):

> Avoiding the cut-and-dried dramatic technique that introduces dialogue with routine announcements, Welles will serve as genial host to his radio audience. As narrator, he will build himself directly into the drama, drawing his listeners into the charmed circle. He reasons: "This method frees the script writer from the necessity of attempting to introduce a description of the locale into the dialogue. . . . A radio audience is apt to be bored when it hears someone say, 'Once upon a time.' Not so if you say, 'This happened to me.' "

This first-person technique was carried over into subsequent Welles radio series; it was even used prominently in the second half of the *War of the Worlds* broadcast—which few people heard at the time. Apart from anticipating the use of subjective camera, and implying an autobiographical link between Welles and his heroes, this method leads to a form of narrative economy—encapsulating exposition and bridging scenes— that is essential to Welles's early film work. (The use of overlapping dialogue—as prominent in the HEART OF DARKNESS script as in his subsequent films—also derives from radio.)

The opening of the script seems particularly rich with radio devices. Over a long shot of the New York harbor at dusk, Marlow's voice begins with a passage drawn from the sixth paragraph of Conrad's story, converted from past to present tense:

> The old river in its broad reach rests unruffled at the decline of day, after ages of good service done to the races that people its banks, spread out in the tranquil dignity of a waterway leading to the utmost ends of the earth.

The narration continues over dissolves showing the river traffic and Manhattan Island, and "lap dissolves" of the "great bridges of both rivers," "parkways," "boulevards" and "skyscrapers," each seen at the instant that their lights are illuminated. In the next sequence, "as we move down the length of the Island"—a passage more impressionistic in visual detail than most of the rest of the script—Marlow's voice is joined by "snatches of sound and music, the beginning of life of the city at night":

> In Central Park, snatches of jazz music are heard from the radios in the moving taxicabs. The sweet dinner music in the restaurants of the big hotels further West. The throb of tom-toms foreshadow the jungle music of the story to come. The lament of brasses, the gala noodling of big orchestras tuning up in concert halls and opera houses, and finally as the camera finds its way downtown below Broadway, the music freezes into an expression of the empty shopping district of the deserted Battery—the mournful muted clangor of the bell buoys out at sea, and the hoot of shipping.

The continuing narration is basically an abridgement of Conrad's text, adapted from a European to an American context:

> I was thinking of very old times when our fathers first came here, four hundred years ago—the other day. . . . Imagine the feelings of a skipper [. . .], a civilized man, four hundred years ago, hove to off the Battery here—at the very end of the world. Imagine the trip up this river. With death skulking in the air, in the water, in the bush. They must have been dying like flies[. . .].

(In the original, "our fathers" was "the Romans," "four hundred" was "nineteen hundred," "skipper" was "commander," and "the Battery" was "the sea-reach of the Thames.") Towards the end of this lengthy speech, we arrive at Marlow's boat and see Marlow leaning against the mast while he speaks, the Manhattan skyline glimpsed behind him. As he relights his pipe, there is a dissolve to a reflection of him lighting his pipe in a shop window while the narration continues offscreen, and Marlow's story and the subjective camera treatment both begin: "I was over in Europe"—(the match flares; dissolve)—"loafing around one of the big port towns looking for a ship—when I saw that map in a shop window." Throughout this opening, the narrative continuity is guided and controlled by the sound.

The legacy of Welles's radio work is vast—from July 1938 to March 1940 alone, he adapted, directed, narrated, and acted in nearly eighty radio plays.[4] Unfortunately, the only recording from this period that is generally available today is *The War of the Worlds*. And according to Welles, even *that* performance is not the one that was broadcast, but one given at another time.

The likely impact of this broadcast on HEART OF DARKNESS cannot be overstressed. It is estimated that 6 million people heard the program and 1,200,000 of them took it literally, believing that America had just been invaded by Martians; an unknown number of people who didn't hear the broadcast were likewise caught up in the hysteria.[5] At the age of 23, Welles was suddenly catapulted into a position of nation-wide fame and notoriety, which led to both a commercial radio sponsor (Campbell Soup) and a Hollywood contract granting him an unprecedented degree of artistic and financial control. When he arrived in Hollywood thirteen months after the broadcast—four months prior to the completion of the script—he was an unusually controversial and powerful figure, and the immediate dislike he attracted in the movie colony undoubtedly amplified this image. During the same month that he signed with RKO, Germany signed a nonaggression pact with the Soviet Union and invaded Poland; while he was preparing HEART OF DARKNESS, the war broke out; and the relation between his own rapid ascendancy and (in his case, unwitting) sway over the masses and Hitler's was surely not lost on him. Marshall McLuhan's description of this relation in *Understanding Media* is, like many of his pronouncements, somewhat facile; but as an evocation of radio's power during this period, it bears repeating:

The subliminal depths of radio are charged with the resonating echoes of tribal horns and antique drums. This is inherent in the very nature of this medium, with its power to turn the psyche and society into a single echo chamber. . . . The famous Orson Welles broadcast about the invasion from Mars was a simple demonstration of this all-inclusive, completely involving scope of the auditory image of radio. It was Hitler who gave radio the Orson Welles treatment for *real*.

Hitler is never cited by name in the HEART OF DARKNESS script, but his relation to Kurtz is nonetheless unmistakable—coming to the fore in the final pages, when Kurtz remarks, "There's a man now in Europe trying to do what I've done in the jungle. He will fail." A bit earlier, we find this exchange:

KURTZ: I have another world to conquer.
MARLOW'S VOICE: What world?
KURTZ: Down the river. Five more continents and then I'll die—

More generally, the alliance is expressed indirectly, as in Marlow's medical examination near the beginning, when Welles's two major additions to Conrad are explicitly racist remarks from the doctor to be played by Everett Sloane* (while examining Marlow's head: "Mmm . . . Good Nordic type . . . the superior races you know") and an early reference to Kurtz, whom the doctor identifies as "our next leader." Later, when Marlow and the company men (who are all Germans in the script) come upon a row of poles supporting human heads in a foggy swamp, the station manager De Tirpitz, to be played by George Coulouris,* says, "That's how Kurtz and the rest of them got their power back in Europe. This shouldn't surprise you. You've seen this kind of thing in the city streets."

Conrad's story, largely based on his experiences in the Congo, has a political tonality of its own, and one critic has argued persuasively that it can be read—at least in part—as a critique of imperialism.[6] (It is interesting to note that Welles originally wanted to shoot the film on location, and designed it for studio shooting only after RKO rejected the idea.*)

At the same time that Welles was writing the script, Chaplin was beginning to shoot THE GREAT DICTATOR, another project centered around a double role of dictator and putative hero. But while Chaplin, the more extroverted of the two, was using himself to confront Hitler, it appears that Welles, the more introverted and intellectual artist, was partially using Kurtz to confront the darker side of himself. The climactic speech of Chaplin's film is delivered by the Jew; the equivalent speech in Welles's script is given by Kurtz, immediately before his death:

KURTZ: [. . .] I'm a whole nation's long, golden dream.—And to you—a miserable wretch you once caught, grubbing for ivory in the bush, crazy with disease, who died on you in captivity.

MARLOW'S VOICE: You're more than that.

KURTZ: Or less?

MARLOW'S VOICE: Or worse.

KURTZ: Or worse. . . .

MARLOW'S VOICE: How do you know you're going to die?

KURTZ: What I've had is fatal—it's called power. . . . Do you understand that? I think so—

MARLOW'S VOICE: You said I never would.

KURTZ: You'll never understand Kurtz—the statue in the public park. And there'll be one—a big one in very bad taste, and on this day, every year, they'll make speeches and lay wreaths at my stone feet. And then the young men will go off and get drunk singing a song about me.—No, you'll never understand that.—Not what they make of me. But you can see what I've made of myself.

MARLOW'S VOICE: You said you ran away. I don't understand that.

KURTZ: I was afraid.—Understand this much.—Everything I've done up here has been done according to the method of my Government.—Everything. There's a man now in Europe trying to do what I've done in the jungle. He will fail. In his madness he thinks he can't fail—but he will. A brute can rule only brutes. Remember the meek—the meek.—I'm a great man, Marlow—really great—greater than great men before me—I know the strength of the enemy—its terrible weakness. The meek—you and the rest of the millions—the poor in spirit. I hate you—but I know you for my betters— without knowing why you are except that yours is the Kingdom of Heaven, except that you shall inherit the earth. Don't mistake me. I haven't gone moral on my death bed. I'm above morality. No, I've climbed higher than other men and seen farther. I'm the first absolute dictator. The first complete success. I've known what the others try to get. I've gotten it in the one place in the world where it could be got. I'm the man on top—the one man. All the rest are six feet underground where I buried them. That's the game. Bury the rest of them alive. Stay on top yourself. I won the game, but the winner loses too. He's all alone and he goes mad. (There is a flash of lightning, followed by a clap of thunder.)

KURTZ (continued): That's why I ran away. I ran from the face of darkness, and then as I started back down the river I saw that there was darkness there, too, and failure. So I hid in the charnel house where you found me, and then I ran again. Madness is better than defeat. Down the river is the light of reason, showing still behind the darkness, marking the evil, marking the shape of the original lie. I sound moral again. I'm not. I'm just practical. I know when to die. (Lightning and thunder.)

KURTZ (continued): I thought the time had come for me. The sun was low over the world, and my shadow was long, it would cover everything. I know now it's not long enough. No man's is long enough. The strong die with their dream. I am the first to die awake. (Lightning and thunder.)

KURTZ (continued): Our shadows are dark like night, and where they fall the jungle grows again. But the sun always goes down. Mine did. And the world has a darker shadow—darker than mine. I'm going to die before day-break—I'm afraid to live. The dawn might find me a very little man. (Kurtz has shifted his gaze. Now he is staring, not towards camera lens, but beyond it, his eyes very wide.)

MARLOW'S VOICE: Kurtz!—Kurtz! (Lightning and thunder.)

MARLOW'S VOICE (continued): What are you looking at?

KURTZ: The horror!—The horror!

II: The Eye

> The yarns of seamen have a direct simplicity, the whole meaning of which lies within the shell of a cracked nut. But Marlow was not typical (if his propensity to spin yarns be excepted), and to him the meaning of an episode was not inside like a kernel but outside, enveloping the tale which brought it out only as a glow brings out a haze, in the likeness of one of these misty halos that sometimes are made visible by the spectral illumination of moonshine.
>
> —Conrad's *Heart of Darkness*

> The cinema is an anti-universe where reality is born out of a sum of un-realities.
>
> —Jean Epstein

Since the release of Robert Montgomery's LADY IN THE LAKE in 1946, the critical consensus about continuous use of the first-person camera has been consistently negative. To inquire whether HEART OF DARKNESS would or could have changed these objections is to ask an unanswerable question: scripts are blueprints, not finished works, and even to discuss one that was never filmed is to give it an identity of its own that was never intended.

Considering RKO's reluctance about HEART OF DARKNESS, it is possible that the script's introduction was partially designed to placate the studio about the film's commercial possibilities, leavening its experimental nature with a heady dose of showmanship. One of its showier aspects is the use of color—the gun that "goes off with a cloud of smoke and a shower of brightly colored sparks," and the "blinding red stain" and "dirty violet" during the electrocution sequence. Welles explained to me that color was planned only for separate shots such as the above; the remainder of the film was to be in black-and-white.

Whatever the ultimate strategies behind the introduction, it remains a remarkable document, and a useful path leading into the script proper. For one thing, it serves the ingenious function of demonstrating the playful and gimmicky aspects of the technique *before* the story begins, thus clearing the way for its subsequent use as a serious narrative device. In the remainder of the script, aside from a few comic moments—such as in Marlow's medical examination, when the doctor, in close-up, extends his calipers toward the camera "like an enormous insect threatening its victim with legs and antennae"—the technique remains functionally neutral throughout, rarely calling attention to itself. An attraction between Marlow and Elsa is faintly implied, but the script spares us the embarrassment of any kissing scenes.

Indeed, despite the heated rhetoric of the Conrad-derived narration that he delivers, Marlow usually figures in the action as a neutral, uncommitted observer, thus enabling the camera to serve a relatively modest role as recording instrument. ("What are your politics?" he is asked by Eddie, the English representative at the company's First Station, to be played by Gus Schilling.* He replies, "I have no sympathies one way or another. I'm just here to run a boat.") The semi-invisible reporter in CITIZEN KANE, also emotionally detached, is probably an outgrowth of this idea. Two striking uses of subjective camera in THE MAGNIFICENT AMBERSONS—shots from Wilbur Minafer's coffin and from the viewpoint of

George walking home near the end—each depend on a sense of numbness in the unseen character: literal death in the first case, emotional alienation in the second.

When I asked Welles how he felt about the technique today, he expressed skepticism and explained that he became somewhat disillusioned with it after shooting a long subjective sequence in AMBERSONS—one moving through the family mansion, apparently meant to follow George's final walk home, which was cut from the film. An obvious drawback to the technique for Welles is that it would have restrained the use of the camera as an independent expressive device—a central aspect of his later style. At one point in the script, as if in anticipation of this development, the camera *does* break away from Marlow's impassivity to forge a statement of its own, in a passage that exemplifies Welles's attempts to illustrate the narration cinematically. At the end of a long sequence detailing Marlow's arrival at the First Station—after meeting Elsa and Eddie, and witnessing the maltreatment of natives, the pettiness of the company men (mainly shown as comic bumpkins), and the callowness of Blauer, the station manager, to be played by Robert Coote,* who complains that the groans of a dying man on a mattress outside his office "make it difficult to work"—Marlow leaves Blauer's office, and the transition is effected in the following way:

Blauer's voice which has started to fade from the soundtrack is now overwhelmed by MUSIC. This music makes reference to Blauer's voice, to the groans of the dying man, to the tinkle of Eddie's piano [featured prominently in the previous scenes—J. R.], to the somber overtones of the New York harbor. Blauer is seen to be still talking, but we cannot distinguish what he says. As this happens CAMERA STARTS TO PULL BACK smoothly but swiftly. Simultaneously [. . .], Blauer's image begins to wash out. CAMERA MOVEMENT SLOWS UP a little when it gets outside door of Blauer's office and then CAMERA STARTS TO RISE (ON THE CRANE) slowly and solemnly, but ANGLES DOWN to the floor so that we again see the dying man.

This is the last clear impression we get on the fading interior.

Dissolve

Exterior Settlement, Harbor and Jungle-Night—(Miniature) CONTINUATION OF CRANE SHOT. CAMERA CONTINUES THE UPWARD MOVE (matching its rising action on the interior shot). It MOVES UPWARD from the Manager's building and takes into the shot a view, from above, of the whole settlement. Still MOVING UPWARD, CAMERA PANS to take in the harbor, with the steamer far below loading in the glare of electric lights. CONTINUING THE MOVE UP-WARD, it clears the harbor and takes in the black wall of the jungle beyond.

Wipe

Exterior Starry Sky—Night—(Painting) CAMERA, MOVING UPWARD, comes now to a shot of the starry sky, which fills the entire frame.

Dissolve Out

Exterior Starry Sky—Night—(Painting) The dark gray shadow of Marlow SUPERIMPOSES itself over the shot of the starry sky. He is leaning against the mast of his boat and smoking his pipe. The shadow takes the pipe out of its mouth and the music introduces Marlow's voice.

MARLOW'S VOICE (narrating): That man inside jabbered about his Mr. Kurtz, and outside the silent wilderness surrounded this cleared speck on the earth, great and invincible, like evil or truth—waiting patiently[. . . .]

Montgomery's use of subjective camera floundered on the mistaken notion that it would permit the audience to "identify" with his hero. Welles's concept, while partaking of this notion, seems based on an attraction-repulsion principle that is not only much more complex, but—unlike Montgomery's—organically related to the concerns of the plot. This, too, is prefigured in the introduction: in quick succession, the viewer is isolated from his neighbors, caged, shot, electrocuted, turned into an incompetent golfer, and then replaced by a movie camera. The disquieting image of an audience composed of cameras attests to the solipsistic nature of the conception, yet the spectator is teased and cajoled in such grand style that he is theoretically seduced into playing the game—without being allowed to forget that he *is* playing it.

In the story that follows, the sensationalism of the technique is partially supplanted by the sensationalism of the plot, and the attraction-repulsion principle becomes central to the dialectic between Marlow and Kurtz. Thus, while we are trapped within Marlow's circumscribed gaze as he travels through a studio-built Africa, hearing awed reports about the power and grandeur of Kurtz, we are gradually lured into wanting to share Kurtz's vision instead. And when we come upon the depraved person of Kurtz, we are presumably driven back by fear into an identification with Marlow—or, more likely, compelled to form a split identification be-

tween the two of them. The climactic meeting of Marlow and Kurtz is rich
with suggestions:

Exterior Lake and Temple—Moonlight—(Fog)
[. . .] CAMERA MOVES toward the temple as the canoe glides toward it,
HOLDING on it, ANGLING from below until the canoe nears its base. CAMERA finally COMES CLOSE to ladder which extends up to floor of temple. Now, indicating that Marlow is climbing the ladder, CAMERA TRAVELS UPWARDS. We
catch in the background the texture of the water and light, as well as the pattern of the pilings under the temple. As CAMERA MOVES UPWARDS, it TILTS UP
to SHOT of the temple ceiling, showing it is covered with skulls. Then CAM-
ERA PANS DOWN off the ceiling and we

> **Feather Wipe**
> **Interior Temple—Moonlight—(Miniature)** CONTINUATION OF PAN DOWN

from skull-covered ceiling to a LONG SHOT of the temple. The skull-and-bone
decoration is carried throughout the interior. The place is dark, the source of
light coming from the moon which shines in through the open front. At the
far end of the structure, we discern a throne on a platform, and seated on the
throne, the figure of a man—Kurtz. CAMERA TRUCKS FORWARD as Marlow
starts walking toward the throne, and we

> **Dissolve Out**
> **Dissolve In**
> **Interior Temple—Moonlight—(Set)** CAMERA is now much closer to

Kurtz on the throne and is still MOVING FORWARD, Marlow having covered
the long walk from front of temple in the dissolve. Kurtz is more distinct,
and as we near him CAMERA TILTS UP SLIGHTLY to indicate that he is on a
higher level than Marlow. We end up in a MEDIUM CLOSEUP of Kurtz.

KURTZ: Have you a cigarette? (He reaches out for the cigarette. His hand
goes below frame of camera. He brings his hand back with the cigarette in it
and puts the cigarette into his mouth.)

KURTZ (continued): Light it for me—CAMERA MOVES FORWARD and UP-
WARD into EXTREME CLOSEUP of Kurtz's face. There is the flare of a match as
Marlow lights the cigarette.

KURTZ (continued): I'm dying—(he looks keenly into lens of camera,
straight into Marlow's eyes): You're American. What's your name?

MARLOW'S VOICE: Marlow.

KURTZ: I'm Kurtz. You look like me—a little—(On the words "a little"
CAMERA MOVES BACK SLIGHTLY and LOWERS a TRIFLE from the extreme
closeup of Kurtz's face, indicating that Marlow has stepped down and back.
Kurtz settles back on his throne.)

KURTZ (continued): (looking straight at Marlow):—The image of God—I can use you—[. . .]

Throughout my conversation with Welles, it was clear that the HEART OF DARKNESS project was still very dear to him, despite the pain and frustration it had cost him, and his later disenchantment with the subjective camera technique. As he wondered at length why no good film has ever been made from Conrad—regarding Brooks's LORD JIM and Reed's OUT-CAST OF THE ISLANDS with equal disdain—and discussed his prolonged efforts to find another actor to play Kurtz, it was easy to see the fascination that the project still held for him. He stressed the fact that he was just on the verge of beginning to shoot the film when the project was cancelled—having already shot tests of the first-person technique with Sloane, Schilling, Coote, and himself*⁷—and it seemed to linger in his memory as one of many Rosebuds, a dream that he had continued to nurture even after the completion of CITIZEN KANE.

Perhaps, in the confrontation between Marlow and Kurtz, we would have wound up identifying with *neither* character. To have brought off such a scene without eliciting a single snicker would have required genius. Yet given the scope of Welles's talent—and the rare energy and enthusiasm with which he attacked his first Hollywood project—can we claim with absolute assurance that he couldn't have done it?

Notes

1. According to Joseph McBride (*Orson Welles,* London: Secker and Warburg, 1972), Welles wrote the script with John Houseman; in "Raising KANE" (*The CITIZEN KANE Book,* Boston: Atlantic-Little Brown, 1971), Pauline Kael writes that "it was reported in the trade press that [Welles] was working on the script with John Houseman and Herbert Drake, who was Mercury's press agent." However, John Houseman's recent memoir, *Run-Through* (New York: Simon and Schuster, 1972), makes it clear that he did not share in the authorship; and Richard Wilson has written me that the revised estimating script "is entirely by Welles."
2. This information was conveyed to me by Richard Corliss, the editor of *Film Comment,* who learned it from Koch himself.
3. Welles used the name Elsa again for the heroine of THE LADY FROM SHANGHAI, played by Rita Hayworth. The Elsa in HEART OF DARKNESS was to have been

played by Dita Parlo, an Austrian actress; but this subsequently became impossible when she was interned in France as an enemy alien (Roy A. Fowler, *Orson Welles: A First Biography* [London, Pendulum, 1946]). In the script, Elsa insists on accompanying Marlow and the company men down the river, but Marlow sends her back to the First Station for safety after De Tirpitz reports back that the members of the Third Station have been decapitated, and they start to hear war drums.

4. In *Run-Through*, Houseman gives a fascinating account of the radio shows, and describes the Mercury recordings Welles made for Columbia Records of *Julius Caesar*, *The Merchant of Venice*, and *Twelfth Night*—complete performances, with music and sound effects—in 1938. Welles's production of Marc Blitzstein's *The Cradle Will Rock* was available on a long-playing record released several years ago. Cf. Joseph McBride's *Orson Welles* for an extensive (though "probably incomplete") listing of Welles's radio work.

5. These figures come from *Invasion from Mars*, a study by Hadley Cantril and his research staff at Princeton; cited in *The Panic Broadcast*, by Howard Koch (Avon Books, 1970).

6. "Imperialism: Conrad's Heart of Darkness," by Jonah Raskin, *Journal of Contemporary History*, vol. 2, number 2, April, 1967.

7. According to Charles Higham (*The Films of Orson Welles* [Berkeley: University of California Press, 1970]), the film was to be shot with hand-held Eyemo cameras. Ray Collins and Erskine Sanford were also to have figured in the cast.

Appendix:
Introductory Sequence to the HEART OF DARKNESS Script by Orson Welles

This has no direct connection with the motion picture itself. It is intended to instruct and acquaint the audience as amusingly as possible with the special technique used in the HEART OF DARKNESS.

INTRODUCTION

After regular RKO trademark title, followed by Mercury title,
Fade Out
Dark Screen
WELLES' VOICE: Ladies and Gentlemen, this is Orson Welles. Don't worry. There's just nothing to look at for a while. You can close your eyes, if you want to, but—please open them when I tell you to. . . . First of all, I am going to divide this audience into two parts—you and everybody else in the theatre. Now, then, open your eyes.
Iris into
Interior Bird Cage—(Process)

1   SHOOTING FROM inside the bird cage, as it would appear to a bird inside the cage, looking out. The cage fills the entire screen. Beyond the bars can be seen chin and mouth of Welles, tremendously magnified.

WELLES' VOICE: The big hole in the middle there is my mouth. You play the part of a canary. I'm asking you to sing and you refuse. That's the plot. I offer you an olive.

A couple of Gargantuan fingers appear from below cage and thrust an enormous olive toward CAMERA, through bars of the cage.

WELLES' VOICE (cont'd): You don't want an olive. This enrages me.

Welles' chin moves down and his nose and eyes are revealed. He is scowling fiercely.

WELLES' VOICE (cont'd): Here is a bird's-eye view of me being enraged. I threaten you with a gun.

Now the muzzle of a pistol is stuck between the bars of the cage. It looks like a big Bertha.

WELLES' VOICE (cont'd): That's the way a gun looks to a canary. I give you to the count of three to sing.

Welles' head moves up, showing his mouth on the words, "one, two, three." His voice is heard over echo chambers and the narration is synchronized on the count with the movement of his lips.

WELLES' VOICE (cont'd): One—(on normal level) That's the way I sound to you, you *canary*. (on echo again) *Two—three*. (on normal level, cheerfully) You still don't want to sing so I shoot you.

The gun goes off with a cloud of smoke and a shower of brightly colored sparks. As this fades out,

WELLES' VOICE (cont'd): That's the end of this picture.

Fade Out
Fade In
Credit Title
RKO Caption, THE END. Conclusive chords of music finishing off as we
Fade Out
Black Screen

WELLES' VOICE: Now, of course, this movie isn't about a canary and I am not going to threaten you with firearms just because you don't feel like imitating birdcalls, but I do want you to understand that you're part of the story. In fact, you are the star. Of course, you're not going to see yourself on the screen but everything you see on the screen is going to be seen through your eyes and you're somebody else. Understand?—No?—Let's take a screen test: Close your eyes. Now,—*open up*.

Iris into
Interior Prison Corridor and Death Chamber

2   SHOT of prison bars. Welles appears on other side of bars. This time, what he says is synchronized.

WELLES: This isn't a bird's-eye view again. This is a *convict's*-eye view. You're in jail.

Welles puts on a Warden's cap.

WELLES (cont'd): I'm the warden.

Welles unlocks cell door. Bars swing away from CAMERA. Welles moves in to CAMERA, staring directly into lens.

WELLES (cont'd): (as Warden) All right, it's time now. Come on. (pause; then fiercely) *Come on!*

CAMERA TRUCKS thru doorway into corridor. Welles steps aside. CAMERA, on normal eye level, MOVES AROUND and confronts prison attendants and Chaplain who are moving toward CAMERA. Very legitimate. CAMERA STOPS.

WELLES' VOICE (cont'd): Let's go.

Jailers turn directly away from CAMERA and start moving away.

WELLES' VOICE (cont'd): Let's go.

Chaplain steps slightly aside to make way for CAMERA, still looking into it.

WELLES' VOICE (cont'd): Come on, march!

CAMERA DOLLIES down corridor after guards and past Chaplain, who disappears from frame. Footsteps to match this action. After CAMERA MOVES several feet, a voice is heard.

PRISONER'S VOICE: Hey!

CAMERA CONTINUES moving forward, but somewhat slower.

PRISONER'S VOICE (cont'd): Hey! (louder) *Hey!*

Guards turn around, look at CAMERA, then turn to their left in direction of the voice.

PRISONER'S VOICE (cont'd): You!

CAMERA PANS around and centers on a very murderous looking customer peering through the bars of a cell.

PRISONER (cont'd): Yes, you. (he smiles) I'm next.

WELLES' VOICE: Shut up, Riley.

PRISONER: Yes, sir.

WELLES' VOICE: Keep marching, you.

CAMERA PANS BACK to corridor and TRUCKS FORWARD, the guards preceding it. After a while the prisoner's voice is heard in the distance.

PRISONER'S VOICE: Happy landings!

A colored baritone commences a typical spiritual routine. CAMERA CONTINUES moving forward. The guards in front of CAMERA come to a halt. One guard turns toward CAMERA, the other starts opening an iron door.

PRISONER'S VOICE (cont'd): I'll be seeing you.

The baritone stops. The prisoner's wild laugh comes over on soundtrack.

CAMERA has STOPPED for a moment and now, as the door opens, it TRUCKS into death chamber, confronting more attendants and registering on the far wall, a large clock.

Sound of iron door closing cuts off sound of wild laughter. CAMERA PANS QUICKLY to the left, taking in gallery of grim-looking witnesses, and finishing on other side of the iron door which attendants have just closed.

CAMERA suddenly LISTS sharply to port and then starts toward floor.

WELLES' VOICE: Steady!

CAMERA'S PLUNGE to the floor is arrested by Warden's voice. CAMERA SLOWLY RIGHTS ITSELF, still holding on the door.

A clock is heard ticking ominously. CAMERA PANS SLOWLY past witnesses again to the clock, then PANS AROUND to other side of the death chamber to attendants and electrician seated beside his paraphernalia. Attendants, still looking at CAMERA, move aside and disclose electric chair.

The clock continues its ominous ticking. As CAMERA MOVES, we also hear footsteps to match. CAMERA TRUCKS SLOWLY to electric chair. When we are next to it and looking down at it, CAMERA STOPS.

WARDEN'S VOICE: Sit down!

CAMERA PANS AROUND taking in clock but not focusing on it, and confronts witnesses. Then LOWERS a couple of feet to height of sitting position.

WELLES' VOICE (cont'd): Straps!

Attendants move into frame, make adjustments. They are very close to CAMERA. Sound of straps being fastened.

WELLES' VOICE (cont'd): Feet!

More sound to match. Then Attendant rises slightly and looks above CAMERA, somewhat to the side.

FIRST ATTENDANT: Yes, sir.

First Attendant straightens and moves out of scene. Second Attendant rises and does the same.

WELLES' VOICE: Fasten the head cap!

Sound to match.

WELLES' VOICE (cont'd): (quietly) Prisoner doesn't want blindfold. (raising his voice) Have you anything to say? (pause) All right, Joe, take it on the minute.

CAMERA PANS to electrician, then PANS SHARPLY to clock whose long hand is moving towards 12:00.

Ticking louder. Sound of witnesses moving forward in their seats.

CAMERA PANS SHARPLY to their faces. They look into lens, completing their move. One witness takes out a watch, looks at it, looks at his left and towards the clock. Witness next to him follows his eyes toward clock. CAMERA FOLLOWS their move and PANS BACK to clock.

Ticking still louder. The long hand gets to 12:00.

WELLES' VOICE (cont'd): All right.

Sound of current being turned on. Screen goes into blinding red stain. CAMERA BLURRING ITS FOCUS at the same time, moves quickly to electrician whose outline distorts terribly, melts into dirty violet, and sound of current magnified into terrific metallic ring which completes sound, dies as we

Fade Out

Fade In

Black Screen

WELLES' VOICE: Ladies and Gentlemen, there is no cause for alarm. This is only a motion picture. Of course, you haven't committed murder and believe me, I wouldn't electrocute you for the world. Give yourself your right name, again, please. It might help. All right, now, I think you see what I mean. *You're not going to see this picture—this picture is going to happen to you.*

3   A moving picture camera appears, contrasted sharply against the original black of the screen.

WELLES' VOICE (cont'd): That's you. You're the camera. The camera is your eye.

A human eye appears, completely filling the lens of camera on the screen. OUR CAMERA MOVES toward the eye until it completely fills the screen. As the eye is moving towards us, a sky full of clouds fades into the pupil of the eye. The outline of the eye, the lashes and then the pupil, become too large for the screen. By this time, all we see is the sky full of clouds.

WELLES' VOICE (cont'd): You're looking at the sky, and remember *you're* looking at it!

CAMERA PANS DOWN from the sky—

Wipe

Exterior Golf Course

4   CONTINUATION OF PAN SHOT DOWN from the sky with clouds, showing the fairway of a golf course and a distant green. PAN QUICKLY DOWN to the ground immediately below, on CLOSEUP of a golf ball and a driver which are in the proper relation to each other under CAMERA. The club starts away from the ball. CAMERA FOLLOWS the club slightly, but is arrested by Welles' voice:

WELLES' VOICE: Keep your eye on the ball!

CAMERA PANS BACK to the ball. Club goes up for another drive, moves out of the frame and into it, striking the ball. CAMERA PANS, following the ball as it sails back up into the sky and then descends into a very palpable rough.

WELLES' VOICE (cont'd): Topped it, didn't you?

CAMERA PANS QUICKLY past fairway and AROUND to Welles' face. He is standing a few feet away, smiling, but as CAMERA settles on him he wipes smile off his face.

WELLES (cont'd): I'm sorry. It was the wind.

Welles moves forward, stopping when he fills frame with MEDIUM CLOSEUP of himself.

WELLES (cont'd): (looking straight into lens) Now, if you're doing this right, this is what you ought to look like to me.

Dissolve

Interior Moving Picture Theater (Painting)

5   SHOT of inside theatre as it would appear from the stage *or rather from the center of the moving picture screen!*

Beginning on the projection booth, CAMERA PANS DOWN taking in the orchestra floor of the theatre, dimly lit by the reflected light from the screen. *The audience is entirely made up of motion picture cameras.* When this has registered:

WELLES' VOICE: I hope you get the idea.

Fade Out

Fade In

Black Screen

6   A human eye appears on left side of screen. Then an "equal" sign appears next to it. The capital "I." Finally, the eye winks and we
Dissolve

—*Film Comment,* November–December 1972

3

Notes on a Conversation with Welles

The following notes appeared in the same issue of Film Comment *as the pre-ceding article, at the end of my regular column, titled "Paris Journal," for that magazine, which typically dealt with several different topics. Though these notes largely replicate things said elsewhere by Welles, two details for me stand out as significant additions to the record: that Welles regarded his* DON QUIXOTE *as nearly completed in 1972 — which corresponds fairly closely to the conclusions of* "DON QUIXOTE: *Orson Welles's Secret" by Audrey Stainton (who worked "on and off" as Welles's secretary in the late 1950s) in the Autumn 1988* Sight and Sound — *and that he remained convinced that the deleted footage of* AMBERSONS *was destroyed by RKO (a belief I regretfully share, though legends continue to circulate about another copy of the longer cut that may survive somewhere in Brazil).*

■

In the course of a conversation with Orson Welles about his HEART OF DARKNESS script, which is detailed elsewhere in this issue, I asked Welles about his more recent projects. Since a great deal of speculation has been circulating about these projects, the following details may be of some in-terest:

THE DEEP—which was shot in Yugoslavia, 1967–69, in Eastman Color, starring Welles, Jeanne Moreau, and Laurence Harvey—is completed, but Welles prefers to hold it back for the time being, waiting until he has released something else first. He describes it as a "melodrama," adding that "it won't date."

THE OTHER SIDE OF THE WIND is not yet finished, but Welles indicates that he would like to release it before any of his other new films, because "movies are a popular subject now"—the story concerns a film director— and he has some doubts about how long this interest will last.

Welles's Don Quixote film, which he began shooting in 1955, is now virtually complete, except for some music and additional sound that is still to be added. Welles noted with a grin that the film now has a new title, WHEN WILL DON QUIXOTE BE FINISHED? (or something to that effect; I quote from memory), and described a previously announced title, DON QUIXOTE GOES TO THE MOON, as a "put-on." Joseph McBride has suggested that one of the reasons why Welles has taken so long with the film is that he was unable to think of an ending: "how can the modern world, in which the film is set, tolerate Quixote's existence . . . but how too could Quixote ever cease to exist?" In this respect, the new title seems ideal. Welles is still undecided about whether to release the film fairly soon, in "competition" with the two other Quixote films that are currently being prepared by others, or to wait still longer.

Still another project that remains close to Welles is shooting a new ending of THE MAGNIFICENT AMBERSONS "with the surviving actors, showing the characters ten years later," replacing the unspeakable final scene as it now exists (directed, according to Peter Bogdanovich, by Freddie Fleck), and releasing this version as a new film. According to McBride, the original deleted footage of AMBERSONS "reportedly exists in the Paramount Studios film library (which acquired RKO's films in 1958), but a scholar would have to dig through literally millions of feet to find it." When I cited this quote to Welles, he remained unconvinced. "No," he said, "I'm sure they burned it all."

—From "Paris Journal," *Film Comment,*
November–December 1972

4

First Impressions of F FOR FAKE

The following piece is closer to a newsbreak than an article—a postscript attached to the end of yet another "Paris Journal" for Film Comment *at a time when I was contributing one to every issue.*

■

[. . .] A last-minute flash: Less than 24 hours after writing the above, I was able to attend a private screening of FAKE, a remarkable new film by Orson Welles. I'm afraid at least one or two more viewings of the film will be necessary before I can determine whether it's merely the least boring film I've seen in months or a great deal more than that. For the moment, steeped in the decidedly un-objective afterglow of sheer admiration, I can only stammer out a few points:

(1) FAKE concerns art forgery in general; Elmyr de Hory, Clifford Irving, Howard Hughes, and Welles himself in particular. Its point of departure is simple: if the distinction between real art and fakery is one that can only be made by "experts," then the faker who outwits the "experts" is a real artist. To all appearances, Welles turns this premise into a concerto.

(2) A few rumblings have already been heard to the effect that FAKE is "not really a Welles film"; don't believe a word of it. It is true that he uses a lot of material shot by François Reichenbach, from a film about de Hory that was made before Clifford Irving's own hoax was uncovered. (Other footage used includes excerpts from a sci-fi film—EARTH VS. FLYING

51

SAUCERS, if I'm not mistaken.) But it would be inadequate to suggest that all he does with this footage is re-edit it. More precisely, he sets up a complex dialogue with and between various fragments of it, interlaces this with sounds and images of his own, and comes up with something entirely different. . . . Another unwarranted dismissal would be to assume that it's "just a documentary." On its most serious level, it is an essay on cinematic illusionism expressed by simultaneously exploding illusions and reveling in them, mixing "fact" and "fiction" so subtly in some cases that it confounds our ordinary definitions of both terms, and creating as many Chinese-puzzle-paradoxes as a tale by Borges.

(3) The film begins, appropriately enough, with Welles performing magic to a group of children. With various forms of wizardry, he goes on to manufacture conversations with other people (de Hory, Irving) that never existed, counterfeit part of his own *War of the Worlds* broadcast, remake the newsreel opening of CITIZEN KANE, zip us around the Western Hemisphere—from his editing studio to Ibiza to Hollywood to Las Vegas and back again, with many side trips—without letting us pause for breath, make his leading actress (Oja Kodar) disappear, and levitate someone who may or may not be her grandfather (who also promptly disappears). The exhilaration of FAKE derives not so much from the more overt tricks that Welles pulls—some of these we see through (and the biggest, alas, is given away by John Russell Taylor in the Autumn [1973] *Sight and Sound*)—but the pleasure that Welles communicates in performing them. Artifice and playfulness are the most prominent characteristics of his magic, and he makes them into primal emotions.

(4) I suppose what I like most about FAKE is how deeply it digs into Welles's sources, all the way back to the radio shows of the Thirties and the headlong exposition and comic-strip velocity in his early features; the crazy-quilt cutting patterns, and the comedy too—I don't think he's made me laugh so much since his films in the Forties. The more somber aspects of his later work, from TOUCH OF EVIL to THE IMMORTAL STORY, are mainly reflected in a few terse aphorisms and anecdotes. Shakespeare aside, it is the most verbal film he has made since he left Hollywood, and its sustaining thread is his symphonic voice. . . . The most moving moments all come from recreations of Welles's past: recounting his experiences as a

bohemian painter in Ireland at 16; reflecting on the consequences of *The War of the Worlds* with devastating irony ("I didn't go to jail—I went to Hollywood"); picking up the lift in Arkadin's accent when he imitates a Hungarian; and in a particularly ghostly moment, turning luminous long shots of Chartres into another version of Kane's mansion. . . . Whether or not Welles has actually reinvented his toy train in a Paris editing studio and various other locations, he conveys so much joy in the very act of movie-making that he momentarily persuades us of the fact.

(5) "Cinema is the most beautiful fraud in the world," Godard says in LE GRAND ESCROC. Welles doesn't include this in his collection of epigrams, but he brought the statement back to memory and then made me wonder whether Godard might have lifted it from somewhere else. Why not?

Department of Mystification: Two days after completing and sending off the above, Les Films du Prisme sends me a *fiche technique* of the new Welles film. According to them, the title is QUESTION MARK, Welles and Reichenbach share the director's credit, and the script is by Oja Palinkas (Kodar), the leading actress. Elmyr de Hory and Clifford Irving (but not Welles) are listed as the leading actors. On the credits of the film that I saw, the word FAKE appears, followed by a question mark, and afterwards the title, "a film by Orson Welles." For the time being, I am content to call it THE NEW ORSON WELLES FILM, co-directed by Irving and de Hory, written by Jorge Luis Borges, and produced by Howard Hughes. . . . As Welles remarks about Chartres, the most important thing is that it exists.

—From "Paris Journal," *Film Comment*,
January–February 1974

5

The Butterfly and the Whale

Orson Welles's F FOR FAKE

During my two-and-a-half-year stint at the British Film Institute, working as assistant editor on the Monthly Film Bulletin *and staff writer on* Sight and Sound, Time Out *was the main local outlet for my freelance writing; Chris Petit, who was* Time Out's *film editor for much of that time, made the assignments. To clarify for American readers, the orientation of the original London version of that weekly magazine was countercultural and relatively laid-back when it came to editing—not at all like the more recent New York and Chicago versions, unless one factors in the occasional crudeness of the headlines. (The original one given to the following article, which I've been happy to suppress, was "Floats Like a Butterfly, Looks Like a Whale.") The "Pseuds Corner" mentioned in the following article was a regular section of the satirical London gossip magazine* Private Eye *that quoted pretentious passages from local journalists; by the time this article was published in* Time Out *in late 1974, I believe I had already made it into "Pseuds Corner" twice—once, as I recall, for my enthusiastic review of Michael Snow's experimental film* WAVELENGTH.

I suspect that the hilarious howler that part of THE OTHER SIDE OF THE WIND *was shot in Teheran came directly or indirectly from the fact that one of the film's funding sources was Mehdi Bousheri, the brother-in-law of the shah of Iran. Meanwhile, I was continuing to perpetuate my inadvertent scrambling of Welles's jokey title for* QUIXOTE—WHEN WILL YOU FINISH DON QUIXOTE?— *that I'd already done in* Film Comment.

As for my expression of a preference for F FOR FAKE *over* CHIMES AT MID-

54

NIGHT, *which may shock some readers, I should confess that the first time I saw the latter film, in Paris during the mid-60s, I was mainly disappointed—unlike my first reaction to* THE TRIAL *in New York a few years earlier, when I was bowled over. Undoubtedly this can be accounted for by my thwarted expectations of something more visually baroque, with better production values, which* THE TRIAL *met more than* CHIMES AT MIDNIGHT *had (apart from the battle sequence). Although I value the film much more today (and value* THE TRIAL *a bit less), I recognize that my own initial response is a typical example of even a dedicated Welles fan feeling unprepared for what Welles had to offer.*

■

A tale is told of a lecture delivered on Orson Welles at the Cuban Cinematheque, sometime during the mid-fifties. The speaker is G. Cabrera Infante, who later went on to write a remarkable novel set in Havana during the Batista period, *Three Trapped Tigers*. It is announced that the lecture will be given in two parts, on successive weeks. An audience gathers for Part One; Cabrera Infante steps up to the podium and delivers it: "Orson Welles is a whale." Then he steps down.

General consternation and outrage. Due to the uproar about the event, an even greater number of people turn up the following week. The curtains part. Cabrera Infante is nowhere in sight, but in his place there is a poster running across the entire length of the stage that says: "Orson Welles is a butterfly."

Whether or not this story is partially or wholly apocryphal—and a Cuban friend has insisted it's the unvarnished truth—it says a lot more about Welles and his latest film FAKE than anything else I could possibly hope to add here. (You can put that in your Pseuds Corner and smoke it.) It is the combined whale-like and butterfly-like qualities of Welles that make him into such a paradoxical, complex, and unpredictable director, difficult to classify and often easy to misunderstand.

In TOUCH OF EVIL, Welles in front of the camera is the very essence of a whale—Leviathan and Moby Dick rolled into one—while behind the camera he is light, mobile, and airborne (think of the opening shot). Even the physical absence of Cabrera Infante from Part Two of his lecture is an appropriate touch, expressing something about the public identity of

Welles as well as his style: if the whale is implacably present, the butterfly is perpetually flighty and elusive.

When I had the unexpected opportunity to interview Welles the summer before last, he said he was in the midst of editing a film about Elmyr
de Hory, Clifford Irving, and Howard Hughes called HOAX. (Later the title
was changed to FAKE.) "A documentary?" I asked him. "No, not a documentary—a new kind of film," he insisted. Then last October, a little over
a year after receiving this cryptic explanation, I got to see FAKE at a private
screening, and discovered that he was right.

A documentary, to be sure, was its starting point. While Clifford Irving was writing his book about the art forger Elmyr de Hory, shortly before launching his own hoax about Howard Hughes's autobiography,
François Reichenbach traveled to Ibiza to make a film about de Hory, and
interviewed Irving as well as de Hory in the process. Welles has juggled
with Reichenbach's footage, added some of his own, and come up with a
delightful string of fresh hoaxes—inventing conversations that never
took place, introducing himself into the discussion, and expanding the
theme of art forgery until it embraces the careers of not only de Hory and
Irving, but Hughes and Welles himself in the bargain. It is autobiography
and reflection in the form of a magic show, a whale of a subject that is
given the butterfly treatment. And not incidentally, it's one of the most
entertaining films I saw last year, and certainly one of the funniest.

When will you get to see it? I wish I could tell you. At the moment, nobody appears to know for sure when it will open anywhere. The sad fact
of the matter is that the film already appears to be regarded by people in
the trade as a commercial disaster—a curious attitude to take towards a
film before it's released, but far from an uncommon one. Indeed, Welles's
career as a director has been plagued by such attitudes. (The most interesting films, after all, are usually the unclassifiable ones, and "unclassifiable" in the movie business usually means unmarketable.) When he
made TOUCH OF EVIL, his last Hollywood film, Universal Pictures was apparently so convinced that the movie was worthless that it didn't bother
to arrange screenings for the press, and one of the central works of the
American cinema was denied even a first-run in the States.

TOUCH OF EVIL was made sixteen years ago, and Welles has not had a chance to work with the technical resources of Hollywood since. Considering his stature, it is almost as if Picasso were forbidden to paint with anything but watercolors for a major portion of his career. Thus Welles occupies the anomalous position of a mainstream artist who is forced to work in underground conditions.

Apart from FAKE, he has made two other features on restricted budgets which remain unreleased: a DON QUIXOTE begun in 1955 and completed fairly recently (which Welles told me he intends to call WHEN WILL DON QUIXOTE BE FINISHED?), and a melodrama, THE DEEP, starring Jeanne Moreau, Laurence Harvey, and himself, shot in Yugoslavia over five years ago. He is currently in the process of completing still another film, THE OTHER SIDE OF THE WIND, about a Hollywood director, which he has been filming in locations as diverse as Los Angeles and Teheran.

What will happen with these films? If the past offers any clues, one suspects that they will each be released in less than ideal circumstances, will fail at the box office, and the same critics who dismissed TOUCH OF EVIL for not being CITIZEN KANE will undoubtedly dismiss the new films for not being TOUCH OF EVIL. Twenty years later, the films may be accepted as classics, but it won't help Welles any: by that time, one imagines, his new films will be criticized for not being as good as THE OTHER SIDE OF THE WIND.

I'd be the last one to argue that all Welles films are equal, or that it's a simple matter to evaluate any of his works when they first appear. On the basis of a single viewing of FAKE, I don't think it's a masterpiece, although parts of it moved me and enthralled me to the point where I really didn't care whether it was one or not. In some ways I prefer it to THE TRIAL, CHIMES AT MIDNIGHT, and THE IMMORTAL STORY, his three previous films, if only because it avoids some of their sobriety and solemnity—what some critics call their "maturity"—to take us figuratively and literally back into Welles's own past, to the time when he used to be known as the Wonder Kid.

The exhilarating speed and razor-sharp comedy animating much of FAKE, particularly its first half, is a kind of high-powered showmanship and wit that no one else in the world can approximate, although many have tried. It can be traced back to his early films and radio shows, and it works hand in glove with his skills as a magician. The delight of magic re-sides in the lie that becomes a truth and the truth that becomes a lie, and this principle dictates the method of FAKE, as well as its subject. The theme is clearly stated: if the difference between "real art" and "fake art" can be determined only by experts, the charlatan who can fool the experts is an artist in his own right.

Playing the sage and elder statesman, Welles becomes a whale; as-suming the role of charlatan, he becomes a butterfly. In FAKE he plays both roles to the hilt, undercutting his own aphorisms with sleights of hand and then turning these sleights of hand into a form of wisdom. The joy he takes in this exposition is the joy of a brilliant amateur—a young director who is still exploring, still discovering. (It comes as a surprise to some spectators to learn that Welles is still under sixty.) Will he be allowed to share this pleasure with more than a few movie fans? That remains the biggest enigma of all.

—*Time Out* (London), December 6–12, 1974

6

Prime Cut

(The 107-Minute TOUCH OF EVIL)

This is probably the most erroneous text to be found in this collection—predicated on the false assumptions that (a) there was such a thing as a final cut by Welles of TOUCH OF EVIL, and (b) the version I was describing was essentially this mythical object. It was corrected by a letter from Joseph McBride in the Spring 1976 Sight and Sound *that rightly surmised that my error was largely traceable to a story of his own in* Variety *the previous June. McBride also alluded to the memo written by Welles to Universal about the film's recutting that he had read at this point, and which I wouldn't come across myself for at least a dozen more years. Interestingly enough, McBride's letter also defended the original release version of the film as "a more effective piece of storytelling" —anticipating the criticisms that would be made of the recut and remixed version that attempted to make the changes suggested in Welles's memo over two decades later (see chapter 21).*

■

In its broad outlines, the footage missing from the 1958 release version of TOUCH OF EVIL has never exactly been a secret: after a festival screening of the film in Brussels, Orson Welles described the major deletions to Charles Bitsch in *Cahiers du cinéma* no. 87. Nor has it ever been assumed that these cuts were nearly as serious as those suffered by THE MAGNIFI-CENT AMBERSONS. Nevertheless, it was good to have a chance to see for oneself—an opportunity afforded by the recent appearance in England of the original 107-minute version, in the Universal season at the NFT and then on the BBC. Fourteen minutes longer than the TOUCH OF EVIL one knew, it is apparently identical to Welles's final cut except for the credits, which still appear over the opening shot instead of the last.

As luck would have it, this "definitive" version turned up shortly after the publication of the second half of Stephen Heath's nearly book-length study of the film in the Summer *Screen*. Drawing on the Freudian and semiological disciplines that have been informing most of that magazine's recent work, Heath's consideration of the narrative mechanisms and their psychological implications—undoubtedly the closest reading that the movie has been given in print to date—offers at once a useful preparation to a viewing of the complete cut (through its attentiveness to the plot and "text" of the shorter version) and a fascinating investigation into methodology.

On the basis of a single look at the new print—weighed against memories of the old version rather than an instant replay for comparison—a few specifics and generalizations can be noted. The most substantial additions, in order, are: (1) A scene between Charlton Heston and Welles just after the latter's first scene with Marlene Dietrich: called away from Tania's by Menzies (Joseph Calleia), Quinlan is confronted by Vargas in front of some oil derricks, lodging a complaint about the treatment of his wife by the Grandis. The first extended dialogue between these rival heroes, it establishes their central conflict with biting directness—Vargas impugning Quinlan's behavior and attitude as a cop, the latter retaliating with insinuations about Susan Vargas (Janet Leigh) having been "picked up."

(2) Vargas sets out with Susan for the motel and a romantic scene ensues; he stops the car and they kiss. A police car pulls up and Menzies gets out to drive Susan the rest of the way so that Vargas can return to the investigation. Menzies explains to Susan how Quinlan wounded his leg by stopping a bullet for him, we see Grandi (Akim Tamiroff) following in another car. Cut to Quinlan, Vargas and Schwartz (Mort Mills) arriving at the construction site (which appears in the shorter version after Susan reaches the motel). Then we see Menzies parked in the middle of the highway to apprehend Grandi; a quick fadeout takes us to the arrival at the motel—Grandi asking what he's being charged with, Menzies replying

that Quinlan will think of something—and they drive off again, leaving Susan. A crane over the motel shows them receding into the distance, and her subsequent meeting with the "Night Man" (Dennis Weaver) now runs longer to include some remarks about Grandi, so that Weaver's manic giggles follow Susan's comment, "He's under arrest!"

(3) Schwartz takes Vargas to the Hall of Records, noting that he may lose his own job as assistant district attorney before the case is over. (4) Quinlan's second visit to Tania's is somewhat longer, so that Vargas is now briefly seen spotting him from outside, near the oil derricks; and Vargas's preparation of the recording equipment with Menzies is also extended a bit.

Along with several additional continuity shots—including at least two which announce the arrival of Tania, in the last scene—these supplements give the narrative a much cleaner fluidity, making both the plot and the physical layout of Los Robles much more legible. The movements of Grandi, the relation of Menzies to Quinlan, the role of Schwartz, and the oil derricks outside Tania's all register in a more integral fashion; and Vargas's sense of ethics—including compunctions about the final trap he sets for Quinlan—is given further attention, justifying Welles's 1958 remark that the "moral" scenes were reduced while the violent ones were left intact. Otherwise, the sound-mix is rather more complex and one has the added benefit of seeing more of all the central characters: all in all, a happy bonus demonstrating that the most densely plotted of Welles's films is a lot more lucid than one had formerly supposed.

—*Sight and Sound,* Autumn 1975

7

André Bazin and the Politics of Sound in TOUCH OF EVIL

The following is a fragment from a longer piece, and I've included it both because of its relevance to the version of TOUCH OF EVIL *that I subsequently worked on (see chapter 21) and because it was originally published in an abbreviated form in* Film Comment *that I don't think did justice to either my argument or the issues involved. Furthermore, it allows me to give an account here of my translation of André Bazin's* Orson Welles, *which would otherwise be unrepresented in this book.*

Let me begin by confessing that in spite of my five years of living in Paris, my grasp of French has always been mediocre—a weakness that over the years I've come to regard as a sort of disability, because I've made many efforts to overcome it. That François Truffaut had a similar (and similarly embarrassing) problem with his English set the stage for a rather awkward and uncomfortable afternoon in Mayfair between the two of us—with his assistant Suzanne Schiffmann often serving as mutual interpreter—after I'd signed with Harper & Row to carry out this translation of Bazin's book on Welles, including the new foreword to that book that Truffaut was writing. Truffaut undoubtedly came away from that afternoon with some understandable skepticism about why I'd been hired to do this job, while I emerged, somewhat defensively, with the impression that he was closer to being a nervous and irritable businessman than the sort of critic and director that I had formerly revered.

I hasten to add that I wasn't bluffing when I had praised Bazin's 1950 monograph on Welles in 1971 as the best criticism published about him—or at least not entirely. (This was a few years before I encountered James Naremore's The Magic World of Orson Welles, *the first edition of which was published in 1978.) Like many other American film buffs of that era, I had spent long hours reading it and many other French critical texts with what I had retained from my college French courses and a French-English dictionary. During my years in Paris, I also read such books as Noël Burch's* Praxis du cinéma *and Roland Barthes's* Le plaisir du texte *and paged through countless issues of* Cahiers du cinéma, Positif, *and other magazines and film books in the same manner.*

So when, shortly after I moved from Paris to London, I received an offer from Harper & Row to translate Bazin's Orson Welles—*specifically, the posthumously published book of that title brought out by Éditions du Cerf in 1972, which I knew less well than the 1950 Chavane monograph—I was faced with a quandary: the job was too appealing to turn down, but I also knew that I could perform it adequately only with enormous effort, as well as help from some of my more bilingual friends in London. I also rationalized that here at last was the sort of challenge that could hopefully force me to master the language once and for all. So with a queasy mixture of optimism and resolve, I gritted my teeth and plunged in.*

Ultimately, I used all the possible means at my disposal. After protracted stretches of wrestling alone with the text, I commissioned literal translations of some chapters from the late Jill Forbes—a fellow film buff in Paris who taught French literature in London—and spent many hours revising them, then annotating or correcting many of Bazin's factual errors, which proved to be far more numerous than I had anticipated. (I also commissioned my Paris friend Gilbert Adair, a passionate Cocteauvian, to translate Jean Cocteau's charming preface, and credited him for it.) Finally, and most importantly, I benefited from the generosity of my flatmate at the time, Tom Milne—a superb translator who had already tackled Godard's criticism and regularly subtitled French films for the BBC—who went over my drafts line by line with the original and made many revisions and suggestions.

During the same period, I wound up having a much much easier time corresponding with Truffaut, especially once we hit on the logical procedure of writing one another in our respective languages. While he was working on his own excellent foreword and both soliciting and following most of my editorial suggestions (such as my arguments on behalf of THE LADY FROM SHANGHAI, *which he had treated somewhat dismissively in his first draft), he was also furnishing me with other texts of Bazin about Welles on a regular basis and encouraging me to incorporate the most interesting passages from them as footnotes. I was nevertheless a bit put off by a couple of details in his foreword, which appeared towards the beginning and at the very end. He concluded the essay with the line "On the plane between Paris and Los Angeles," which was sheer invention (if memory serves, he was on Guernsey, one of the Channel Islands, at the time, shooting* L'HISTOIRE D'ADÈLE H.)*—not a serious fib, but still somewhat perturbing to me at the time. What bothered me more was the sentence concluding his third paragraph: "This little volume, superbly prefaced by Jean Cocteau, quickly went out of print and became a collector's item, and in 1968, shortly before his death, sparked by enthusiasm for* TOUCH OF EVIL, *Bazin prepared a revised and expanded edition, published here in Jonathan Rosenbaum's translation."*

Though I was ridiculously slow to realize this, this sentence was not only a fib—in this case an unwitting one—but one that revealed that Truffaut hadn't bothered to read or at least reread the two Bazin volumes in question, because the 1968 book wasn't at all a "revised and expanded edition" of the 1950 one but a completely different text. It was also a markedly inferior one—written in obvious haste, and in some cases copying out passages from a poorly translated French version of an already not very reliable book in English by Peter Noble. But given my embarrassment about not having spotted this sooner, and my even greater sense of intimidation about confronting Truffaut with this discovery, I kept silent about it.

This led in turn to a growing resentment against Truffaut that eventually found expression in a brief diatribe in a "London and New York Journal" for the July–August 1976 Film Comment, *reprinted on pages 26–27 of my collection* Placing Movies: The Practice of Film Criticism *(University of California Press, 1995). This diatribe, in turn, provoked an exchange with Truffaut that can be found on pages 462–64 of his collected* Letters *(Faber & Faber, 1989), in which he responds to my own explanatory letter by saying (in Gilbert Adair's translation), "If I had known that you regarded the Chavanne edition as superior, Janine Bazin and I would have given you the go-ahead to combine the two editions. Now it's too late."*

I take no pride in this episode, since it seems to me that Truffaut and I were both to blame for what finally emerged as Orson Welles: A Critical View

(Harper & Row, 1978)—the product, I now conclude, at least in part, of our mutual paranoia stemming from my poor grasp of French (even though it still includes a mainly first-rate foreword by Truffaut, and some passages of considerable interest by Bazin). But I've recounted this story in such detail because it seems to me emblematic of the kind of misapprehensions and misunderstandings that sometimes yield what we call film history, which includes the history of film criticism. And the degree to which Welles and our view of him have often been casualties of this kind of carelessness shouldn't be underestimated.

In the following excerpt, where I attack a brief passage from the book that I translated, I anticipate a charge made by Welles himself, in This Is Orson Welles, *against some of the critical discussions of* TOUCH OF EVIL *in France: "The French are convinced [that* TOUCH OF EVIL *is] the absolute proof that I'm a fascist. It's because an awful lot of the* Cahiers du cinéma *people are fascists, and they wanted it to prove that I was fascist—not as an attack" (2nd edition [Da Capo, 1998], 299).*

■

André Bazin's defense of Orson Welles's Hank Quinlan in TOUCH OF EVIL, which I had the job of translating a few years ago, shocked me at the time for what seemed to verge on a fascist argument in the midst of a humanist discourse. Acknowledging, with his customary scrupulousness, that his moral interpretation differs from that of Welles, Bazin implies that Quinlan is justified in his framing of suspects, not only because "without him . . . the guilty would pass for innocent," but also because of his innate superiority:

> Quinlan is physically monstrous, but is he morally monstrous as well? The answer is yes and no. Yes, because he is guilty of committing a crime to defend himself; no, because from a higher moral standpoint, he is, at least in certain respects, above the honest, just, intelligent Vargas, who will always lack that sense of life which I shall call Shakespearean. These exceptional beings should not be judged by ordinary laws. They are both weaker and stronger than others. Weaker: "When I start out to make a fool of myself, there's little enough can stop me," confesses the sailor Michael O'Hara at the start of THE LADY FROM SHANGHAI. But also so much stronger because directly in touch with the true nature of things, or perhaps one should say, with God.[1]

Much as Bazin's taste for Welles's low camera angles often seems to have an unstated affinity with the position of someone kneeling in church, this curious apologia for Quinlan's swinishness has never convinced me.

What has any of this to do with sound? A lot. Phyllis Goldfarb has ably shown how the repeated "fragmentation of the relationship between a sound and its source" in TOUCH OF EVIL produces a series of visual and aural dislocations—a material counterpart, one might add, to the moral ambiguities that undeniably infuse the film.[2] And one of the fascinations of the longer version of the movie that surfaced recently is its somewhat different sound mix—including, for the first time, the off-screen sound of Sanchez (Victor Millan) being slugged by Quinlan during the latter's interrogation of the former.

The point is that this single addition to the soundtrack—preceded by Quinlan saying, "Back in the old days we gave it to them like this," and followed by a cry of pain from Sanchez—*might* have tipped the scales for Bazin against Quinlan, had he seen this longer version. The ironic "footnote" that Sanchez proves to be guilty after all[3] remains unchanged; the crucial issue here is Quinlan's police methods. And the sound of a fist hitting a stomach while the camera focuses on Vargas (Charlton Heston) and Schwartz (Mort Mills) in another room is only one more instance of the moral difference that a sound can make.

Notes

1. *Orson Welles: A Critical View* (New York: Harper & Row, 1978), 124.
2. "Orson Welles's Use of Sound," *Take One,* vol. 3, no. 6, July–August 1971, 10–14. [2006: A considerably revised version of this essay is printed under the name Penny Mintz in the collection *Film Sound: Theory and Practice,* edited by Elisabeth Weis and John Belton (New York: Columbia University Press, 1985), 289–97.]
3. An afterthought from 2006: As James Naremore astutely points out, the fact that Sanchez offers a confession after protracted police brutality is hardly conclusive proof of his guilt.

—From "Sound Thinking," *Film Comment,*
September–October 1978

8

The Invisible Orson Welles

A First Inventory

I was living in Santa Barbara when Welles died on October 10, 1985, teaching what I believe was the first of the three Welles courses I taught at the University of California, Santa Barbara, and lecturing on THE MAGNIFICENT AMBERSONS *that same day. On November 2, I attended a lengthy Welles tribute held at the Directors Guild in Los Angeles, and recall sitting with a few other Welles fans, including Todd McCarthy and Joseph McBride, at a restaurant for many hours afterwards, holding what amounted to a kind of personal wake.*

This wasn't long after I'd managed to read and acquire xeroxed copies of two late, unrealized Welles screenplays, THE BIG BRASS RING *and* THE CRADLE WILL ROCK, *and one of the idées fixes I had after his death was that both of them should be published, along with the* HEART OF DARKNESS *script (another fixation that had persisted since the early 70s); if memory serves, I even wrote a letter soon after Welles's death to Paola Mori, Welles's widow, expressing this wish, but never got a response. Around November or December, I received a call from the Rotterdam Film Festival, which I had started attending regularly in early 1984, asking me how they could get in touch with Agnes Moorehead, Joseph Cotten, and other Welles associates in order to invite them to a Welles tribute they wanted to put together for late January. After explaining that Moorehead had passed away over a decade earlier, I did my best to persuade them that Oja Kodar, Gary Graver, and Peter Bogdanovich—all three of whom I'd just seen speaking at the Directors Guild—were the sort of people they should be inviting.*

Meanwhile, knowing that my friend Bill Krohn had recently interviewed

Kodar for Cahiers du cinéma *and was still in touch with her, I enlisted his help as a go-between, and in fact owe it entirely to him and his persistence that she was persuaded to attend. Bogdanovich, who was going through a bankruptcy at the time, reported back that he could only attend if his accountant came along, which caused the festival to demur, and I don't recall whether we ever got around to contacting Gary. I also gathered several videos and audiotapes of Welles materials to bring with me to the festival, including a professional taping of the entire DGA tribute that came courtesy of Richard Wilson. What I didn't realize, however, until I arrived in Rotterdam, a few days ahead of Oja, was that Huub Bals, the festival director, was expecting me to produce the tribute.*

Oja arrived at the Rotterdam Hilton with Dominique Antoine, the French producer of F FOR FAKE *and* THE OTHER SIDE OF THE WIND, *as well as a few videos of her own containing Welles material, and it was quickly decided that the festival would drive the three of us to an editing studio in Amsterdam to put together a 90-minute compilation that could be presented towards the end of the festival's ten days. And by the time we made our presentation a few days later, Oja had also gotten the festival to bring another friend, José Maria Castellvi, a Spanish still photographer who had taken some production photos on* THE OTHER SIDE OF THE WIND.

During the same few days, while becoming acquainted with Oja, I tried unsuccessfully to broker a deal whereby Raúl Ruiz, an ardent Welles fan who was also attending the festival, could film Welles's screenplay for THE DREAMERS *in a way that would incorporate the footage that Welles had already shot. Unfortunately, the Ruiz feature that happened to be showing at the festival,* L'ÉVEILLÉ DU PONT DE L'ALMA, *proved to be a less than ideal résumé as far as Oja was concerned, and she and José Maria lasted only about a third of the way through it.*

Above all, it was my conversations with Oja (with Dominique's input) over several days in Rotterdam that yielded the following article and also paved the way for our three eventual joint publishing ventures: THE BIG BRASS RING, THE CRADLE WILL ROCK, *and* This Is Orson Welles *(the first two at my instigation, the third at Oja's). But in the short run, once I was back in Santa Barbara, I first had to cope with a couple of disappointments. After writing the article and making an appointment with Oja to show it to her for her approval, I drove the hundred miles to her house on Stanley Avenue in Los Angeles, the one she had shared with Welles, one Sunday morning only to find an apologetic note from Oja on the*

front gate saying she'd had to go out to meet with her lawyer. (I left behind my
draft, and she conveyed her comments and minor corrections somewhat later,
over the phone.) And a plan for Oja to attend the Santa Barbara film festival,
where I was presenting the same compilation video that we'd edited with Do-
minique, was also canceled at the very last minute. I wound up regarding both
incidents as loyalty tests of some kind, even if they may not have been consciously
intended as such—comparable to the sort of things that Welles himself had often
done—so I made a point not to raise a fuss about them.

Some corrections and updates: The 16mm reels of MOBY DICK *alluded to here*
proved to be not Welles's (unfinished and aborted) film of his English stage pro-
duction but a subsequent incomplete solo performance of that play with Welles
playing all the roles, shot by Gary Graver in Orvilliers (where Welles lived with
Oja at the time) in 1971. LIFE OF LOLLOBRIGIDA *proved to be only the working*
title of VIVA ITALIA!, *shown in its entirety under the latter name on German tel-*
evision a few years ago. For more material on DON QUIXOTE, *see the final chapter*
of this book. The obstacles preventing a completion of THE DEEP *have included the*
failure of Jeanne Moreau to dub her own part, the disappearance of an edited work
print, and the loss of other materials due to unpaid lab costs, though the Munich
Film Archives have put together a feature-length restoration with a good many
patches that are either silent or with live (as opposed to dubbed) sound and/or
stretches in black and white. The mysterious missing reel of THE MERCHANT OF
VENICE *remains unrecovered, although theories and rumors about its where-*
abouts continue to circulate. The F FOR FAKE *trailer is nine minutes long, not*
twelve. And the principal obstacle to completing THE OTHER SIDE OF THE WIND,
despite many attempted deals, has been the inability for Oja to obtain a contract
allowing herself and Gary Graver to have final creative control. Given Gary's
shooting of the entire film and Oja's substantial input as writer, actress, and even
director (in a climactic sequence of the film-within-the-film), I consider them the
only ones with the knowledge and sensitivity as well the moral right to carry out
this work, but other egos and power positions have periodically argued otherwise.

In the spring of 1999, shortly after the Munich Film Archives acquired the
unfinished and other film material of Welles that was then in Oja's possession
(not including DON QUIXOTE, *which had by then already gone to the Filmoteca*
Española in Madrid, or, in the case of other materials, remained with Mauro
Bonnani in Rome or with the Paris Cinémathèque), I had the rare privilege of

coming to that city (for the first time) at the invitation of Robert Fisher-Ettel and spending six days with him and other Archive employees going through a good many reels of film on flatbeds, assessing as well as we could part of what was there, and meanwhile helping to plan a four-day Welles conference to be held in Munich half a year later. (One of the first and most delightful discoveries I made on that visit was that Jakob Zouk's attic in MR. ARKADIN was actually located across the street from the site where the Archives would later be built—purely by coincidence. Although the building has since been rehabbed, it remains recognizable.)

Among the many things that we looked at—including several reels from THE DEEP without sound and the unedited FILMING "THE TRIAL"—was THE MAGIC SHOW, and Robert arranged to copy all of THE MAGIC SHOW material for me on video so I could present a very tentative "rough cut" at the conference. My reasoning was that because Oja would be there, this crude assembly, which I put together in Chicago with two VCRs over the ensuing months, could trigger enough of her memories about the project to evoke corrections and other key indications about the intended order of sequences. But this strategy failed completely, because Oja was so distressed by the visual quality of the dubs that she promptly walked out of the auditorium shortly after my presentation started. Many months later, Stefan Drössler, who had meanwhile taken over Robert's (temporary) position as director of the Archive, put together a shorter assembly of his own, on film, and I regret that he omitted my favorite part of the footage—a hilarious stretch of silent slapstick featuring magician Abb Dickson as a Southern sheriff, preceded by a brief monologue from him—because there was no obvious place for it in the performances of magic tricks. More recently, the young American Welles scholar Peter Tonguette has been researching THE MAGIC SHOW, THE DREAMERS, and other late projects much more thoroughly via interviews for a book scheduled to appear before this one. (Portions of this work have already appeared in the online journal Senses of Cinema.) At the Locarno Welles conference in August 2005, Dickson accompanied the silent footage with his own clarifying commentary, and revealed that Welles had left other portions of the footage with him as well as some script materials. (At the same event, I resaw a roughly half-hour assembly of the materials shot for THE DREAMERS, which I continue to find the most effective and convincing of all of restorations carried out by the Munich Archive—material I even prefer in some ways to THE IMMORTAL STORY, despite its unfinished and incomplete state.)

In my synopsis of THE BIG BRASS RING, *I erroneously identify Kim Meneker's former lover as "a basket-case casualty from Vietnam" rather than from the Spanish Civil War.*

■

All films today are unfinished—except, possibly, those of Bresson.
—Râúl Ruiz in conversation

You don't imagine that posterity's judgment, do you? Posterity is a whim. A shapeless litter of old bones: the midden of a vulgar beast: the most capricious and immense mass-public of them all—the dead.
—Kim Menaker in THE BIG BRASS RING

It seems typical of the misunderstandings which plagued Orson Welles's life that he died, as a working artist, in almost total obscurity. The director of CITIZEN KANE, to be sure, taped a lengthy TV talk-show appearance the day before he died which summarized a substantial portion of his career—as magician, actor, director, one-time political aspirant, show-biz personality, and, most recently, the subject of a biography by Barbara Leaming. Yet such is the nature of our media and its discreet omissions that this generous glimpse of Welles failed even to hint at the artistic activity that consumed the last two decades of his life. The closest the program got to this reality was a passing acknowledgment of CHIMES AT MIDNIGHT, released in 1966, as an unjustly neglected film.

It's an unpleasant but unavoidable fact that according to the logic of capitalism, which tends to define reality exclusively in relation to marketable items, Welles as an artist died in disgrace—the butt of endless fat jokes, has-been references, and morose reflections about what would or could or should have been had the man not gone so distressingly to seed. This wasn't, of course, the general response outside the U.S.; in Paris, to cite the other extreme, only two days after his death by heart attack on October 10, 1985, *Libération* came out with a twelve-page tribute. But, by and large, the American response was remorseless in its verdict. Decline, failure, inactivity, endless "taking meals" at Ma Maison in Los Angeles, and hack TV appearances by a one-time genius were mostly what one read about, often with a reference to Pauline Kael's pejorative "Raising KANE" thrown in for good measure.

Why was Welles hated and feared so much on his native soil? Was it because he was perceived as the man who had it all, and then threw it away? But of course Welles never had it all to begin with; despite the strength of his original RKO contract, only one of his many projects there ever got made and released to his satisfaction, and that one came dangerously close to never getting made or released at all. The legend embraced the boy wonder in power, but fell aground as soon as it had to cope with him as deposed royalty—which is what he remained for the next forty-five years. For the most part, critics and public alike remained loftily indifferent to this second Welles, at least until it was too late to make any difference: if it wasn't another CITIZEN KANE, made with the virtually limitless resources of a major studio and released by a major distributor, they weren't interested—until the film was revived as a classic a decade or so later.

Considering the brashness of Welles, it would be foolish to claim that he was entirely blameless in what happened, yet no less foolish to assume that he should somehow have tempered his brashness in order to stay in the game. (He tried that in THE STRANGER, and only an anti-Wellesian like James Agee could have been very pleased with the results.) And it is important to remember that he was brash as an artist, not as a celebrity or public figure; he never shocked anyone on a TV show—which is perhaps part of what made the periodic need to shock in his art so palpable. TOUCH OF EVIL, THE TRIAL, and (as scripted) THE BIG BRASS RING are all like the volcanic eruptions of a caged beast kept too long in confinement—excessive at times to the point of losing control over their own meanings, yet richer and more thrilling for the headlong risks they take.

If Welles, along with Murnau, was the most poetically gifted master of camera movement in the history of cinema, this was largely because he wasn't a rationalist like Mizoguchi or even Ophüls in his charted arabesques and flourishes, but an explorer of unconscious and semiconscious drives and transports. The bravura of the descent into and eventual ascent away from the El Rancho; the giddy, fleeting entrance into the last of the Amberson balls; the almost prenatal backward probe down a dark courtyard passageway, away from Van Stratten on his way up the stairs through the snow towards Jacob Zouk; the swoops and dives of a crane across a Mexican border town, or the serpentine chase around the pillars of a ruined building outside a strip joint—always the elation of a Victorian imagination run riot.

Significantly, at a tribute to Welles held at the Directors Guild in Hollywood last November, Charlton Heston described Welles as the most gifted director he ever worked for, but demurred when Peter Bogdanovich labeled TOUCH OF EVIL (1958), Welles's last Hollywood film, "a masterpiece." Heston said that he preferred to call it "the best B picture ever made." In America, to make the best B picture ever made means, on the bottom line, to be a failure; acutely aware of this fact, even as he railed against it, Welles could not transform himself into a mainstream figure, and wound up subsidizing most of his late work himself. Quite simply, to "succeed" in the 80s, he would have to have been someone else.

Yet during the last week of his life, at age 70, he was working on at least four of his own features, and even died while typing stage directions for the last part of one of them, which he planned to shoot later the same day. And since his death, an accumulating legacy of invisible works has slowly yet obstinately been rising to the surface, giving the lie to the cherished industry fiction that all those legendary titles—DON QUIXOTE, THE DEEP, THE CRADLE WILL ROCK, THE DREAMERS, KING LEAR, and still others—were merely (or mainly) apocryphal alibis from an artist who was no longer producing. The new counter-evidence, at once heartening and appalling, is that Welles's phantom filmography really exists, and is larger than anyone expected.

Thanks to computers, economic balance sheets are available in a flash. Aesthetic balance sheets take much longer, and we are still years away from the point when the "entire" Welles legacy can simply be *seen*, much less studied and assessed. In the meantime, a certain amount of clarification seems both possible and desirable. Even the fragmentary evidence already becoming available suggests a different Welles from the one we have become accustomed to calling our own, and clearly this is as it should be: was there ever a film in his career that *didn't* confound our expectations? And for starters, it is now evident that Welles continued to produce for half a century at very nearly the same alarming rate which he had sustained in his youth, however and whenever he could. It was only the rest of us who had slowed down.

Indeed, one could argue that it was precisely this non-stop production which aborted Welles's career and led to so many unfinished, unrealized and/or invisible projects—to the same degree that it yielded the substantial (if partially mangled) *oeuvre* which we already know. Living on the wire, Welles saw life and work alike as a treacherous balancing act requiring constant improvisation, meaning that no script, however elaborate, could be simply executed, and no footage, however successful, could be simply edited—a style of work which sent chills up investors' spines, but one not incompatible with the ordinary working methods of many painters, composers, and novelists. The resulting martyrdom has usually been rationalized in one of two ways, neatly summed up by the two Welles biographies which appeared last year: either by blaming everything on Welles (the Charles Higham formula) or by blaming fate or the world (only a slight exaggeration of Barbara Leaming's approach). Surely the fact that Welles's subjective private world tended to be split between fidelity and betrayal only added to this polarization. But the truth has to be somewhere in between, and no single or simple Rosebud can be produced satisfactorily to dissolve the dilemma. Perhaps it isn't a dilemma that *should* be dissolved; perhaps, on the contrary, it is the peculiar strength of Welles's work to keep it alive and worrying—a continuing rebuke and challenge to the way the world usually goes about its business.

In love with process rather than product, Welles triumphed as well as suffered by postponing deadlines; it is worth recalling that the most celebrated works of his career—*Julius Caesar* on stage, *The War of the Worlds* on radio, CITIZEN KANE—all thrived on last-minute delays and revisions. The only thing that changed, really, was our tolerance for such activity, and the loss is mainly ours. Welles, after all, had a thousand and one Welles films in his head and at his disposal; we only have the ones we allowed him to make.

■

In the latter part of his film career, Welles took a dramatic turn towards privacy that makes many of his late works more intimate and personal and less tied to his public image than the earlier ones. As an integral part of that life and work, the figure of Oja Kodar is likely to disconcert many of those Welles aficionados who assume that they had the master all figured out years ago. Until very recently, she has remained a willing stranger to the world of cinema, and apart from her appearance in F FOR FAKE, unknown to most of Welles's audience. Yet insofar as there is an invisible Orson Welles to contend with, she is clearly, along with cinematographer Gary Graver, a major collaborator, witness, and resource.

A Yugoslav sculptor who met Welles in Zagreb during the shooting of THE TRIAL in 1962, and lived with him for the better part of the last two decades of his life, she worked on at least a dozen of his late features and projects—beginning with the dubbing of Jeanne Moreau's lovemaking sighs in THE IMMORTAL STORY and proceeding through a major part in THE DEEP, script collaboration and lead parts in F FOR FAKE and THE OTHER SIDE OF THE WIND (films whose titles are incidentally hers), work on many other scripts (including THE HONORARY CONSUL, THE SURINAM, A HELL OF A WOMAN, THE BIG BRASS RING, and THE DREAMERS) and some projected or semi-realized parts (Pellegrina, the lead role in THE DREAMERS; Cela Brandini in THE BIG BRASS RING; Cordelia in LEAR). Apart from this, she assumed such varying tasks as props and wardrobe on F FOR FAKE, assistant director on THE MAGIC SHOW, and everything from slate holder to focus puller on still other projects.

The Welles legacy, such as it is, consists of works in different forms and different stages of realization and completion, ranging all the way from scripts to finished films. Most of the films require lab and/or restoration work before they can be seen at all, and when this will happen depends on several factors, most of them legal and/or financial. Omitted from the inventory below, the order of which is roughly chronological (and often misleadingly so, for many projects were worked on concurrently), are several late projects or scripts about which I know little beyond their titles or subjects: adaptations of *Catch-22*, Conrad's *Lord Jim* and *Victory* (the latter of which, entitled THE SURINAM, Bogdanovich once planned to produce), Greene's *The Honorary Consul* (co-scripted by Kodar), Jim Thompson's *A Hell of a Woman* (co-scripted by Kodar and Gary Graver); films about Chaplin, San Simeon and Central America; and a couple of Kodar stories, *Blind Window* and *Crazy Weather*—not to mention the twenty or so earlier scripts listed in an appendix to Peter Cowie's *The Cin-*

ema of Orson Welles, as well as other titles which we may both have missed.

One further caveat. In what is conceivably the last draft of Welles's script for THE MAGNIFICENT AMBERSONS before shooting started, dated 7 October 1941, one encounters the following:

THE MIDDLE-AGED CITIZEN

Sixty thousand dollars for the woodwork *alone!* Yes, sir—hot and cold running water upstairs and down, and stationary washstands in every last bedroom in the place!

Pretty much the same dialogue occurs in the film, but split between no less than four gawking townspeople, two men and two women. A small change, perhaps, but rhythmically and musically a crucial one in terms of the line's delivery and impact, and only one of the countless examples of Welles's creativity on a set. Bearing this in mind, it is impossible to read any of his unrealized scripts and confidently imagine that one can conjure up the film that would have been from the printed evidence. Yet the remarkable thing about the scripts I've read for THE CRADLE WILL ROCK and THE BIG BRASS RING—unlike the first and ninth drafts of THE DREAMERS, which leave more to the imagination—is that they often register like living, breathing and *finished* works on the page, almost as if Welles had suspected that they might never be allowed to live elsewhere. As such, they virtually cry out to be published, and one hopes eventually they will be.

IT'S ALL TRUE. Although much has already been written about this doomed Latin American venture of 1942, including articles by Charles Higham and Richard Wilson in this magazine, a considerable portion of the unprocessed and unedited silent footage had not until very recently been seen by anyone. In *Cahiers du cinéma* last autumn, Bill Krohn reported at some length on the tortuous history of this episodic documentary and its partially recovered footage. Since then, Richard Wilson and Paramount executive Fred Chandler have been working on a documentary about IT'S ALL TRUE which will incorporate much of the available footage, primarily a version of the *jangadeiros* episode edited by Wilson, as well as interviews with some of the surviving participants on the project.

While hardly any of the three-strip Technicolor carnival sequences ap-

pears to have survived (unlike much of the black and white coverage of
the same events), the most important material to have been uncovered
this year is said to be the footage shot in Fortaleza with a silent Mitchell
camera and a skeleton crew of four (Wilson and his wife Elizabeth, cameraman George Fanto and Welles's secretary Shifra Haran) during
Welles's last six weeks in Brazil, which Krohn finds comparable in some
respects to Eisenstein's QUE VIVA MEXICO! rushes. (Whether Welles would
have appreciated the comparison is doubtful; according to Kodar, whose
anticinéphilia runs as deeply as Welles's did, my own suggestion that the
beginning of OTHELLO is Eisensteinian wouldn't have pleased him either.)

MOBY DICK. A few sources cite a film made of Welles's celebrated 1955
stage version of Melville's novel, done in the form of a stage rehearsal, at
London's Hackney Empire and Scala Theatre. According to some reports,
the film was never finished. Kodar has recently uncovered three very old
and fragile reels of 16mm footage labeled MOBY DICK; if this *is* in fact the
material, we can perhaps look forward to a unique film record of Welles's
stage work.

LIFE OF LOLLOBRIGIDA. In my translation of André Bazin's second book
about Welles (Elm Tree Books, 1978), I said in a footnote that this TV film
was never completed. But according to Jean-Pierre Thibaudat in *Libération*
last February, three more moldering reels comprising a half-hour personal "essay" by Welles about Lollobrigida have recently surfaced in
Paris. The story recounted by Thibaudat is quintessentially Wellesian.
Circa 1958, probably on his way back from Rome, Welles stopped off at
one of his favorite hotels in Paris, and left the film cans behind when he
departed. As the canisters bore no name or address, they wound up in the
hotel's lost property department, were never reclaimed, and were eventually transferred to another storage area, where they remained for a further two decades.

The film was made for CBS and, according to Welles in a 1982 interview, "sent to them, where there were cries of horror and disgust from
[James] Aubrey there, whose nickname you remember was 'The Smiling
Cobra.' And that was the end of that." Apparently done in a manner that
anticipates F FOR FAKE and FILMING OTHELLO (as well as some of Fellini's
film journals), the film has Welles ruminating on other Italian stars, pin-

ups, and Rome, speaking onscreen and off over Steinberg drawings and Italian landscapes, including brief encounters with his wife Paola Mori, and with Rosanno Brazzi and Vittorio De Sica, and finally visiting Lollo-brigida in her native village (Subiaco) in the third reel, after being greeted by her three wolfhounds at the door.

DON QUIXOTE, aka WHEN WILL YOU FINISH DON QUIXOTE? The film with the longest production history in Welles's career, this adaptation of Cer-vantes's novel in a modern setting, financed entirely out of Welles's own pocket, was worked on intermittently for thirty years. He started it in France in 1955, with Mischa Auer as Quixote and Akim Tamiroff as San-cho Panza, continued it in Mexico over three months in 1957 (replacing Auer with Francisco Rieguera), and added further material (shot in Mex-ico, Spain and Italy) in the 60s and early 70s, the last of which was footage of the Holy Week Processions in Seville, shot by Graver. He edited a more or less complete version in Rome in the mid-70s, and shortly before his death had the work print shipped to Los Angeles, planning to discard the film's original framing device (Welles, as himself, telling the story to a young Patty McCormack) and add a color prologue and epilogue—work which was never completed.

The film is currently in the process of being restored. When it finally becomes visible, one wonders to what degree it will reflect the varying conceptions Welles had of it as he progressively developed the project. According to Bazin, the original material shot in Mexico followed "a prin-ciple of complete improvisation inspired by the early cinema." Kodar re-ports that Welles, apart from supplying the narration, dubbed the voices of both Don Quixote and Sancho Panza. At one point in the early 80s, Welles hoped to return to Spain and add material about changes since the death of Franco, giving the film more of an essay form. It would appear that part of his reluctance to conclude the project stemmed from his changing attitudes towards Spain, where he lived for many years during the 50s (and which is the principal setting of THE BIG BRASS RING). Do-minique Antoine, the French co-producer of THE OTHER SIDE OF THE WIND, recalls that he once told her he could finish DON QUIXOTE only if he ever decided *not* to go back to Spain—apparently because each return visit suggested further revisions.

THE DEEP. Not to be confused with Peter Yates's 1977 feature of the same title, this adaptation of Charles Williams's thriller *Dead Calm*, scripted by Welles, was shot in color off the Dalmatian coast at Hvar, Yugoslavia, between 1967 and 1969, with Welles, Laurence Harvey, Jeanne Moreau, Oja Kodar and Michael Bryant. Most of this film was shot and edited, but gaps remain due to the death of Laurence Harvey in 1973 and the still undubbed part of Jeanne Moreau. Welles, Kodar and others have regarded this as the least of his features, so one imagines that it has a low priority on the list of works to be completed and/or released—although, as Kodar points out, priorities may change on any project if investment is forthcoming.

At the Rotterdam film festival last January, Kodar, Dominique Antoine and I compiled a 90-minute videotape of Wellesiana to be shown there, and among the clips we included was a two-minute trailer for THE DEEP— an early action sequence including brief glimpses of all five of the characters on two yachts and an effective use of percussive jazz (bass and drums) on the soundtrack. Crisply if rather conventionally edited, it does not suggest major Welles, although a look at Williams's novel suggests an intriguing tension between the characters of Hughie Warriner (Harvey), a psychotic hijacker, and Russ Brewer (Welles), an acerbic macho writer, which in some ways parallels the charged relationships between older and younger men in CHIMES AT MIDNIGHT, THE OTHER SIDE OF THE WIND, and THE BIG BRASS RING. (If the theme of mothers and sons seems to inform the early features—KANE, AMBERSONS, THE LADY FROM SHANGHAI, MACBETH—the emphasis on fathers and sons seems no less prevalent in some of the later projects.)

THE MERCHANT OF VENICE. The most unknown of all Welles's invisible features, shot in color (by Giorgio Tonti, Ivica Rajkovic and Tomislav Pinter) in Trogir, Yugoslavia, Asolo, Italy (the villa of Eleonora Duse), and Venice in 1969. The film was completed—edited, scored and mixed—over fifteen years ago but has not yet seen the light of day because two of the work print reels, including the sound elements (which are now missing from the original negative) were stolen from the production office in Rome.

The last of Welles's realized film adaptations of Shakespeare, featuring himself as Shylock, Charles Gray as Antonio, and Irina Maleva as Jessica, it is set in the 18th century and, according to Kodar, reflects Welles's interest in Judaism, as well as his belief that the play is neither anti- nor pro-semitic. "It's impossible to believe that [Shakespeare] didn't know Jews," Welles told Bill Krohn in 1982, during the interview in which he first acknowledged the film's existence. "And there were few of them in England at the time. But there was the theory that he'd been in the Low Countries and doing military service, and it would have been there that he'd run into a lot of Jewish people. Because the rhythms of speech are so Jewish." (It is worth noting that in THE DREAMERS Welles also cast himself in an explicitly Jewish role.)

Welles originally wanted Kodar to play Portia, but she refused, at that stage considering her English inadequate, and Welles wound up eliminating Portia from the story altogether—a startling move, but one not inconsistent with some of his other drastic changes in Shakespeare throughout his career. One of the segments planned for ORSON WELLES SOLO was an abridged one-man performance of *Julius Caesar* eliminating Brutus!

The F FOR FAKE Trailer. Before the disastrous American release of Welles's 1973 feature (but after its successful run in Europe), he filmed a promotional trailer with completely new material, featuring Kodar and Gary Graver. Because the film runs about a dozen [nine] minutes, the American distributor indignantly refused to process it; it remains in black and white work print form, with sound and image on separate reels, and was shown in that form at a Welles tribute in Los Angeles a few years ago.

THE OTHER SIDE OF THE WIND. If DON QUIXOTE has the longest production history, this color and black and white feature, prefigured to run about three hours, has certainly had the most complex and nightmarish vicissitudes; Kodar has remarked that the correspondence file alone is as long as WAR AND PEACE. (See the lengthy account in Leaming's biography, which co-producer Antoine informs me is entirely accurate.) Started well before F FOR FAKE, in 1970, and continued for years afterwards, in Arizona, Los Angeles, and elsewhere, the film was very nearly completed: Antoine recalls Welles putting together a rough cut with the aid of no less than eleven moviolas, arranged in a semi-circle. But for the last decade it has remained unseen, either in the possession of the brother-in-law of the late

Shah of Iran or in the French courts, where Kodar is trying to retrieve it, hoping to complete it with the assistance of Graver (who shot the entire film and worked on the editing) and Peter Bogdanovich. From all accounts, it would appear to be both Welles's last satiric word on the world of cinema and one of his most adventurous stylistic experiments.

"When we started writing the script," Kodar says, "we had two stories. Orson's was called JAKE HANNAFORD and it was too long, because it was based on the life of movie director Rex Ingram, and on Hemingway following the bullfights through Spain, and on some of Orson's own experiences. Orson came to the conclusion that the bullfights had become just a tourist attraction and had lost whatever sincerity they once had.

"So after he discovered his script was too long, and cut everything he wanted to cut, he discovered it was too short. This is how we decided to make a sort of osmosis of his story and my story, and began working together on a new script. My story is that there is a man who is still potent— it's not that he is impotent—but gets a real kick from the idea of sleeping with his leading man, sleeping really with the woman of his leading man. So he is not a classic homosexual, but somewhere in his mind he is possessing that man by possessing his woman. And at the same time, just because there is a hidden homosexuality in him, he is very rough on open homosexuals, as so many of those guys are.

"This is one reason why the script is so complicated and has so many chords. When you see the film, you will feel that somebody else worked with him because there are things that he never would have done alone, and never did before. He was a very shy man, and erotic stuff was not his thing. And in this film, you will see the erotic stuff. He kept accusing me with his finger: 'It's your fault!' And he was right—it's my fault!"

Part of this film's formal interest is that it incorporates two separate styles, neither of which can be associated with Welles's customary signature (apart from the almost subliminally rapid editing which characterizes his "late" manner from OTHELLO to portions of THE TRIAL to F FOR FAKE). One style belongs to an unfinished, rather arty film which Jake Hannaford (John Huston) is screening at his birthday party; the other derives from the diverse 16mm, Super-8 and video footage being shot by several TV and documentary crews at the party.

Centered round the night of July 2nd (which, Joseph McBride has noted, "is not coincidentally the date of Hemingway's suicide"), and reportedly employing a somewhat KANE-like flashback structure, the film features TV actor Bob Random as Hannaford's leading man, Kodar as his leading actress, Lilli Palmer as the friend giving the party, Peter Bogdanovich as a younger director (patterned in part after Bogdanovich himself) and, among others, Norman Foster, Curtis Harrington, Henry Jaglom, Joseph McBride, Mercedes McCambridge, Paul Mazursky, Cameron Mitchell, Edmond O'Brien, Paul Stewart, Susan Strasberg, Dan Tobin, and Richard Wilson. Two excerpts from the film—both witty and frenetic—were shown by Welles at the AFI's Life Achievement Award banquet held in his honor in 1975, in an unsuccessful attempt to raise completion money, and these are described in some detail in the closing pages of James Naremore's excellent *The Magic World of Orson Welles.* Which affords us a match cut to

THE MAGIC SHOW. Shot intermittently between 1969 and 1985 with Graver, Kodar, and fellow magician Abb Dickson, in Los Angeles, Atlanta, and Kodar's home in Orvilliers, France, this is the project Welles was working on when he died. The centerpiece of this theatrical smorgasbord, which seems to bear some resemblances to Tati's PARADE, is an assortment of some of his best acts of prestidigitation, all done without camera tricks. According to Graver, this portion of the program runs about half an hour and is more or less edited.

The remainder consists of *The Orson Welles Special,* completed, a 90-minute talk-show with Burt Reynolds, Angie Dickinson, and the Muppets; and ORSON WELLES SOLO, scripted but regrettably unrealized, which Welles wanted to shoot partially with a Beta cam—a one-man show that would have included the abridged *Julius Caesar* without Brutus and the telling of an Isak Dinesen story, "The Old Chevalier," which Welles had originally planned to include as part of a sketch feature for Alexander Korda in the 1950s, PARIS BY NIGHT. Other cast members in THE MAGIC SHOW as a whole include Senta Berger, Artie Johnson, Lynn Redgrave, Mickey Rooney (whom Welles once expressed an interest in casting as the Fool in KING LEAR), and restaurateur Patrick Terrail.

THE BIG BRASS RING. Although this project never got beyond the script stage, it is unquestionably one of the most remarkable and revealing works in the entire Welles canon. Written at the urging of his friend director Henry Jaglom, ostensibly as a "commercial" Hollywood screenplay, it is in fact nothing of the sort—though no less brilliant for that. The settings are New York, a yacht in the Mediterranean, North Africa, Barcelona, and Madrid. Senator Blake Pellarin, a Texas Democrat, has just lost out to Reagan in a presidential election, to the bitter disappointment of his ambitious wife, Diana. On a yachting trip, he spies a Portuguese maid about to steal his wife's emerald necklace and impulsively urges her to take it. Then, even more impulsively, he offers to find her a fence for it, snatches it back, and sets off on a wild goose chase leading him to his beloved Harvard mentor Kimball Menaker (Welles), holed up at the Batunga Hilton with a sickly, dying pet monkey and two black, nude female bodyguards.

Having thus in effect gone AWOL from his wife and political entourage, Pellarin asks for Menaker's help in fencing the necklace, which eventually leads to secret meetings between the two in Madrid. As the story shuttles in ARKADIN-like fashion between Pellarin, wife and entourage, and Menaker, and their occasionally parallel trajectories, the major go-between is Cela Brandini, a jet-set journalist in army fatigues clearly patterned after Oriana Fallaci. Rather like the faceless reporter in KANE, she probes the painful half-secret that has helped to undo Pellarin's political career and continues to bind him to Menaker—the fact that Menaker, once a prized member of F.D.R.'s Brain Trust, has belatedly come out of the closet and, in a letter to his former lover, now a basket-case casualty from Vietnam, declared his love and lust for Pellarin.

The above barely summarizes the plot's point of departure, but cannot begin to do justice to the manic energy of this demonic, tragicomic thriller, which Welles hoped to shoot in black and white. (Most of the members of Pellarin's entourage are comic grotesques worthy of the Grandi clan and night watchman in TOUCH OF EVIL.) Shortly after Welles's death, Jaglom complained bitterly to the *Los Angeles Times* about the circumstances which sank the project. Producer Arnon Milchan agreed to put up the money if Jaglom and Welles could find a bankable star to play Pellarin for two million dollars, but all seven of the stars who were approached—including Warren Beatty, Clint Eastwood, Jack Nicholson, Robert Redford, and Burt Reynolds—turned them down, each for a different reason. The script manages to convey complex feelings about Spain since the Civil War and the U.S. from the New Deal to Watergate, as well as a Goyaesque view of powerless and helpless suffering (which "rhymes" Menaker's pet monkey with a blind beggar whom Pellarin kicks to death), and a delirious depiction of sexuality which comes to the fore in Pellarin's reunion with a former Vietnamese mistress (another contribution by Kodar of "erotic stuff"). Overall, the plot gradually develops from a kind of bouncy naturalism to a nightmarish phantasmagoria, before returning to mischievous comedy. It is clearly too advanced, too sophisticated, and too candidly personal for anything that Hollywood in the 80s could begin to handle, much less imagine. Forty years earlier, Welles had RKO and all its resources at his disposal; with a fraction as much today, he might well have come up with a feature just as startling.

THE CRADLE WILL ROCK. Like TOUCH OF EVIL, this was a project not initiated by Welles, but one which he was able to take over after it had been developed separately—in this case, scripted by Ring Lardner Jr. for producer Michael Fitzgerald. According to Kodar, Welles's version of the script, written during the fall of 1984, was entirely original.

Set in New York City and environs in 1937, THE CRADLE WILL ROCK depicts Welles's life and career at the age of twenty-two: performing *Dr. Faustus* on Broadway, meeting composer Marc Blitzstein and launching his leftist musical *The Cradle Will Rock,* and meanwhile performing weekly on radio shows ranging from *The Shadow* to soap operas to *The March of Time,* proceeding from one studio to the next in a rented ambulance. The plot is candid enough to comment on some of the problems in Welles's first marriage as well as his ambivalent relation to Blitzstein's radical politics. Members of the Mercury Theatre such as John Houseman, Augusta Weissberger, black actor Jack Carter, and Welles's first wife, Virginia Nicolson, figure prominently; and the script begins with Welles himself as narrator, succinctly evoking the mood of the Depression of the mid-30s.

After Welles cast Rupert Everett as the young Welles and Amy Irving as Virginia, sets were constructed at Cinecittà in Rome and exterior locations selected in New York and Los Angeles; but three weeks before shooting was scheduled to begin, the budget evaporated after some difficulties between the investors. Tragically, not even Steven Spielberg, Amy Irving's husband, who once paid a princely sum to purchase one of the original Rosebud sleds, was willing to lift a finger to save the project. Apparently Fitzgerald is still interested in filming Welles's script, with another director. A fascinating and highly critical self-portrait, it tells a lively story whose interest goes well beyond its autobiographical aspects in its nostalgic evocations of the period.

Whether a film of the script could overcome the problem of casting young actors as Welles, Agnes Moorehead, and other Mercury figures without alienating older viewers remains an open question (Welles himself was apparently concerned about this issue). But for any reader of the script who can fill in the names with the appropriate faces, it remains an exciting and crucial document—possibly the most extensive exercise in literal self-scrutiny that Welles has given us. And considering the over-40-year feud between Welles and John Houseman, it is worth noting that Welles's depiction of his Mercury producer is in fact rather benign; the script even paraphrases Houseman's description of Welles as a Faustian obsessive in his memoir *Run-Through*—a view hotly contested in Leaming's Welles biography.

KING LEAR. I haven't read Welles's screenplay for the last of his projected adaptations of Shakespeare, which he planned to shoot in black and white, with himself as Lear, Kodar as Cordelia, and Abb Dickson (the magician in THE MAGIC SHOW) as the Fool. But going by Kodar's description, it is a good deal more detailed than the other scripts which I have read—indicating every move of the camera and actors, and supplemented by many drawings for the costumes and constructed models for the sets. And Welles's proposal for LEAR in the form of a six-minute videotape, shown in Rotterdam last January, gives provocative and tantalizing clues about the form and style that his film would take.

After powerfully evoking the play's theme of old age, he begins to describe what the film *won't* be like. It will not, he promises, be "what is called a costume movie" in any sense of the word. "That doesn't mean that the characters are going to wear blue jeans; it *does* mean that a story so sharply modern in its relevancy, so universal in its simple, rock-bottom humanity, will not be burdened with the time-worn baggage of theatrical tradition. It will be just as free from the various forms of cinematic rhetoric, my own as well as the others, which have already accumulated in the history of these translations of Shakespeare into film. What we'll be giving you, then, is something new: Shakespeare addressed directly and uniquely to the sensibility of our own particular day. The camera language will be intimate, extremely intimate, rather than grandiose. The tone will be at once epic in its stark simplicity and almost ferociously down to earth. In a word, not only a new kind of Shakespeare, but a new kind of film." Conceived of largely in close-ups, Welles's LEAR, one imagines, would have been a logical successor to CHIMES AT MIDNIGHT.

Although LEAR was ostensibly to have been financed by French television, Kodar firmly believes—as did Welles—that they never sincerely intended to make the film. Speaking in a barely controlled rage at the Directors Guild tribute to Welles last November, she read a cable of condolence from François Mitterrand stating that Welles "may not have been able or may not have wanted to have followed to an end this film." "I am sorry," Kodar then remarked, "that M. Mitterrand, even at this sad hour, has had to play politics and defend his establishment. . . . Who would be the best person to help French Minister of Culture Jack Lang to take his foot out of his mouth for openly declaring his dislike and disdain for existing imperialism of nonexistent American culture? Who else? Welles."

Speaking of an artificially inflated budget, impossible production conditions, and broken promises, Kodar read the last part of Welles's own message to Paris in May 1985: "In the fifty-five years of my professional career I have never, not even in the worst days of the old Hollywood, encountered such a humiliating inflexibility. Need I say that this is a bitter disappointment to one who has until now received so much heartwarming and generous cooperation in France. To my profound regret, therefore, I must accept that your own last Telex is the last word about LEAR and that there is no longer any hope that in this affair a constructive relationship is possible."

Despite this loss of finance, Welles continued to hope to make the film by other means, and had himself photographed in his Lear costume and makeup shortly before his death.

THE DREAMERS. "The last of Orson's dreams," Kodar describes this color adaptation of two Isak Dinesen stories, worked on between 1978 and 1985. While trying unsuccessfully to raise money for this project, Welles shot various tests and a few scenes, totaling about twenty minutes, in and around the house he shared in Hollywood with Kodar, with Graver as cinematographer and Kodar in the lead part of Pellegrina—an opera singer who, having lost her voice, decides to live many other lives. In the first story, "The Dreamers," three men who have fallen in love with her—a young Englishman, a Danish cavalry officer, and a young American—converge on an inn, each in search of her, and during a blizzard pass the time by telling one another about their affairs with this elusive woman, only gradually discovering that they are all in pursuit of the same person. In the second story, "Echoes," Pellegrina arrives in a remote mountain village, and, in a church, encounters a young boy named Emmanuele whose singing voice seems identical to the voice she once had. She proceeds to give the boy voice lessons and falls in love with him, until he denounces her as a witch.

In the earliest version of the script, entitled DA CAPO, Welles introduces the film by speaking of his lifelong infatuation with Dinesen's work. In the last version, the introduction is given over to Warren Beatty, who introduces Welles, who introduces in turn Lincoln Forsner, the young Englishman in search of Pellegrina—who is himself only the first of many narrators in Welles's intricate Chinese box structure of tales within tales.

Probably the most romantic of Welles's late projects, THE DREAMERS would almost surely have embodied his most exquisite and developed use of color. Over two years in Madrid, still photographer José Maria Castellvi worked as Welles's "color scout" by photographing precise changes in the colors of the leaves in a park at different times of day and recording the time and date of each photograph, all in preparation for sequences to be shot in Spain. (Shortly before Welles's death, Castellvi told me, a trunk arrived containing all the costumes to be worn by Kodar.)

A three-minute scene filmed in 1982 in Welles and Kodar's backyard in Hollywood, describing Pellegrina's departure from her life as a famous opera singer, represents as much of a quantum leap from THE IMMORTAL STORY, Welles's previous Dinesen adaptation, as OTHELLO does from MACBETH. Admittedly, the scene is no more than an unfinished fragment: Welles never got round to shooting his own close-ups (in the part of Marcus Kleek, the elderly Dutch Jewish merchant who is Pellegrina's only friend), and the dialogue—a lovely duet of two melodious, accented voices, accompanied by the whir of crickets and even the faint hum of passing traffic—is recorded in direct sound. But the delicate lighting, lyrical camera movement, and rich deployments of blue, black and yellow, combined with the lilt of the two voices, create an astonishing glimpse into the overripe dream world that Welles envisioned for the film.

■

As suggested earlier, the above list is far from exhaustive; but clearly it is more than enough to vindicate Welles from the charge of idleness in his late years. The range of the work is as remarkable as the breadth, and the fact that virtually all this legacy has remained buried gives the film industry and media a lot to answer for. But a tentative hypothesis or two about how this happened might help to shed some partial light.

A man who was deeply moved when he was once recognized as Falstaff (rather than as Orson Welles) by a driver on the Champs-Elysées, Welles felt he belonged more to the public than to the film specialist. After the fame that carried him through his mid-twenties, conceivably the most galling aspect of his subsequent career was the lack of a clear mainstream success. The only time that I met him, in 1972—having unexpectedly been invited to lunch by him in Paris two days after writing a modest letter of inquiry about HEART OF DARKNESS, his first feature film project—I was surprised to hear him say that he was reluctant to release DON QUIXOTE then because he didn't want it to compete with MAN OF LA MANCHA. No less surprising was the discovery that not even the earliest of his film dreams, HEART OF DARKNESS, was regarded by him as abandoned; he still nurtured hopes of making it one day. Yet as the projects accumulated and the investments dwindled, he steadily refused to accept the status of a marginal artist—a decision which undoubtedly spurred his creative activity at the same time that it edged him further and further away from the mainstream, except as an entertainer.

Thus, even while his work grew more inward and self-reflective in its resonance for Welles fans—with characters as diverse as Russ Brewer, Don Quixote, Shylock, Hannaford, Pellarin, Menaker, Lear, Pellegrina, and Kleek all taking their places beside the direct self-portraits in F FOR

FAKE, FILMING OTHELLO, and THE CRADLE WILL ROCK—the conscious address grew ever more expansive and generous in its appeal to the general public. This discrepancy may finally have less to do with Welles than with the shrinking and diminishing culture around him; but whatever its source, it could only be judged one way while he was alive—as creative blockage. Ironically, now that he is dead, the floodgates can open—demonstrating once again that what a culture wants of an artist at any given moment may at best be only incidental to the range of his or her talents.

As we know now from Leaming and Higham, Welles grew up trying to please parents who were diametrically opposed and eventually became estranged from one another, both of whom expected him to be entertaining and "grown up." Considering how well he succeeded with both of them, it is scarcely surprising that he extended these talents to the outside world, which initially rewarded him no less handsomely for his deceptions. Like Pellegrina, he became more than the sum of his roles, even if his public career afforded him less than the sum of his reputation.

With this background in mind, the standard objections to Welles's "character" remind one of René Clair's fatherly advice to Preston Sturges, cited and admirably glossed by Manny Farber and W. S. Poster: "Preston is like a man from the Italian Renaissance: he wants to do everything at once. If he could slow down, he would be great; he has an enormous gift, and he should be one of our leading creators. I wish he would be a little more selfish and worry about his reputation." "What Clair is suggesting," note Farber and Poster, "is that Sturges would be considerably improved if he annihilated himself." This is more or less what we tended to expect from Welles, and although it took him the better part of seventy years, he finally obliged us.

There are only two things it is ever seemly for an intelligent person to be thinking. . . . One is: "What did God mean by creating the world?" And the other? "What do I do next . . . ?"
—The end of THE DREAMERS

—*Sight and Sound,* Summer 1986

9

Reviews of Biographies by Barbara Leaming and Charles Higham and a Critical Edition of TOUCH OF EVIL

It's embarrassing to admit to an error in this piece—in the second of the five book reviews included here—that I subsequently charge David Thomson with making in chapter 20, namely the mistitling of FILMING OTHELLO *as* THE MAKING OF OTHELLO. *For all I know, he could have copied this mistake from me (or from Gary Graver, who has also made it).*

It seems lamentable that most Welles biographers have tended to stay away from academic conferences about Welles. Based on those I've attended myself (listed in my introduction to chapter 11), the chief exceptions appear to be Simon Callow in Venice and Joseph McBride and Bart Whaley in Locarno. I especially regret the absence of Barbara Leaming and Frank Brady at the Welles conferences I've been to because I've always been hoping to clarify certain questions I've had about their sources. The advantages of Welles scholars being able to exchange notes and leads with each other has always struck me as a major reason for bringing them together—at least if one assumes the existence of a community of shared interests—and I've been somewhat disappointed that Brady and Leaming have remained relatively isolated from this community. (The only time I've ever seen Leaming was when she spoke at the Directors Guild's Welles tribute shortly after his death.)

■

Orson Welles: A Biography, by Barbara Leaming (New York: Viking, 1985)
Orson Welles: The Rise and Fall of an American Genius, by Charles Higham (New York: St. Martin's Press, 1985)

TOUCH OF EVIL, edited by Terry Comito (New Brunswick, NJ: Rutgers University Press, 1985)

If Orson Welles had been chiefly known as a composer, poet, playwright, novelist, painter, or sculptor, it is an open question, at least, whether any notion of artistic or moral decline would ever have attached itself to his name. Over the forty-six years that comprised his career as a filmmaker, it appears that there was hardly ever a time when he was not actively pursuing or working on a film project of his own; the very week that he died, he was working directly on at least four of his own features, and he even died while typing stage directions for one of them. Yet such is the nature of our product-happy media—which defines reality almost exclusively on the basis of what is "finished" and out on the market—that most of Welles's later career as an artist was invisible to the public, at the same time that he remained almost constantly visible as a show-biz personality. Given this split, it is hardly surprising that the contrast between public and private selves should be a major theme in his work, or that the responses to his death in this country should so often only add insult to injury.

As David Ehrenstein (among others) has pointed out, from the point in the early fifties when Welles began to finance many of his own films, he became an independent, "underground," filmmaker—a move which helped to deprive him of a mainstream success in this country with either critics or the public, although it often regained him some of the freedom and autonomy that he had (uncharacteristically) found in a Hollywood studio on CITIZEN KANE. But because he remained at least peripherally in the public eye (through acting jobs which supported the movies) and continued to hanker, perhaps unrealistically, after mainstream success, he was labeled a failure in terms of the marketplace—a judgment with which many of his highbrow critics concurred. It is a label, unhappily, that followed him to his grave and continues to haunt his memory, and with that label comes a very American form of moral censure that conveniently attaches itself to obesity—as if to compensate for the sheer lack of information we had and continue to have about the last thirty-five years of his career as a filmmaker. It is as though we fixed on the image of

Welles as immoderate consumer in order to assuage our consciences and paper over the gaps in all that we didn't know about Welles as producer and creator.

In different ways, this incomplete, troubled image crucially informs all three of the books under review. It figures in the ways that we regard such late Wellesian figures as Hank Quinlan, Falstaff, Mr. Clay, and Welles himself in F FOR FAKE. It helps to account for the understandably defensive tone of Leaming's biography, the unfortunately loaded subtitle of Higham's, and the shocking naivety of the following sentence from the last paragraph of Terry Comito's introduction to his generally helpful TOUCH OF EVIL reader: "In the [1958] interview with Bazin, [Welles] says he is thinking about giving up film and theater altogether, though he was not to do so for another decade, at least." The chilling ease with which this sweeps into oblivion THE MAKING OF OTHELLO, THE MERCHANT OF VENICE, THE DEEP, DON QUIXOTE, THE OTHER SIDE OF THE WIND, THE DREAMERS, KING LEAR, THE HONORARY CONSUL, THE CRADLE WILL ROCK, and THE BIG BRASS RING (to cite only some of the films and film projects that engaged Welles since 1968—apart from F FOR FAKE, which Comito mentions—the first half of which actually got made) is certainly matched in many of the more recent Welles obituaries; but it is doubly depressing to find the same blinkered assumptions in an academic textbook.

A handicap suffered by all three of these books is the fact that they were published when Welles was still alive, and are now being reviewed after his death—meaning that one now has to speak in the past tense about a life and career that were still in the present when these texts were written. Yet it should be stressed at the outset that we are still years away from any capacity to grasp Welles, much less assess him. At best, these books can only expose the enormous obstacles—ideological as well as practical—that continue to stand in our way. For starters, to begin with either the premise that "Hollywood destroyed Welles" or the premise that "Welles destroyed himself" is already to embark on a process of glib oversimplification that serves ideological needs more than it allows us to understand the issues involved in all their complexity. And until we are able to see at least the unreleased DON QUIXOTE, THE MERCHANT OF VENICE, THE DEEP, and THE OTHER SIDE OF THE WIND in their complete or incomplete states, any critical summations will have to be held in abeyance. The fact that some things were never finished hardly justifies dismissal; would we ever think to rule out Kafka for that reason?

Partially because of this problem, both biographies are unsatisfying as total statements. Yet each is indispensable in providing information not readily obtainable elsewhere; and together they offer important clues about why Welles's career is so notoriously difficult to research. Leaming's, the longer and more readable of the two, was written with Welles's full cooperation, and is inflected throughout by the author's budding friendship with her subject, which began two years after she started her research. Although Welles helped Leaming promote the book by appearing on TV talk shows with her, he reportedly never read it, and stressed that it was not an authorized biography. Leaming admirably contextualizes her own strategies and biases by chronicling her efforts to track Welles down and her eventual success. Including lengthy conversations with Welles, she even reveals that the book's basic form—chronological chapters occasionally interspersed with passages in italics describing her own progress—was directly prompted by Welles himself. And while her book passionately and often persuasively counters the less sympathetic earlier accounts of Welles given by Higham, Houseman, and Kael, her evidence (and, by extension, Welles's) is still too various not to concede some occasional points to the opposition, even though they're seldom acknowledged as such.

Higham's book, unfortunately, contains no account of how its own biases were formed, and readers who wish to contextualize his positions are advised to read his introduction to the last chapter in his *Celebrity Circus* (Delacorte Press, 1979)—describing his ongoing feud with Welles (whom he never met) since the publication of his *The Films of Orson Welles* (University of California Press, 1970)—before even starting the present work. Many of the factual errors in Higham's previous Welles book are silently corrected in the new one, but the overriding thesis remains the same— that Welles was "the brilliant architect of his own downfall." A considerable portion of the new book is devoted to exploring Welles's family history, which Higham traces all the way back to the Mayflower, meanwhile exposing a good many of Welles's autobiographical statements as falsehoods. To his credit, Higham also interviewed a good many more people than Leaming did, especially regarding the later periods, including composer Francesco Lavignino (yielding some fascinating material about the shooting and scoring of OTHELLO) and cinematographers Edmond Richard, Willy Kurant, and Gary Graver; and a particularly welcome Welles discography is included as an appendix.

A significant paradox about these biographies is that while Higham's is almost certainly more factually accurate than Leaming's, it is on the whole less useful. Because Welles is usually a good deal more intelligent, insightful, and interesting than either his associates or his commentators, there are times when a lie told by him is more valuable than a truth reported by a drudge. The fact that Welles's father wasn't a friend of Booth Tarkington's certainly has some importance—but less, one could argue, than the fact that Welles preferred to believe otherwise. Furthermore, Welles's late self-portraits from Falstaff to his versions of himself in F FOR FAKE and his remarkable script for THE CRADLE WILL ROCK are all depictions of transparent liars, suggesting that his mythomania may have been a bit less sinister than Higham tries to make it seem. And sometimes Higham's tattling adds up to little more than petty malice. Thirty-four pages after he proudly reports that, contrary to Welles, there never was a horse named Dick Welles which won the Kentucky Derby, one discovers in a footnote that there was indeed a horse of that name which won races at Harlem, Washington Park, Chicago, Morri Park, Hawthorne Park, and Latonia. Needless to say, this information is not offered as a vindication of Welles for merely getting his horserace wrong, but figures instead as an independent piece of trivia offered for its own sake—a bit along the lines of other little eurekas such as "William Alland was Thompson (shades of Virgil Thomson)" in CITIZEN KANE; and naturally we hear about a horse named Rosebud too.

For a figure with the theatricality and imagination of Welles, exaggeration, hyperbole, and flights of invention often took the place of solid facts (though not always—see below), and it is certainly understandable that Higham would want to cut through all the camouflage and search out the truth. Regrettably, however, facts never speak for themselves. If Welles often told lies as a raconteur in order to entertain, Higham often cites facts in order to demonstrate that Welles was a liar (as opposed to, say, an entertainer). If Leaming, on the other hand, tends to give Welles the benefit of almost every doubt, not always with happy results, there is a somewhat more defensible rationale for her doing so: (1) she is trying to entertain (and her gestures towards best-sellerdom perhaps account for the irritating fact that there is probably more here about Welles's sex life than about his films, much of it improbable), and (2) unless or until Peter Bogdanovich's *This Is Orson Welles* is ever published, her biography offers the only book-length account of Welles's career given mainly from his own viewpoint—making it a valuable resource for this reason alone.

Having once interviewed Welles myself, at his own invitation (in response to a letter), in 1972, and having subsequently discovered from Robert L. Carringer's recent *The Making of* CITIZEN KANE, among many other sources, that apparently everything he told me about his career was accurate, I can certainly sympathize with Leaming's own position, even if I regret some of its consequences. Because her book is not quite coauthored by Welles yet not quite independently researched in many areas either, it is difficult to know in some cases who to blame for the misinformation. At one point in my own interview with Welles, he volunteered the information that he had never written a novel—explaining that *Une Grosse Légume* (Gallimard, 1953) was actually a translation and adaptation of a film treatment, and *Mr. Arkadin* (Gallimard, 1954; W. H. Allen, 1955) a ghosted novel. Apparently following the lead of Peter Cowie's *The Cinema of Orson Welles*, both Leaming and Higham assume that both books are by Welles, and that the film CONFIDENTIAL REPORT/MR. ARKADIN was adapted from the novel. Other sources have reported that Welles disowned only the novel's English translation—implying, still more improbably, that either he wrote the novel in French or that it was retranslated back into English.

Nor is this the only confusion regarding ARKADIN. Leaming quotes Welles's assertion that not only was the film taken away from him, but "more completely than any other picture of mine has been hurt by anybody, ARKADIN was destroyed because they completely changed the entire form of it: the whole order of it, the whole point of it. . . . AMBERSONS is *nothing* compared to ARKADIN!" But about his original form for the film,

Leaming reveals precisely nothing, and Higham is equally no help. Yet if we refer back to the (otherwise equally unhelpful) ARKADIN chapter in Higham's earlier book, we discover that the version described there differs in its chronology from the version in circulation today. (The present version opens after the credits with Van Stratten visiting Jacob Zouk, leading to flashbacks which begin with Branco's death; the earlier version opens after the credits with Branco's death, and doesn't get to Zouk until much later.) Having seen both versions of the film at separate times, I am still at a loss about whether either bears any relation to Welles's original conception; and to complicate matters still further, Herman G. Weinberg's 1956 review of the film in *Film Culture* describes a different credits sequence as well.

It is in areas such as these that Welles scholarship remains in a primitive state. At this point we are fairly knowledgeable about KANE, AMBERSONS, and TOUCH OF EVIL but are on relatively shaky ground regarding most of the rest; and a major limitation of both biographies is their relative lack of curiosity about ARKADIN, THE IMMORTAL STORY (which gets less than a paragraph from Leaming), and F FOR FAKE (for Higham, "an exercise in film journalism" and evidence of "a certain moral corruption"). Terry Comito's TOUCH OF EVIL reader admirably summarizes most of what we know about that film (although Leaming offers much fresh material). Disappointingly, Comito's book includes the film's cutting continuity rather than Welles's original script; as partial compensation, however, he reprints John Stubbs's helpful recent study of the Wade and Miller novel, Monash screenplay, *and* Welles screenplay in relation to the film. Other contributions include a lengthy essay and biographical sketch of Welles by Comito and reprints and/or translations of interviews with Welles and Charlton Heston, three contemporary reviews, and articles by William Johnson and Jean Collet, as well as a fragment of Stephen Heath's massive study of the film in *Screen.*

Returning to the dynamic and nearly dialectical duo, Leaming and Higham are sometimes at odds about facts as well as interpretations. According to Leaming, Welles studied a print of THE CABINET OF DR. CALIGARI (along with STAGECOACH) before shooting KANE; Higham, somewhat more plausibly, reports that he saw it before shooting THE LADY FROM

SHANGHAI (whose funhouse set comes closer to suggesting a CALIGARI influence). Elsewhere, Leaming mislabels FOLLOW THE BOYS as THREE CHEERS FOR THE BOYS, and devotes over a couple of pages to expounding what initially seems like a crackpot interpretation of THE LADY FROM SHANGHAI as a Brechtian film, primarily based on a reading of the Chinese theater sequence in conjunction with Welles's previous anticipation of working with Brecht on *Galileo*. This is one of many instances in Leaming's book in which Welles is not quoted yet one suspects that his influence is still the guiding force. Recently reseeing the film, I found that her (and/or his) interpretation becomes much more plausible if seen in relation to the foregrounding of audience reactions in the trial sequence—suggesting that Welles's own statements about his work are usually well worth attending to, even if they sometimes have to be recast before they can be clearly understood.

Leaming also offers a rather persuasive autobiographical reading of CHIMES AT MIDNIGHT in relation to Welles's own rejection of his alcoholic father for his teacher Roger Hill, while Higham strives to relate the stammers of Silence in that film and the night man in TOUCH OF EVIL to those of Welles's much maltreated older brother, Richard. In general, the critical and analytical talents of both biographers are variable—sensitive to certain issues, but without the kind of precision or thoroughness found in the excellent Welles studies of Joseph McBride and James Naremore, or the theoretical dimensions broached in André Bazin's two books on Welles.[1] Higham misdescribes a memorable shot in TOUCH OF EVIL proceeding "through a hotel lobby, into an elevator filled with people, up two floors, and along a hallway without a single break" (in fact, there's a cut and angle change when the elevator is at ground level) while Leaming, perhaps motivated by a desire to improve Welles's Hollywood profile, omits any mention of some of his film projects—LORD JIM, VICTORY, and THE HONORARY CONSUL, among others—which never found any backers (although these are not mentioned by Higham either). Oddly, neither biographer mentions the film of THE MERCHANT OF VENICE shot by Welles circa 1969–70, described in his 1982 interview with Bill Krohn for *Cahiers du cinéma,* and unreleased because the second of its three reels was stolen. Yet if research into Welles's career still hasn't advanced enough beyond the tactics of the "News on the March" team in KANE, Leaming's and Higham's biographies, whatever their faults, are still much more substantial than anything we have had up until now, and future biographies will have to build upon them.

Notes

1. To correct belatedly a widespread misunderstanding, the second of these books by Bazin, written in 1958, which I translated for Harper & Row, was not a "revised and expanded" version of his 1950 monograph, as François Truffaut stated in his foreword, but essentially a separate work—further demonstrating that in matters Wellesian, casual obfuscation is almost a commonplace occurrence.

—*Film Quarterly* 40, no. 1, Fall 1986

Afterword to *THE BIG BRASS RING*, a Screenplay by Orson Welles (with Oja Kodar)

When I presented my Welles tribute at the Santa Barbara film festival in 1986, one person in the audience who introduced himself to me afterwards was James Pepper, a local rare book dealer who, in response to my assertion that the Welles screenplay for THE BIG BRASS RING should be published, expressed some interest in bringing out a limited edition of 1,000 copies. Having already brought out a handsome volume devoted to Robert Towne's original screenplay for CHINA-TOWN in a similar way, he seemed to know what he was talking about, and I conveyed his proposal to Oja.

The following year, around the time I was preparing to make a permanent move to Chicago to write for the Chicago Reader, the book appeared. And it was roughly two years after then that Gore Vidal published a rave review in the New York Review of Books ("Remembering Orson Welles," June 1, 1989, vol. 36, no. 9) that finally accorded the screenplay the literary attention and respect I always believed it deserved—in an engaging (if not exactly scholarly) autobiographical piece about Welles that also reviewed Frank Brady's more recent biography. The same essay has subsequently been reprinted in a couple of Vidal's collections and elsewhere (including Orson Welles Interviews, edited by Mark W. Estrin [Jackson: University Press of Mississippi, 2002]). That all its multiple appearances have come long after the book went out of print and disappeared from sight has seemed to me a paradigmatic illustration of "Wellesian" mistiming—a problem that dogged his film career and continues unabated posthumously. (My major regret about Vidal's essay is his lack of familiarity with

Oja Kodar and F FOR FAKE, *which limits his lucidity about some of the script's more personal elements.)*

I hasten to repeat my earlier assertion, however, that anyone who wants to track down this book can still do so. In 1989, it came out in Italian as La posta in gioco, *but I only learned about this edition two years later. Shortly after I gave the keynote address at a Welles conference in Venice, Guido Fink, the conference's organizer, told me that his wife, Daniela, had translated it, and then Daniela herself generously made me a gift of her own copy. That same year, the original screenplay was reprinted as a paperback by Black Spring Press in England.*

In 1999, George Hickenlooper released a film of the same title, adapted very loosely with F. X. Feeney from the Welles script, with the characters, plot, and much of the dialogue radically altered and the locales shifted to St. Louis from parts of Spain and to Cuba from Africa. Having expressed my regrets about this feature in "Fables of the Reconstruction: The Four-Hour GREED" *(reprinted in my collection* Essential Cinema: On the Necessity of Film Canons *[Baltimore: Johns Hopkins University Press, 2004]) as well as in chapter 24, I see no point in repeating them here, except to say that I tried very hard to get the Welles script reprinted around the same time by the University of California Press, partially in order to clarify that Welles couldn't and shouldn't be blamed for the film. Although Oja agreed on principle to this reprint both times I lobbied for a contract, she failed on both occasions to sign the contract that emerged, with the lamentable consequence that the Hickenlooper film continues to have much more visibility and currency than the work by Welles that inspired it. Since this protracted frustration, I haven't tried to promote any more publications or reprints of works by Welles.*

Because the afterword that follows assumes the reader's detailed familiarity with the screenplay, it may not always be easy to follow. A perusal of the partial synopsis in chapter 8 and the much more complete one in Vidal's essay should clear up most of these difficulties.

■

He is a great man—like all great men he is never satisfied that he has chosen the right path in life. Even being President, he feels, may somehow not be right. He is a man who has within him the devil of self-destruction that lives in every genius. You know that you're absolutely great, there is no question of that, but have you chosen the right road?

Should I be a monk? Should I jerk off in the park? Should I just fuck everybody and forget about everything else? Should I be President? It is not self-doubt; it is cosmic doubt! What am I going to do—I am the best, I know that, now what do I do with it?

Hannibal crossed the Alps with the second greatest army in classical history. He arrived at the outer gates of Rome and Rome was in his hands, ready to be taken. At the outer gates, he stopped and went back. What made him stop? That same devil—this thing that always stops conquerors at the moment of victory. That is what THE BIG BRASS RING is about. Also: There is this foolish, romantic side of us all, that puts us into these absurd, even ridiculous situations and positions in life. That is what the circumstances of the film are about—the theft of the necklace, the situation with the monkey, etc. All these idiotic events that one's romantic nature leads one into.
—Orson Welles to Henry Jaglom, in a memo from Jaglom to Jack Nicholson, dated May 20, 1982, during the efforts to launch THE BIG BRASS RING

The rift between public and private life that figures so prominently in the work of Orson Welles, from CITIZEN KANE to THE BIG BRASS RING, is ironically a factor that has tended to obscure substantial portions of his own life and work. An intensely private man himself, in spite—or should one say because?—of his expansive public image, especially during the latter portion of his life, Welles played Menaker to his own Pellarin (and vice versa) in more ways than one. While he remained in the public eye throughout his career, principally as an actor and performer, a large portion of his creative work as writer and director was kept firmly under wraps, for a number of reasons.[1]

If it seems likely that the closest we will ever get to a spiritual autobiography of Welles will be the work he left behind, it will probably be a good many years before we can even begin to see the full shadow of his profile, much less assess it. Since his death at age 70 on October 10, 1985, it has become increasingly clear that the legacy he left behind—a wealth of material including countless films, scripts, and projects, scattered over many years and countries, in different stages of completion or realization—is immeasurably larger and richer, and more full of potential surprises, than any of us had reason to suspect.

Oja Kodar—Welles's companion, muse, and major collaborator over the last two decades of his life, to whom he entrusted this legacy—has dedicated herself to the formidable task of making available as much of this work as possible. But the obstacles she has to face, many of them continuations of the same financial and logistical difficulties that blocked these projects when Welles was alive, are a good deal more daunting and complex than one might initially assume. Welles essentially left behind two estates—one of them controlled by his wife, Paola Mori, and daughter Beatrice (complicated still further by the death of Mori in 1986), the other controlled by Kodar, and it is only recently that a final settlement has been reached. This is one reason why the publication of *The Big Brass Ring* represents a major step forward in the clarification of the invisible Orson Welles, even though it comprises only a piece of the iceberg (or jigsaw puzzle, if one prefers).

As a sample of Welles's creativity in his mid-sixties, this original screenplay offers ample evidence that he was continuing to move in fresh and unexpected directions. Yet to call it "characteristic" of his late work in any but the broadest terms would be misleading, if only because every Welles project represented a fresh departure—a virtue that regrettably kept him "unbankable" as a director throughout most of his career. Spectators looking forward to "another" CITIZEN KANE would be confounded by the challenges of TOUCH OF EVIL, and by the time they had caught up with the brilliance of the latter film, Welles would be somewhere else again—thereby frustrating the principle of supply and demand that could sustain a Chaplin, a Hitchcock, or even a Godard.

By conservative estimate, in the 1980s alone Welles was working on at least a dozen separate film projects, no two of them alike—including a film set in Hollywood in the early 1970s, THE OTHER SIDE OF THE WIND (which was begun during that period), THE MAGIC SHOW (a collection of some of his best acts of prestidigitation, all done without camera tricks), DON QUIXOTE (which he had been working on intermittently since the 1950s), a fiction film about Sirhan Sirhan (THE ASSASSIN), adaptations of Graham Greene (THE OTHER MAN, based on *The Honorary Consul*) and Jim Thompson (DEAD GIVEAWAY, based on *A Hell of a Woman*) and Isak Dinesen (THE DREAMERS), a radically conceived KING LEAR to be shot in black and white close-ups, an exercise in autobiographical self-scrutiny set in the mid-1930s (THE CRADLE WILL ROCK), and a development of a short story by Kodar (MERCEDES, based on her "Blind Window") which he started work on the summer before he died. While only some of these— THE OTHER SIDE OF THE WIND, THE MAGIC SHOW, DON QUIXOTE, and THE DREAMERS—advanced beyond script and preproduction stages, nearly all of the scripts went through countless revisions; there are nine drafts of THE DREAMERS alone.

THE BIG BRASS RING was a unique project of this period insofar as it sprang from material that was completely original with Welles and was started at the urging of a friend, director Henry Jaglom—rather than at Welles's own instigation. Jaglom had already been trying without success to help Welles secure financing for THE DREAMERS, one of the latter's most cherished projects, and one day, in February or March 1981, he suggested that Welles write something more commercial and contemporary—an original script which could entice producers. After some reluctance, Welles began telling him stories over a series of lunches, and Jaglom describes the outcome as follows:

> . . . Finally he told me one he'd been thinking about for years, about an old political advisor to Roosevelt who was a homosexual, and whose lover had gotten crippled in the Spanish Civil War fighting the fascists. Now he was in an African kingdom, advising the murderous leader and back in the U.S., a young senator, who'd been his protégé, was going to run against Reagan in 1984, as the Democratic nominee. And I said, "Great! My God! That's great! Write that!" And he said, "Oh, I can't. I can't possibly." And I said, "Please write that." And he said, "No, there's no way."
>
> One night, about six days later, I got a phone call. He said, "I've got four pages." He was sweating; I could hear it: "Could I read them to you?" I said, "Sure," and he read to me—and I said, "My God, they're brilliant! Please keep on writing. And he said, "What are you, crazy? It's four in the morning; I've got to go to sleep."
>
> The next day he came to lunch, and he had 12 pages. And the next day he had 23. And in three months he had a script, one which I just could not believe. It was called THE BIG BRASS RING. It was absolutely the bookend to CITIZEN KANE. It was about America at the end of the century—socially and politically and morally—as KANE and AMBERSONS are about America at the beginning of the century.[2]

After some casting about, Jaglom eventually found a willing and enthusiastic producer, Arnon Milchan, who was working at the time on THE
KING OF COMEDY (his subsequent credits include ONCE UPON A TIME IN
AMERICA and BRAZIL), and agreed to furnish an eight million dollar
budget, pre-selling the film in foreign markets, if a "bankable" male star
could be found to play Blake Pellarin. "He was amazingly clear about his
job as a director in helping a producer," Milchan recalls today, remembering lengthy phone conversations with Welles (whom he never met
face to face) on subjects ranging from technical matters about the shooting to the treatment of sex—which would be "clear and felt" but not
graphic. "He was really on top of it," Milchan states with conviction.

Welles estimated that he needed six million to shoot the film—figuring
on location work in Spain, filming the yacht scenes near Los Angeles, and
a limited amount of studio work (possibly in Rome) for the hotel interiors—so it was decided that the remaining two million plus ten per cent of
the profits would be used to lure the male star. To Milchan and Jaglom,
the strategy seemed foolproof, and with Welles a list of six possible actors
was drawn up: Warren Beatty, Clint Eastwood, Paul Newman, Jack
Nicholson, Robert Redford, and Burt Reynolds. (At earlier stages, before
the "bankable" star strategy was hatched, Welles contemplated using a
real-life couple to play Blake and Diana Pellarin—John Cassavetes and
Gena Rowlands at one point, Cliff Robertson and Dina Merrill somewhat
later; James Caan was also considered, but never approached.) But over
the next year or so, they made the unhappy discovery that none of the six
actors was willing to accept the offer unconditionally. Eastwood, Newman, Redford, and Reynolds all simply declined, each giving a separate
reason. Nicholson, who was Welles's first choice, asked for a larger sum,
arguing that, after working hard for years to raise his asking price, he
could not settle for two million without reducing his future fees. Beatty,
Welles's second choice, fresh from having just shot REDS, agreed to play
the part if he could produce the film and have final cut—a condition that
he realized that Welles would find impossible. By late 1982, the project
was effectively dead.

The version of the script printed here, the last of many drafts, is dated
June 22, 1982. An undated early version, probably written about a year

before, follows the same general plot outline except for one very striking difference: the climactic murder of the blind beggar is committed by Kim Menaker, not Blake Pellarin. Except for this change, the description of this scene is almost identical, apart from some echoes of the children's chant "Quiene tiene miedo del tri-mo-tor" (sung to the tune of "Who's Afraid of the Big Bad Wolf?"), recalled earlier by Menaker in the Retiro Park— hoarsely half whispered by Menaker as he enters the neighborhood, and later heard as a ghostly echo in his brain (along with laughter and a "scampering of little feet") after he kills the beggar.[3]

Although Welles ultimately chose to have Pellarin commit the murder, for a number of reasons, he significantly reassigned the crime to Menaker in one or more of the intermediate versions of the script, apparently on the basis of whether he thought the male star being approached could convincingly carry off the scene or not. The fact that he contemplated both alternatives is certainly revealing both of the flexibility of his conception and of the larger sense that Pellarin and Menaker (like Marlow and Kurtz in *Heart of Darkness*, his first Hollywood project) are different sides of the same coin, both of them Wellesian self-portraits. It is important to recall that, like Menaker, Welles had been a friend of Franklin Roosevelt and occasionally wrote speeches for him—and that, like Pellarin, he was once regarded as a serious political hopeful, having come very close in the mid-1940s to running against Joseph McCarthy in Wisconsin as a Democrat for a seat in the Senate.

Kodar recalls a political conversation with Welles which had a particular bearing on this scene, and helps to explain one of the reasons why Pellarin (whose name, accented on the first syllable, suggests *pélarin*, the French word for pilgrim) was the one who finally committed the crime: "You see, Orson did not like symbolism—nor do I." Once, however, he admitted to Kodar that he was guilty of symbolism in his depiction of the murder of the blind beggar. After he complimented Kodar on her smile and the whiteness of her teeth, she remarked that this was partially thanks to America, recalling the aid packages she received as a child in Yugoslavia. They then discussed the dubious wisdom of the U.S. having showered Vietnam with bombs instead of aid packages, as well as the behavior of America after destroying much of Germany and Japan in World

War II, "throwing candies" at them and suffocating them with its "good intentions." At which point Welles remarked, "I'm afraid I'm going to get into some symbolism in THE BIG BRASS RING. Because this beggar is going to be killed by this enormous wealth and health."

Kodar's collaborative role on the script basically centered on the parts of Cela Brandini, which she was to play herself, and the unnamed French Cambodian woman whom Pellarin re-encounters in an empty house. But before examining her specific contributions, it would be useful to sketch in a bit of her own background. Coming from an intellectual family grounded in the visual arts, based mainly in Dalmatia—her Hungarian father and older sister are architects, another sister paints and makes tapestries, and her Yugoslav mother wanted to be a sculptor—she aspired to be a chemist (after seeing Greer Garson in MADAME CURIE) and writer (having published poetry when she was very young) before she settled on sculpture in her teens, and was the first woman ever admitted to the sculpture department of the Academy of Visual Arts in Zagreb. Sculpting mainly in stone and bronze, and more recently in African teak, her work is at once abstract, monumental and erotic. As a reviewer in the *Tufts Observer* wrote, "Kodar conveys, through abstract forms worthy of Matisse, the human form in all its malleable transigence." She has had shows in Zagreb, Amsterdam, Paris, Rome, Boston, New York, and Los Angeles.

When she met Welles in Zagreb in 1962, while he was shooting THE TRIAL, she had just finished acting in a Yugoslav feature called A PIECE OF THE BLUE SKY, was working as an anchorperson on Yugoslav TV, and had recently written a story called "Girl-Watching" (which years later became the Picasso episode in F FOR FAKE). She accompanied Welles when he returned to Paris, but eventually left him to return to Yugoslavia. Two or three years later, she returned to Paris to attend the École des Beaux Arts, met Welles again, and then remained with him for the next two decades.

Her first script collaboration with Welles was an unrealized adaptation of Poe's "The Cask of Amontillado," originally intended for a film collection of shorts by different directors, released in English as SPIRITS OF THE DEAD in 1969. Their work together on scripts—including F FOR FAKE, THE OTHER SIDE OF THE WIND, THE SURINAM (an adaptation of Conrad's *Victory*), DEAD GIVEAWAY, THE ASSASSIN, THE DREAMERS, and MERCEDES—

often consisted of Welles presenting a situation to her and getting her to ask questions and suggest alternatives. As she describes the process between them, it was a bit like playing Ping-Pong; sometimes she would improvise an idea while he took notes, avoiding interruptions which would unbalance her English: "When I felt it was still too murky and too fragile to be touched or manipulated by words, I would go into my room and talk into my tape recorder. And then, when it was wrapped and safe in this little box, I would bring it out and let him listen to that, and we would talk again about it." On some occasions—including work on F FOR FAKE, THE OTHER SIDE OF THE WIND, and THE BIG BRASS RING—it involved combining stories which each of them had composed independently.

In the case of THE BIG BRASS RING, Welles decided to incorporate certain elements from an autobiographical story written in English by Kodar seven or eight years earlier—a story which he had originally titled himself, called "Ivanka" (a Yugoslav name which means "little Joanna"). "The story of the Asian girl and part of Cela Brandini come from 'Ivanka,'" Kodar explains. "There is something of Orson and myself in the story of the Asian girl, something that we lived. It's not exactly that, but something like that happened." When Pellarin describes to Menaker over the muted noises of the feria his former lover's way of walking (page 114), this passage comes from a letter written by Welles to Kodar after they separated in Paris, a letter which was never sent, but which Welles continued to carry around with him for years, and which he showed Kodar only after he unexpectedly encountered her again in Paris. "When I met Orson again in Paris a few years later, he did not know that I was going to see him; it was a surprise. But he still had the letter, and that was the first time that I read it." One might say, in other words, that it was the Pellarin in Welles who wrote the letter, and the Menaker in him who failed to send it.

"What I had in 'Ivanka' which we decided not to use—actually he fought for it at first, and I must say I didn't want to give it to him, because I was keeping it for my story—was a scene in which Blake comes up from the cellar and pours his heart out to the girl, tells her everything—and finally discovers that she's not there anymore. It's a wonderful love declaration, and in a way a love scene, but he tells it to nobody." This declaration would have been spoken in French, with English subtitles; its absence probably accounts, at least in part, for the scene's sketchiness as it now stands. "He was going to have Blake explain himself—not only what he did to her, how he hurt her and how he needed her back, but he was going to say much more about himself. He came to a certain realization of himself—what he really was—because he was in too much pain at the moment, and when people are in pain they lose control. The pain opened all the sore spots in his soul, and he was saying everything—what he thought of himself, his future and his past.

"When I took away this declaration and scene, in a way I was glad. Because I think—and actually it was Orson's decision, but he wanted my opinion—it was better for Pellarin to remain partly an enigma to himself. This is why he is capable of going off singing on that train. Because he would become a better and cleaner man, an angelic guy, if he emptied himself. But if we wanted Pellarin to continue in his striving for the Presidency, he had to remain who he was: if he confessed, if he cleaned himself, he would have been left naked, he would have lost his armor."

The character of Cela Brandini, on the other hand, was based on two independent sources. One was a somewhat comic character from "Ivanka," based on a rather flashy member of the production crew on THE TRIAL who had a penchant for interviewing the directors she worked for as well as sleeping with them, and who tried unsuccessfully to seduce Welles—an event which Kodar witnessed herself. The other was the Italian journalist Oriana Fallaci, whom Kodar never met but read and watched on TV. To develop the part, she and Welles improvised scenes with a tape recorder in which her Cela would interview his Blake or Kim.

For the seasoned Welles enthusiast, THE BIG BRASS RING offers a tempting but ultimately deceptive trap: an apparent profusion of earlier touchstones in Welles's career. Starting on the first page with the evocation of KANE in the depiction of Pellarin's failed political campaign, the references continue with HEART OF DARKNESS (page 13), Welles's radio persona (in the voice on Cela's tape recorder, preceding Welles's first appearance), TOUCH OF EVIL (in the opening dialogue of Jerry Kinzel on page 19 about leaving behind his wife, Susie, on a holiday trip) and DON QUIXOTE (page 35). When Menaker remarks that "In a perfect world, all of us should be allowed some short vacations from our own identities," the theme and world of THE DREAMERS—written just before THE BIG BRASS RING, and developed concurrently—is immediately conjured up. Even the scandalous handkerchief of Pellarin (pages 121 and 129–130) may make some readers think of the pivotal handkerchief in OTHELLO.

Carrying this principle further, many readers will be compelled to visualize certain scenes with images gleaned from a fast-forward tour through Welles's filmography. But one should bear in mind that stylistically, Welles seldom repeated himself ("We should never borrow from ourselves," remarks Jake Hannaford, the director played by John Huston in THE OTHER SIDE OF THE WIND), and at best we have to patch together our own movie out of the script rather than the one that Welles never made, which we can never hope to know. Specifically "cinematic" moments are few, although what is probably the supreme one—Menaker's voyeuristic Ferris wheel ride (pages 115–116)—might be taken as a startling metaphor for the cinema itself, bringing us all the way back to its zoetrope and peepshow origins while replicating the vicious circles of the nearby wheels of fortune and carousel; from this standpoint, the primal scene of Menaker facing the naked Pellarin, "like a great child rocking in its cradle," has the illuminating shock of a freeze-frame.

Such scenes, however, are rare, and for the most part we are obliged to read the script as a libretto for the music that Welles's direction would have brought to the material. Even more, we should acknowledge the relative poverty of our own imaginations if we should happen to think of THE TRIAL, as I did, when we read, "Buildings like big ugly boxes are crammed together on the barren earth where not a tree or blade of grass is growing." When I confessed this thought to Kodar, a pragmatic anticinéphile with a vengeance, she responded Socratically by proposing, "Let's try to play a symbolism game. What do those buildings in THE TRIAL represent to you?" After reflecting, I replied, "The crushing weight of institutions." "Yes," she said, "and what do those buildings of Franco in THE BIG BRASS RING represent to you?" Clearly, I admitted, they were not the same thing.

The moral of this story is that most of THE BIG BRASS RING comes from life, not other movies. The mention of "the illegality of the mass slaughter of the elephant" by the agreeably named Buckle (page 59) derives not from THE ROOTS OF HEAVEN, a John Huston film in which Welles acted, but from a news item which Welles and Kodar saw on television. Allusions in the dialogue to Reagan, Gay Liberation, survivalists, Kissinger, Nixon, Watergate, Vietnam, and "Batunga" (identified as Uganda in an earlier draft), as well as eerie intimations of Irangate and Contragate, may create some of the newsreel immediacy of KANE, but their focus is the contemporary world rather than a film made in 1941. (Queried by a French film student about whether THE BIG BRASS RING would be about Reagan, Welles tersely replied. "No . . . there's not enough there for a feature movie.") A good deal more novelistic than the other Welles scripts I have read—and it is worth noting that Welles at one point planned to adapt it into a novel, exploring certain facets of the story in greater depth—it bristles with references to Welles's life, which only incidentally included the movies he made.

Menaker's monkey, for example, is an exact likeness, down to the same urinary disorder, of a baby wool monkey named Mimi which Welles bought in the early 1970s in a pet store on the Quai de Seine after she refused to let go of his finger, and took to the house of Kodar in Orvilliers, where the lack of proper heating made the creature miserable. Hoping that Mimi would get better in a sunnier climate, Welles took her along to Spain when he acted in (and co-wrote) TREASURE ISLAND—and indeed, one can see Welles with both Mimi and his pet parrot in that film—but unfortunately the cold climate in Spain made Mimi even sicker, and eventually she died of pneumonia.

It seems possible that the ambitions of Diana Pellarin for her husband were suggested in part by Paola Mori—although her "huge, tirelessly adoring eyes," resembling to Blake "a pair of lightly poached eggs," were directly inspired, according to Kodar, by Nancy Reagan. The Hasty Pudding Club Review plausibly has some relation to the early amateur theatricals of Welles at the Todd School with his teacher and lifelong friend Roger Hill. The necklace and cigarette lighter which wind up in the Mediterranean are connected to an incident involving Kodar which also found fictional form in "Ivanka," the baby eels in Menaker's beard can be traced back to a meal with Henri Langlois in Barcelona, and even the "prestigious firm of Pellarin, Loeb, Leibowitz and Cirello" [*sic*] (page 70) has some autobiographical significance in its nod to Welles's loyal chauffeur in the 1940s, a hunchbacked dwarf named "Shorty" Chirello.

Similarly, the deserted house with covered furniture where Blake meets his long-lost lover, along with the carnival and fireworks outside,[4] were suggested by specific places where Welles and Kodar had stayed in Spain and France. More generally, the importance of the Spanish Civil War in the script can be related to Welles's own intense political involvements during that period, which led to him being labeled (along with certain other leftists) a "premature antifascist"; Kodar points out that he surely would have fought in that war if his poor health had not excluded the possibility.

By contrasting the Spanish Civil War with Vietnam, Welles is doing something more than juxtaposing the moral watersheds of two generations some thirty years apart. The lost lovers of Menaker and Pellarin alike are viewed as casualties of those wars, and the libidinal sense of guilt and irrationality which charges through the screenplay like a live wire—culminating in Pellarin's murder of the blind beggar—underlines the relations between the powerful and the powerless, the haves and the have nots, which inform the plot like variations on a musical theme. From Tina (the Portuguese maid) to the monkey to the boy asleep in the Retiro Park to Vanni to the French-Cambodian woman to the blind beggar, the gallery of the helpless confronting Menaker and Pellarin register like phantoms of liberal guilt as well as agents of their tortured trajectories. For all the big shots surrounding the two leads, most of them comic grotesques, it is these marginal figures who form the major pivots of the narrative, propelling the heroes forward.

While Cela Brandini might initially seem to belong to the haves rather than the have nots, she is in fact the only go-between, serving as the reader/spectator's guide into the world of the film. Significantly, she is the only European character in the film who speaks at any length. While she shares with Menaker and Pellarin an international status, she remains a perpetual outsider, serving as the film's European conscience (and consciousness). Like the others, she is left behind at the station while the American innocents charge off, scot-free—despite the blood and semen on their hands—to their elusive destinies.

Playing against the contemporaneous aspects of THE BIG BRASS RING are many facets of Welles's artistic personality which seem to belong to earlier historical periods. In one of the most suggestive recent essays about Welles, "The Force of the Work" by Bill Krohn—available in French as the introduction to *Cahiers du cinéma*'s most recent special Welles issue *"hors-série,"* but unfortunately unpublished in English—it is argued that his art expresses a nostalgia for the Middle Ages on many different levels: the "economy governing [his] system of production . . . resembles the economy of feudalism," his form of storytelling evolves from that of the resident farmer to that of the trading seaman (forms which "intermingled for the first time in the medieval trading cities"), and "the popular 'carnivalesque' forms of the Middle Ages" are reflected throughout his films— not only in such obvious instances as DON QUIXOTE and CHIMES AT MIDNIGHT, but elsewhere as well. Formally his films "recreate the scene of the carnival, where disparate members of society collide, commingle and converse"; thematically they recreate what Mikhail Bakhtin calls "the great carnival theme, 'the pathos of shifts and changes' evoked by the crowning and uncrowning of a mock king . . ."—a process that brings to mind Menaker as well as Pellarin.

At the same time, it should be noted that THE BIG BRASS RING seems equally grounded in Anglo-American fiction of the nineteenth century. Even without the mediating narration of a Marlow, the guilt-ridden darkness of Pellarin and Menaker suggests the universe of Conrad, and it is worth recalling that Welles's script adaptations of *Heart of Darkness, Lord Jim,* and *Victory* span three decades of his career. On another plane, the gallery of fools comprising Pellarin's political entourage owes something to the caricatural energy of Dickens—think of the aforementioned J. Sheldon Buckle, or Dinty Benart—reminding one that a PICKWICK PAPERS with W. C. Fields was one of Welles's earliest Hollywood projects.

Against these European antecedents, one must also consider the spirit of Mark Twain, especially *Tom Sawyer* and *Huckleberry Finn* (the latter of which was adapted into one of the most brilliant of Welles's radio shows). Clearly the childish mischief of Pellarin and Menaker belongs to a myth of freedom and innocent intrigue that relates to Huck and Jim's raft and the male camaraderie it fosters, while some of the more gratuitous and contrived capers of Pellarin evoke certain machinations of Tom. The bittersweet ending of the departure on the train ("If you want a happy ending, that depends, of course, on where you stop your story") carries some of the ambiguity inherent in Huck's closing words, and the very title of the screenplay conjures up a child's playful endeavor and hellbent toy vehicle which belong in the company of Charlie Kane's sled and Georgie Minafer's carriage.

Yet in spite of all this literary parentage, it could be argued that the acuteness of Welles's grasp of international politics and blustering American dominance reveals a maturity of moral viewpoint that is less apparent in the flippant references to Kane's war-mongering and other forms of demagoguery over four decades earlier. Without the benefit of charismatic performances and concrete images, the screenplay belongs to literature more than film history, and on that level it certainly bears comparison with the depiction of power and solitude essayed by Welles and Herman J. Mankiewicz. The enigma of personality is no less apparent, and a sense of America existing in the world rather than within the confines of its own solipsism suggests a broader and more sophisticated frame of reference.

"I'm bored with stories that don't seem to be balanced dangerously," Welles remarked in a 1981 interview, speaking about THE LADY FROM SHANGHAI. "If you walk down a highway with a story instead of on a tightrope, I'm bored with it." The sense of reckless danger informing both the writing of THE BIG BRASS RING and the action contained inside it testifies to the fierce persistence of Welles's creativity and nerve, in defiance of the industry's conservatism and cowardice that kept him unemployed as a Hollywood director over the last twenty-eight years of his life, at the same time that he was almost universally revered as his country's greatest filmmaker.

The desire to shock is as palpable here as in the seediness and violence of TOUCH OF EVIL, which even in 1958 was the first Hollywood film he had been able to make since MACBETH, an experimental three-week cheapie shot at Republic studios a decade earlier. (In the interim, Welles had embarked on the alternative route of financing his own filmmaking with OTHELLO—a dangerous departure in its own right, but one that proved to yield more results than his efforts to work within the Hollywood system.)

Clearly not all of Welles's late works carry this rebellious and daring spirit—although reportedly portions of the still unfinished THE OTHER SIDE OF THE WIND, which Kodar and cinematographer Gary Graver are determined to complete, are equally hair-raising and unexpected. Judging only by the screenplays that I have read, THE CRADLE WILL ROCK, apart from its elements of autocritique, is surprisingly benign towards its characters, while THE DREAMERS reads like the apotheosis of Welles's lyricism and romanticism. According to both Kodar and Jaglom, Welles felt personally closer to THE DREAMERS than to THE BIG BRASS RING, which leads one to the intriguing yet paradoxical postulate that he tended to identify more with his adaptations than with his original scripts—THE MAGNIFICENT AMBERSONS rather than CITIZEN KANE, CHIMES AT MIDNIGHT rather than MR. ARKADIN. Perhaps this can be attributed to the Sancho Panza side of his personality—the desire to locate himself within an existing world rather than construct an alternative one. But as the Wellesian oeuvre continues to expand, even after his death, in all directions, with a frenzy of invention that will keep us chasing after its meanings for years to come, altering our sense of the works we already know, THE BIG BRASS RING allows us the rare privilege of hearing his voice, resonant and unmistakable, still in the present, addressing us directly.

Notes

1. An earlier investigation into some of this work and some of these reasons can be found in my article "The Invisible Orson Welles: A First Inventory," *Sight and Sound,* Summer 1986.
2. "The Scorpion and the Frog" by Michael Wilmington, *L.A. Style,* June 1987, vol. 3, no. 1.
3. Kodar reports that Welles wanted to use the barely audible echo of tiny bells rather than voices to evoke this chant. Apart from this, he did not want to use many musical effects in the film; the music used would be Spanish and rather stark—basically *verbena* (fairground music) and *zarzuela* (a kind of Spanish operetta).
4. Developing a bold idea first sketched out in the prologue to HEART OF DARKNESS, Welles planned to show the reflected lights of the fireworks in the room where Blake rejoins his lover in color—a unique moment in an otherwise black and white film. References to the "little color bombs" and "colored lights" on page 118 suggest that color may have been used there as well.

> —From *THE BIG BRASS RING,* a screenplay
> by Orson Welles with Oja Kodar (Santa
> Barbara: Santa Teresa Press, 1987)

11

Wellesian

Quixote in a Trashcan
(New York University
Welles Conference)

The following is an account of the first of the eight international Welles confer-
ences I've attended, which was held in New York in the spring of 1988. (The oth-
ers have been in Venice [1991], Rome [1992], Munich [1999], Mannheim [2002],
Locarno [2005], Udine [2006], and at Yale University [2006].) A very rich and
well-planned event, it included much more than I had space to discuss adequately
in this news story. I gave a paper about Welles's 1940 radio adaptation of Huckleberry Finn *that I have never published (and may not even still have a copy of),*
and the contributions of Michael Denning and Robert Sklar, referenced respec-
tively in their published forms in chapters 18 and 24, were originally presented
at the same event (see Persistence of Vision, *no. 7, 1989, for these and other pa-*
pers). I also met Jim Naremore, a good friend ever since, for the first time at this
conference, and we attended together both of the screenings of clips selected by
Oja that are described in the second half of this piece. His keynote address became
the afterword to the second edition of his The Magic World of Orson Welles
(op. cit.).

I should add that Oja's screening of clips at this event remains by far the best
presentation of Welles's unfinished work that I've seen to date in terms of both
selection and arrangement. This is partially why I continue to consider her more
qualified to complete THE OTHER SIDE OF THE WIND *than anyone else (quite*
apart from her roles on the film as cowriter, actress, and even, in one sequence,
director or codirector)—a position that hasn't always been shared by some of my
colleagues. It's true that she was also lamentably responsible, at least indirectly,

for allowing Jess Franco to take over the final edit of the monstrosity known as DON QUIJOTE DE ORSON WELLES *four years later. But that didn't prevent her from exercising exquisite taste in selecting what scenes to show in New York in 1988. (One minor point I wasn't aware of at the time is that what I call "contemporary Spain" was actually contemporary Mexico in terms of the shooting, because Francisco Reiguera, an anti-Franco rebel, could no longer enter Spain at the time.)*

According to Catherine Benamou in a recent email, the plan in the late 80s for the Brazilian government to help finance the IT'S ALL TRUE *documentary, which would have been done through the newly formed Fundação do Cinema Brasileiro, was squelched "in March 1990, [when] Brazilian President Fernando Collor de Melo (who was later impeached) abolished Embrafilme and practically all central state funding for film; the Lei Rouanet was not yet in place to give private enterprises a tax break on film investments. So the Fundação was reduced to a repository for existing films, and could only participate nominally in Dick [Wilson]'s project, by cutting bureaucratic red tape and the like."*

■

"I earn a good living and get a lot of work because of this ridiculous myth about me," Orson Welles told Kenneth Tynan in the mid-60s. "But the price of it is that when I try to do something serious, something I care about, a great many critics don't review that particular work, but me in general. They write their standard Welles piece. It's either the good piece or the bad piece, but they're both fairly standard."

Standard Welles pieces were for once not the main bill of fare at a major Welles retrospective and conference held last May at New York University and the Public Theater. A welcome amount of concrete research into Welles's work in radio, theatre and film was aired, along with the obligatory theoretical exercises. Sidebars included an extensive exhibition of Welles's radio shows and materials documenting stage productions, and an effectively staged reading of *Moby Dick—Rehearsed,* a prime instance of how Wellesian magic could be conjured out of suggestively minimal sounds and images.

In his keynote address, James Naremore offered some fascinating glimpses into the Welles archive in Bloomington, Indiana. The original

version of THE STRANGER was half an hour longer, with a flashback structure, a surreal early scene set on a dog-training farm in Argentina, and a
nightmarish dream sequence. Even more tantalizing was the description
of the original design of THE LADY FROM SHANGHAI, based on a 1947 cutting continuity of a pre-release version that was about an hour longer.
Among many finds: Michael O'Hara's first encounter with Elsa Bannister
in Central Park was depicted in a lengthy camera movement charting the
separate trajectories of both characters and a cruising police car, similar
to the opening shot of TOUCH OF EVIL.

Some papers concentrated on lesser-known aspects of the Welles oeuvre. William Simon, the conference organizer, focused on two wartime
propaganda radio series, *Hello Americans* and *Ceiling Unlimited*, which
used some of the pseudo-documentary techniques of *Julius Caesar* on
stage, *The War of the Worlds* on radio, and the KANE newsreel, and anticipated such essay films as F FOR FAKE. Andrea Nouryeh gave a detailed description of the 1941 stage adaptation of *Native Son*, which featured the
Rosebud sled among the props in the Thomas tenement flat, and had Big-
ger Thomas firing a gun into the audience as actors dressed as policemen
proceeded to the stage from the balcony.

Perhaps the most remarkable instance of reinterpretation based on
fresh information came from Robert Stam's account of the ill-fated IT'S
ALL TRUE. Drawing on an array of Hollywood and Brazilian documents,
including the research conducted and commissioned by Welles at the
time, Stam persuasively argued that most of the complaints about
Welles's profligacy in Brazil can be attributed to his radical pro-black
stance, including the fact that he enjoyed the company and collaboration
of blacks, as well as his insistence on featuring nonwhites as the pivotal
characters in both of the film's Brazilian episodes. Stam also examined
how "in his interest in the northeast, in the *cangaceiros* (rebel bandits), in
millennial cults, in popular culture and rebellion, Welles managed to anticipate many of the themes subsequently taken up by Brazilian Cinema
Novo in the 60s and after." Indeed, the Brazilian government recently
voted to finance the feature about IT'S ALL TRUE that is being planned by
Richard Wilson, Welles's assistant in Brazil, including Wilson's reconstruction of the remarkable Fortaleza episode.

The climax of the weekend was Oja Kodar's screening of excerpts from four unfinished or unreleased films—an event that was well attended, although oddly enough not by many of the conference's more prominent academics. There was a short scene from THE DREAMERS, already discussed in these pages (*Sight and Sound*, Summer 1986), and one reel of THE MERCHANT OF VENICE. This is a provocative sample—fully edited, scored, and mixed—of a finished film whose soundtrack was stolen in Rome in 1969, soon after the film was completed, for reasons that remain mysterious. (Kodar possesses the complete negative, but without sound, apart from this reel.) Featuring Welles as a heavily made-up Shylock, a spectacular array of festively decorated boats, and a use of color that is distinctly different from that of THE IMMORTAL STORY (with gold predominating in the harbor), the reel is too fragmentary to constitute more than a teaser.

The three reels from THE OTHER SIDE OF THE WIND offered three complete scenes. Earlier versions of the first two were shown at Welles's 1975 AFI Tribute, and are described in James Naremore's *The Magic World of Orson Welles*. The third charts an unsettling series of exchanges between director Jake Hannaford (John Huston), surrounded by members of his entourage at his birthday party, and a prissy schoolteacher (Dan Tobin), clearly out of his depth, whose former student is the lead actor in Hannaford's film-in-progress. Hannaford's banter is basically macho gay-baiting, and the musically timed reverse-angles which alternate between his gibes and the teacher's embarrassed rejoinders or giggles finally give way to simple exchanges of looks. Relentlessly prolonging and exacerbating the queasy tension, this sequence is the most aggressive employment that I know of *champ contrechamp*.

But the major revelation was the four reels of DON QUIXOTE. This series of fully edited but only partially dubbed black and white sequences, in no apparent order, already provides strong evidence of why Welles never wanted to let go of the film: it is so fully Welles and Cervantes at the same time, and so close to the wellsprings of his inspiration, that it must have served as his ultimate plaything. Completion would only have put an end to the game.

The materials at hand are simple and unadorned: Quixote (Francisco

Reiguera) and Sancho Panza (Akim Tamiroff), both in ragtag period costume, and contemporary Spain all around them. When they pass through a town, with crowds waving, the continuing relevance of Quixote is ironically underlined by the presence of his name on shop signs and billboards, including one for Quixote Beer. The rural landscapes are worthy of Dovzhenko, with a similar dominance of sculpted sky over ground. There are no sound effects. When voices are heard, they belong exclusively to Welles—as both of his characters and in one sequence as himself offscreen, addressing a querulous Sancho, who speaks back to the camera.

The interplay between master and servant is perhaps most hilariously expressed in a scene on a city rooftop, where Sancho is washing his master in a trashcan next to a TV aerial, calmly soaping and scrubbing Quixote's arms while they wildly gesticulate in the midst of nonstop pontifications. The earthiness and physicality of the characterization parallel that of Falstaff, reminding one of the paradox that Welles's most personal work came in literary adaptations—Tarkington, Shakespeare, Dinesen—rather than in original scripts such as KANE and ARKADIN.

—*Sight and Sound*, Autumn 1988

12

Reviews of *Citizen Welles* and a Critical Edition of CHIMES AT MIDNIGHT

Citizen Welles: A Biography of Orson Welles, by Frank Brady (New York: Scribner's, 1989)

CHIMES AT MIDNIGHT, edited by Bridget Gellert Lyons (New Brunswick, NJ: Rutgers University Press, 1988)

In overall approach as well as attitude, Frank Brady's hefty (655-page) and readable Welles biography represents a certain advance over the previous efforts of Barbara Leaming and Charles Higham, which I reviewed in these pages exactly three years ago. Eschewing the gossip of Leaming and the petty malice of Higham, Brady concentrates on Welles's work and career almost exclusively, with a balanced sympathy towards his subject that avoids either special pleading or thesis mongering. The book's jacket informs us that Brady, who has also written biographies of Bobby Fischer, Aristotle Onassis, and Barbra Streisand, worked on this one for a decade, and the breadth of his research is often impressive: a mine of interesting information is on view here, and much of it has not been available before.

Yet as soon as one descends from this overview and starts to deal with the nuts and bolts of this book, problems begin to crop up. It pains me to say this, because Brady, whom I've never met, devotes a very flattering paragraph to my own work on Welles in his acknowledgements, and, as I've already suggested, displays an overall seriousness of attitude in dealing with Welles that deserves to be recognized; as other reviewers have noted, he has no particular ax to grind, which is something of a rarity in writers about Welles. But his handling of facts is wildly uneven. Some areas of this biography—in particular, the sections dealing with CITIZEN KANE and radio—appear to be researched much more thoroughly than others, and it won't be obvious to the unspecialized reader which sections are the more reliable ones. Not only do we rarely know Brady's sources; we're also not even sure much of the time where information stops and speculation begins. (The bibliography, by omitting a substantial number of sources alluded to in the text, comes across more like a perfunctory afterthought than as a useful tool for other Welles researchers.) And in certain areas, Brady is either confused or simply wrong about his facts.

I suspect that much of this problem comes from the difficulty of relying too much on diverse documents and trying to reconcile them all in a fluid narrative. Although it's clear that some individuals were interviewed for the book, including Roger Hill, John Houseman, Beatrice Welles, Richard Wilson, and Welles himself in one phone conversation, there is only occasional evidence of Brady checking the information imparted in these interviews against other sources; and it's equally clear that many key individuals, such as Oja Kodar, Gary Graver, and Peter Bogdanovich, were never contacted at all.

Citing a six-minute video proposal made by Welles about his KING LEAR project—a tape of Welles speaking directly to the camera which I described and quoted from in the Summer 1986 issue of *Sight and Sound*—Brady gets this mixed up with a spurious account of Welles filming bits and pieces of this proposed film on the sets of other directors, so that what he winds up with is a fanciful conflation of my account and someone else's—a six-minute tape which somehow manages to incorporate several nonexistent filmed scenes as well as a talking head describing the project. In the case of THE BIG BRASS RING, another unrealized late project, Brady seriously misdescribes the plot so that the unrequited love of one man for another becomes a "secret love affair," and turns a comment by Henry Jaglom about the project into a sentence which begins, "Orson began to believe that. . . ." (In fact, Brady is often rather cavalier about reporting to us what he supposes went on in Welles's mind.) Brady states that Welles's controversial beard in Hollywood was grown for *Five Kings*; Welles himself told me it was grown for *The Green Goddess*. An alleged exchange of wisecracks between Welles and Herman Mankiewicz about the Oscar they shared for the script of CITIZEN KANE was actually an exchange imagined by Welles in a note that he sent to Mankiewicz. Brady claims that Welles "was pleased" by the Leaming biography, but everyone I know who was close to Welles asserts that he never read it.

In relation to a purported Welles biography by Bogdanovich, Brady writes that "Orson's only wish was that Bogdanovich would have the book published before Orson's death." Having recently begun to edit this very lengthy manuscript—which is not a biography, but an interview interspersed with numerous documents (including articles, studio memos, letters, and script extracts) and illustrations—I can state with assurance that Brady has it backwards: it was Welles and not Bogdanovich who delayed the book's publication.

It could be argued that most of the above errors are relatively minor, and many are understandable, given the notorious difficulties of researching Welles's career. But what about Brady's handling the whole complex episode of the editing of THE MAGNIFICENT AMBERSONS, which is sabotaged at the outset by his apparent assumption that Welles did all of his editing of this film in Rio, while he was organizing and shooting IT'S ALL TRUE? Although Brady frequently gives indications of having studied other accounts of this crucial period, he seems unaware of the well-documented information that (1) Welles assembled a rough cut of the film with Robert Wise before he left for Rio, and (2) RKO promised and then failed to send Wise to Rio so that the editing of the fine cut could be accomplished there. While it is true that Welles received a copy of the rough cut in Rio and sent many lengthy detailed instructions to Wise from Brazil about further editing changes (only a few of which were heeded), Brady's repeated claim that Welles edited AMBERSONS in Brazil seriously muddles one's grasp of the whole episode; and his descriptions of Welles struggling with "tens of thousands of feet of unedited film" on a moviola in Rio—without any acknowledgement, for instance, of the prior editing done by Welles with Wise over three days and nights in Miami, immediately before Welles flew to Rio—only adds to the confusion.

Elsewhere, Brady perpetuates some misinformation from Higham

about THE FOUNTAIN OF YOUTH—that Welles spent a month and an un-
seemly amount of money making this extraordinary TV pilot for Desilu—
which should be definitively laid to rest. Bill Krohn, who recently went to
the Desilu records for clarification, discovered that the pilot took only five
days to shoot (May 8, 9, 10, 11 and 14, 1956), and that the final, all-
inclusive cost was $54,896—about $5,000 more than the $49,832 Welles
was originally budgeted for, but still only slightly more than half the cost
of the first episode of I Love Lucy (about $95,000).

Even more disorder informs Brady's account of the filming of THE MER-
CHANT OF VENICE. According to both Oja Kodar, who was present at the
filming, and Welles himself, who spoke about it to Krohn in a 1982 interview for Cahiers du cinéma, this filming took place in Italy and Yugoslavia
in 1969. A reel of this color film was recently shown by Oja Kodar in both
Honolulu and New York at separate Welles events. Brady implies that he
has seen this reel, but without any visible evidence, he asserts that "these
fragments," which he claims were filmed "as a promotional device," were
all that Welles ever shot on the project, and that they were filmed over ten
years earlier, shortly after Welles appeared in THE ROOTS OF HEAVEN
(1958); in addition, through the placement of this event in his chronology,
he implies that the filming was done in either England or Ireland. Assuming that any of these facts could possibly be true (and it is hard to
imagine how they could be), what is one then to make of Brady's later
claim that, in 1966, "Outside of acting, all of [Welles's] experience with
film, for almost thirty years, was in black-and-white"?

Other confusions seem to come about because of a faulty understanding of film in general. Consider this sentence about OTHELLO: "Although
any particular scene might appear to have been filmed at one time, in one
place, it was only through the patching together through the editorial
process that it appeared to be an uninterrupted take." Assuming that
what Brady means by "uninterrupted take" is "continuous scene," the
sentence makes sense; read literally, it is unfathomable.

While it would be accurate to say that the original release version of
TOUCH OF EVIL contains less of Harry Keller's footage than the longer version which has since been found and released, it is surely wrong to state,
as Brady does, that it contains none of Keller's footage. More debatable,

but still curious, is Brady's contention that a Welles project to film *Crime and Punishment* "was eventually blue-penciled partially because everyone realized, with the possible exception of Orson, that it might have been difficult to have improved on Josef von Sternberg's 1936 classic adaptation of the story." (Has Brady seen it recently?)

After devoting this much space to carping, it is important to reiterate that the overall extensiveness of Brady's research frequently helps to make up for the unreliability of certain details. One of Brady's most fascinating and valuable discoveries involves the origins of MR. ARKADIN in two of the episodes scripted by Welles for his Harry Lime radio series, which clarifies a link between that film and THE THIRD MAN which no former commentator has managed to tease out. And his account of Welles's original two-picture contract with RKO, which appears to be backed up by a careful perusal of the relevant documents, includes several pertinent facts which are at variance with previous accounts.

There's also some valuable fresh information to be found in Bridget Gellert Lyons's impeccably researched critical edition of CHIMES AT MIDNIGHT in the Rutgers Films in Print series—above all, Lyons's lengthy interview with Keith Baxter, who played Prince Hal in the film and was around during virtually all of the shooting and most of the post-synching of the dialogue, and who imparts much more information about the film's production than is available anywhere else. Lyons has also taken the trouble of annotating the continuity script in order to pinpoint which lines come from which Shakespeare plays (or from Welles himself, in a few cases), and has gathered together an excellent selection of other materials, including eight contemporary reviews of the film, and critical commentaries by C. L. Barber, Dudley Andrew, and Michael Anderegg. Truthfully, no serious Welles scholar can afford to be without this book; the same goes for Brady's biography, however cautiously and circumspectly one has to proceed with it.

—*Film Quarterly*, Winter 1989–90

∎

If I were reviewing Brady's biography today, I'd be sorely tempted to link it to Clinton Heylin's recent Despite the System: Orson Welles versus the Hollywood Studios (*Chicago: A Cappella, 2005*), *another well-intentioned study that is very flattering to my own work but is nonetheless full of obfuscations and distortions—in part because the author, like Brady, isn't a film scholar and can't adequately fight his way through the swamp of misinformation that confronts even some specialists. Because of all the Welles books that have appeared since Brady's, Heylin's offers fewer discoveries, but his valiant efforts to refute writers like Higham and Thomson still give his study a timely polemical value as well as much information that's bound to be fresh to nonspecialists. But the errors and misjudgments that I find throughout, a few of which are cited in the final chapter of this book, still give me pause even when I find the book sympathetic. How could Heylin be expected to know, for instance, that Oja Kodar didn't direct any part of THE ONE-MAN BAND, the 1995 documentary about Welles's "lost" films, despite the fact that she appears in much of the film and is sometimes credited as codirector with Vassili Silovic? The only reason why I happen to know this is that both Kodar and Silovic told me, on separate occasions, and this is close to being a routine example of the sort of confusion a relative outsider to Welles scholarship is likely to encounter the moment he or she plunges in.*

I was sent a copy of Heylin's book in manuscript in an effort to solicit a back-jacket endorsement from me, and I regretfully passed on this option because of all the factual problems I encountered. I cited about a dozen of these in an email to the book's editor—some of which were debatable, though many clearly weren't—and was disappointed to discover when I received a finished copy of the book that none had been heeded and that Peter Bogdanovich, evidently seeing none of the problems that I did, had offered an extravagant back-jacket endorsement of his own.

13

Review of *Orson Welles: A Bio-Bibliography*

Orson Welles: A Bio-Bibliography, by Bret Wood (Westport, CT: Greene Press, 1990)

Issued without dust wrappers and priced beyond the range of most individuals, this 364-page book is clearly intended for libraries, and not likely to get much attention outside of specialized publications. But as a multifaceted research tool for anyone investigating the career of Orson Welles it is a veritable godsend—more valuable in some ways than any of the Welles biographies published so far.

Not counting introduction, endnotes, index, a skeletal Welles chronology, an invaluable section devoted to special sources, and ten well-chosen illustrations, the book is divided into eight sections: Biographical Sketch, Theatre Credits, Radio Credits, Film Credits, Welles as Author, Discography (a brief section that regrettably excludes commercial releases of radio broadcasts), Books and Monographs on Welles, and Articles on Welles. Probably the most valuable of these sections in terms of fresh material are the two longest, Radio Credits (74 pages) and Film Credits (120 pages), containing not only listings but, in many cases, descriptive and critical annotations. (The length of the film section can largely be accounted for by the fact that Wood is as attentive to unrealized projects as he is to finished works, and it is chiefly his accounts of the former that make this section so useful.)

I don't mean to suggest that Wood's research skills are infallible or that his book doesn't contain its share of typos, syntactical ambiguities, factual errors, and glaring omissions. But given the difficulty and intricacy of Welles's career as an object of study, he has generally acquitted himself admirably. Welles scholars have neglected particularly the bulk of the radio work and such lesser known film projects as DON'T TOUCH ME, CARMEN, and SALOME.

Regarding Welles's radio work, he offers the first thing that even remotely approaches a comprehensive account, with a keen sensitivity to how that work relates to Welles's work in both film and theater. Apart from a few patches in John Houseman's *Run-Through* and Frank Brady's fascinating but unreliable *Citizen Welles*, virtually all of Welles's chroniclers and critics have paid only glancing lip-service to this vast, undiscovered continent in Welles's oeuvre. Although many people still believe that Welles's film career essentially began and ended with CITIZEN KANE, there are surely even more who assume that his radio career began and ended with *The War of the Worlds*. Considering the fact that Welles did hundreds of radio broadcasts, educated and detailed commentary on this work has been by far the most gaping lacuna in Welles studies.

Wood has listened to all of Welles's groundbreaking, seven-part adaptation of *Les Miserables* in 1937, can pinpoint many of the individual highlights of *First Person Singular* and *Mercury Theatre on the Air* (1938), *The Campbell Playhouse* (1938–1940), and subsequent shows through the later forties, and is able to trace (for instance) the style and format of *The Orson Welles Almanac* in 1944 back to Welles's several appearances on Jack Benny's show in 1943. He clearly qualifies as the first serious scholar to write at any length about these matters. While one can differ with some of his individual judgments—I happen to rank Welles's controversial and political 1941 radio play *His Honor, the Mayor* much higher than he does, largely because of Welles's remarkable neo-Brechtian narration—there's no question that Wood dwarfs all his predecessors in his detailed assessments of Welles's radio work.

The bibliographical sections, on the other hand, while they contain many entries that were unfamiliar to me, are as notable in some ways for what they leave out as for what they include. Although Wood neglects to mention this, his list of books and monographs completely excludes non-English works, and most other items are also in English. The principles for inclusion often seem curious and haphazard: two pieces in *Confidential* about Welles's love life are cited, but neither of the two prominent manifestos by Welles and Houseman about the Mercury Theater that appeared in the *New York Times;* and even Peter Bogdanovich's celebrated "The Kane Mutiny"—published in *Esquire* and reprinted in a volume Wood cites elsewhere—goes unmentioned.

Wood fails to note that Fletcher Markle was the credited author of the SALOME treatment he discusses and incorrectly states that Welles's TV documentary about Gina Lollobrigida was "never completed" (when it was both discovered and shown in its entirety at the Venice film festival a few years ago). Many of these and other errors or omissions can be traced back to printed sources elsewhere—a recurring problem that is especially acute when it comes to Wellesian matters—although it also suggests that some matters received much more of Wood's attention than others. (Curiously, he seems completely unaware of the bulk of Welles's work for European TV—including such series as *Orson Welles Sketchbook, Around the World with Orson Welles,* and *In the Land of Don Quixote.*) But these are only niggling reservations about an indispensable resource for all Welles scholars.

—*Film Quarterly,* Winter 1990–91

14

Orson Welles's Essay Films and Documentary Fictions

A Two-Part Speculation

The following essay, the most formally playful in this collection, is also the one in which my periodic impulse to practice a mimetic "hommage" form of criticism is most pronounced. It is also one in which, at the end, I enact a kind of revenge via ridicule against academic film study for its seemingly unlimited capacity for self-validation even (or perhaps especially) when it lacks information about film or intelligibility—following an overall anti-academic bias that Welles shared. (Call it my own way of tweaking the "experts.")

The many numbered lists utilized in this piece deliberately come in matching sets: two sets of two propositions; lists of a dozen and two dozen film titles; and the eight parts of Deleuze's summary of the beginning of F FOR FAKE *replicated both by the eight parts of my own summary and by my eight notes at the end. The latter joke was blunted at Stefan Drössler's insistence when the piece got reprinted in* The Unknown Orson Welles *(op. cit., see introduction) with nine notes. (The additional note pointed out that* FOUR MEN ON A RAFT *was eventually converted into* IT'S ALL TRUE: BASED ON AN UNFINISHED FILM BY ORSON WELLES*—a fact that the reader of this book can discover elsewhere, in chapter 17 as well as in this sentence.) Rather than repeat his alteration, I've stuck to my eight notes while updating and/or upgrading this piece in a few other particulars (something I haven't generally done elsewhere in this book): eliminating a factual error unrelated to Welles in the first section, retaining the page numbers added by Stefan to some notes, and anachronistically alluding to and quoting from Stefan's own collection (which contains the first publication of Krohn's Welles in-*

terview in English) in the very last note. I should add that the shifts between italic and roman fonts, retained here, are part of the piece's original design.

Having had an opportunity to see much more of THE OTHER SIDE OF THE WIND *after writing this piece, I'm sorry now that I wasn't able to delve into some of the implications of the use of pseudodocumentary in that film—a topic I subsequently discussed on a panel at the Locarno film festival's Welles conference in August 2005. One of the biggest challenges offered by the character of Jake Hannaford, played by John Huston, as seen through countless pseudodocumentary snippets, is that his unfinished film-within-a-film, which we see a great deal of over the course of the narrative, doesn't seem to be a film that he could or would have made, even though we can even hear him directing the two lead actors at one crucial juncture. (The film we see is quite arty and often seems conceived as a parody of Antonioni during this period, and this doesn't gibe with Hannaford's macho, "all-American" persona in any legible way.) Although some might construe this discrepancy as a flaw, I see it as one of the purest expressions of Welles's radical sense of human personality being contradictory and inexplicable—a theme that haunts his work from* CITIZEN KANE *onwards, and one which only deepens the mysteries of character being explored here.*

Although I still regard Naremore's The Magic World of Orson Welles *as the best critical study of Welles in any language, I should add that Youssef Ishaghpour's massive and highly intelligent* Orson Welles Cinéaste, Une Caméra Visible *(Paris: Éditions de la Différence, 2001)—which arrives at the same conclusion about the Naremore book, and which I haven't yet read in its entirety (its three volumes run to almost 2,000 pages!)—certainly deserves to be regarded as* hor concors.

■

> I want to give the audience a hint of a scene. No more than that. Give them too much and they won't contribute anything themselves. Give them just a suggestion and you get them working with you. That's what gives the theatre meaning: when it becomes a social act.
> —Orson Welles, quoted in *Collier's*, 29 January 1938

Two propositions:

1. One of the most progressive forms of cinema is the film in which fiction and nonfiction merge, trade places, become interchangeable.

2. One of the most reactionary forms of cinema is the film in which fiction and nonfiction merge, trade places, become interchangeable.

How can both of these statements be true—as, in fact, I believe they are? In the final analysis, the issue is an ethical one. In support of 2, there are docudramas that use spurious means to grant bogus authenticity to fiction (MISSISSIPPI BURNING is a good example), and documentaries that employ fictional devices in order to lie more effectively (consider the studio retakes in Leni Riefenstahl's TRIUMPH OF THE WILL, which are well documented in Albert Speer's *Inside the Third Reich*).

In support of 1, there are masterpieces collapsing, combining, and/or juxtaposing fiction and nonfiction in order to facilitate and broaden a filmmaker's grasp on a subject in the interests of truth. This is a highly subjective matter, of course, but a few of my own key touchstones in this category would be:

1. Josef von Sternberg's THE SAGA OF ANATAHAN (1953)
2. Alain Resnais and Marguerite Duras's HIROSHIMA, MON AMOUR (1959)
3. Jean-Marie Straub and Danièle Huillet's THE BRIDEGROOM, THE COMEDIENNE, AND THE PIMP (1968)
4. Jacques Rivette's OUT 1: NOLI ME TANGERE (1971)
5. Orson Welles's F FOR FAKE (1973)
6. Jacques Tati's PARADE (1973)
7. Jean-Luc Godard's ICI ET AILLEURS (1974)
8. Chris Marker's SANS SOLEIL (1982)
9. Françoise Romand's MIX-UP (1985)
10. Râúl Ruiz's MAMMAME (1987)
11. Joris Ivens and Marceline Loridan's A TALE OF THE WIND (1988)
12. Leslie Thornton's PEGGY AND FRED IN HELL (still in progress)

■

Two propositions:

1. *All of Orson Welles's film and television work can be divided into two categories, fiction and nonfiction.*

2.   *All of Orson Welles's film and television work can be divided into two cate-
     gories, stories and essays.*

*This leads us into certain semantic problems from the outset: stories, after all, can
be fictional or nonfictional, and essays can make use of fiction as well as nonfiction. Then there is the equally vexing question of how we define a "work" by
Orson Welles, which has been addressed in some detail by James Naremore:[1] if
we include only works that were both completed and publicly shown, we narrow
our scope considerably, but if we decide to broaden our list, we invariably come
up with a different set of problems.*

*Let us try to make do with four separate lists, all of them necessarily somewhat
tentative and incomplete, none of which includes the (now lost) films done by
Welles as interludes in many of his stage productions, but still comprising two
dozen works in all:*

(a)   *nonfiction or essay films by Welles that were completed and shown:*
      CITIZEN KANE *trailer (circa 1940)*
      ORSON WELLES'S SKETCH BOOK *(BBC-TV, 1955, six 15-minute
          programs)*
      AROUND THE WORLD WITH ORSON WELLES *(ITA-TV, 1955, six
          26-minute programs)*
      NELLA TERRA DI DON CHISIOTTE (IN THE LAND OF DON QUIXOTE)
          (RAI, 1964, nine 30-minute programs)
      F FOR FAKE *(film, 1973)*
      FILMING OTHELLO *(film, 1978)*

(b)   *nonfiction or essay films by Welles that were completed but not publicly
      shown:*
      condensed first act of Wilde's The Importance of Being Earnest *and
          last scene of Shakespeare's* Henry IV *(filmed record of performance in
          Munich, 1950)*
      ORSON WELLES AND PEOPLE *(independently produced television pilot
          about the life of Alexandre Dumas, 27 minutes, circa 1956)*
      PORTRAIT OF GINA *(ABC, 1958)*
      SPYING IN VIENNA *(sketch done for unshown CBS television special,
          ORSON'S BAG, 1969)*
      F FOR FAKE *trailer (1976, 9 minutes)*

(c)   *nonfiction or essay films that were started but not completed:*
      IT'S ALL TRUE *(film, 1942)*
      MOBY DICK—REHEARSED *(film record of London stage performance, 1955)*
      THE DOMINICI AFFAIR *(program for* AROUND THE WORLD WITH ORSON
          WELLES *television series, 1955)*
      THE MAGIC SHOW *(film record of magic performance without camera
          tricks, 1969–1985)*
      FILMING THE TRIAL *(film, circa early 1980s)*

(d)   *fiction films of Orson Welles that utilize documentary, pseudodocumen-
      tary, or essayistic elements:*
      CITIZEN KANE *(1941; pseudodocumentary* News on the March *segment)*
      THE MAGNIFICENT AMBERSONS *(1942; essayistic narration)*
      THE STRANGER *(1946; documentary footage of concentration camps)*
      MR. ARKADIN *(1955; pseudodocumentary prologue)*
      DON QUIXOTE *(1955–1985, unfinished; essayistic narration)*
      THE FOUNTAIN OF YOUTH *(television pilot, 1956; essayistic narration)*
      CHIMES AT MIDNIGHT *(1966; essayistic narration from Holinshed's*
          Chronicles*)*
      THE OTHER SIDE OF THE WIND *(1970–?, unfinished; pseudodocumentary
          form throughout)*

∎

The process-oriented methods that permitted at least four Welles features
and a number of short works to be left unfinished are easier to understand
than they would be if we adopted the mental habits of producers, which is
exactly what more and more critics today seem to be doing; but that is no
comfort to those of us eager to understand, and eager as critics always are to
have the last word, which we are not about to have with this filmmaker. At
least our direction, as always, is laid out for us: as long as one frame of film
by the greatest filmmaker of the modern era is moldering in vaults, our work
is not done. It is the last challenge, and the biggest joke, of an oeuvre that has
always had more designs on us than we could ever have on it.
—Bill Krohn, *Cahiers du cinéma*, 1986[2]

Any investigative foray into the legacy of Welles that is undertaken
today, including this one, has to be at once historical research and an ex-

ercise in science fiction. With a substantial part of Welles's work still un-available to us, each "new" work has to serve double duty as a fresh chap-ter in his tangled oeuvre and as an additional skeleton key for unlocking some of the mysteries in his other works, visible and invisible alike. In the case of FILMING OTHELLO—the last feature of his to have been completed and shown publicly before his death in 1985—we have an additional com-plication of confronting an extended meditation on an earlier Welles fea-ture that is currently unavailable in the United States (although this situ-ation may change in the near future: Welles's youngest daughter, Beatrice, who has inherited the American rights to OTHELLO, is currently planning to rerelease the film, and, as I write, Michael Dawson is in the process of restoring the film for this purpose). But while this meditation is clearly no substitute for the 1952 OTHELLO it describes, it is a fascinat-ing enough essay in its own right.

FILMING OTHELLO was planned as the first in a series of films in which Welles would re-examine some of his earlier works; the second in the se-ries, which he had already started (again, with cinematographer Gary Graver), was devoted to THE TRIAL. Why did he choose these films rather than, say, CITIZEN KANE or TOUCH OF EVIL? Partially, it seems, because these were the two of his released features on which he had final cut which were most governed by chance and the financial vicissitudes that required last-minute changes and improvisations. Indeed, both films were initially designed to be shot in studios and then had to be completely redesigned in relation to found locations once the initial financing evap-orated. And both films outline the radical change in Welles's aesthetics that accompanied this readjustment—the realization that if he wanted to make films his own way, as he had once before been able to do only on KANE, he would have to do them differently.

OTHELLO, in particular, inaugurates the whole "second manner" of Welles's film career, which might be called the *bricolage* or *caméra-stylo* manner (in contrast to the studio shooting that dominates nearly all of his 1940s work)—a manner that persists with only a few exceptions (i.e., TOUCH OF EVIL) to the end of his life. Because Welles found himself peri-odically running out of money during the shooting of OTHELLO—obliging him to go off and act in commercial films in order to raise the money to continue—he found himself adopting a number of new strategies in order to make his stop-and-start procedures more viable. Some of the major characteristics of his second manner include the spirit of *bricolage* (the most famous instance in OTHELLO being the restaging of the killing of Roderigo in a Turkish bath after the costumes for the scene failed to show up), the increasing importance of editing over camera movement (largely due to the loss of such studio equipment as tracks and cranes), the increasing use of doubles (for actors and locations alike), a certain loss in sound depth, and Welles's growing tendency to dub other actors' voices himself—all characteristics that tended to increase the spatial disorientation of the viewer and minimize the long takes of Welles's earlier work.

Conceivably the most modest of all the films in the Wellesian canon (unless one counts the nine-part television series IN THE LAND OF DON QUIXOTE done for RAI in 1964, a conventional and relatively uninteresting "home movie" travelogue), in budget as well as aspiration, FILMING OTHELLO can itself be read as a kind of shotgun marriage between chance and control. In contrast to both Welles's carefully composed monologues beside a moviola and an impromptu question-and-answer session in Boston is the "dialogue" with Michael Mac Liammóir and Hilton Edwards over lunch which forcibly combines these modes: on the one hand, three colleagues ruminating about Shakespeare's play around a table; on the other, isolated and carefully composed shots of a conversing Welles seated at another table—clearly inserted later, though with no attempt to disguise the mismatches of sound as well as image. (Earlier examples of this doggedly "unprofessional" technique can be found in the 1958 television film PORTRAIT OF GINA, cited above—a rambling personal essay about Gina Lollobrigida and pin-ups in Italy which was made for and rejected by CBS in 1958, and which is conceivably as full of digressions as this parenthesis. The checkered history of this particular *film maudit*, moreover, has plenty of mismatched discontinuities of its own: almost eighteen years after Welles left it behind in his hotel room in Paris, it was rediscovered by chance in a storage area in the mid-1980s; after a lengthy excerpt was shown on French television—the only portion I've been able to see—the film was screened in its entirety at the Venice film festival before promptly vanishing again, reportedly due to legal objections from

Lollobrigida.) According to Gary Graver, these mismatches can partially be explained by the fact that several years passed between the lunch with Mac Liammóir and Edwards and the inserted shots of Welles, and the film stock that was used for the former was no longer being made when Welles came to shoot the latter. Even here, however, the apparent dialectic between an impromptu documentary method and a more "composed" form of discourse is not as clear-cut as it may first appear: Welles's allusion at one point during the lunch to a woman's remark made between takes foregrounds that this "documentary" is far from random, while the gist of his inserted remarks blends smoothly with the logical flow of the discussion.

If many of Welles's late films gravitate toward the essay film ("The essay does not date," he remarked in a 1982 interview, "because it represents the author's contribution, however modest, to the moment at which it was made"), it should be kept in mind that the forms of essay and documentary are inscribed in his fictional work from the beginning, even before he turned to movies. (The news bulletins in his famous 1938 *War of the Worlds* radio broadcast are the most obvious example, but a careful examination of his other work in radio and theater during the 1930s would surely turn up others.) More specifically, it is the ambiguous merging of fact and fiction which engages Welles the most—providing the basic principle behind his DON QUIXOTE (to judge at least from the forty-five minutes or so that I've seen, which plant Cervantes's fictional characters in a documentary version of contemporary Spain), becoming the very subject of F FOR FAKE, and actually forming more of the texture of FILMING OTHELLO than Welles's candor as a monologist might at first suggest. For most of what we see of OTHELLO in FILMING OTHELLO is not excerpts preserved intact but an intricate re-editing of the original material—the scrambled shards of a dream of OTHELLO, oddly akin to the dreamlike prologue of KANE, rather than the film itself. Apart from the precredits funeral sequence that opens OTHELLO and FILMING OTHELLO alike, the footage is re-edited and shown silent over Welles's 1978 commentary, giving a complex and ironic twist to Welles's remarks about "quoting or misquoting" critical comments by Jack Jorgens and André Bazin about OTHELLO.

Creatively misquoting his own film at the same time that he misquotes his critics, Welles thus continues his projects of candid concealment and continuous revision which have already made his filmmaking career as labyrinthine and as mysterious as it is. And transposing some of the same giddy continuity of OTHELLO whereby Iago crosses continents "in the middle of a spoken phrase" and the separate thrusts in a skirmish between Roderigo and Cassio occur a thousand miles apart, Welles reshuffles and reorders much of the material in his own commentary, and revises the performances of himself and Mac Liammóir by reciting some of the same speeches—performing a creative dance around an object that is never allowed to remain fixed and static. Such work-in-progress, with both the subject and the object of the discussion in a perpetual state of becoming, seems only fitting as a contribution to an oeuvre which, as Bill Krohn points out above, refuses to allow us the last word, even while it actively and generously invites our participation.

■

The position of power enjoyed by the storyteller/essayist/narrator in much of Welles's work is more than a simple or seamless technique; considering the multiple and complex changes that are wrung from this position, it deserves to be treated as a preoccupation of the work itself, a notion of media as mirror whereby the performer paradoxically becomes the spectator of himself, the drama at hand providing the individual lens for his latest exercise in self-scrutiny. It is a narcissism always mediated and/or contested by a moral inquiry: HEART OF DARKNESS, *Welles's first Hollywood project, revolved around the notion of playing both Marlow (off-screen narrator and first-person camera) and Kurtz (on-screen demagogue/villain)—that is, witness as well as subject.[3] From* KANE *through* TOUCH OF EVIL, *the Welles character that we see on screen is never as moral (virtuous or truthful) as the Welles persona who might be telling the story off-screen—even if, as in* THE LADY FROM SHANGHAI, *the Welles character is narrating his own story (and thereby registers as a sadder and wiser version of the Michael O'Hara that we see).[4]*

In THE FOUNTAIN OF YOUTH, *Welles's first television pilot—an adaptation of John Collier's short story "Youth from Vienna" that begins as an essay on the subject of narcissism—the dialectic is given a new pattern. For once, the narrating Welles persona is intermittently visible as well as audible; he begins the show, in effect, as a slide show lecturer, and reappears periodically to remind us of his privileged position. But as he basks in both his fictive power to give his static slides motion and his essayistic authority to freeze his characters again in order to digress about Narcissus or Ponce de Leon, the visibility of his manipulation undermines certain aspects of his narrative authority, turning his fiction into a documentary about himself (much as* FILMING OTHELLO *begins as a documentary about the actual* OTHELLO, *and partially winds up as a documentary about a re-edited, hence fictional,* OTHELLO). *By speaking for the characters as well as about them—literally lip-synching Joi Lansing, Dan Tobin, and Rick Jason, his three stars, at certain junctures to mock their role as puppets—his moral fallibility (that is to say, his narcissism) becomes identified with theirs, and the implicit nastiness of Welles's amused, glacial detachment consciously boomerangs.*

It seems fairly likely that ORSON WELLES AND PEOPLE—*Welles's second unsold television pilot, made after* THE FOUNTAIN OF YOUTH *and before* TOUCH OF EVIL—*is a lost work that will never be recovered. According to Fletcher Markle, a good friend of Welles during this period who is one of the few people to have seen it, it was a pilot about the Dumas family, done for a half-hour biographical series that would in theory eventually include such disparate figures as Winston Churchill and P. T. Barnum; Welles financed it himself on a minuscule budget, using the $5,000 he had been paid for appearing (paradoxically, as himself) and performing part of a magic act on* I Love Lucy, *and the entire thing was shot in a single day, in "a cheap, non-union 16mm studio—a converted garage, as I recall, somewhere off Hollywood Boulevard," with Welles as narrator, armed with "masses of period photos and drawings of Dumas and the Paris of his day" that were "blown up for use on the insert stand."*[5] *One imagines that it might have been a somewhat elaborated version of the simple talking-head format of* ORSON WELLES'S SKETCH BOOK, *a British television series done a year or so earlier, just as* IN THE LAND OF DON QUIXOTE *can be regarded as a close cousin of the British television series* AROUND THE WORLD WITH ORSON WELLES (*to judge from the single episode I've seen in the latter—a chat with Kenneth Tynan about bullfighting, shot in Spain). Like* PORTRAIT OF GINA, *it seems likely that most or all of these television works, with the striking exception of* THE FOUNTAIN OF YOUTH, *qualify as ephemera, but they are significant insofar as they represent the seeds or offshoots of more important works—much as the methodology of* F FOR FAKE *can already be seen in embryo in* PORTRAIT OF GINA, *for instance.*

■

The two major documentary forays of Welles on film, standing roughly at opposite ends of his film career, are IT'S ALL TRUE (1942) and F FOR FAKE (1973), two projects whose very titles together express a dialectical relationship to the documentary. The first of these, which occasioned the disastrous turning point in Welles's Hollywood career away from creative control and studio support, was in some respects as ambitious as CITIZEN KANE and THE MAGNIFICENT AMBERSONS in its conception. But for many years, some of the facts about this work have been repeatedly misrepresented in books about Welles, so a brief description of the project is in order.

Originally planned at RKO as a collection of sketches on diverse North American subjects—including a history of jazz, a love story about Italian immigrants, and a Robert Flaherty tale about the friendship between a Mexican boy and a bull—IT'S ALL TRUE quickly turned into a film about Latin America when Nelson Rockefeller, Coordinator of the Office of Inter-American Affairs and RKO board member, appointed Welles as Good Will Ambassador to Brazil in late 1941. Welles was encouraged to speed up the production of both THE MAGNIFICENT AMBERSONS and JOURNEY INTO FEAR so that he could arrive in Rio in time to shoot the Carnival for a history of the samba. The Mexico episode, which Norman Foster had already started shooting in September 1941, was temporarily suspended so that Foster could direct JOURNEY INTO FEAR, and Welles was assured by RKO that he could complete the editing of AMBERSONS in Rio. Welles also planned episodes about the conquest of Peru and another Brazilian episode re-creating the journey of four Northeastern fishermen, or *jangadeiros*, on a raft from Fortaleza to Rio (over 1,500 miles) to petition the Brazilian president for social benefits. All four episodes seem to have been conceived somewhat after Flaherty's documentary methods—that is, a mixture of genuine documentary with re-creations. Unfortunately, RKO failed to honor its promises about AMBERSONS (Welles was not able to do the final cutting), and the leader of the *jangadeiros* accidentally drowned during the re-creation of their journey to Rio. RKO had meanwhile gone through a massive reorganization during Welles's absence, and the film was abruptly called off and shelved after Welles had shot a great deal of footage. (Welles made many subsequent unsuccessful efforts to buy back the footage and complete the film after his return to the United States.)

Paradoxically, it wasn't until many years after the release of F FOR FAKE that enough information about IT'S ALL TRUE came to light to make a limited critical assessment of this project possible. This information came in two parts. First came the discovery in the mid-1980s of about two-thirds of the unedited material shot by Welles in Fortaleza at the very end of his Brazilian sojourn, with a silent Mitchell camera and a skeleton crew of five (cameraman George Fanto and his assistant Reginaldo Calmon, Richard and Elizabeth Wilson, and Shifra Haran)—material which possibly represents the most ambitious footage shot by Welles in Brazil, most of which had never been seen (even by Welles) or even processed prior to its relatively recent discovery. (Samples of this footage are visible in Richard Wilson's 1986 short FOUR MEN ON A RAFT, which he is still hoping to expand into a feature.) Then came the revelatory research carried out in both Brazil and the United States by Robert Stam and others[6]—research which is still in progress, but which has already yielded some fascinating discoveries. Drawing on an array of Hollywood and Brazilian documents, including the research conducted and commissioned by Welles at the time, Stam persuasively argues, for instance, that most of the complaints about Welles's profligacy in Brazil can be attributed to his radical pro-black stance, including the fact that he enjoyed the company and collaboration of blacks, as well as his insistence on featuring nonwhites as the central characters in both of the film's Brazilian episodes. Based on this reading, which Stam explores in detail, one is encouraged by Stam to reread most disapproving biographical accounts of Welles's "Brazilian episode," especially those of Charles Higham and John Russell Taylor, as unconsciously but unmistakably racist. (It should be noted, incidentally, that the style of photography in the Fortaleza rushes bears certain relationships to the visual styles and rhetoric of both Flaherty and Dovzhenko; variations in this style can be found in both OTHELLO—also shot by Fanto—and certain passages in DON QUIXOTE.)

Certainly the ideological issues raised by Welles's encounters with Hollywood are rich in unexplored subtexts, from the relatively recent canonization of CITIZEN KANE as a safe Hollywood classic to the widespread hostility expressed by American critics toward Welles for the remainder of his life because he failed to match up to industry standards, yielding him a "failure" after KANE in the eyes of the middlebrow press.[7] If the progressive lucidity of Stam's research, converting fiction into fact, helps to clarify to what degree the radical political thrust of Welles's work as a whole—on radio and in theater as well as in film—has been either ignored or actively concealed by most Welles research, it is worth examining briefly another kind of routine obfuscation in academic film studies that has helped along some of the same process: converting fact into fiction.

It is almost an axiom in contemporary academic film theory that the fewer films one has seen or knows about, the better and clearer the academic mind is in following its own theoretical bents. As a French cinéphile, Gilles Deleuze is rather atypical in this respect, as the numerous film titles cited in both *Cinéma 1: L'image-mouvement* and *Cinéma 2: L'image-temps* demonstrate. Although he is not always meticulous, he at least gives some evidence that he usually knows something about what he is discussing. This is less true, alas, of many of his readers, including the English translators of *Cinéma 2: L'image-temps*, and thanks to the weird collusion of Deleuze, his proofreaders, the aforementioned translators, and *their* proofreaders, *Cinéma 2: The Time-Image* (University of Minnesota Press, 1989) offers detailed commentary on a good many nonexistent films—a Borgesian bounty that inadvertently echoes all the fake masterpieces that are created, exhibited, and discussed in F FOR FAKE.

Among the many intriguing items found in the index are Mankiewicz's THE BLOODHOUND, Minnelli's THE PERFECT WIFE, Donen's PAJAMA PICNIC, Ophüls's HOUSE OF PLEASURE, Murnau's THE LAST MAN (not to be confused with THE LAST LAUGH, which is listed separately), Straub's RESISTENZA, a CABINET OF DR. CALIGARI directed by Fritz Lang (which also crops up in Peter Gidal's recent *Materialist Film*, giving it further credence), and even a Marguerite Duras Western (DESTRY SHE SAID).

In the case of Welles, this has the rather grotesque consequence of collapsing IT'S ALL TRUE and F FOR FAKE into the same film (although, to complicate matters further, they are listed separately in the index). The French title of F FOR FAKE is VÉRITÉS ET MENSONGES; Deleuze—who is, after all, only a film theorist—calls it VÉRITÉS ET ILLUSIONS; and his translators, apparently finding at least half of both titles problematical, solve this difficulty by calling it IT'S ALL TRUE. (They have also faithfully preserved all of the misspellings and typos in the French edition, so that two of Welles's leading costars in F FOR FAKE—Elmyr de Hory and Oja Kodar—are now Elmer and Kadar.)

Collapsing the distinctions between truth and fiction in more ways than one, Deleuze's semigibberish text in English about Welles in *The Time-Image*, mixing titles, mauling names, and inverting the order of sequences in F FOR FAKE, creates a mad, tantalizing weave that is positively Wellesian (the bracketed comments in italics are my own):

> . . . a becoming, an irreducible multiplicity, characters or forms are now valid only as transformations of each other. And this is the diabolical trio of THE LADY FROM SHANGHAI, the strange relay-characters of Mr. Arkadin [*sic*], the chain which unites those in TOUCH OF EVIL, the unlimited transformation of those in THE TRIAL, the journey of the false which constantly passes through the king, his son, and Falstaff, all three imposters and usurpers in some way, culminating in the scene where the roles are exchanged. It is finally the great series of IT'S ALL TRUE, which is the manifesto for all of Welles's work, and his reflection on cinema. F for Falstaff, but above all *F for fake.*
>
> . . . This great series of Welles, the story that is continually being modified, may be summed up as follows:
>
> 1. 'presentation of Oja Kadar, whom all men turn to look at in the street'; 2. 'presentation of Welles as conjuror' [*Deleuze has inverted the order of sequences here*]; 3. presentation of the journalist, author of a book about a forger of paintings, but also of false memoirs of Hughes, the millionaire forger with a multiplicity of doubles, whom we do not know if he has himself harmed the journalist [*why no more inverted commas, and why no more coherent syntax?*]; 4. conversation or exchange between the journalist and the forger of paintings; 5. intervention of Welles who assures that, for an hour, the viewer will neither see nor hear anything else false [*again, out of sequence*]; 6. Welles recounts his life, and reflects on man in front of Chartres Cathedral; 7. Oja Kadar's affair with Picasso at the end of which Welles arrives to say that the hour has passed and the affair was invented in every respect; 8. Welles wishes his audience a good evening.

■

F FOR FAKE remains one of Welles's most controversial works insofar as for many spectators, including some Welles enthusiasts, it is not really a "Welles film" at all. (To clarify Deleuze's garbled description a little, the film, visibly narrated by Welles in a manner that suggests at times both THE FOUNTAIN OF YOUTH and FILMING

*OTHELLO, is mainly concerned with art forger Elmyr de Hory, Clifford Irving—
who wrote a book about de Hory called* Fake *before he successfully forged Howard
Hughes's autobiography—and diverse elements of fakery in Welles's own past,
such as his* War of the Worlds *broadcast and his own entry into professional acting in Dublin . . . not counting several hoaxes and digressions of its own.)*

*There has even, ironically enough, been some confusion regarding the au-
thorship of* F FOR FAKE, *as there has been with* FILMING OTHELLO *(occasioning,
in the case of the latter film, one of the few gaffes in the updated edition of Naremore's* The Magic World of Orson Welles, *the best critical study of Welles in
any language). Simply because Welles refuses to include what are generally
thought to be "typically Wellesian" shots in* F FOR FAKE—*a deliberate ploy, one
learns, from his extended interview with Bill Krohn in 1982,[8] and a strategy that
can also be found somewhat less systematically in* THE IMMORTAL STORY *(1968)
and (for contextual reasons)* THE OTHER SIDE OF THE WIND—*viewers who insist that they know who Welles is better than Welles does himself wind up feeling that they've been sold a bill of goods. The legend of Welles has always had
much more potency for many people than the reality and, in more ways than one,*
F FOR FAKE *seems to have been both inspired by this paradox and structured
around it.*

One of the first "tricks" (or ruses, or fakes) in F FOR FAKE *occurs during the
opening credits sequence, a few minutes into the film—a complex découpage
with very musical articulations and transitions between and within shots, all to
the strains of Michel Legrand's theme song. The following titles appear in the following forms:*

1. *"François Reichenbach presents" (painted in red with a brush against a
    white background, the brush painting the last letter just as we cut to);*
2. *"?" (painted in white with a brush on a moviola screen that has just shown
    a flying saucer atomize a building, followed by a freeze-frame of the explo-
    sion—a clip in black and white from the film* EARTH VS. FLYING SAUCERS—
    and followed by the shot going out of focus);
3. *"about Fakes" (coming into focus and shown already painted on a label on a
    film can; several more film cans clatter on top of it, the top can saying);*
4. *"a film by Orson Welles" (shown already painted on a label on a film can;
    the camera pans to the left to a stack of adjacent multicolored film cans and
    moves up to);*

5.   *"WITH THE/COLLABORATION/OF CERTAIN"* (*shown already painted on the sides of three separate film cans; the camera moves up to*);

6.   *"EXPERT/PRACTIONERS"* (*shown already painted on the sides of two separate film cans; the camera moves up to*);

7.   *"and INTRODUCING"* (*shown already painted on the side of one film can; the camera moves up to*);

8.   *"OJA KODAR"* (*shown already painted twice on two separate film cans; the camera moves up to frame the top version in the center*).

One of the first questions raised by this assembly—and the only one which I intend to address here—concerns the word "practioners." No such word exists in the English language; it cannot be found, at least, in any of my dictionaries. Yet because of the speed with which we read it (the hand or the film frame is quicker than the eye), most of us assume that the word is probably "practitioners." We read it, in other words, as if it makes sense.

Does this qualify as a typo like one of those in the "Deleuze text" quoted above? Hardly. Appearing only four shots after an allusion to Welles's War of the Worlds *hoax on radio, the first of his major pseudodocumentaries, it is one of the earliest signs in the film that our own gullibility is this film's principal subject. Gullibility, after all, is only just another form of imagination, and the imagination of the audience remains the essential tool in Welles's box of tricks throughout his career—the central factor that makes everything else possible. What we think is what we get, and what we think is not so much what we see as what we think we see.*

Notes

1. "Between Works and Texts," *The Magic World of Orson Welles,* rev. ed. (Southern Methodist University Press, 1989), 261–276.

2. *Orson Welles,* edited by Alain Bergala, Jean Narboni, and Claudine Paquot, 2nd ed. (Paris: Les Editions de l'Étoile, 1986), 13.

3. It should be stressed, however, that Welles's plan to play Kurtz wavered, unlike his determination to play Marlow. As he expressed this uncertainty in separate conversations with Peter Bogdanovich in 1969 (for an interview book scheduled for publication by HarperCollins in 1992) and myself in 1972 (for an article, "The Voice and the Eye," published in *Film Comment,* November–December 1972), he contemplated playing Kurtz only because he was unable to find anyone else for the part. This same ambivalence is reflected in the fact that

he assigned the Kurtz role to Ray Collins the first time he presented *Heart of Darkness* on the radio, and played the part himself the second time.

4. It should be noted, however, that Welles's narration in both THE LADY FROM SHANGHAI (1946) and MACBETH (1949) was occasioned by the recutting of the original versions; in neither case was it part of the original conception. ("A director," Welles was fond of saying, "is someone who presides over accidents.")

5. Letter to the author, 10 February 1987.

6. See, in particular, Stam's "Orson Welles, Brazil, and the Power of Blackness," as well as articles by Catherine Benamou and Susan Ryan, in *Persistence of Vision*, no. 7, City University Press of New York, 1989 (special Welles issue).

7. A further exploration of this subject can be found in my own reply to an article by Robin Bates in *Cinema Journal* 26, no. 4, Summer 1987.

8. In response to Krohn remarking that "As the most recognizable stylist in the American cinema I think it's very interesting that you turned around and criticized this idea of the signature," Welles says, "I got fed up with that about the time that people told me THE TRIAL was an *'anthology of Wellesian visual ideas.'* At that moment I thought, *'Well, we've had enough Wellesian ideas!'* . . . On camera, at eye level, I did nothing that you could parody as Wellesian at all in F FOR FAKE. . . . There isn't a Wellesian shot in it." (" 'My Favorite Mask Is Myself': An Interview with Orson Welles" by Bill Krohn, in *The Unknown Orson Welles*, edited by Stefan Drössler [Belleville/Filmmuseum München, 2004], 64.)

—*Cinematograph* 4, 1991

15

The Seven ARKADINS

The following article, like the preceding one, was partially written as a way of conserving space while editing This Is Orson Welles (1991). A particular problem I had throughout this project was having more material that I wanted to use than I had room for. So I figured that if I could write and publish articles elsewhere that incorporated portions of this material, all I had to do in the book was allude to them. This strategy was carried out less purely in the case of writing about Welles's "essay films" (where I had other fish to fry) than it was here.

ARKADIN has always been the most difficult to research of the Welles films that were finished in some form while he was alive—partially because it remained such a painful memory to Welles due to his friendship with Louis Dolivet, the producer, that he avoided discussing it. Indeed, there was barely any material at all about it in the tapes and drafts for This Is Orson Welles that I had to work with. So as I tried to expand what I had via research, I eventually hit upon the idea of publishing a piece in Film Comment.

By necessity, much of what I included in this article was provisional. (The same applies to a lesser extent to the dual commentary I recorded with James Naremore in early 2005 to the film's "Corinth version" [no. 3 in the article] for a Criterion DVD box set released in April 2006.) But I didn't realize how provisional it was until the Welles conference held at the Locarno film festival in August 2005, when French Welles scholar François Thomas, who had recently examined the files of Dolivet, generously went to the trouble of making out a list of all the errors in this piece that he was then aware of. Since much more detailed *and comprehensive accounts will appear in a book on the production and post-production histories of Welles's films that François is writing with Jean-Pierre Berthomé, which is likely to appear in English translation, as well as a series of articles François is planning for the biannual French journal* Cinéma *in 2006–2007, he has asked me to omit a couple of his findings here, but otherwise his list, most of which is paraphrased in this preface, is virtually complete:*

It's now certain that Welles didn't attend the Paris premiere of ARKADIN, *and it's certain that Louis Dolivet produced other films afterwards, including Jacques Tati's* MON ONCLE *and* PARADE. *He also coproduced* LA DOLCE VITA. *There are at least two Spanish versions of the film, not one (by now I've seen both), and the shot of a dead woman's body on a beach is the second in one of these, not the first. Welles spent more than four months editing the film, and the "Christmas 1956 deadline" was only one among several. There is now documented proof that Maurice Bessy wrote the novel. Amparo Rivelles and Irene Lopez Heredia are the only two Spanish actors used specifically in the Spanish versions, and it's now certain that Welles directed both of them. The bats seen behind the credits of* CONFIDENTIAL REPORT *can also be glimpsed at the masked ball. The seventh* ARKADIN *identified in the article is actually a truncated version of no. 3, not a truncated version of* CONFIDENTIAL REPORT *(no. 6), and one can further argue that, apart from its chronological structure, no. 6 contains more of Welles's editing than no. 3. Furthermore, it appears that the project's postproduction history is far more complex than most Welles scholars have assumed, and the process by which Welles lost control over the film was partially a matter of his own initiatives, motivated or at least inflected by his friendship with Dolivet—though to understand this more properly, we'll clearly have to wait for Berthomé and Thomas's book and Thomas's article.*

On the issue of how critical scholarship and commercial interests can sometimes come into conflict with one another, the following anecdote may be somewhat instructive. When I wrote liner notes for the Voyager laserdisc of CONFIDENTIAL REPORT *(no. 6) in the early 1990s, my assertion in those notes that no. 6 was the second-best version of* MR. ARKADIN *was censored. Roughly 15 years later, when I was commissioned to write liner notes for what I'd previously thought to be the best version (i.e., no. 3) for a DVD box set of* ARKADIN *released by Criterion, a company that grew out of Voyager—a version that Thomas persuaded me may not have been the best after all, at least in all particulars—I wasn't censored about my preferences. But it's amusing to note that in the interests of both clarity and symmetry with the two other versions of* ARKADIN *included in the box set and their respective liner notes, I was still asked to revise my notes in order to make them more supportive.*

Spanish film scholar Esteve Riambau has contributed much to our knowledge of Welles's work on this film (and others) in Spain, including many of the precise locations, though lamentably this work has been available mainly in Spanish or at Welles conferences, without wider circulation (apart from the excellent documentary in 2000 he made with cowriter Carlos F. Heredero and director Carlos Rodriguez, ORSON WELLES EN EL PAÍS DE DON QUIJOTE—*the only treatment of Welles in Spain I'm familiar with that brings some critical perspective to his willingness to live in Franco Spain and part of what this entailed). And from German film scholar Hans Schmid, who produced a German version of the Harry Lime radio series in the 1990s (and who once took me on a tour of all the major Munich locations used in* MR. ARKADIN, *during my first visit there—the most startling of which is the building that houses Jakob Zouk's attic, rehabbed but still recognizable, and by pure coincidence located today across the street from the Munich Film Archives), I've learned much more about what shows the film derived from. All of them survive in two versions, some of which have separate titles, which has led to many confusions. The principal source was the second version of "Man of Mystery," not "Greek Meets Greek," and other elements in the film came from "Murder on the Riviera" (called "Cigarettes" in its earlier version), "Blackmail Is a Nasty Word" (called "Givrolet" in its previous version), and, to a lesser extent, some others.*

■

> I wanted to make a work in the spirit of Dickens, with characters so dense that they appear as archetypes. . . . I thought it could have made a very popular film, a commercial film that everyone would have liked. In place of that . . . I'm afraid to see it! It's terrible, what they did to me on that. The film was snatched from my hands more brutally than one has ever snatched a film from anyone . . . it's as if they'd kidnapped my child! They brought in another cutter who pretended to have "saved" the film!
> —Orson Welles in *L'Avant-scène du cinéma,* no. 291–292 (1–15 July 1982) (my translation)

It's generally known that, for a variety of reasons, some of the films of Orson Welles survive today in two or more versions. James Naremore has told me he once saw a print of THE LADY FROM SHANGHAI in Germany that included alternate takes of certain scenes and somewhat different editing, plus a few shots he hadn't seen before or since. (This sounds roughly comparable to the "Italian" version of Stroheim's FOOLISH WIVES, apparently sent overseas before the domestic version was completed.) Better known are Welles's two separate versions of MACBETH, running 107 minutes and 86 minutes. (The second was prepared after Welles was asked to cut two reels and redub the "Scots" dialogue; it contains offscreen narration missing from the long version but *doesn't* contain the single take lasting an entire reel which preceded Hitchcock's ROPE by a year.) Still better known are the two editions of TOUCH OF EVIL—the 93-minute version originally released and the 108-minute version discovered in the mid-70s that has virtually supplanted it. Since Welles was barred from the final stages of editing, neither can be considered definitive; indeed, it's impossible to speak of a definitive TOUCH OF EVIL.

The same is true of MR. ARKADIN (1955). But in this case the consequences are much more confusing because of the number of ARKADINS we have to choose from—plus the fact that the version best known in this country is very far from the best.

Here, in simplified form, is more or less how the story line goes.

In Naples, a man, Bracco (Grégoire Aslan), mysteriously knifed in the back, whispers two names while dying: "Gregory Arkadin" and "Sophie." The only people to hear are Guy Van Stratten (Robert Arden), an American smuggler, and his girlfriend, Mily (Patricia Medina). Hoping to snare a fortune via blackmail with these names, Guy tracks the fabulously wealthy Arkadin (Welles) to a castle in Spain and, against the man's wishes, woos his sheltered and beloved daughter, Raina (Paola Mori). Unexpectedly, Arkadin, who claims to suffer from amnesia, hires Guy to prepare a confidential report on his activities prior to 1927. Guy conducts interviews all over Europe and in Mexico, basically tracking down former members of a gang of white slavers to which Arkadin belonged. These include Oskar (Frederick O'Brady) and Sophie (Katina Paxinou) in Mexico and Jakob Zouk (Akim Tamiroff) in Munich; Mily helps out by speaking with a black marketeer (Peter van Eyck) in Tangiers and with Arkadin himself on his yacht. As Guy uncovers Arkadin's past, he gradually discovers that his employer, afraid Raina will learn who and what he once was, is having his old associates murdered, as well as Mily. Fearing for his own life, Guy flies to Raina in Barcelona ahead of Arkadin, who is following in a private plane. Guy convinces Raina to tell her father, over the plane's radio, that she now knows everything, at which point Arkadin kills himself by leaping from the plane. Raina leaves Guy in disgust.

In 1958 the editorial board of *Cahiers du cinéma* collectively decided that MR. ARKADIN—more precisely, CONFIDENTIAL REPORT, as they knew it—was Welles's greatest film, the one that belonged on their list of the twelve greatest films ever made. At the time, not long after the film's appearance in Europe, there was no public awareness that Welles had lost editorial control over it; the director had lent his presence at the Paris premiere, and apparently made no public statements about his creative difficulties until some time later. Even now we have less information about the making and the editorial reworking of ARKADIN than we have about any of the other Welles narrative features released during his lifetime.

What we *do* have is a tantalizing panoply of texts—for the purposes of this discussion, seven—in a variety of media. They range from the stylistically conventional to the stylistically radical, from the tossed-off to the aesthetically intricate. The *Cahiers* editors' odd preference notwithstanding, I don't consider ARKADIN a masterpiece in any of its versions or incarnations. But I find most of it fascinating and much of it beautiful and exciting—"it" in this case being a conflation of ARKADINS nos. 3, 6, and 7 (in descending order of importance) among the exhibits I propose to submit for consideration.

What's offered below isn't so much a map of a "definitive" ARKADIN as an exploration of a few of the processes that the story and film went through. It is, if you will, a kind of detective story without a denouément, but with plenty of clues. The mode is tentative historical inquiry, selective and suggestive in intention rather than exhaustive, with a few critical remarks appended.

In pursuit of my own confidential report, I have greatly benefited from three invaluable sources in addition to the primary texts: an after-noon spent with a good many loose pieces of the producer's work print materials—examined on a moviola with two other Welles scholars, Ciro Giorgini and Bernard Eisenschitz—thanks to the exceptional gen-erosity of Fred Junck and Marco Müller; a phone interview graciously granted me by Patricia Medina; and *This Is Orson Welles* by Orson Welles and Peter Bogdanovich, a book I have been editing for Harper-Collins. I'd also like to thank Geoff Andrew, Tag Gallagher, James Pep-per, Bill Reed, and Bret Wood for furnishing me with some of the pri-mary materials.

Pre-Texts

1: "Greek Meets Greek"—half-hour episode of the London-based radio series *The Adventures of Harry Lime*, a spin-off of the Welles character in the 1949 Carol Reed/Graham Greene film THE THIRD MAN. Written by and starring Welles, directed by Tig Roe, and probably recorded in 1951, the segment is quite unremarkable except as the source for ARKADIN's skele-tal plot and key themes.

2: *Masquerade*—an early version of Welles's script for ARKADIN, dated March 23, 1953, the year before shooting commenced. *Masquerade* differs from most or all of the later versions in the following ways:

(a) The opening quotation is not an aphorism about a king and a poet and a fatal secret, but a quotation from Emerson:

> Commit a crime, and the earth is made of glass. Commit a crime and it seems as if a coat of snow fell on the ground, such as reveals in the woods the track of every partridge and fox and squirrel and mole. You cannot recall the spo-ken word, you cannot wipe out the foot-track, you cannot draw up the lad-der, so as to leave no inlet or clew.

This also appears in the French and Italian editions of the novel, but ap-parently none of those in English. As Richard T. Jameson has pointed out to me, the same quotation is recited by Edward G. Robinson in Welles's THE STRANGER (1946).

(b) Apart from the precredits sequence of the riderless plane—which exists in every version of the film but not the novel—there are no flashbacks and no offscreen narration. The plot progression is strictly chronological.

(c) The investigator is called "Guy Dumesnil" and is described as "young and attractive" and "an Americanized European" (not an American called Guy Van Stratten). The Jakob Zouk character (played by Akim Tamiroff in the film) is called "Jakob Nathansen."

(d) Most of the major scenes in the script are in the film, although some are set in different countries. Arkadin's masked ball is in Venice, not Spain ("This is clearly an attempt on Arkadin's part to out-do the famous Bestigui Ball, and is in fact, in many ways, a duplication of it. . . . The canals are filled with illuminated gondolas carrying Arkadin's guests, all in costumes of the Venetian 18th century . . ."). Similarly, the pawn and junk shop of Burgomil Trebitsch (Michael Redgrave) is located in Marseille, not Amsterdam. A few scenes in the film, such as the one featuring the flea circus director (Mischa Auer), are not in the script.

(e) Perhaps the most extended material available here but missing from all the other versions of ARKADIN (except for the novel, where it figures in a somewhat different form) involves Van Stratten's adventures when he first arrives in Mexico, before he questions Oskar and Sophie. He attends the funeral of Sophie's elderly toy poodle Ki-Ki,[1] and tracks down Oskar in a "kosher café" run by Sophie, where he plays the accordion for tips. Van Stratten lures Oskar onto a rented boat by offering him a high fee to entertain guests on an alleged pleasure cruise, at which point he begins to torture him for information by depriving him of heroin. Only a brief version of this boat scene survives in the film.

(f) In the film, there is a confrontation between Van Stratten, Arkadin, and Raina in Guy's hotel room in Paris; the script sets the scene in Van Stratten's flat, and Arkadin appears only belatedly. (In the workprint, Welles conducts a rehearsal for part of this scene and, in instructing Mori how to deliver some of her lines, gives the setting as New York.)

Films and Filming: "A Phenomenon of an Age of Dissolution and Chaos"

> I was developing the rushes of ARKADIN in a French lab. Can you imagine that I had to have a special authorization for every piece of film, even if only 20 yards long, that arrived from Spain? The film had to go through the hands of the customs officials, who wasted their time (and ours) by stamping the beginning and end of each and every roll of film or of magnetic sound tape. The operation required two whole days, and the film was in danger of being spoiled by the hot weather we were then having. The same difficulties cropped up when it came to obtaining work permits. My film unit was international: I had a French cameraman, an Italian editor, an English sound engineer, an Irish script girl, a Spanish assistant. Whenever we had to travel anywhere, each of them had to waste an unconscionable amount of time getting special permissions to stay to work. . . . Similar complications arose when, for example, we had to get a French camera into Spain. . . .
>
> The true culprits are the producers. They prefer the security of a limited but certain profit from a national or regional market to the infinitely wider possibilities of a world market, which would of course entail, at the outset, certain supplementary expenses.
> —Orson Welles, "For a Universal Cinema," *Film Culture* 1, no. 1 (January 1955)

A few words about the making of MR. ARKADIN. Louis Dolivet, the French producer, who died not long ago, was a good friend and political mentor to Welles in the United States during the mid-40s. (See Barbara Leaming's biography *Orson Welles* [New York: Viking Penguin, 1985], for particulars.) Dolivet never produced a feature prior to ARKADIN and, to the best of my knowledge, never produced another afterward. The little evidence we have suggests that ARKADIN's production was an exacerbating experience for him and Welles alike and that their friendship ultimately proved to be one of its casualties. To make matters worse, Paola Mori—the professional name of the Countess di Girfalco, who later became Welles's third and last wife—was criticized so harshly for her performance by Dolivet and others that she gave up acting, appearing again only in cameos in THE TRIAL and the unfinished DON QUIXOTE. (Again, the workprint rehearsal footage is suggestive: Mori's musically accented voice is distinct from the English-accented voice we hear in the released films, raising the possibility that "Raina's" voice was subsequently dubbed by another actress.)[2]

It appears that most of the film was shot in Spain—much of it in a studio in Madrid—with a certain amount in Munich and Paris locations and probably a few pickup shots elsewhere in Western Europe. (One can't take seriously any of those accounts claiming that part of the shooting was done in Mexico.) On the basis of my interview with Patricia Medina and the slates visible in certain outtakes, we know that many scenes were shot, wholly or partially, in or near Madrid. These encompass such fictional settings as a hotel in Mexico City, the docks in Naples, Arkadin's yacht, the interior and environs of his Spanish castle, a café in Tangiers, a nightclub on the Riviera, and the inside of a Munich cathedral!

Patricia Medina has never seen ARKADIN, so all her memories are tied exclusively to her own participation in the film. She was under contract to Columbia at the time, and when Welles phoned her in London to ask her to play Mily, she had very little time to shoot because she was due back in the states to act in something else (probably MIAMI EXPOSÉ). Welles replied jokingly, "Then we'll have to kill you off." (Mily's murder, alluded to offscreen in the film, was never shot in any form.) Medina flew to Madrid and all her scenes were shot there, most of them in a studio, over about ten days.

Overall, she remembers the shoot as a happy event. The first scene she did was on the yacht with Arkadin. The night before shooting, Welles showed her the set, asking scornfully, "Doesn't it look just like the Staten Island Ferry?" The yacht set was up in the air; one had to climb up into it. After Medina returned to her hotel, Welles phoned to ask her if there was anything in her hotel that "belonged in a yacht." She looked around and found very little. When she arrived for filming the next morning, she discovered that Welles had been up all night redressing the set with furniture temporarily swiped from the lobby of the Madrid Hilton, where he himself was staying. He announced that they had time for only two takes because the furniture had to be returned before it was missed. (One detail in this scene was improvised: when Mily says "Shut up!" to a screeching bird in a cage, neither the screech nor her line was in the script.)

Medina's participation in the scene featuring the procession of penitentes near Arkadin's castle was all done in a studio. Interestingly, although Paola Mori appears in the same sequence, Medina never met her
during the shooting. If one examines this scene closely, it becomes clear
that Mily and the procession never appear in the same shot; the illusion
of proximity is supplied and intensified by the shadows—ostensibly of
the penitentes—flickering across Mily and Guy.

When she left for the States, Welles asked her to send a still of herself
that could be blown up for a poster advertising Mily as a bubble dancer.
She neglected to do so. When she arrived in Paris sometime later to do the
dubbing with Welles, she was appalled by the still that he had found and
used on his own. (When Van Stratten learns of Mily's death later in the
film, this picture recurs in some versions, identified in the dialogue as
"the only available photo taken before death.") And that marked the end
of her involvement, save that much later she was contacted by Dolivet to
act in some additional scenes; learning that Welles wouldn't be directing
them, she refused.

But back to the seven ARKADINS. . . .

3: MR. ARKADIN, the film—that is to say, the version of the film closest to
Welles's conception. This became available in the United States through
Corinth Films; we owe the original existence of this version in the United
States to Peter Bogdanovich, who discovered it in Hollywood in 1961, and
to Dan Talbot of New Yorker Films, who acquired it for the belated U.S.
premiere and release of ARKADIN the following year.

According to the film's editor, Renzo Lucidi (recently interviewed by
Ciro Giorgini), the first four sequences of this version correspond precisely to Welles's intentions. It opens with Van Stratten visiting Jakob
Zouk in Munich, then continues as a series of flashbacks narrated off-
screen by Van Stratten, periodically returning to Zouk's attic flat.[3]

Welles spent four months editing, averaging (according to Lucidi) two
minutes of finished film per week. He was barred from the cutting after
failing to meet Dolivet's Christmas 1954 deadline, but continued to communicate his intentions to Lucidi. Once Lucidi had finished editing this
version, however, Dolivet apparently asked for the film to be reedited

without most of the flashbacks—in chronological order after the opening sequence—and this was the principal version released in Europe as CON-FIDENTIAL REPORT. (See no. 6, below.)

In *This Is Orson Welles*, Welles maintains that at least two important scenes of his were eliminated from all the released versions of ARKADIN. This would seem to be corroborated by Frank Brady's citation, in his Welles biography, of an undated *New York Herald Tribune* story in which Welles complained that fourteen minutes were removed from his version. To Bogdanovich, Welles cited another party scene and an additional scene between Arkadin and Van Stratten, both of which showed Arkadin "as a sentimental, rather maudlin Russian drunk"; Arkadin's character, he added, was inspired to some extent by Stalin.

Given Welles's relative unfamiliarity with the release versions of his film—which he clearly found painful to watch—these remarks *may* have alluded to further material in Arkadin's masked ball, or at the Christmas party in Munich (where we do see Arkadin drunk). Alternately, they may refer to two complete scenes of which we no longer have any record in any of the seven ARKADINS. Since Welles had a penchant for revising his scripts while shooting—and even, on occasion, revising dialogue while postdubbing and editing—both hypotheses are plausible.

Apparently one of the reasons why ARKADIN was so late—seven years!—in opening in the United States was a $780,000 legal suit filed by the European production company Filmorsa against Welles in New York, claiming that Welles's behavior was responsible for the film's ultimate commercial failure. This action was launched on April 7, 1958, but papers weren't filed until September 28, 1961; on the following day brief news stories were run in the New York papers, citing "drinking excessively on and off the set" as the principal charge. In the *Times*, Welles called the charges "blunderbuss, catch-all phraseology, naked generalizations, un-supported inferences and patent irrelevancies," while one of his lawyers maintained that it was Filmorsa rather than Welles that had broken the contract. The charges, in any case, were eventually dropped.

4: *Mr. Arkadin*, the novel, signed by Welles but not written by him—al-though the version available in English is an anonymous translation of a

French novel ghostwritten by Maurice Bessy that was based, in turn, on a version of Welles's film script, in English, that was written at some point after no. 2. The novel was originally composed for newspaper serialization in France, and first appeared in book form there at the time of CON-FIDENTIAL REPORT's French release.

The novel is divided into three sections, entitled "Bracco," "Sophie," and "The Ogre." Narrated in the first person by Van Stratten, it most closely resembles no. 7 in its overall form. The most significant material missing from all other versions relates to Van Stratten's mother, a professional gambler who, at the time of the novel, is occupying "a tiny two-room flat at Beausoleil with Myrtle," an English gambling companion, and appears briefly, along with Myrtle, in the second chapter.

Although Lucidi has recently maintained that Welles wrote the novel, all the other available evidence—including a conversation I had with Welles in 1972—refutes this. A comparison of the novel's dialogue with the film's suggests in virtually every case that the former is a retranslation back into English of French dialogue adapted from an English script; the meanings of lines are generally the same, but the words and phrasings are almost always different.

5: The Spanish version of the film. If the current "Spanish version" is identical to the one that opened in Madrid in March 1955, then this is probably the first version that premiered anywhere. I've been able to see only a few parts of this version—presumably the most significant parts—in Ciro Giorgini's invaluable TUTTA LA VERITÀ SU MR. ARKADIN, a 1991 TV documentary for Italy's RAI.

The Spanish version was apparently shot simultaneously with the principal production. It features different actresses playing the parts of Sophie and Baroness Nagel (and perhaps other Spanish actors as well), as part of the arrangement made for a Spanish coproduction. A different editor is also credited, Antonio Martinez. In the precredits sequence, the pilotless plane is said more vaguely to have been sighted somewhere in Europe rather than "off the coast of Barcelona"; in the glimpses of the actors shown in the credits, we see Amparo Rivelles instead of Suzanne Flon as the Baroness Nagel, Irene Lopez Heredia instead of Katina Paxinou as Sophie; Robert Arden is inexplicably identified as "Bob Harden." As for the scenes involving Rivelles and Lopez Heredia, the first of these alternates shots of Welles (dubbed by someone else) with reverse angles of Rivelles in what appears to be a crude approximation of the same set (a fancy Paris restaurant); it seems highly unlikely that Welles directed these reverse angles. But in the scene with Lopez Heredia and "Harden," the set appears to be the same one used in the English-speaking versions, and the lighting and mise en scène, while not quite identical, are sufficiently Wellesian to suggest that Welles himself might have directed this alternate version of the scene.[4]

6: CONFIDENTIAL REPORT—the version of the film that opened in London in August 1955 and apparently the main version that was and is shown elsewhere in Europe, including France.

It seems quite possible that an early draft of Welles's script was used as a guide in reediting this version, a detailed description of which is available in French in the issue of L'Avant-Scène du cinéma cited at the beginning of this article. (This description includes annotations about materials found in the work print). As Giorgini shows in his documentary through a split-screen technique, the differences between this version and no. 3 are more than just a matter of chronological sequence; they involve variations in editing and dialogue and/or narration within scenes, and in a few instances may even involve different takes.

There are at least two brief scenes in CONFIDENTIAL REPORT that are missing from both no. 3 and no. 7—a scene in which Van Stratten speaks to a black American pianist in a bar on the Riviera while looking for Mily and Arkadin's "Georgian toast" near the end of his masked ball, in which he recounts a curious dream set in a cemetery. This also happens to be the only version containing shots of hanging papier-mâché sculptures representing bats in the opening credits sequence. (As to what they refer to in the film, they could be either objects in Trebitsch's junk shop or part of the décor at Arkadin's masked ball; when queried about these bats by Bogdanovich, Welles had no recollection of them.)

Another major difference between CONFIDENTIAL REPORT and all other versions is a block of offscreen narration by Van Stratten, quoted below, that accompanies four shots of him approaching a rundown house in the snow (shots visible in all the versions). I haven't been able to determine whether Welles wrote or recorded this exposition; if he did, it seems probable that this was later superseded by the different sort of exposition he employed in no. 3. The end of this narration certainly blunts the power of the film's most beautiful camera movement, a backward retreat down a dark tunnel of a hallway:

> Here I am at the end of the road. Naples, France, Spain, Mexico, and now Munich. Sebastianplatz 16. In the attic of this house lives Jakob Zouk, a petty racketeer, a jailbird, and the last man alive besides me who knows the whole truth about Gregory Arkadin. My confidential report is complete now. My original fee for this job was $15,000, and it looks like a little bonus will be tossed in—like a knife in my back. But Zouk will get his first unless I can save him. And then me—the world's prize sucker.

7: The principal public domain version that circulates in this country on video; it may also still be available on film. With the probable exception of the Spanish version, no. 5, and the possible exception of the radio show, no. 1, and the novel, no. 4, it is the least satisfactory version of ARKADIN that we have. But because of its wide availability on video and its frequent showings on TV, it is more than likely the ARKADIN that most Americans know.

For the most part, this qualifies as a clumsily truncated version of no. 6, with many of the significant losses occurring at or near the beginning. Characteristically, the offscreen narration that begins after the credits starts in the middle of a sentence, with Van Stratten on the docks in Naples (which is where no. 4 begins as well).

A Tentative Conclusion: "Give the Gentleman His Goose Liver"

In his preface to the English translation of André Bazin's *Orson Welles*, François Truffaut divides all of Welles's films into those made with his right hand and those made with his left hand, adding, "In the right-handed films there is always snow, and in the left-handed ones there are always gunshots; but all constitute what Cocteau called the 'poetry of cinematography.' " ARKADIN is the only Welles film with both snow and gunshots, but I think Truffaut is probably correct in considering it one of the left-handed films. Its moments of poetry are intense and indelible, but the feeling of chaos that it imparts, while fundamental to this poetry, is at times less than adequate to the more prosaic needs of the narrative. Eric Rohmer was right to classify the film as a tale or fable rather than a realistic story or a thriller, and it might be argued that the relative hospitality of French criticism toward unrealistic narrative helps to account for the relative favor ARKADIN has found in French criticism.

Anglo-American critics have generally been put off by the same elements. Dwight Macdonald characteristically complained about the lack of attention paid to Arkadin's business dealings and the visible artifice in Welles's makeup for the part; others have seized on the superficial plot resemblances to CITIZEN KANE to berate the film for its incoherence, its performances, and/or its production values.

I share some of these biases, although a few seem misplaced. For all the film's lack of realism, it still has some validity and interest as a cold war allegory, as James Naremore has suggested. Naremore notes Robert Arden's "uncanny resemblance to a young, athletic Richard Nixon," and if one connects this with Arkadin's resemblance to Stalin—a resemblance underlined by Arkadin's habit of killing off former associates and witnesses—the struggle of the two over Raina, who might be said to represent Western Europe in the mid-50s, is full of suggestive and subversive possibilities. The fact that Arkadin and Van Stratten are presented as moral equivalents—older and younger versions of the same unscrupulous lout—is central to this reading.

Arden's performance as Van Stratten is commonly singled out for abuse, even by most of Welles's defenders, but after repeated viewings it seems to me that it's the unsavoriness and obnoxiousness of the character rather than the performance itself that is responsible for most of this attitude. A comparable syndrome applies to Tim Holt's George Minafer in THE MAGNIFICENT AMBERSONS: because both characters occupy the space normally reserved for charismatic heroes, we feel we're supposed to like and/or sympathize with them, and when their respective films make this impossible, we wind up blaming either the actors or Welles's casting rather than accept the premise that we're meant to have a difficult time with these people.

This is not to suggest that the performances in ARKADIN are above criticism. I agree that the film has one debilitating performance, but this is given by neither Arden nor Paola Mori (who may be relatively unskilled but still seems quite adequate to the demands the script makes of her). I'm afraid it is given by Welles himself. The falseness of his makeup and the variability of his Russian accent can't be rationalized by the elusiveness of Arkadin's character, because no norm is ever established for these traits to deviate from. One can accept the film's premise of presenting us with a gallery of grotesques, but not a title ogre whose face is little more than a Halloween mask. At separate junctures, Arkadin is linked to Neptune and Santa Claus, and at his own ball he hides behind a mask; most of the plot is devoted to uncovering his original identity as a lowlife named Akim Athabadze. But even this latter phantom, glimpsed in a faded photograph belonging to Sophie, lives more in our minds than Gregory Arkadin does on screen. (Mainly this is because of Sophie herself; she and Zouk wind up providing most of whatever soul the movie has, thanks in large measure to Paxinou and Tamiroff.) Welles appears to have conceived of Arkadin as a tissue of paradoxes, but his own performance, even if it contains some lovely line readings, doesn't bridge or embrace those paradoxes. At best it only alludes to them.

The character's silliest moment comes when he informs Van Stratten in a Munich cathedral, "I no longer think of you at all." Considering the fact that he has already trailed Van Stratten across the Atlantic and back, and followed him not only to and around Munich but even to this very spot, it would be an understatement to call this remark disingenuous. Maybe the missing scenes alluded to by Welles would have provided more of a context for such anomalies; or maybe not. Either way, it's worth noting the degree to which stubborn irrationality plays a major role in Welles's work, from Kane and George Minafer to Iago and Othello, from most of the characters in THE LADY FROM SHANGHAI and TOUCH OF EVIL to all of the characters in THE TRIAL.

Perhaps the most underrated feature of ARKADIN is Paul Misraki's wonderfully evocative and rhythmic score, which sometimes plays even more of a shaping role in the film than the plot, dialogue, or mise en scène. Nostalgia for a lost innocence plays as important a role in ARKADIN as it does in KANE, AMBERSONS, and CHIMES AT MIDNIGHT (where it is also tied to snow), although the site of this innocence is less localized than the nineteenth century or the Middle Ages is in those films (not to mention Tanya's bordello in TOUCH OF EVIL). Like Arkadin himself, it's anywhere and everywhere, sometimes where we least expect it. It's Christmas and goose liver and the last time someone said "Come to bed" to Jakob Zouk. It's the youths and romantic yearnings of the Baroness Nagel and Sophie, and a scruffy little Salvation Army band in the street. More mysteriously and disturbingly, it's the sudden, irrational, backward retreat of the camera down a dank tenement corridor, into a dark womb of oblivion.

Notes

1. Oddly enough, Welles had a beloved small dog of that name in Hollywood at the end of his life.
2. I've subsequently learned that the young Billie Whitelaw did the dubbing.
3. Welles's own testimony to Bogdanovich (*This Is Orson Welles,* 237) contradicts Lucidi to the extent that Welles recollects his version beginning "with a shot of an enormous empty beach and a naked girl [Mily] being washed in by the sea"—a brief shot that appears in no. 6 immediately after the yacht scene, is missing from nos. 2, 3, and 7, but actually *does* begin no. 5, the Spanish version, as I've just discovered. (June 1997)
4. Apparently he didn't. See the invaluable companion volumes Esteve Riambau's *Orson Welles: Un España inmortal* and Juan Cobos's *Orson Welles: España como obsesion* (Valencia: Ediciones Filmoteca, Filmoteca Española, 1993). (1995)

—*Film Comment,* January–February 1992,
with updates incorporated into a reprint of
this article in *Movies as Politics* (Berkeley:
University of California Press, 1997)

16

OTHELLO Goes Hollywood

Although some of the factual material in the following review for the Chicago Reader *has been amplified, extended, and in some cases superseded by the chapter on* OTHELLO *in Michael Anderegg's* Orson Welles, Shakespeare, and Popular Culture, *I feel that it remains, along with chapters 1, 2, and 8, one of the texts in this book that's had the most impact. It even prompted a friendly phone call at one point from Julian Schlossberg, who spoke with some embarrassment about the removal of the monks' chants in the opening sequence (subsequently restored on video).*

But I'm sorry to say that it only briefly had the effect of helping to make an "unrestored" version of the film available again in the mid-90s, when Voyager brought it out on laserdisc (for which I wrote the liner notes, a text I've been unable to track down). Because of objections raised by Beatrice Welles, a second pressing of this laserdisc wasn't allowed, and in subsequent years, versions of the film with Welles's original soundtrack have effectively been outlawed.

When a print was once shown at the University of Chicago's Doc Films, I was told that dire threats ensued, and an equally grotesque consequence of this banning has been the unavailability of FILMING OTHELLO, *apparently because it contains footage from this version (and perhaps also because Oja rather than Beatrice holds the U.S. rights to this film and is afraid of a lawsuit).*

Although Welles is most often (and here) credited with the idea of staging Iago's murder of Roderigo in a Turkish bath, Betsy Blair—who was on location in Mogador at the time, and whom I met at Il Cinema Ritrovato in Bologna in

July 2005—plausibly maintains it was Alexander Trauner, OTHELLO's *art director who suggested it. And Jean-Pierre Berthomé has pointed out to me that Turkish baths recur frequently in Trauner's films, including, for starters,* LES ENFANTS DU PARADIS.

■

> Sustained until death at 70 by his fame as the prodigy with the baby face, Orson Welles always appeared to abide by words he put in the mouth of Citizen Kane: "There's only one person in the world to decide what I'm gonna do—and that's me."
> —From a two-page magazine ad for the Dodge Shadow that appeared last month under the heading "Amazing Americans . . . a celebration of people who have lifted our nation's pride"

I guess this describes the official Orson Welles we're all supposed to love and revere. The ad demonstrates how even the recalcitrance of a wasted and abused artist can wind up as a handy marketing tool. Chrysler, a corporation that never would have dreamed of sustaining, much less supporting, Welles as an artist when he was alive—and surely wouldn't pay a tenth of what this ad cost to help make his unseen legacy available today—proudly invites us to join it in celebrating his artistry. Clearly they're onto something: loads of money can be made sustaining our self-applause for recognizing Welles's genius. But let's not be too quick about defining what this genius consists of. If we aren't careful, we may wind up honoring something quite different from what he accomplished.

Indeed, part of what continues to be fascinating about the unruly genius of Welles, seven years after his death, is how much it confounds the norms of commercial movies and conventional artistic careers on every conceivable level. Explaining who he was and what he did is a task that has already stumped at least half a dozen ambitious biographers, because the ordinary definitions, categories, and patterns of understanding generally prove to be not only inadequate but downright misleading.

Take CITIZEN KANE. At least three books on the film exist, and all three assume a priori that it's a Hollywood classic—an assumption that winds up determining almost everything they have to say about it. But while it was made in and released by a Hollywood studio, it shatters so many

Hollywood norms that it seems debatable whether it's best understood as a Hollywood picture like CASABLANCA or SINGIN' IN THE RAIN as opposed to, say, an independent feature that uses certain Hollywood facilities (which is arguably how it was considered before the books came along). Yet it's in the interests of the Hollywood propaganda machine—which operates 24 hours a day, 365 days a year, in every branch of media and most branches of academia—to silence that debate. Central to this self-protective agenda is proving that serious alternatives to Hollywood don't exist—ergo CITIZEN KANE was not an alternative but part of the mainstream.

This even became a concern when KANE was reissued in a "restored" version last year; actually the only changes were in the brightness of some shots, so that the opening newsreel wasn't as grainy and the projection-room sequence wasn't as dark—both obvious efforts to bring the movie closer to Hollywood norms. (The changes were made by Robert Wise, a onetime Welles associate who collaborated on Hollywood "improvements" of Welles's work as far back as THE MAGNIFICENT AMBERSONS.)

For these and related reasons, Welles is almost invariably considered a Hollywood director—and sometimes a failed one because he directed only six studio pictures over nearly half a century. But the six represent only about a third of his completed movies and a fourth of his film output—even though, thanks to the nonstop publicity mills and their gospel of production values, they're vastly better known and distributed than all the others. You might say that a yellow brick road has been paved by the media to allow us to reach those six Hollywood movies, but to make it to most of the others we still don't have dirt paths or even maps. When it comes to unreleased unfinished independent features such as DON QUIXOTE, THE DEEP, and THE OTHER SIDE OF THE WIND, we may have to wait many more years for someone to put up the money to make them available. (The Spanish government has already agreed to preserve the dozen or so hours of DON QUIXOTE, and a feature-length film carved out of this material will premiere in Barcelona this spring. But how long will we have to wait before American distributors show any interest?)

If we consider just the completed films over which Welles had final and complete artistic control, only KANE and the 50s TV pilot THE FOUNTAIN OF YOUTH even begin to qualify as Hollywood products. All the others—

OTHELLO, THE TRIAL, CHIMES AT MIDNIGHT, THE IMMORTAL STORY, THE MERCHANT OF VENICE, F FOR FAKE, FILMING OTHELLO, and a few other TV works—qualify as independent.

OTHELLO was the first of these, and in many ways it remains the most important and exciting of them as well. It's more significant to Welles's work as a whole than KANE, because it leads to much more in his subsequent oeuvre—and its long absence from American screens has been a major obstacle for anyone wishing to understand that oeuvre. Originally designed as an Italian studio production in 1948, the movie underwent a radical conceptual transformation after the producer went bankrupt and Welles decided to finance it out of his own pocket. Other changes followed; when the costumes failed to arrive for the shooting of Iago's murder of Roderigo, Welles spontaneously decided to film the scene in a Turkish bath, which allowed him to go on working without the costumes.

Shooting it piecemeal at diverse locations in Morocco and Italy between 1948 and 1951—with bouts of acting and investor chasing to pay the bills—Welles literally reinvented and recast the rudiments of his style in relation to this new method of filmmaking, which he continued to develop over the remainder of his life. In place of the long takes of his Hollywood work, he fragmented shots into jagged crazy-quilt patterns and syncopated rhythms, often favoring jarring discontinuities in the editing over the dovetailing continuities of KANE and AMBERSONS. Without benefit of studio tracks or cranes, he opted for a rougher, more vertiginous form of camera mobility that was arguably more physical as well as more intimate (as in the evocations of Othello's epilepsy). The abnormal distances between people artificially created on RKO soundstages for Kane's mansion were rediscovered, then explored and amplified, in the architecture of Moorish castles and a Portuguese cistern—and thereby put to vastly different uses, as were the low angles composed in relation to this architecture. (Even a studio movie like TOUCH OF EVIL is radically different in its uses of locations and disorienting sound direction and distance from what it might have been without the experience of OTHELLO.)

Without the resources of Hollywood sound equipment, Welles aimed for a rawness in such sound effects as crashing waves, colliding curtain rings, and echoing footsteps. Drawing from his prodigious radio experience (which entailed producing a weekly show for almost nine years as well as two previous years of acting), he partly compensated for his inferior equipment with subtle atmospheric effects that were dubbed in later and integrated with the music. Ciro Giorgini, who has been interviewing OTHELLO crew members for an Italian documentary, wrote me that one of the production assistants told him that Welles stroked the strings of a piano to achieve a sound effect for the opening sequence and ordered a spinetta, an old form of harmonium, from Florence for other effects.

OTHELLO originally had no nationality; it was assigned one—Moroccan—only when this became a legal necessity at the 1952 Cannes film festival, where it shared the top prize with TWO CENTS WORTH OF HOPE. Though Welles periodically lost financial control over the film afterward, it was never, to my knowledge, significantly altered or recut by others. After he made his essay film FILMING OTHELLO in the 70s for German television, he suggested that a stipulation for showing the two films together at festivals—which he hoped would happen—would be showing OTHELLO in a decent print.

This point seems worth emphasizing to counter the erroneous impression, created for advertising purposes, that OTHELLO was ever a "lost" film. Good 35-millimeter prints still exist abroad, and the film was lost here only in the sense that FILMING OTHELLO still is: for an unconscionable number of years it had no American distribution. In other words, out of sight, out of mind—and anything not for sale is out of sight.

Welles was never a good businessman or salesman, but this hardly accounts for the cool American response when United Artists released OTHELLO in the fall of 1955. Reviewers tended to compare it unfavorably to Laurence Olivier's Shakespeare films, finding it amateurish and self-indulgent in relation to the polish and production values of HENRY V and HAMLET. In some ways this response only repeated and amplified the objections to Welles's MACBETH seven years earlier: that Welles had done violence to the Shakespeare text, indulged himself, and made many of the lines unclear.

The main reason they were supposedly unclear was the Scots accents, and Welles was obliged to edit and redub a second, shortened version without them. In the process we lost the first ten-minute take in a released

Hollywood movie. (The original version is now available on video, ten-minute take and all, and the lines are perfectly clear.) The lack of clarity of many lines in OTHELLO was blamed partly on faulty lip sync, most of which has been eliminated thanks to the painstaking work done in Chicago on the new version. Frankly, I've always thought that both of these "problems" were partially excuses for people intimidated by Shakespeare or by Welles's refusal to approach the playwright on his knees. There was a widespread conviction back then that the best thing movies could possibly do was serve up Shakespeare straight. But if we recall that the Latin root of "amateur" is *amare*, "to love," Welles's romantic, impractical, and passionate commitment to his own work—quite the opposite of Olivier's bloodless professionalism—was the real scandal. "Fear of completion" may have been the charge that dogged him for most of the rest of his career, but it was clearly fear of *in*completion that brought him to the end of this particular adventure.

I saw OTHELLO on TV in Alabama in my early teens—by sheer luck it was the first Welles *or* Shakespeare movie I ever encountered—and was blown away by its dizzying mise en scène, its creepy horror-movie atmosphere (including the dank Moorish locations and the near-somnambulism of Welles's underplayed performance), and the eerie and awesome power of the modernist score (still one of the best in movies). When I later read American "experts" on the subject—people such as drama critic Eric Bentley—I was shocked by their violent disagreement:

> A film bad from every point of view and for every public. Technically, it is gauche, the dialogue being all too obviously dubbed. . . . To connoisseurs of Shakespeare, it can only be torture. . . . If Mr. Welles's failure as director is partial, as actor it is complete. . . . He never acts, he is photographed. . . . I don't know what *The Daily Worker* said, but it missed a trick if it didn't hold up Mr. Welles as a prize example of individualistic, bourgeois culture in decay. To which I suggest adding that the whole film is a precise example of formalistic decadence.

In retrospect, I think I can see now what made Welles's first unambiguously independent film an act of even more courage and defiance than CITIZEN KANE. In KANE he was bucking only Hollywood and Hearst; with OTHELLO he was defying both Hollywood and academicians—not to mention the whole institutional setup for picture making itself, as it was then dimly understood by Bentley and others. Properly speaking, he had entered the treacherous domain of the avant-garde—probably against his own conscious wishes—and a substantial portion of the American intelligentsia never forgave him for it. From then on he would make features only with the support of European producers (with the exception of TOUCH OF EVIL)—and not very many of those. Then he died, and folks like the Chrysler people came along to explain how much we'd loved, appreciated, and *sustained* him all along.

Some people wonder today how a leftist like Welles managed to escape or elude the McCarthy witch-hunts and blacklists of the early 50s. The answer is that he was abroad at the time, striking out on his own— and not coincidentally filming a tale of treachery and paranoid suspicions, of jealousy and betrayal that reflected some of the traumas back home. Maybe some leftists got the message all too well, whether they consciously admitted it or not, and resented Welles's bid for freedom while they were suffering humiliations in the states.

It may not have been until the 70s that a sober assessment of the film as a Shakespeare adaptation was offered, in Jack J. Jorgens's excellent *Shakespeare on Film:* "Welles's OTHELLO is one of the few Shakespeare films in which the images on the screen generate enough beauty, variety, and graphic power to stand comparison with Shakespeare's poetic images. His visual images compensate for the inevitable loss of complexity and dramatic voltage accompanying heavy alterations in the text."

A later part of Jorgens's analysis is so acute that Welles quotes it in FILMING OTHELLO: "The visual style . . . mirrors the marriage at the center of the play—not the idyllic marriage of Othello and Desdemona, but the perverse marriage of Othello and Iago. . . . If the film's grandeur, hyperbole, and simplicity are the Moor's, its dizzying perspectives and camera movements, tortured compositions, grotesque shadows, and insane distortions are Iago's, for he is the agent of chaos."

As you can see, I'm more than a little excited by the prospect of a movie as wonderful as OTHELLO getting a second chance in this country. If any doubts remain, they mainly have to do with differing opinions about what Welles's OTHELLO is—and what its "restoration" consists of.

When Francis Coppola proudly presented the "complete" NAPOLEON of

Abel Gance at Radio City Music Hall in 1981, an entire subplot was excised so that the screening wouldn't run past midnight and jack up the theater's operating costs. If I'm not mistaken, the same subplot is missing from the NAPOLEON that's now shown on video and cable in the U.S., but not from the versions shown in Europe. Thanks to the complicity or indifference of the American press, most Americans who've seen NAPOLEON are completely unaware of this tampering. But considering that Coppola's name was much larger than Gance's in the ads—even though it was Kevin Brownlow who carried out the restoration—maybe they assume that it's Coppola's film, to do with it as he wishes.

No such deception has been carried out in the restoration of OTHELLO; all the shots and 91 minutes are present and accounted for. But the aesthetic and historical issues raised by this new version are by no means simple, and the degree to which they've been mystified, obfuscated, and distorted in the press is unfortunate, because very few people who've seen the film in its present state have known what they were getting. Thus I'm fully in agreement with the *New York Times'* Vincent Canby, who reviewed "an expertly restored print that should help to rewrite cinema history"—though not, I suspect, in the way Canby intended.

I've known Michael Dawson, the local coproducer (with Arnie Saks) of the restoration, for almost four years, and thanks to him was able to meet Beatrice Welles-Smith—Welles's youngest daughter, who authorized the restoration—two years ago. In connection with my own research projects on Welles, Dawson and I have found many occasions to exchange information and thoughts; while our philosophy of film restoration is not the same, it's been a friendly disagreement. Dawson's approach is almost exclusively technological, and his aim has been to bring OTHELLO's soundtrack in line with current commercial norms. But I believe state-of-the-art technology should ultimately be subservient to historical research that pinpoints as much as possible what's being preserved, altered, or discarded. Significantly, though Dawson eventually discovered that at least two distinctly different Welles-edited versions of OTHELLO exist—the first premiered at Cannes and the second in New York—he researched this point only after the restoration of the second version was virtually complete.

In short, rather than concentrate on the film's history, Dawson concentrated on the technical challenges of the assignment—a job, I should add, that he and his collaborators have carried out most impressively, especially given the limited time and money they had. Yet no serious attempt was made to acquire the late Francesco Lavignino's score (though a friend of mine who knows Lavignino's family tells me it exists—contrary to claims made in the *Chicago Tribune* and elsewhere). Instead, conductor Michael Pendowski was asked to annotate what he heard to the best of his ability and then rerecord the music with members of the Chicago Symphony and Lyric Opera. The "redoing" of the sound effects in stereo was carried out by others in the same fashion. (This is considerably different from how the *Village Voice* reviewer claimed it was done: "The musical score was remastered . . . it's a bit like encountering a grimy monument that's recently been sandblasted." But then practically no press account I've read has accurately or adequately described the work done.) Consequently, while the visual work on the negative conforms mainly to a dictionary definition of restoration, the sound work obviously doesn't—qualifying instead as a highly subjective reworking of some of the original materials, a postmodernist dream inspired by the original OTHELLO soundtrack.[1]

To make matters more complicated, the film's New York distributor, Julian Schlossberg—whose name is as prominent in some ads as Francis Coppola's was in some ads for NAPOLEON—has altered some of the sound work done in Chicago. I won't even attempt to sort out who made which decisions, but I should stress that the protechnological, ahistorical approach adopted at the outset was not significantly deviated from. The underlying assumption appears to be that contemporary sound technology can only improve Welles's original work because he had inferior equipment to work with. My own assumption is that Welles's aesthetic decisions are impossible to isolate from what he had to work with—and that includes a single microphone when the score was first recorded. Hollywood buffs might judge these results substandard, but when you start to tamper with the original choices it's hard to know where to stop. (You might as well reshoot CITIZEN KANE in 3-D or Cinerama on the theory that if those technologies had been available to Welles in 1940 he surely would have used them.)

There are multiple consequences to this approach. While one could again quarrel with the brightness or darkness of particular shots, there's no question that the new OTHELLO looks magnificent in terms of overall clarity. It also sounds wonderful, particularly if you place clarity and texture of voice and musical instrument over other criteria. Nearly all of the dialogue is in sync now, which is clearly an improvement, and Welles's own voice has never sounded better. But in many crucial respects, it's no longer a soundtrack by Welles. At best it's a soundtrack using or imitating some elements from the original film and not using or imitating others—and changing the relationships between those elements in the bargain.

The atmospheric effects cited above (such as Welles stroking piano strings and the use of a spinetta) are of course missing, though I suppose it could be argued that they weren't sufficiently audible in the original to inspire imitation. My problem is that what the original sounds like is more a matter of personal interpretation than one of scientific analysis, and I'd rather trust Welles on this matter than Pendowski (who freely admitted to me that he's not familiar with Lavignino's other work, which includes three other scores for Welles productions of Shakespeare). Even with the best will and mimicry in the world, most of the precise elements of the music and sound effects as supervised by Welles—specific performances, textures, and tonalities—are no longer part of the film. Neither, for that matter, is the chanting of Latin by monks in the funeral procession in the film's remarkable opening sequence—a prolonged hushed recitation that serves effectively both as a diminuendo after the music ends and as a tapering sound bridge to the silence that follows in both Welles-edited versions of the film. Why this major part of Welles's sound design was simply deleted is anyone's guess, though I'm told it may be restored in the video and laser-disc versions.[2]

Where Welles and his crew got the sound of their crashing waves straight from the Mediterranean, the Chicago crew uses Lake Michigan. Where Lavignino's score at one point, according to Welles, used 40 mandolins at once, Pendowski's approximation never uses more than 3 or 4. Moreover, Pendowski had nothing to do with the rerecording of the sound effects, and one could argue that the sense in the original of music and sounds being aesthetically integrated is significantly reduced. The use of stereo adds further complications, involving many aesthetic choices Welles never had to make.

Interestingly enough, Welles briefly explored the possibility of recording MACBETH—the film before OTHELLO, done entirely in a studio—in stereo, but I've found no clues about how he might have used it. Considering his eclecticism and originality, I seriously doubt that he would have followed the standard contemporary Hollywood practice of placing all the voices behind the screen and dispersing the sound effects and music through the other speakers, as has been done in this version. This has the effect of "normalizing" OTHELLO in a way analogous to the mainstreaming of KANE—making it conform to a current Hollywood model of correctness. Certainly the dynamic relationship between dialogue, music, and sound effects is profoundly altered from the OTHELLO I know and love; the percussive assault of the music in the opening sequence, for instance, is substantially reduced by virtue of being spread out like butter rather than brought to a sharp monaural point that pierces one's consciousness. The single most important aesthetic change that results from this—at least in my own subjective impressions—is that the film is no longer as spooky and creepy as it was; the spectral chill in its bones, which once made me think of NOSFERATU, has largely disappeared. (Then again, maybe if NOSFERATU were "sandblasted" and refurbished, it wouldn't remind me of NOSFERATU either.)

These are the negative factors. What are the positive ones? As noted above, the new version looks glorious, and in some cases the effects of the film's checkered production history—such as the use of different kinds of film stock—are emphasized rather than played down by the overall improvement of visual grain, which helps somewhat to counteract the Hollywoodizing of the soundtrack. Yet because the sound is much cleaner, it's possible to appreciate many more aspects of the music and its orchestration, even if some of them are different.

The original OTHELLO hasn't been destroyed (at least not yet). It's simply being kept from the eyes and ears of Americans for business reasons, much as the longer version of Gance's NAPOLEON is. With most of the dialogue now in sync, more of it can be understood than ever before; Bentley's complaint that it is "all too obviously dubbed" still holds true, but to a lesser degree. Whether Europeans, who've never expressed discomfort with the original version, will welcome an "improved" one—albeit in a Welles cut they may not have seen before—remains to be seen. But we should certainly rush out to see the new OTHELLO and marvel at everything Welles brought to it. Whether we should regard it as a model for restorations to come is quite another matter.

Notes

1. At a Welles conference in Rome organized by Ciro Giorgini in October 1992, which I attended, the first reels of three separate versions of OTHELLO, including the "restoration," were screened in succession in the presence of a daughter of Francesco Lavignino, who maintained on that occasion that Pendowski's version of the music was not her father's work. Unhappily, a version of this ersatz score has since been issued commercially in the U.S. with no acknowledgment of any discrepancy and no communication with Lavignino's family. (1993)
2. It was. (1993)

—*Chicago Reader,* April 10, 1992. © *Chicago Reader,* Inc. Reprinted with permission.

17

Truth and Consequence

On IT'S ALL TRUE: BASED ON AN UNFINISHED
FILM BY ORSON WELLES

I'm one of the people who receives an acknowledgment in the final credits of IT'S
ALL TRUE: BASED ON AN UNFINISHED FILM BY ORSON WELLES, but in fact I re-
gret the contribution I made to this film. During a phone conversation with Bill
Krohn, one of the writers, directors, and producers, Bill told me that one of the
French producers, Jean-Luc Ormières, was looking desperately for a composer for
the documentary who wouldn't charge too much money. I suggested Jorge Ar-
riagada—the Chilean film composer who at that point had written the scores for
something like a couple of dozen films by Raúl Ruiz, a filmmaker I greatly admire
as well as a friend—and Arriagada wound up getting hired for the job. I recall
having heard that Arriagada mainly worked for Ruiz because he liked to do so
rather than out of economic necessity, and this fact combined with Ruiz's own
Welles worship and Arriagada's South American background made him seem
ideal. Unfortunately, this conclusion was built on the common Anglo-American
fallacy that Latin America is something like a single homogeneous culture—the
same assumption, I presume, that years later would prompt Colin MacCabe, the
producer at the British Film Institute of a series of national film histories on film
or video assigned to various filmmakers, to assign the whole of Latin American
cinema to one (admittedly very talented and knowledgeable) Brazilian director,
Nelson Pereira dos Santos, yielding his 93-minute CINEMA OF TEARS in 1995.

In this case, my assumption that Arriagada would have been well versed in
samba and Brazilian pop music proved to be erroneous, and his score for IT'S
ALL TRUE, whatever its own qualities, wound up having little to do with

Welles's original designs for the music. I'm fairly certain that if Dick Wilson—who'd been of inestimable help to me while I was editing This Is Orson Welles, *all the way up to his tragic death in August 1991, while keeping his illness a secret from me—had still been alive, such an error would have been averted, because Dick was much more aware of and familiar with the specific music that Welles had in mind.*

For much more material about IT'S ALL TRUE *and Bill's own work on it, see chapter 19. I should add that far and away the most valuable scholarly resource on* IT'S ALL TRUE *remains Catherine L. Benamou's brilliant and definitive book on the subject, adapted from her dissertation, which I've read in manuscript and which will be published eventually by University of California Press, once Catherine allows this to happen. (The many delays and deferments, alas, have already been comparable in some ways to the releases of some of Welles's unfinished films.) Meanwhile, Catherine has recently brokered the acquisition of two invaluable sets of papers by the University of Michigan, where she teaches—those of Welles that were in the possession of Oja Kodar, and those of Richard Wilson, Welles's assistant and associate during much of the 30s and all of the 40s. (She has aptly named both collections "Everybody's Orson Welles.")*

■

> Too much effort and real love went into the entire project for it to fail and come to nothing in the end. I have a degree of faith in it that amounts to fanaticism, and you can believe that if IT'S ALL TRUE goes down into limbo I'll go with it.
>
> —Orson Welles, writing to a Brazilian friend in the 40s

As perverse as it sounds, the work of art that IT'S ALL TRUE: BASED ON AN UNFINISHED FILM BY ORSON WELLES most calls to mind—my mind, anyway—is Vladimir Nabokov's 1962 novel *Pale Fire*. Discounting its tricky foreword and index, this literary tour de force consists of a 27-page, 999-line poem by the fictional dead poet John Shade, followed by 160 pages of annotation by the probably insane and certainly unreliable Charles Kinbote. By contrast, IT'S ALL TRUE consists of about half an hour of entertaining, accurate, and altogether sane commentary on Orson Welles's ill-fated, three-part feature of that title, followed by an hour-long edited version of the silent rushes of one of the episodes, "Four Men on a Raft," originally planned as the feature's centerpiece. (Edited by Ed Marx, who used a few rough outlines by Welles as his main guide, this episode has been furnished with discreet sound effects and music by Jorge Arriagada, Râúl Ruiz's principal composer. The most significant part that's missing—and I wish the documentary prologue had pointed this out—is the narration Welles planned to use but never wrote or recorded.)

One can easily tick off major differences between *Pale Fire* and IT'S ALL TRUE. What then are the similarities? An interdependence of text and commentary that keeps one's mind restlessly scampering between the two, unable to find satisfaction or closure in either. The uncertainty and indeterminacy of the longer section of each work (*Pale Fire*'s commentary, IT'S ALL TRUE's "text"), in contrast to the pithy clarity of the shorter section. The presentation of two complementary and stylistically divergent forays into the same genre (fiction in *Pale Fire*, documentary in IT'S ALL TRUE) that together say and mean more than either could alone, despite the fact that the synthesis is riddled with gaps and raises innumerable questions. Finally, an excruciating rift between what is present and what is absent—between the knowable and the unattainable, the graspable and the unimaginable.

In short, IT'S ALL TRUE generally does such a good job with what it has, journalistically speaking, that it winds up breaking your heart. It doesn't offer up a "new" or "restored" Orson Welles film, because there never was a film. It doesn't even offer an ersatz Welles film cobbled together out of Welles footage, like the distressing version of DON QUIXOTE recently released in Spain. But what it does provide is indispensable: a cogent account of what happened with the project and enough of the original footage to allow one to speculate at some length about what might have been.

The film should leave you feeling vaguely unsatisfied; anything else would have been a lie. And if it presents a quandary, it's neither the first nor the last one posed by Welles's unruly career—a career that constantly brings up the question of what a work or an oeuvre actually is.

■

Among the many film projects Welles had in development just after the release of CITIZEN KANE, in May 1941, were one about Landru, a 20th-century French Bluebeard (a project written for and eventually purchased by Charlie Chaplin, who converted it into MONSIEUR VERDOUX); a life of Jesus set in America at the turn of the century, conceived as "a kind of primitive western"; a political thriller centered around a fascistic news commentator; adaptations of THE MAGNIFICENT AMBERSONS and JOURNEY INTO FEAR; and an omnibus feature called IT'S ALL TRUE, consisting of four true stories—a history of American jazz, a story by John Fante about his Italian parents meeting in San Francisco, and two stories by documentary filmmaker Robert Flaherty, one about a Mexican boy's friendship with a bull ("My Friend Bonito"), the other about a boat captain. An anthology format had served Welles well on radio, and he launched a new weekly show around the same principle in the fall; by then, three of his film projects were in production, with Welles serving as writer-director-producer on AMBERSONS, producer and actor on JOURNEY, and producer on IT'S ALL TRUE. In September Norman Foster began directing "Bonito" in Mexico under Welles's supervision, and the following month Welles began shooting AMBERSONS. In December, two weeks after Pearl Harbor, he received a telegram from the coordinator of the federal Inter-American Affairs office asking him to undertake a goodwill mission to Brazil and make a noncommercial film there without salary to promote "hemisphere solidarity," with RKO studios footing the bill but the government guaranteeing up to $300,000 against potential financial losses. Nelson Rockefeller, a major RKO stockholder, and President Roosevelt, a personal friend of Welles, both urged him to accept; Rockefeller was adamant that Welles arrive in February, in time to shoot the annual Rio carnival.

Welles finally agreed, on condition that he be allowed to finish cutting AMBERSONS in Rio with his editor, Robert Wise. In early January he recalled Foster from Mexico to begin directing JOURNEY INTO FEAR, intending to complete "Bonito" himself on his way back from Brazil and incorporate it into a revamped, South American IT'S ALL TRUE. Speeding up both AMBERSONS and JOURNEY in order to make his deadline, he finished his production work and suspended his radio show by February 1, flew to a briefing with government officials in Washington the next day, and proceeded directly to Miami for a three-day marathon editing of AMBER-SONS with Wise. Then he flew to Rio, where he and his crew immediately began shooting the carnival, in Technicolor and black and white.

Over the next month Welles began to sketch two Brazilian stories to go with "Bonito": an account of the samba at the carnival, to replace his history of American jazz, and a re-enactment of an epic 1,650-mile raft journey taken the previous fall by four impoverished *jangadeiros* (fishermen) from Fortaleza to Rio to speak to President Vargas about their economic exploitation by the owners of their fishing rafts, who collected half of their weekly catch. Welles's celebration of impoverished blacks in both these stories, quite compatible with the emphasis of "Bonito," raised the hackles of Brazilian government officials and RKO studio executives alike, and some U.S. government officials expressed their displeasure as well. The four *jangadeiros* may have become national heroes, but their activist leader, Jacaré, was considered a communist; the film hardly promised to correspond to the touristic propaganda about Brazil the local dictatorship wanted. When Welles took his Technicolor cameras into the *favelas* (shantytowns) to trace the origins of samba, he and his crew were ejected from at least one of them at Vargas's behest. Meanwhile, Welles was commissioning an extraordinary array of research into Brazilian life and culture by a large team of Brazilian (not Hollywood) writers, producing a weighty file of ambitious essays that still exists.

These radical aspects of the project, elided or minimized in most previous North American accounts of IT'S ALL TRUE—or else distorted by racist innuendo, such as reading Welles's friendship and collaboration with blacks as simply "partying" or slumming—have never been forgotten in Brazil. Grande Otelo, the star of "The Story of Samba," whom we also see and hear 50 years later in the documentary, compared Welles to Martin Luther King when he spoke at a Welles conference held at New York University in 1988. And the very fact that such a conference was held became front-page news in a São Paulo newspaper.

Things began to go badly for Welles. Not honoring its promise to send an AMBERSONS rough cut with Wise to Rio, RKO decided to preview the film. A week after the second preview, Jacaré drowned in an accident while he and the other three *jangadeiros* were preparing to restage their triumphant arrival in Rio for the film. Then things got even worse. Rockefeller left the RKO board of directors, and shortly after studio president George Schaefer—the man who'd first lured Welles to Hollywood, had remained his strongest ally, and had even come up with the title for CITIZEN KANE—was forced to resign. More than 45 minutes were hacked out of AMBERSONS by Wise and others, in part to soften some of its harshness, and some scenes were reshot or added. Then Welles's staff was summarily evicted from the RKO lot, and IT'S ALL TRUE was halted in mid-production.

Before returning to the States, Welles was permitted to shoot, from mid-June to mid-July, a revised "Four Men on a Raft," without sound and in black and white, on a minimal budget and with a skeletal crew, in Fortaleza, Recife, and Salvador. But when he returned to the U.S., no one would go anywhere near the project.

It would hardly be an exaggeration to say that Welles's career never fully recovered from RKO's mutilation and dumping of AMBERSONS and JOURNEY, its abrupt scuttling of a third picture, and its well-mounted campaign depicting Welles as irresponsible and out of control—a clear attempt to justify its actions. (The following year RKO's stationery bore the pointed slogan "Showmanship instead of genius.") Almost three years passed before Welles could direct another picture, and the image of him proffered by RKO has become so well entrenched over the past half century that it's still repeated in some quarters like a comforting mantra. Critic and biographer Charles Higham devoted two full books, published in 1970 and 1985, to propounding it, and Robert L. Carringer's THE MAGNIFICENT AMBERSONS: *A Reconstruction*, published this year, argues that nothing could have made AMBERSONS an artistic success because of Welles's oedipal hang-ups and his irrational denials stemming from them. (Speaking of irrational denials, over the course of 307 pages Carringer fails to mention IT'S ALL TRUE once, even in a footnote, and seems to regard the entire Brazilian episode as extraneous to what happened to AMBERSONS.)

Considering the sacred value we accord the bottom line, we shouldn't be surprised that some academics (like Carringer) defend RKO's business sense in eviscerating AMBERSONS and JOURNEY, though both movies lost piles of money anyway. After all, it was the principle of the thing—the pride and honor of the studio system itself—that was at stake.

This isn't to argue that Welles had any business sense or even much common sense when it came to ingratiating himself with that system. Three months before the release of CITIZEN KANE he published an article attacking the functions of most producers, agents, and studio heads, and the implied threat to the system represented by his original Hollywood contract, which granted him almost unlimited control of his pictures, clearly made many in the film industry livid. While he inspired passionate loyalty from most of his staff, one suspects that his business associates, starting with John Houseman, regarded him somewhat more ambivalently. (When he was off in Brazil his business manager was Jack Moss. According to writer-director Cy Endfield—who was working for Moss at the time, and whom I interviewed earlier this year—many of the frantic long cables Welles sent Moss about the re-editing of AMBERSONS went straight into the wastebasket unread.) If Welles's troubling career carries any lesson, it's that the same delirious risk-taking that led to such unmitigated disasters paid off spectacularly in other situations, including KANE.

The dogged efforts of academics to assign a neat, linear progression to Welles's oeuvre are frequently misguided, being generally based on what was released rather than what was filmed. When one reads that THE IMMORTAL STORY (1968) is his first color film, the dazzling, extensive Technicolor footage he shot in Brazil 26 years earlier, some of which we see in IT'S ALL TRUE, is overlooked. Other "experts" acknowledge the Brazilian color footage but assume all of it was devoted to the carnival—a myth that has clung to Welles scholarship so tenaciously that some reviewers of the new documentary have been expressing doubts that the other Technicolor footage briefly visible in IT'S ALL TRUE is Welles's. (A subtle bias about arty black and white being the only proper medium for showing poverty—a bias reflected in most documentaries and neorealist features of the 40s—may be behind this uncertainty.)

Similarly, many critics—myself included—have cited OTHELLO as Welles's first independent feature. It probably is; but it might be argued that IT'S ALL TRUE, which started out seven years earlier as a Hollywood feature with full studio resources, wound up independent, at least when

Welles was shooting most of "Four Men on a Raft," and certainly when he was trying to keep the project alive afterward. (In truth, it's a bit of both; the documentary shows us the Hollywood-ish trickery involved in shooting the men on the boat, but also reveals how crude and improvised such "special effects" had to be.)

■

With the possible exception of Erich von Stroheim, no Hollywood figure better illustrates the incompatibility of art and commerce than Welles. It's an incompatibility that can easily be overlooked or rationalized if one's looking at the careers of certain giants during the heyday of the studios— figures such as John Ford, Howard Hawks, Alfred Hitchcock, and Ernst Lubitsch—but is much harder to ignore today, when the conditions that allowed such careers to flourish no longer exist. (People who cite CITIZEN KANE as a counter-example tend to minimize the fact that on first release it played only at independent theaters and lost money. It was never pre-viewed and came very close to being destroyed: Louis B. Mayer and other studio executives offered to reimburse RKO for the total cost of the pic-ture if it would burn the negative. If RKO president George Schaefer hadn't defied the Hollywood community by rejecting the offer, we wouldn't have the film today.)

Most moviegoers and reviewers would still prefer to ignore this in-compatibility because the business couldn't be run as smoothly if they didn't, and one of the most popular rationalizations for ignoring the in-compatibility of the two is "retrievability." According to this myth, it doesn't really matter how many movies are mutilated by producers or distributors, because they can always be "restored" later, on laserdisc or otherwise. But it's absurd to apply such a myth to Welles. We can't "re-store" AMBERSONS, because all the cut footage was destroyed by the new RKO management in late 1942, and we can't "restore" IT'S ALL TRUE be-cause it was never allowed to exist. That's why the documentary IT'S ALL TRUE needs its awkward subtitle, BASED ON AN UNFINISHED FILM BY ORSON WELLES; without it, the film sounds like a resurrection.

All we now have of the original film are some of the raw materials— those that weren't dumped into the Pacific Ocean when the space at the studio storage facilities was needed. Not only is most of the carnival footage missing, but so also is all of the editing Welles did in subsequent years, done whenever he was attempting to persuade a studio to resuscitate the project in some form. (At one point he even purchased the footage himself, but was unable to keep up the storage payments.) It's worth adding that most of the "Bonito" footage appears to have survived as well—though we see only one sequence of it in IT'S ALL TRUE, a lovely depiction of the blessing of young animals in a village church—and all this undeveloped footage will turn to dust if funds for its preservation aren't made available.

In keeping with Welles's chameleonlike propensity to change some aspects of his style in every film project, IT'S ALL TRUE is atypical. The pagan Catholicism we glimpse in all three projected episodes can be read in light of Peter Bogdanovich's recent revelation in *This Is Orson Welles* that Welles was raised a Catholic—which perhaps also adds a spin to the influence of John Ford's style on this picture. It's hard to find other overt examples of Catholicism in Welles's work. However, the spare expressionist graveyard here is echoed in the Celtic crosses of his MACBETH; some of the heroic, low-angle diagonals look forward to OTHELLO (which used the same gifted cameraman, George Fanto); and the sculpted, spacious sky vistas and cloud formations anticipate those in DON QUIXOTE, which was also improvised and shot silent. (The last two traits suggest the visual styles of Eisenstein and Dovzhenko respectively, but they're also evident in a good many 30s documentaries.)

The profusion of close-ups here, I should note, is at odds with the mise en scène of both KANE and AMBERSONS—movies that resort to close-ups rarely, and then only at climactic junctures. Those films, of course, employed professional actors, and Welles liked to joke that he used close-ups only when the actors weren't good enough; even so, I think Ed Marx's editing favors them too much, leading to an overall dulling effect. "Four Men on a Raft" also lingers over beautiful images in a way that authentic Welles movies, which are too restlessly busy with their narrative and expository agendas, never do. (To my mind, Marx's editing most nearly approximates Welles's during the blessing of the animals in "Bonito.") Nevertheless, having watched about seven hours of the "Four Men on a Raft" rushes on video a few years ago—much of it devoted to repeated takes of the same shots—I don't think it can be said that Marx hasn't respected the material in his editing choices. For the most part, he's simply allowed it to breathe and exist, and by doing so offers us more of the Welles scrapbook to pore over.

■

The new documentary begins with Welles semi-humorously describing a voodoo curse placed on the original IT'S ALL TRUE when RKO closed down the production. (The clip comes from ORSON WELLES'S SKETCH BOOK, an enjoyable weekly TV show Welles did for the BBC in the spring of 1955 that's never been broadcast here.) The curse might appear to have lasted well into the early 1990s if one counts the protracted efforts of the late Richard Wilson—Welles's dedicated key assistant on IT'S ALL TRUE, who worked on most of his stage productions, radio shows, and Hollywood pictures before becoming a filmmaker in his own right—to get this documentary about IT'S ALL TRUE made.

After making a 22-minute trailer [called FOUR MEN ON A RAFT] in 1986 in an attempt to raise money, Wilson spent the last five years of his life struggling to get this story told on the screen. A rare scholar among filmmakers, Wilson was so scrupulously devoted to accuracy in Wellesian matters that only a few months before he died from cancer, when he was keeping his fatal illness secret from everyone but close friends and family, he spent a good six or seven hours on the phone with me making meticulous corrections and additions to a long account of Welles's career I was compiling, undoubtedly aware that he would probably never live to see it in print.

Back in 1985 Wilson was joined on the IT'S ALL TRUE project by critic Bill Krohn, the Los Angeles correspondent of *Cahiers du cinéma*, and two years later by Myron Meisel, a former film critic for the *Los Angeles Reader* and *Chicago Reader*. The following year they were joined by the invaluable Catherine Benamou, a Latin American and Caribbean specialist who's done exhaustive field research with the original participants in IT'S ALL TRUE in Brazil and Mexico (and is preparing a dissertation on the subject) and even speaks the local *jangadeiros* dialect. Only after Wilson's death in

1991 did the project finally acquire the funds, from France, needed to complete it.

I doubt that this documentary deliberately set out to be a modernist text. Its mission was to tell the truth—a task that isn't always as easy as it first might appear—and in the process of honoring this mission became something more complex than a simple news report. (The only textual lapse I'm aware of is a simple gaffe in the opening narration—setting the New York premiere of CITIZEN KANE in Hollywood.) However keenly we may feel the absence of Welles's voice narrating and explaining "Four Men on a Raft," we see this silent footage after half an hour of Welles talking about the film's subject on all sorts of occasions over many decades: on radio shows of the 40s, TV shows of the 50s and afterward, and even in private, taped conversations with Peter Bogdanovich. In addition, Miguel Ferrer's narration alerts us to the central facts we need to know about the narrative of "Four Men on a Raft" before we get to it. The subtle effect of this detailed dossier combined with Welles's voice is to assist us in constructing our own imaginary Welles film out of the key materials available—making this film, like all of Welles's work, interactive moviegoing.

If Welles had completed IT'S ALL TRUE in 1942 it would have offered both a radical contrast to AMBERSONS—a look at the poorest segment of society after a sustained look at the wealthiest—and a certain continuity, insofar as Welles's familiar radio voice would have served as the viewer's intimate tour guide in both. Because the two Brazilian episodes were essentially shot without scripts, they offer early glimpses of the impromptu shooting methods that characterize many of Welles's late film essays, such as F FOR FAKE and FILMING OTHELLO. They also hark back to a much more dated view of documentary associated with early Robert Flaherty pictures such as MOANA, as well as F. W. Murnau's expressionist South Sea tragedy TABU, which Flaherty worked on as a writer—a romantic and pre-Marxist view of noble folk (if not noble savages) living in harmony with nature, with no obvious ties to the industrialized society observing and recording them. (You'd never guess from this picture that Fortaleza was and is a bustling resort city.)

The Flaherty mode of restaging real events and inventing others is fully embraced by Welles; one key strain in the narrative—the romance, wedding, and subsequent drowning of a young fisherman in Fortaleza— is purely fictional, though this drowning alludes to the real drowning of Jacaré. This approach to actuality is worlds away from the synthesis of archival material, recent interviews, and factual commentary provided by Wilson, Krohn, and Meisel in the preceding half hour, even though it consciously strives to honor and do justice to the same people, and this implicit contrast between articulations of "what's all true" in 1942 and 1993 is one of the movie's most valuable history lessons. Equally striking is the sense of separation between what Welles wanted the film to do and how it registers today: the 1942 feature was designed to end euphorically with Technicolor carnival footage recounting the story of samba after the fishermen arrive in Rio, but because of our knowledge of all that happened (or didn't happen), portions of that euphoric footage at the end of IT'S ALL TRUE can't provide the same lift.

Much as one can regard the original IT'S ALL TRUE as an independent venture and a studio project, the extensive collaboration of Brazilians on the film makes it qualify to some degree as part of the history of Brazilian cinema. From this standpoint, the academic critic Robert Stam has argued plausibly that Welles managed to anticipate some of the themes, methods, and "social audaciousness" of Cinema Novo (the Brazilian new wave) in the 60s and afterward.

Indeed, one of the most moving aspects of the film is the evidence of how deeply Brazilian participants in the 1942 film and their relatives today revere Welles for the story he was trying to tell about them. "This film is the only inheritance the four fishermen left us," the grandson of one of the *jangadeiros* says today, just before "Four Men on a Raft" begins—heart-stopping testimony to a loving trust that has endured for 50 years. It's no wonder Welles felt inclined to idealize and exalt these people—people who, as the film makes clear, are exploited as badly today as they were then, but who are still uncynical enough to believe that a truthful documentary about their situation might improve their lot.

"Cheap labor," a skeptical friend of mine scoffed while watching some of the extras in rushes of "Four Men on a Raft" a few years ago. The condescension he found in this footage points to the irreparable damage popular-front attitudes have suffered in our culture since the 30s, when Welles was cutting his teeth on agitprop like Marc Blitzstein's dated socialist opera *The Cradle Will Rock*. Yet the faith shown in IT'S ALL TRUE by the Brazilians leads me to question my friend's cynicism: if we can see "beyond" popular-front optimism today, what is it that's so much more precious to us? The style of the 40s footage may be dated as hell, but in feeling it corresponds pretty closely to what the *jangadeiros* are still saying to us—and if it's the 40s style that keeps us from hearing them, so much the worse for us. This movie, at least, has kept the faith.

—*Chicago Reader*, October 29, 1993. © *Chicago Reader*, Inc. Reprinted with permission.

18

Afterword to *THE CRADLE WILL ROCK*, an *Original Screenplay* by Orson Welles

As I recall, critic Dave Kehr once said to me that encountering THE CRADLE WILL ROCK after THE BIG BRASS RING was a bit like encountering THE MAGNIFICENT AMBERSONS after CITIZEN KANE. I appreciate what he meant—especially when it comes to this script's nostalgia and its sharp autocritique compared to the more narcissistic and irreverent surface of its predecessor. But I hasten to add that this script, unlike THE BIG BRASS RING, is more interesting for its autobiographical elements than for its literary qualities. Perhaps for the same reason, writing an afterword about it was more difficult.

On the subject of Tim Robbins's CRADLE WILL ROCK, I'd like to quote excerpts from an article of mine that appeared in the Chicago Reader on December 24, 1999:

> For the past seven months, ever since Robbins's movie premiered in Cannes, friends and associates who saw it there have been warning me that I, as an Orson Welles specialist, would despise it. Writer-director Robbins does make the character of Welles (Angus MacFadyen) a silly boozer and pretentious loudmouth without a serious bone in his body—something closer to Jack Buchanan's loose parody of Welles in the 1953 MGM musical THE BAND WAGON than a historically responsible depiction of Welles in 1937. Yet Welles is a marginal character in CRADLE WILL ROCK, and he had little to do with its subject, the short-lived glory of American socialist art. Furthermore, the film's depiction of that subject is both historically defensible and rather gutsy.
>
> The heroes of Robbins's movie are Hallie Flanagan (Cherry Jones), head of the WPA's Federal Theater, who defended state-funded art against the stupid (and very

90s-like) attacks of Martin Dies and his House committee; and Aldo Silvano (John Turturro), a populist everyman and somewhat fictionalized Italian-American cast member of Marc Blitzstein's Marxist opera, The Cradle Will Rock, *perhaps suggested by Howard da Silva, who opposed the sliding of his home country toward fascism. Welles, rightly, isn't much more than an irritating speck in relation to these two noble presences. (More questionable is Robbins's letting Dies be a more coherent and dignified character than Welles, though this suits his ultimate strategy.)*

In 1937 Welles was a 22-year-old radio actor who was extremely well paid but usually unbilled; he was just starting to make a name for himself as an innovative theater director who sometimes acted in his own productions, but he hadn't yet become a radio or film director. No matter how highly one ranks Welles as an artist— or as a "premature antifascist," who spoke at a communist bookshop, wrote for the Daily Worker, *and emceed a benefit concert for* New Masses *in 1938—his importance in the history of socialist art is marginal at best. The same could be said of Welles's producer John Houseman (played by Cary Elwes as an improbable blend of Tom Wolfe and William Buckley). Robbins is generally more respectful of Diego Rivera as a leftist artist of this period, but even Rivera, as played by Ruben Blades, comes across like a cartoon radical; Hank Azaria's Blitzstein registers somewhat like an effete version of John Waters or Billy De Wolfe, a light comic actor in 50s musicals. Only Rivera's and Blitzstein's art are accorded any real integrity; the artists themselves are not, perhaps because Robbins hates elitism and star politics—one reason he may distrust Welles. If Robbins had more imagination and more capacity for nuance he might have appreciated the irony of Welles's hefty salary as an anonymous radio actor being fed directly—albeit secretly and illegally—into his Federal Theater productions, making those productions, like all of his movies, unclassifiable hybrids of public art and private enterprise. But then Robbins already had a pretty complex story about art, politics, and patronage—one that doesn't betray the significance of the spontaneous populist premiere of Blitzstein's opera after the government shut it down. This premiere was essentially without a director or sets, and it brought more fame to Welles (who'd directed the production that was shut down) than Welles brought to it.*

Welles fully recognized this paradox in his [screenplay] . . .—a script Robbins says he deliberately didn't read before writing his own. . . . Perhaps because [this] script, unlike Robbins's, is built on personal recollections, its nostalgia for the period registers quite differently: it's the reverse of [Robbins's] in its warm treatment of individuals and its relative indifference to collective expression. Robbins gives the dated Blitzstein opera much more attention, plainly seeing it as the last hurrah of American collectivist art, and to build his case he takes a few pretty dubious historical shortcuts—such as making Nelson Rockefeller the godfather of American abstract painting. Yet regardless of his movie's faults, Robbins's real point is to show us what we lost when we abandoned socialist art rather than what we gained, and that's an

affecting and meaningful story. If Welles gets lost in the shuffle, you can't have
everything.

■

It somehow seems fitting that in order to piece together Orson Welles's autobiography, we have to turn to his creative work. The unceasing desire and energy to produce that coursed through the seventy years of his life, and literally kept him occupied until his final moments, crowded out the opportunity to recount his life in tranquility, at least in any complete form, yielding only a series of tantalizing fragments. There's a moving account in F FOR FAKE (1973) of how, in Dublin at the age of sixteen, he launched his professional career as an actor, and FILMING OTHELLO (1979) describes how, in Morocco in his mid-thirties, he launched his career as an independent—as opposed to studio—filmmaker. A series of extended interviews with Peter Bogdanovich in the late 60s and early 70s—*This Is Orson Welles* (HarperCollins, 1992)—fill in some other parts of his life story, and a film project he worked on intermittently over the last decade in his life, ORSON WELLES SOLO—a sort of scrapbook self-portrait for which he filmed conversations with his old friends Roger and Hortense Hill in 1978, and wrote two brief autobiographical fragments about his parents, "My Father Wore Black Spats" and "A Brief Career as a Musical Prodigy" (both published in the Christmas 1982 issue of the French *Vogue*)—fill in a few more. Very shortly before his death, he began writing an autobiography in earnest, but never got beyond a few pages.

Perhaps the most extended and complete of his autobiographical ventures was written in 1984, the year before his death, and it came about quite by chance. If, as Welles often pointed out, a film director is someone who "presides over accidents," the "accident" that brought about this protracted exercise in self-scrutiny—an original screenplay called THE CRADLE WILL ROCK—is no less striking than the series of chance occurrences charted in the script itself.

Producer Michael Fitzgerald, whose features at this point included two John Huston pictures, WISE BLOOD and UNDER THE VOLCANO, had commissioned a first-draft screenplay from Ring Lardner, Jr., ROCKING THE CRADLE, which dealt with the events surrounding Welles's 1937 stage production of Marc Blitzstein's "play with music," *The Cradle Will Rock*. Fitzgerald then showed this script to Welles in June 1984 for his approval, and over the course of their ensuing discussions, invited Welles to direct the film himself. After showing some initial reluctance about the project (see Barbara Leaming's *Orson Welles* for details), Welles wound up not only agreeing, but completely discarding Lardner's script and writing a new one himself—turning the film in the process into an autobiographical account of his life during the first half of 1937, just before and after he turned twenty-two. (In Lardner's script, Welles was a less central figure—certainly a less developed one—and the emphasis was placed more squarely and exclusively on the production of the Blitzstein play.)

Insofar as this period constituted the time just before Welles achieved his biggest fame—he appeared on the cover of *Time* magazine on May 6, 1938, less than a year after *The Cradle Will Rock* opened—the script can be said to describe an existential point in his career that may have been even more decisive than any of his subsequent adventures in Hollywood, Latin America, or Europe. Indeed, precisely because this pivotal moment is virtually lost today to those who assume that Welles's career "began" with *Caesar* on the stage (November 11, 1937), *The War of the Worlds* on radio (October 30, 1938), and/or CITIZEN KANE in film (May 1, 1941), Welles's focusing on it here carries the force of a resurrection—the summoning up of a forgotten past that implicitly affects our sense of everything that came afterward. Following on the heels of another original screenplay by Welles, THE BIG BRASS RING—written in 1981–82, and published posthumously by Santa Teresa Press in 1987—THE CRADLE WILL ROCK might be said to bear some of the same relationship to its predecessor as THE MAGNIFICENT AMBERSONS has to CITIZEN KANE: after a flamboyant and fearless speculation about corruption, a modest and highly self-critical reflection on the brashness of innocence, tinged with sweetness and nostalgia.

Significantly, *The Cradle Will Rock* was by far the most "directorless" of Welles's stage productions, and in order to ferret out the overall meaning it had in a career that is known mainly for its individuality, it becomes necessary to arrive at an understanding of the overall political and social context in which Welles flourished during the late Depression. As

Michael Denning has argued in an essay that has direct bearing on this issue, "If the Mercury project is representative of the popular front, their productions may be read as allegories of their contradictory populism, a populism worth reexamining in the midst of our own debates over the politics of that contemporary embrace of the popular which has been called postmodernism."[1]

For Denning, the premiere of *The Cradle Will Rock* constituted the first of two events "that prevented the Mercury from becoming merely an avant-garde theater group, from being a radicalism of special effects"— the other event being "the panic caused by the radio broadcast of *The War of the Worlds*" the following year. "The evening [of the *Cradle* premiere] marked the end of Welles's and Houseman's connection to the Federal Theatre; and its notoriety launched the Mercury Theatre that fall. And it served as an emblem of what Houseman and Welles meant as a people's theater, which was less an ideological theater—though despite Houseman's latter-day disclaimers, they shared what Gramsci would call the 'common sense' of the popular front—than a theater marked by a new and wider audience." As Blitzstein himself noted at the time, in a piece written for the *Daily Worker*, "*The Cradle Will Rock* is about unions, but only incidentally about unions. What I really wanted to talk about was the middle class." For all its trappings as a proletarian labor opera, *The Cradle*, which Blitzstein dedicated to Bertolt Brecht, was specifically conceived as a Marxist work that addressed itself to the bourgeoisie.

Furthermore, if we agree with Denning that ultimately, the "Mercury went from an experiment in people's theater to a trademark for a star," the brief period covered in the CRADLE screenplay might be said to be the period when the ambiguities of that contradictory evolution were most apparent—ambiguities that, judging from the screenplay, weren't entirely lost on Welles himself. One thing, for example, that clearly distinguished the Welles-Houseman projects for the Federal Theater—and which serves to account for the fact that they succeeded in forging more productions through the WPA bureaucracy than all the other theater groups—was the fact that they illegally drew funds from Welles's lucrative career during this period as an anonymous radio actor. (It could be argued, indeed, that part of the scandal of Welles's iconoclasm throughout much of his career—encompassing not only the period covered in CRADLE, but such later maverick film productions as OTHELLO, DON QUIXOTE, and THE DEEP—was his willingness to subsidize substantial portions of his own work.) Such details as the political ambivalences of Orson and Virginia about their upper-class habits and attitudes, Orson's reference to his uncollected WPA salary (which was actually $23.86), and his changing an effect in *Dr. Faustus* with the use of a mirror in order to make room for Blitzstein's rehearsal piano, should all be seen in light of the particular conflicts and negotiations provoked by *The Cradle* between Welles's political and entrepreneurial drives.

For conceptual insights into what sort of film Welles wanted to make from his script, Welles's young friend Jim Steinmeyer—a magician he met in the early 80s, saw on the average of once a week and discussed THE CRADLE WILL ROCK with at length—has been especially helpful. About a year and a half prior to the CRADLE script, Welles had already discussed with Steinmeyer a possible film project about magic shows at the turn of the century, and their common interest in magic proved to have more relevance to certain aspects of CRADLE than might first seem apparent. As Steinmeyer put it to me, Welles wanted to present himself in the film as a magician on Broadway.

Take, for instance, the backstage and behind-the-scenes basement glimpses of Christopher Marlowe's *The Tragical History of Dr. Faustus* that are witnessed by Marc Blitzstein towards the beginning. Welles recalled *Dr. Faustus* to Steinmeyer as an "all black-art show," a production whose magical effects were centered on lights and curtains. Discussing with Steinmeyer the relationship between events on the stage and events under the stage, Welles wanted to convey the impression that the under-the-stage operations "explained" the onstage magic without its actually doing so. He didn't feel, moreover, that he had to represent the original *Faustus* production faithfully. In the original, there was a scene featuring "The Seven Deadly Sins" that consisted of Bil Baird's puppets and floating objects, including a pig, that were moved around invisibly by stagehands dressed in black. Although a pig played a minor role in this scene, it wasn't a pig that was big enough for an actor to ride. For the very elaborate, "borderline impossible" floating pig trick in the movie—which

Welles wanted to shoot in Rome for economic reasons, and which was designed and built by John Gaughan—a number of shifting principles were
involved. Steinmeyer declined to go into further details about this (too
many of the principles are currently in use by other magicians), but
stressed that "black art" wasn't involved: the trick would have been performed in bright light.

Steinmeyer recalls Welles saying that the script remained the most important aspect of the film to him; theoretically it could have been directed
by someone else. The most important thing about the casting for him was
getting actors who looked like the original people. (Some of the actors he
contemplated using at various points were David Steinberg as Marc
Blitzstein, Amy Irving as Virginia, Jackie Mason as Moishe the cab driver,
and David Ogden Stiers as John Houseman; Stiers having studied with
Houseman and observed him first-hand was a particular incentive.)

Entertaining some doubts about how Blitzstein's *Cradle* might play for
a contemporary audience, Welles lent an audiocassette of the opera to
Steinmeyer; when his friend reported back that he didn't like it much,
Welles sadly agreed that the play was dated and said that he would endeavor (in Steinmeyer's words) "to write circles around it."

In the August 30 issue of *Variety*, Todd McCarthy reported that production manager Tom Shaw was "lining up locations and crew for a mod-
erately budgeted production" that would require ten weeks of shooting,
with nine weeks in Los Angeles for interiors and another week of second-
unit work in New York. John Landis and George Folsey, Jr. were slated
as executive producers and Michael and Kathy Fitzgerald, assisted by
Prince Alessandro Tasca di Cuto, were announced as "line" producers.
Ted Pedas's Circle Theaters—an eight-screen movie theater chain in the
Washington, D.C. area—were cited as the source of financing, and Mc-
Carthy added that English actor Rupert Everett was cast in the part of the
young Welles.

According to Tasca, the initial budget was $6 million, and the shooting
locations and facilities that had been pre-figured by the fall—while Welles
worked on revising his script in October and November—included a still
wider range of possibilities: one theater south of Long Beach and two theater interiors in Rome, Italy (one of them a cinema called the Olympico);

exterior locations in Staten Island and Hoboken as well as downtown Los Angeles; possible studio work in Los Angeles (without union crews) and/or Utah; and studio work for the film's country house interiors in Rome. The film would be shot on color negative (as a commercial safeguard) but processed in black and white.

But by the end of the year, the expected financing failed to materialize; and what began as a hopeful postponement eventually became a regretful cancellation a few months before Welles's death on October 10, 1985—even after the budget had been reduced to $3 million and various European investors had been sought. (Another story in *Variety* dated May 31, 1985, and filed from Munich reported that the film, now allegedly called LET THE CRADLE ROCK, "may begin within a year's time," with Hans Brockmann of Anthea Films co-producing with Michael Fitzgerald, and shooting to take place entirely in Europe.)

When Welles, in one of his last-ditch efforts to save the project, invited Steven Spielberg and his then-wife Amy Irving (tentatively cast as Virginia Nicolson Welles) to lunch at Ma Maison, there might have still been some cause for hope. Spielberg, after all, had recently spent $55,000 at an auction for the Rosebud sled in CITIZEN KANE, and according to Welles biographer Frank Brady, Spielberg's INDIANA JONES AND THE TEMPLE OF DOOM had even more recently grossed nearly $10 million in a single day. Perhaps Welles assumed that even if Spielberg didn't want to invest in THE CRADLE WILL ROCK himself, he could lend a helping hand in other ways simply by picking up a phone; surely he had the clout to get someone to invest $5 or $6 million in what would have been the first Hollywood studio film by Welles in a quarter of a century, ever since TOUCH OF EVIL. But as Welles discovered to his regret, Spielberg didn't even offer to pay for the lunch. (This story, incidentally, has been confirmed by Welles's daughter Beatrice, to whom Welles recounted it later the same evening, in Las Vegas.)

Other friends or acquaintances in the industry were scarcely any more helpful. When Warren Beatty invited Welles to lunch at the same restaurant, asking him to bring the CRADLE script with him, he insisted on reading the script straight through at the table while Welles sat waiting for him, then offered the suggestion that Welles shoot present-day interviews with surviving real-life participants in the original events—in short, imitate Beatty's own procedure in REDS. . . . A couple of studio reports that I've read on the CRADLE script seem characteristic: both readers complain that the script assumes an interest in Welles's early life that they didn't happen to share.

Far from anything like a settling of old accounts—a frequent motivation for showbiz autobiographies—Welles's look back at his own youth is full of generosity towards others and more than a few skeptical notions about his earlier self, including his marital infidelities and his sexual double standard. Significantly, Virginia Nicolson both read and approved the screenplay during the preproduction, and even Welles's old enemy John Houseman—who read it after Welles's death and not long before his own—commented favorably on its overall fairness and accuracy.

It should be stressed, however, that Welles felt free to adopt a certain poetic license when it came to handling a few specific historical events, as well as some personal ones. A more precise chronology reveals some of the alterations:

Spring 1936: Blitzstein writes *The Cradle Will Rock.*
Fall 1936: Blitzstein meets Welles backstage during the run of the latter's production of *Horse Eats Hat* to discuss Welles directing *The Cradle* for the Actor's Repertory Company. (Soon afterwards, the project is put aside due to lack of funds.)
January 8, 1937: *Dr. Faustus* opens.
March 1937: Houseman and Welles decide to produce *The Cradle* at the Maxine Elliott Theater for Project #891 and rehearsals begin.
May 9, 1937: *Dr. Faustus* closes.
May 23, 1937: John D. Rockefeller dies.
May 30, 1937: Ten Republic Steel strikers are killed by the Chicago police.
June 1937: Technical rehearsals on *The Cradle* begin, despite massive budget cuts in the New York Theatre Project.
June 12, 1937: The production of *The Cradle* is prohibited by government order.
June 14, 1937: Final dress rehearsal for hundreds of invited guests.
June 15, 1937: A dozen uniformed guards take over the Maxine Elliott Theatre.

June 16, 1937: The play is performed at the Venice Theatre.
December 1938: Texas Representative Martin Dies asks Hallie Flanagan, head of the Federal Theatre, if "this Marlowe" is "a Communist."

Not all of Welles's characters in the script can be verified by other accounts of the period, so it seems possible that a few of them—including Solly Pruett, Moishe the cab driver, and Mayzie Katz, among others—are either fictionalized composites or pure inventions. (We have it on good authority, however, that Mrs. J. Sargeant Cram "really existed," as Welles's narration insists.) There's also a likely telescoping of some of Welles's future interests in Hollywood and presidential politics in the final dialogue with Virginia.

Perhaps the most telling calculated departure from history in the script is the name of the theater where the *Cradle* premiered, which was actually called the Venice rather than the Seville. (Subsequently, the same theater was renamed the New Century, then the 57th Street.) In fact, Welles gravitated between calling the theater the Venice and the Seville in separate drafts of the script; Tasca has a script dated November 1984 which calls the theater the Venice, but his call-sheet for the production lists it as the Seville. Like the question of whether Blake Pellerin or Kim Meneker murdered the blind beggar at the end of THE BIG BRASS RING, Welles's uncertainty about this matter, probably based on his autobiographical associations with both cities, evidently carried some potency for him; as his companion and collaborator Oja Kodar pointed out to me when I brought this matter up, "Orson sometimes liked to invent his own superstitions." (A line from movie director Jake Hannaford in the script of Welles's still-unreleased THE OTHER SIDE OF THE WIND: "Seville. That's one of the great places. Venice, Ankorvat, the God-damned Pyramids—they're all so many used-up movie sets.")

Negotiating the complex truces between fiction and nonfiction is a daunting task throughout Welles's work, largely because the CRADLE screenplay is far from being the first time that he works with a fictional or non-fictional character named Orson Welles. Throughout his radio career, for instance, one finds him sharing the same narrative space as his fictional characters. In his radio version of *Huckleberry Finn* (broadcast on March 17, 1940), there are extended dialogues between "Huck Finn"

(Jackie Cooper) and "Mr. Welles"; in his own controversial radio play *His Honor the Mayor* (broadcast on April 6, 1941), where he functions as narrator, he remarks at one point of his hero Bill Knaggs (Ray Collins), the mayor of a town near the Mexican border, "Believe me, I'm not campaigning for Knaggs's re-election. He's a friend of mine, but I don't want to get mixed up in municipal politics, particularly in a town that's almost 2,000 miles away from my own." In 1944, on the variety show *Orson Welles Almanac,* there are even many times when he converses at length with the Disney character Jiminy Cricket.

After the triumphant premiere of Blitzstein's *Cradle,* the show reopened at the Venice in the same impromptu form two days later, where it played through July 1st. During the same period, it was given an extra Sunday performance at an amusement park in Bethlehem, Pennsylvania and a performance in Uncasville, New York, before touring the steel districts of Pennsylvania and Ohio. On June 27, New York radio station WEVD—named after the socialist hero Eugene V. Debs—broadcast it. On December 5, the show was revived in a new "oratorio version" at the Mercury Theatre (formerly the Comedy Theatre, on 110 West 41st Street) on Sunday nights, utilizing the *Caesar* set, two rows of chairs, a reduced chorus of twelve, and Blitzstein himself resuming his original role at the piano. When Random House published the text of the play the following year, Welles began his Preface by saying, "I started producing Marc Blitzstein's music drama the minute it was written almost two years ago, and I have been producing it almost incessantly ever since."

Welles and Blitzstein collaborated on many subsequent occasions over the next two decades, especially during the late 30s. Five months after the *Cradle* opened, Welles's next stage production, *Caesar,* featured music by Blitzstein; the composer performed the same role on Welles's production of *Danton's Death* a year later, and also did the music for the Mercury Text Records of *Julius Caesar* and *Twelfth Night* released in 1939. On February 8, 1938, Welles hosted a benefit concert for *New Masses,* during which Blitzstein's half-hour "song play" *I've Got the Tune,* dedicated to Welles, received its stage premiere (with Count Basie performing in one section), and Welles arranged for the piece to be performed at the Mercury on two Sundays later the same month. In mid-July, Blitzstein played the part of a French barber in the film shot by Welles for his production of the stage farce *Too Much Johnson*. Eight years later, when Blitzstein's *Airborne Symphony*, a cantata for male voices, premiered at the New York City Center, Welles served as the narrator. And ten years after that, in 1956, again at the New York City Center, Blitzstein was in charge of the music for Welles's last American stage production, *King Lear*, and played the harpsichord during its run.[2]

Indeed, considering the symbiotic and reciprocal nature of this friendship over the years, it might not be too fanciful to consider Blitzstein's character as a sort of alter-ego of Welles in the script. (In this respect, Welles as scriptwriter may have been only returning the compliment. Welles was originally cast by Blitzstein as the composer, Mr. Musiker, in the autobiographical *I've Got the Tune* for its CBS radio premiere in October 1937, and Blitzstein wound up taking over the part himself only after Welles proved to be too busy rehearsing *Caesar*.) For all the political differences between these characters, one could argue that Blitzstein not only influenced Welles, but eventually, in certain respects, came to stand for a significant part of his artistic persona—his political conscience and consciousness—over the remainder of his career.

In "The Director as Actor," a paper delivered by James Naremore at a Welles conference in Venice, Italy in October 1991, there is a passage that pinpoints precisely the dual artistic persona that I have in mind:

> . . . I would argue that Welles's major accomplishment as both an actor and director was his ability to synthesize two apparently contradictory forms of theatricality: On the one hand, he was a brilliant practitioner of what John Houseman called "magical effect," and he was clearly indebted to a romantic or gothic tradition of Shakespearian drama, grand opera, and stage illusionism; on the other hand, he was also a didactic, somewhat Brechtian storyteller whose cultural politics were shaped during the period of the Popular Front, and whose technique was visibly rhetorical, strongly dependent on direct address. The tension between these extremes—in other words, the tension between Welles as conjurer and Welles as narrator—accounts for many of the special qualities of his films in general.

Naremore goes on to cite F FOR FAKE—where Welles "appears as a narrator-magician, and where he behaves like a cross between a pedagogue and a con man"—as a prime example of this duality. Very much the same duality is present at the first meeting between Blitzstein and Welles—a Brechtian pedagogue and a magician on Broadway—in THE CRADLE WILL ROCK, defining a kind of friendly ideological tension that continues throughout the script. A similar friendship of symbiotic opposites is defined between Welles and Jack Carter, and it's worth adding that Welles actually did replace Carter in black face in the voodoo *Macbeth* during at least part of its run in Indianapolis in 1936. But if Carter literally played Mephistophilis to Welles's Faust, and if, according to Houseman, Welles himself was also Mephistophilis to his own Faust, it's less certain in the friendship between Welles and Blitzstein precisely who was Faust and who was Mephistophilis. Each clearly inspired the other to do things he never would have undertaken otherwise, and this screenplay shines with the fond memory of what happened when their mutual inspiration took the world by storm.

Notes

1. "Towards a People's Theater: The Cultural Politics of the Mercury Theatre," *Persistence of Vision* no. 7, 1989.
2. See Eric A. Gordon's biography *Mark the Music: The Life and Work of Marc Blitzstein* (New York: St. Martin's Press, 1989), for a comprehensive account of Blitzstein's career.

> —From THE CRADLE WILL ROCK: *An Original Screenplay* by Orson Welles (Santa Barbara: Santa Teresa Press, 1994)

19

Orson Welles in the U.S.

An Exchange with Bill Krohn

*This chapter—the longest in the book, and in some ways my favorite—was orig-
inally written for the French quarterly* Trafic, *and in fact was the first thing I ever
wrote specifically for that magazine. The late Serge Daney (1942–1994)—whom
I'd known since his stint as editor of* Cahiers du cinéma, *when he'd gotten me
to serve briefly as its New York correspondent (after Bill Krohn had shifted from
that post to the same magazine's Los Angeles correspondent)—died of AIDS not
longer after launching* Trafic, *and by my own choice, my first contribution, a
memoir about working for Jacques Tati (see "The Death of Hulot" in my collection* Placing Movies), *was something I'd already written for and published in*
Sight and Sound. *My second contribution was my brief introduction to Orson
Welles's "Memo to Universal" (see note 1 in the introduction), an "outtake" from*
This Is Orson Welles *that had been accepted by Serge's coeditors (Raymond Bel-
lour, Jean-Claude Biette, Sylvie Pierre, and Patrice Rollet) during Serge's illness.*

*Early the next year, at the Rotterdam film festival, Sylvie proposed that I write
something for the journal about Welles. Recalling Bill Krohn's contribution to the
first issue of* Trafic *("Letter d'un ami américain,"* Trafic, *no. 1 [Winter 1991:
121–126]), I thought that our respective recent work on* This Is Orson Welles
and IT'S ALL TRUE *could form the basis of an exchange of letters, and was delighted when Sylvie and Bill both agreed to the idea. And even though it took a
little over eight months for Bill to respond to my first letter, I found it well worth
the wait.*

Bill had previously come to my rescue by reviewing the hasty French transla-

tion of This Is Orson Welles *in the* Cahiers. *He explained in his review that my only serious disagreement with Bogdanovich, which I'd mentioned in a carefully written footnote, was about Peter's suppression or alteration of a few passages from his interviews with Welles that didn't conform to his standards of politesse or political correctness (such as Welles using the word "Negro," as practically everyone else was doing, in 1969 — an example I'm citing now, but couldn't mention then — as well as a few rude comments about Israel and other directors and actors that I hated losing). The careless French translation, to my horror, attributed all these changes to me rather than to Bogdanovich, so I was deeply indebted to Bill for setting the record straight.*

The very title of this translation, I should add — Moi, Orson Welles *— is lamentable, suggesting a form of egotism that's not at all present in* This Is Orson Welles, *derived from the way Welles introduced himself on radio. Retaining this title is one of the battles I'm happiest about having won; at one point Peter wanted to call it* Around the World with Orson Welles, *which I argued against by maintaining that Mexico, the U.S., and two European capitals didn't constitute the world. On the other hand, while going through a carton of memorabilia, Oja once showed me Welles's passport from when he was around sixteen, and I was gratified to discover that they proved his claims about having been a world traveler by that age were not at all exaggerated. If, indeed, he and Peter had been able to follow through on the same pattern while conducting the interviews for this book, the title would have made perfect sense.*

The passage I quote from Cy Endfield in my first letter is taken from the original published version of my "Pages from the Endfield File" in the November–December 1993 issue of Film Comment. *When I revised and updated this piece for* Movies as Politics, *I omitted most of the extended material about Welles because it digressed from Endfield's own story, but for anyone researching this period in Welles's career, I think it's well worth consulting.*

I suspect that "the article from the 1940s" Bill alludes to in his letter (which he hasn't read) that "describe[s] the difference between [Welles's] conception and Eisenstein's" is most likely Welles's May 25, 1945, column for the New York Post *—a fascinating comparative look at two then-current biopics,* WILSON *and* IVAN THE TERRIBLE. *If so, Bill gives a somewhat faulty description, understandable because it's a secondhand account. What Welles is comparing is Russian and Hollywood filmmaking: "Because of the inferiority of Russian film stock, lenses* *and other equipment, the camera must assert itself by what it selects, and by the manner of selection. The Hollywood camera has a merchant's eye and spends its time lovingly evaluating texture, the screen being filled as a window is dressed in a swank department store." (James Naremore, incidentally, not only discusses this column at length in* The Magic World of Orson Welles *but also makes it the point of departure for his provocative monograph on Vincente Minnelli.)*

Along with the following chapter, this article was read by Oja Kodar years after it was published, when I gave her a copy (unlike chapters 8, 10, and 18, which were all vetted by her prior to publication). I should note for the record that she subsequently confirmed my hypothesis that the disastrous misappropriation of footage from Welles's Italian TV documentary series NELLA TERRA DI DON CHISCIOTTE *in Jesus Franco's edit of* DON QUIXOTE *essentially filled the gap left by the omitted Patty McCormack material—which provided the film's original narrative framework but which, based on her own sense of Welles's subsequent plans for the film, she didn't allow Franco to use. Unfortunately, it appears that the few other Welles scholars who've written about his* QUIXOTE *in English have ignored this issue and assumed, like Franco, that* IN THE LAND OF DON QUIXOTE *and* DON QUIXOTE *belong together—when in fact the former was hackwork taken on by Welles to finance and otherwise facilitate the production of the latter. (See the final chapter in this book for more details.)*

■

October 1, 1993

Dear Bill,

I estimate it's been about two years since you wrote Serge a letter for the first issue of *Trafic,* the last part of which was concerned with several anticipated developments concerning "the invisible Orson Welles." By 1992, you correctly predicted, versions of DON QUIXOTE and a "restored" OTHELLO would be appearing, and the interviews with Welles conducted by Peter Bogdanovich in 1969 and 1970, which I had been editing since the late 1980s, would be published. You were also looking forward to the publication of Welles's unrealized script for THE CRADLE WILL ROCK, written a year before his death, and I'm happy to report that while that publication has been twice delayed for financial reasons, it should finally be appearing next year, fall 1994, if all goes well. And while your hopes that THE MERCHANT OF VENICE might finally surface haven't yet been fulfilled, and our prospects for seeing THE OTHER SIDE OF THE WIND or THE DEEP will continue to look dim until (or, rather, unless) some wealthy philanthropist can come up with the money to lure them out of hiding, there is the exciting news that the documentary on IT'S ALL TRUE started by Richard Wilson in the 1980s, including most of the newly discovered Fortaleza footage, is finally in the process of being completed by you and a few others; in fact, I look forward to seeing a press show in Chicago within a fortnight, shortly after it premieres at the New York film festival.

So generally speaking, the windfall of Wellesiana that you evoked in your letter is genuinely coming to light. But the consequences of this windfall remain somewhat ambiguous, especially in an American context—which is to say that none of these works is appearing in a neutral climate. More specifically, this is the curious form of hostility shown by certain American intellectuals towards Welles, a phenomenon that Welles himself commented on to Peter Bogdanovich: "Basically I've always been completely at odds with the true intellectual establishment. I despise it, and they suspect and despise me." Considering the degree to which American academics now often take sides with the Hollywood studios and against Welles, extolling not only "the classical Hollywood cinema" (scarcely a neutral term in this context) but also the so-called "genius of the system," it seems clear that what we're facing once again, as you pointed out, is one institution (academic film study) paying homage to another (the studio system) over the body of an artist.

One indication of this is the publication of *This Is Orson Welles*, the Welles-Bogdanovich interviews, in the U.S. one year ago, which had all the status of a non-event. In the same issue of the *New York Times Book Review* that carried lengthy front-page reviews of the latest biographies of Yves Montand and David O. Selznick, the book received a flippant one-paragraph notice from a reviewer who, to all appearances, never got further than Peter's introduction, and devoted 95% of his space to the book's inception as it's recounted there: "Like so many Wellesian projects . . . this one had a long and fitful history. It tottered through Welles's lavishly documented decline even as Mr. Bogdanovich went on to direct such films as THE LAST PICTURE SHOW and PAPER MOON." In short, every effort made in the book's 533 pages to counter the myth of Welles's decline counted for so little that the reviewer was apparently unaware that such an effort had even been made. All in all, the book received so little attention that I was hardly surprised when, at the Rotterdam film festival last winter, a Portuguese friend asked me about the book—having read about its publication in an Italian newspaper—while one of New York's leading film programmers was completely unaware of its existence. So it's hardly surprising that fewer than 7,000 copies of the hardcover edition have been sold. On the other hand, I expect the paperback edition, due out this month, to sell much better, and while I don't know the sales figures for any of the European editions, it's already been apparent that the English and French reviews of the book, including yours in the *Cahiers*, have generally been more serious. (The best edition of all, I should add, is the just-published Italian translation brought out by Baldi & Castoldi—if only because they, unlike the others, were eager to incorporate all the factual corrections I've been able to gather from diverse sources over the past year.)

The conclusion is inescapable: in a climate where works are literally equated with markets, most of the works of Orson Welles continue to be not only invisible in the American marketplace, but non-existent; so a work by Welles about his own work necessarily has to follow the same law of non-presence, because who wants to read about works not currently showing? Actually, this ties in with your reference to Paramount's commercially successful fiftieth anniversary rerelease of CITIZEN KANE in 1991, in prints that were so overlit (by Robert Wise, as you noted) that Joseph Cotten's face became incorrectly recognizable in the projection room sequence. A related problem, one should add, was that the newsreel was made to look less grainy than it did in the original prints. These are relatively small matters, perhaps, but they seem to me highly symptomatic of a much wider problem when it comes to the understanding of Welles in the U.S. today. This is a period, after all, when the latest Hollywood releases are automatically guaranteed free publicity (usually disguised as journalism) on not only every TV and radio network, but on virtually every cable channel and in every newspaper and newsmagazine, simply as a matter of course—a privilege not extended to independent distributors who can't afford junkets or TV interviews. Insofar as KANE itself was distributed in 1941 as an independent film that showed only in independent theaters—and, due to either pressure or feared pressure from the Hearst press, was not booked by any of the chains—I think it would be fair to conclude that if KANE were released in the same conditions in 1991, it would have suffered a similar fate at the box office. (How fortunate that your IT'S ALL TRUE is being distributed by Paramount!)

The crucial point to be made here, I think, is that CITIZEN KANE in 1991 was regarded as a Hollywood feature, and the "timing" or lighting of the print by Wise was done accordingly. But half a century earlier, what KANE mainly represented in the American cinema was an independent feature that made brilliant use of Hollywood studio facilities and some Hollywood conventions—which is hardly the same thing. In my opinion, the crucial ideological turning point in this change in public perception was Pauline Kael's essay "Raising KANE," originally published in *The New Yorker* thirty years after the film's release. Explicitly conceived as a polemical riposte to *la politique des auteurs* as it was then understood in the U.S., popularized and somewhat modified by Andrew Sarris as "the auteur theory," Kael's essay set out to prove that the most important auteur of KANE was not Welles but Herman J. Mankiewicz. And despite the fact that her main piece of dubious evidence to support this contention—that the script of KANE was almost exclusively the work of Mankiewicz—was later definitively disproved, by Robert L. Carringer and many others, the principal *subtext* of her argument—that KANE belonged in the mainstream of Hollywood cinema (specifically as a culmination of the Hollywood "newspaper comedies" of the 1930s), a cinema that she and the American film industry alike regarded as a collaborative art—was eventually accepted by the public at large. Significantly, this subtext is also the principal thesis of Carringer's *The Making of CITIZEN KANE* (1985), a book now commonly regarded in this country as the standard, authoritative work on the film (along with the published script, to which Kael's essay serves as the preface). And once this thesis became generally accepted, KANE was safe to become an unthreatening and much beloved Hollywood classic, a mainstream fetish object on the order of CASABLANCA—no longer a challenge or alternative to

Hollywood but, on the contrary, a vindication of Hollywood, a virtual proof that disparate talents such as Welles, Mankiewicz, Gregg Toland, and others could be brought together to yield a single, satisfying, and ultimately relatively impersonal industrial product.

Of course, in order for a classic to become "timeless," it has to be liberated from history and ideology, which is characteristic not only of the sort of treatment KANE gets from mainstream critics, but also what one finds in the fourth edition of David Bordwell and Kristin Thompson's *Film Art: An Introduction,* currently a standard classroom text. Over the course of 25 pages about the film, devoted to narrative form and style, the relation of KANE to William Randolph Hearst is only alluded to, not explored, in two short sentences about what 1941 spectators would have been looking for—the implication clearly being that such a relation needn't concern us today—while the issue of ideology, broached only under "notes and queries" as "the ideology of form," is treated even more cursorily. From this standpoint, Laura Mulvey's recent monograph on CITIZEN KANE in the "BFI Film Classics" series, arguing that "quite beyond Bazin's conception of the 'democratic' nature of deep focus, the film is juggling with American myth, politics, and the collective psyche," is especially welcome, persuasively tracing much of the film's meaning and value to Welles's anti-isolationism and anti-fascism before America's entry into the war—a factor that indeed played a major role in all of Welles's film projects apart from AMBERSONS and IT'S ALL TRUE that were most developed during this period: HEART OF DARK-NESS, THE SMILER WITH THE KNIFE, "Mexican Melodrama," and JOURNEY INTO FEAR.

In fact, I believe that the avoidance of ideological meaning has direct bearing on the so-called "restorations" of both OTHELLO and DON QUIXOTE, on Carringer's new book on AMBERSONS, and, perhaps most relevantly of all, on the work that you're currently engaged in—defining both what IT'S ALL TRUE might have been and what the public perception (or, rather, misperception) of this project did to the remainder of Welles's career. I realize, of course, that all these cases involve separate histories and circumstances, but at the same time I think they all have immediate bearing on the same fundamental issues.

How does one account for the fact that Orson Welles is mainly regarded in the U.S. today as a failed artist? To cite the fact that none of his American features was a commercial success when first released only begins to touch on the problem; far more significant, it seems to me, is the widely held belief that every feature after CITIZEN KANE represents some sort of betrayed promise, a dream deferred or denied. On the other hand, it's likely that in certain contexts financial considerations merge imperceptibly into aesthetic judgments. At the tribute to Welles held at the Directors Guild in Hollywood in November, 1985, not long after his death, which we both attended, you'll recall that Charlton Heston unhesitatingly described Welles as the most gifted director he ever worked for, but then demurred when Bogdanovich, who served as the host for the tribute, described TOUCH OF EVIL (1958), Welles's last Hollywood film, as "a masterpiece." Heston said that he preferred to call it "the best B picture ever made." What he was saying, in effect, was that in America, to make the best B picture ever made means, on the bottom line, to be a failure. On some level, this strikes me as being at the root of the problem that kept Welles from making another Hollywood feature for the three decades of his life that followed TOUCH OF EVIL.

To inquire more deeply into the ideological ramifications of Heston's belief is to ask a question about the difference between French and American responses that ultimately go beyond the issue of Welles as a special or isolated case. In the U.S. no one appears to be very curious about why the French take a different view of Welles, but in the case of Jerry Lewis, the so-called "French taste" has taken on some of the dimensions of a scandal and outrage—a position that manages to overlook the salient fact that Lewis's entire career as a cineaste could never have been launched, much less sustained, if his American popularity during the 1950s hadn't been strong enough to support at the very minimum two Lewis features a year. To my mind, the refusal in America to take Lewis seriously is intimately connected to a reluctance to accept the embarrassing fact that on some level the Lewis persona and all that he represents *is* America: infantilism, retarded adolescence, nouveau riche taste and behavior, sexual hysteria, megalomania, and so on.

It appears that one can only get away with making a comparable sort of equation between America and Welles in the U.S. if one believes that his career basically began and ended with CITIZEN KANE. (One is reminded of the quote from F. Scott Fitzgerald—"There are no second acts in American lives"—that prefaces Eastwood's BIRD.) And I'm sorry to say that Carringer's recent book on THE MAGNIFICENT AMBERSONS, published by the University of California Press, mainly seeks to confirm this hypothesis. Both this book and *This Is Orson Welles* offer reconstructions of Welles's original, 132-minute cut of AMBERSONS, and I should add that Carringer had full access to the RKO files while I had access only to materials relating to a book worked on by Bogdanovich and Welles twenty years ago (some—if not all—of which duplicated Carringer's sources), which gives his work value even when his scholarship is debatable. (I'm especially grateful for his transcription of the full text of the comedy record playing in the background of Welles's original ending, set in a boarding house.) Nevertheless, given these substantial *material* differences between our two projects, it is also worth asking what the theoretical and ideological differences are.

Now that I have the book before me, the answer is plain: Carringer's critical position is an unqualified defense of RKO and just as unambiguous an attack on Welles's position as neurotic and self-destructive. In many ways, his book is the ultimate tribute to Welles's continuing potency as an ideological threat to the status quo of American film culture, the film industry in particular. Clearly, two books of vilification by Charles Higham, Pauline Kael's "Raising KANE," and Carringer's own previous book were not enough to catalog the full range of Welles's character defects, so yet another effort in this direction had to be made.

Carringer's introduction is entitled "Oedipus in Indianapolis," and he accurately summarizes it as follows: "The critical introduction is likely to be controversial. THE MAGNIFICENT AMBERSONS has traditionally been considered a prime instance of the Hollywood system's total disdain for mature artistry and its unrelenting commitment to destruction. To the contrary, I argue that Welles himself must bear the ultimate responsibility for the film's undoing. While it is undeniable that [studio head George] Schaefer's decision to recut THE MAGNIFICENT AMBERSONS was primarily a business judgment, I believe it was a string of question-able judgments and rash actions on Welles's part that predisposed this outcome."

Significantly, the issue of whether Schaefer's business judgment was questionable even from a business standpoint—AMBERSONS, after all, still lost money after being recut—is never raised. (On the other hand, apparently on the basis of a single humorous anecdote, Carringer claims that "Welles liked to depict Schaefer as something of a buffoon"—directly contradicting everything Welles said to me about Schaefer, all of it informed by obvious respect and gratitude, when I interviewed him in Paris about his HEART OF DARKNESS project in 1972.) Carringer's agenda is simply to show how Welles's irrationality and bad decisions—the consequences of his own Oedipal fixations and his unwillingness to work through them—paved the way for disaster: "This is not to say that Welles acted irresponsibly; that he behaved *evasively* would be a more accurate characterization. Regarding each action, a vexatious personal involvement in the material was at play, and this factor overrode Welles's aesthetic judgment." If only Welles could have had Carringer around in the 1940s to force him to face up to his aesthetic obligations, one is made to feel, film history would have been radically different and everyone would have been happy.

Unfortunately, in order to evaluate Welles's aesthetic judgment in such a context, one has to consider Carringer's; and Carringer's—hinging largely on Welles's decision to cast Tim Holt rather than himself as George Minafer, and to keep this character out of the film's final scenes—is so simpleminded and unreflective that it leads one to suspect that his ideal AMBERSONS would be even less interesting than the studio release version. The mere possibility that an uncharismatic, even grating treatment of George's character might have suited Welles's artistic purposes, or that Eugene Morgan (Joseph Cotten) and Aunt Fanny (Agnes Moorehead) might be equally important characters, isn't even acknowledged. (Speaking as someone who regards Welles's highly prissy performance as George in his 1938 radio version of *Ambersons*—included on Carringer's excellent "deluxe" laserdisc edition of the film—to be anything but charismatic, I think the casting of Holt in the film could be defended even on these questionable commercial grounds; but Carringer won't admit that such an argument can be made, so the discussion stops there.) Indeed, by never admitting that artistic and commercial concerns regarding AMBERSONS (both defined very simplistically) could ever be in serious conflict, Carringer bases his own analysis on an identification with Schaefer rather than an identification with Welles—the same bias adopted in his previous book, *The Making of* CITIZEN KANE. Without ever owning up to the fact, his new book is yet another attempt to rationalize the Hollywood studio system in relation to Welles, which means that every executive decision is taken at face value while every artistic decision becomes potentially suspect for "evasiveness." To cite one random example of each: the first preview of AMBERSONS in Pomona is typically deemed "disastrous" without considering the fact that 53 of the 125 "comment cards" filled out were favorable and that some of these were as rapturous as anyone could wish. (These cards were preserved, as you know, by Dick Wilson, and a representative sampling is included in *This Is Orson Welles*.) On the other hand, Welles's "puzzling " failure to direct a stage or film version of *Hamlet* is deemed to be of major significance in pointing out his Oedipal defects, including his "evasiveness." (In the latter discussion, one also encounters some slipshod scholarship: Welles's "first directorial credit on network radio" was not "for a two-part *Hamlet*"—a program directed by Irving Reis—but for a seven-part *Les miserables*. And in his notes to the reconstruction, Carringer completely overlooks Welles's stated reason—given in my 1972 interview in *Film Comment*—for his decision to omit an extended, virtuoso subjective shot of George Minafer exploring the empty Amberson mansion.)

It seems to me that any serious scholarly investigation into the matter of AMBERSONS has to move beyond simple blame and consider a complex of factors much wider (as well as more verifiable) than Welles's attitudes towards his dead parents, Carringer's principal obsession. Obviously, the work on IT'S ALL TRUE that Welles was doing in Brazil during the previews, recutting, and reshooting of AMBERSONS at RKO is of central importance, but Carringer, while arguing that Welles "behaved evasively," is himself so unwilling to address this subject that he can't bring himself to cite the words "IT'S ALL TRUE" once in his book, even in the bibliography. The implications of such a highly selective form of scholarship are embarrassing but inescapable: arguing that AMBERSONS was an "acting out" of Welles's unresolved Oedipus complex, Carringer raises the question of whether he, like so many others, might simply be projecting onto Welles certain Oedipal fixations of his own.

I realize that my own fumbling efforts to defend the original ending of AMBERSONS in *This Is Orson Welles* by alluding to the endings of THE LIFE OF OHARU and GERTRUD—inspired in part by simplistic assumptions about this ending by Carringer and others—are also probably suspect from a historical viewpoint, for no one can truly offer a critique of a sequence one hasn't seen. In this respect, my recent interview with the former writer-director Cy Endfield (best known in France for THE SOUND OF FURY/TRY AND GET ME! and ZULU), who entered the film business as an apprentice working for the Mercury unit at RKO while Welles was away in South America, is highly instructive. For whatever it's worth, Endfield himself defends Welles's original cut of AMBERSONS. It's true that he hasn't seen it for half a century, but at least he was present at all the original previews and many of the deliberations that went into the reshooting and recutting, unlike either Carringer or myself. He even recalls crying out in pain when he heard that the kitchen scene between Agnes Moorehead and Tim Holt—later to become one of the cornerstones of Bazin's theory of deep focus!—was about to be cut, and speculates that his spontaneous display of grief may have even played a role in saving this sequence.

Endfield—a highly skilled magician, with some experience in theater directing, who had already attracted Welles's attention through his card tricks—was hired by Jack Moss, who was left in charge of the Mercury during Welles's absence, in exchange for teaching Moss at least one card trick that would succeed in confounding Welles when he returned from South America. This already tells one a little something about the kind of power plays that were at work in such a complex situation, even among Welles's supposed Mercury allies. Let me quote just a single passage from Endfield's comments about this experience, which leaves one with a very different impression from every other account I've read of how Welles's instructions were being received at the time:

> I sat with Jack Moss most days [in his office]. The poor man was spending his money on me wastefully, because he was not learning very much. He was naturally clumsy, and had no skill or aptitude for the card moves I was showing him. In the meantime, Orson was showing his anxiety in a number of long-distance calls he made to Jack. A telephone with a private line had been installed in Moss's office in the Mercury bungalow that had a number known only to Orson in Brazil. For the first few days that I was with Moss, he had a few discussions with Orson and tried to placate him; then, they had started arguing because there were more changes [in AMBERSONS] than Orson was prepared to acknowledge. After a few days of this, the phone was just allowed to ring and ring, and I conducted many magic lessons when the phone was ringing constantly and uninterruptedly for hours at a time. I saw Jack Moss enter the office carrying 35 and 40-page cables that had arrived from Brazil; he'd riffle through the cables, say, "This is what Orson wants us to do today," and then, without bothering to read them, toss them into the wastebasket.

I cite this passage not to offer any clinching evidence about ultimate blame in the AMBERSONS matter, which Carringer is so eager to have settled, but merely to point to the sort of personal testimony that often gets left out of the more "official" accounts. Needless to say, the surmises that we have to make about the original AMBERSONS are mere child's play next to the deliberations you have to go through in making a documentary about a Welles film that was never even edited, much less brought to a rough cut form. I'd be eager to hear some of your own thoughts about this dilemma, especially now that you're concerned with them on an active and daily basis.

As ever,
Jonathan

June 7, 1994

Dear Jonathan,
Sorry to have been so long replying. As you say, much has happened since you wrote your letter. We both started out years ago in a series of

polemical articles to correct received ideas of Welles, and we seem to be making progress. *This Is Orson Welles* and IT'S ALL TRUE will be more widely read and seen than those articles ever were. Already Richard Combs, writing about F FOR FAKE in the January–February 1994 *Film Comment*, acknowledges the thesis of Welles the independent filmmaker advanced by you in "The Invisible Orson Welles" as a corrective to the idea of Welles the great failure, then proceeds to propose a new theory of the work, with failure of another kind inscribed in it from the start. That article would have been unthinkable a few years ago, when what might be called the vulgar theory of failure was still dominant.

The work on the Welles legacy is going well: Oja is set to co-direct a documentary that will include several of the important fragments; THE DEEP and THE OTHER SIDE OF THE WIND may be finished in the next couple of years, and hope springs eternal where THE MERCHANT OF VENICE is concerned. I don't rule out the possibility that someday we'll see DON QUIXOTE finished properly, when all the pieces of the negative are finally assembled in one place and scholarship and craft replace the rush to release that resulted in the embarrassing version that was shown at Cannes in 1992. And, hopefully the "restored" CHIMES AT MIDNIGHT won't repeat the mistakes of the "restored" OTHELLO—in large part because of the campaign for fidelity to Welles that you started in the pages of the *Chicago Reader* and Todd McCarthy carried on in *Variety*.

I don't know if you've noticed, but we seem to be in an era of salvagers. As the future of cinema looks dimmer, the makers of laserdiscs are scrambling to rescue "directors' cuts" of mutilated films and other lost work from the past to recycle them into our home viewing spaces. Some of this is bogus, motivated by capitalism's "new and improved," or worse: by the video equivalent of the wave of technomania that swept the country when stereo record players were the new fad, and the words "woofer" and "tweeter" were on every hobbyist's lips. On a recent visit to a big video store in L.A. with Marco Müller, I suddenly felt sad at seeing everything from CLIFFHANGER in letterbox format to the director's cut of THE FEARLESS VAMPIRE KILLERS, neatly ranged on shelves in packages where they will be joined shortly by IT'S ALL TRUE and inevitably by the other Welles "phantoms." The museums are replacing theatres. The Centenary looms.

Which is not to say that IT'S ALL TRUE didn't need to be finished. So does THE BIG RED ONE, which promises to be a masterpiece if Sam Fuller is ever allowed to do his four-hour cut. I'm quite sure Susan Ray will find a way to finish WE CAN'T GO HOME AGAIN, which has so many affinities with THE OTHER SIDE OF THE WIND. And the work on Welles must go on. But how these things are written about is as important as the work of reconstruction, restoration, and "finishing" itself, and that's where the issues you raise are still important.

I'm grateful that this interrupted correspondence of ours gives me a chance to look back at Welles's first great unfinished work and draw some conclusions. Very little has appeared in the press yet about IT'S ALL TRUE, the film. For the most part, as I expected and rather hoped, reviewers have retold the story we told in the documentary, which is essentially the Richard Wilson–Catherine Benamou version of what happened to Welles in Brazil, the reasons for the film not being finished, and so forth. That serves the first purpose: getting our version of these events out, to counteract the self-serving myth created by the RKO publicity department and recycled by the likes of Charles Higham. Now what about the film Welles was making down there, and the part of it that has survived? As with *This Is Orson Welles,* where reviewers mostly wrote about the preface rather than the book, the film is being swallowed up by the tale of its long finishing, which at least has a happy ending. But the film is much more subversive than its preface.

"Four Men on a Raft," the only part of IT'S ALL TRUE that could be finished, is still a political film—or at least it will be when it opens in Brazil tomorrow, where the descendants of the *jangadeiros* Welles filmed are worse off than their ancestors fifty years ago. Then, they were poor; today, pushed off the beach into *favelas* by real estate developers and faced with industrial fishing and worse—new forms called predatory fishing that are exhausting their traditional fishing grounds—they see their very way of life threatened with extinction. Yet, when four men very much like the ones you see in the film sailed on a *jangada* from a village near Fortaleza to Rio in April–May–June of 1993, while we were working on the editing of the film, the President of Brazil wouldn't even meet with them to hear their grievances. When I spoke to him, Welles was very concerned about how films date; he would be happy to know that "Four Men on a Raft" is one of the few militant films that escapes Daney's Law: that good militant films only arrive when they are no longer needed. This one seems to have arrived just in the nick of time.

I hope there will be a debate in Brazil, and that we will be allowed to add our two cents to the *jangadeiros'* side. An American journalist working on the story of the 1993 voyage told me the attitude of the Brazilian right: that these people, and their way of fishing, are anachronisms and that Brazil has enough problems without trying to preserve a way of life 400 years old. They're not wrong about their facts, and the facts are worth remembering. Actually, we interviewed the descendants of the *jangadeiros* in Fortaleza (with the help of a simultrans system *bricolé* by our wonderful sound man, Jean-Pierre Duret) without realizing who they really were. And yet all the pieces of the puzzle were in plain view: an invisible people living within the boundaries of a large city, linked by ties of blood and craft, eking out a living as maids or construction workers, but still apart from the larger society, in danger of forgetting their cultural traditions. It was only when Catherine Benamou and I sat down to a surprisingly tasty dinner in a Rio McDonald's with Aloysio Pinto, brother of Fernando Pinto, the businessman who financed the 1941 voyage, that the pieces came together.

"The people you interviewed in the Northeast are Indians," said Aloysio, an ethnomusicologist who has spent a lifetime recording their songs and dances. "The raft they sailed on, the hammock in which the boy is buried, are Indian inventions, which existed in the same form before the Portuguese arrived in Brazil." In fact, the *jangadeiros* are examples of the *caboclo* culture that sprang from the intermingling of the indigenous tribes with black slaves, although the aridity of the Northeast, as Aloysio explained to us, kept the Indian bloodlines purer, because the colonists there were too poor to be able to afford many slaves. The crew of the raft that sailed in 1941 were two black men, Tatá and Manuel Preto ("The Black"), led by two men who look to me like full-blooded Indians, Jeronimo and Jacaré—the São Pedro symbolizes *cabo-*

clo culture, for anyone who is attentive to the images of Welles's film. But everything about that raft was already a symbol.

What we have said to the Brazilian journalists we've met here is that the *jangadeiros* of Fortaleza were anachronisms when Welles met them in 1942, and that was certainly the reason he filmed them. He had just filmed AMBERSONS, the story of a world that disappeared before he was born, and he was in the midst of filming the people's Carnival in Praça Onze, a public square that had been demolished by the government to make way for Getulio Vargas Boulevard, which he was therefore obliged to reconstruct in a studio for the filming of "The Story of the Samba." Welles was not a radical, even though there were radical writers around him in Brazil; he was a man of many nostalgias, whose greatest film, made a quarter of a century later, is a film of nostalgia and regret at the passing of the "merry old England" of Falstaff. DON QUIXOTE, he told me, had taken so long to finish that it could not be finished as a film about the Eternal Spain, but only as a meditation on its disappearance. Maybe that's what he was really waiting for.

Today, we were told by our friends in Fortaleza that the Castelo Encantado *favela* where many of the *jangadeiros* live is slated for demolition to make way for the Avenue of the Jangadeiros, a name which will have a certain allure for tourists coming to this city where every imaginable adjunct of their leisure activities, from the beach towels at our hotel to the annual beer festival, is decorated by the triangular sail of the *jangada*. Welles would certainly have appreciated the irony of real heroes still living, invisible and in danger of annihilation because of their invisibility, in a town where their rafts have become the totem of tourism, like his Don Quixote and Sancho Panza riding past a shop window displaying Don Quixote knick-knacks and even beer bottles bearing their likenesses.

What his film makes visible is the *jangadeiros* themselves, and their way of life. What his film says, and what we have said every time we've spoken to the Brazilian press, is that that way of life has value precisely because it is an anachronism, founded on a harmonious relationship with the natural world that we have lost. Today, the *jangadeiros* and their allies, like the late Chico Mendes and his allies, use ecological arguments: whereas the predatory fishermen who dive for lobsters (drugged on marijuana because their employers don't give them wet-suits to protect them against the cold) take everything including the young, the *jangadeiros* have always known what to take and what to leave so that the species can continue to propagate. Harmonious rela-tions of man with Nature, and, I might add, of man with man. The mar-ginal or artisanal fishermen of every stripe along the Atlantic Coast have in their heads a complex webwork dividing up the sea into territo-ries where each fisherman has the right to fish. The industrial fishing boats and the predators ignore this web, which is invisible because it is woven of oral traditions, but that doesn't mean that it doesn't exist.

Of course, Welles doesn't show that. His way of expressing the idea of the collectivity is through what our editor Ed Marx calls "conver-gence": the community converging in the cove where the drowned boy has washed up, or at the top of the hill where he is buried; the "orches-tra with a moving conductor" (Ed's expression again) of the political debate, where the camera hops around from one speaker to another as each in turn becomes the center of a little group of listeners, who are scattered among the drying sails until a larger group coalesces, first around Jacaré's double, then around Tatá, Jeronimo and Manuel Preto as they decide abruptly to sail to Rio and set off to Francisca's hut to tell her, followed by the entire community; *and* in the last scene, the fleet of vessels converging on the lone *jangada* sailing into Rio Harbor. A sym-phonic conception of montage, based on the idea of the whole rather than the fragment—the terms Welles used, Catherine tells me, in an ar-ticle from the 1940s that I haven't read, to describe the difference be-tween his conception of cinema and Eisenstein's.

Welles also doesn't show the other network of social relations that bound the *jangadeiros* to the bourgeoisie of Fortaleza. Not only did Fer-nando Pinto raise money to finance the expedition; when the raft set sail, both communities turned out to watch, and choirs from the local seminary sang hymns on two platforms erected for the occasion; a fleet of *jangadas* saw them out to sea, and planes sent out by the harbor au-thorities followed their voyage, while journalists, led by a radical of *jan-gadeiro* origins, Edmar Morel, pumped up enthusiasm for their exploit through newspaper and radio coverage, until a fleet of modern vessels came out to greet them in Guanabara Bay. Welles leaves all that out, and when he films the *jangadeiro* colony on Mucuripe Beach, he finds angles that erase the flourishing modern city around them, except for one shot, which we used, which shows the returning fishermen on the beach at sunset with a silhouetted battleship in the background. Those omissions add up to a strong misreading of the Flaherty tradition, with which he is aligning himself against Eisenstein—Eisenstein, whose influence is visible in every shot, and especially in those close-ups you think we overused, on the evidence of Welles's other films. But I don't think there is another Welles film quite like this one.

We chose the same approach, in a way, in our documentary preface, which focuses on Welles and tells the story from his point of view. There is another documentary to be made about the *jangadeiros* themselves, who continued making voyages after Welles left, and even planned to build a big raft to sail to Hollywood to see him one more time before they died and ask him why the film was never finished. Maybe we'll make that one some day, but in this one we chose to tell the story of an invisible people being filmed by a filmmaker who was himself on the way to becoming, as you say, invisible: here is the result. Through the images of his film we can still read the other text, the one written by the *jangadeiros* in the breathtaking trajectory of their voyage, which symbolized their desire to become part of the Brazilian nation. They were using the only means of communication available to them; so was he, when he filmed in Fortaleza with a silent Mitchell and the whole improvised apparatus you see in the documentary, and the experience transformed his cinema.

I'm happy with our choices, which I assure you were made after trying just about all the possibilities. One which I never liked enough to really explore it was to play games with the title—I always felt that the title would play games with us without our making any special effort, and it did. For political reasons, we chose to give a false date for when the negative was found (in fact, I'm not sure myself of the real one), but it was a sheer mistake to identify the newsreel images of the KANE premiere at the beginning as Hollywood, when they are really Times

Square. So the narrator's first and last words—"Hollywood, 1941" and "Then, in 1985 . . ."—are false, a symmetry which pleases me no end.

If we made a big mistake, it's one that I think you and I may also have made in our long polemic, which any good polemicist risks incurring. I mean special pleading, of course—we've discussed this. I've told you about the sudden doubt that seized me when I saw MONTPARNASSE 19 for the first time last fall: Becker's portrait of Modigliani made me wonder if we—you and I—haven't been blinded in our own way to the reality of the man we've been writing about all these years by the necessity of making a defense of him that will satisfy, or at least refute his accusers, when an artist's acts are to be judged in another court altogether, by laws which we only dimly understand.

And I've tried to convey to you the vertigo that sometimes seized me when we were plowing through the mass of documents on the making of IT'S ALL TRUE, the difficulty of knowing what happened and why, particularly when we were in Brazil. No one we interviewed in Fortaleza, even Welles's friends in the local bourgeoisie, could tell us what was in his head while he was shooting "Four Men," clearly because he had never confided in them, but at least in Fortaleza you didn't feel as if the ground was about to open under your feet every time you took a step. In Rio, perhaps because of something about the place itself, you did.

Take the famous furniture-throwing incident, which isn't in the documentary for good reasons. We know that before leaving Rio to film in Fortaleza, after RKO had publicly disowned him in the Brazilian press, Welles threw some furniture out of the window of a room he had been living in, attracting a crowd and bad notices in the local press. We have two eyewitness accounts: Betty Wilson, who was outside, looking up at the window as a sofa poked out and, after a moment of hesitation, was withdrawn, and a waiter who walked in while the thing was going on. And we have George Fanto's recollection of Welles telling the story in the plane on the way to Fortaleza, laughing so hard that the plane shook and the three surviving raftsmen took off their shoes in preparation for a crash at sea. But none of our research was able to establish whether the incident took place at the Copacabana Palace Hotel or at a nearby apartment which Welles was also renting, or even, supposing that it was the hotel, which room: we were shown one overlooking the street, but we were also shown one overlooking the pool, which is where the more colorful accounts say the furniture landed, with a great splash.

It was like that all the time in Rio. Not only were we shown two hotel rooms; we were shown two apartments, and two houses where Herivelto Martins entertained Welles and Grande Otelo till the wee hours of the morning while they planned the next day's shooting, not to mention two bars near the Casino Urca where Welles went in protest to join his non-white friends when they weren't allowed to attend his birthday broadcast at the casino in honor of Vargas's birthday. Then there's the story Catherine heard in Bahia about a furniture-throwing incident that allegedly happened there. How many times did it happen? I'm not sure, and I certainly couldn't tell you why it happened, although I've heard as many explanations as I've heard reasons for Jacaré's death, which occurred in broad daylight in front of witnesses. We can assume that the *New York Times* story that he was eaten by a shark, at least, is untrue, although Welles himself repeated it to Peter, so that you had to cut it out of the book.

My powers of description are simply inadequate to convey the experience of walking around Rio with the Brazilian filmmaker Rogerio Sganzerla, the first person to research this subject, who can show you all the places where everything happened, including the lovely canal (today reeking with sewage) where the government supposedly dumped the Macumba footage that Dick said was never shot. The nonstop vertigo is partly caused, I'm absolutely sure, by something about Rio itself, and partly by the fact that Rogerio and I have to communicate in French, which he doesn't speak very well—not to mention the brilliant associative patterns of Rogerio's mind, which I only began to appreciate when we played back our interview with him, accompanied by Catherine's voice-over translation.

That's why I recommend, if you want another version of the making of IT'S ALL TRUE, that you look at Rogerio's two films about it, NEM TUDO E VERDADE and LINGUAGEM DE ORSON WELLES. We all know NEM TUDO's faults, but at least Rogerio tried—for example, in his dramatization of the furniture-throwing incident—to give a well-rounded portrait of the artist as Dionysus, one that supplies a needed corrective to our filmed brief for the defense. And I'm very eager for people to see LINGUAGEM DE ORSON WELLES, Rogerio's short sequel to NEM TUDO, which as far as I know has never been shown anywhere.

Not having access, as we did, to Welles's own images and his voice, which we got from Peter's tapes and the BBC archives, Rogerio used what was ready to hand in his short: mainly the Brazilian newsreels, which he was the first to unearth; and a color film made in the 1960s about the *jangadeiros;* and for the voice, statements by and about Welles read by Grande Otelo and sound-bites from the films and radio plays. Unnarrated, the stew of sound and picture Rogerio concocted gives off a powerful aroma of paranoia, with Welles as the sacrificial victim. He even manages to insinuate, as an impression spun off a series of aural and visual associations, the conspiracy theory of Jacaré's death, which he shares with angrier members of the family of the deceased. And indeed, is it just a coincidence that when the drowning occurred, the press was elsewhere, covering a photo opportunity thoughtfully supplied by President Vargas? I couldn't say.

Like any essay film worthy of the name, LINGUAGEM DE ORSON WELLES is really a lyric poem, one which concludes with a *trouvaille* that is breathtaking in its simplicity and efficacy: over images of *jangadeiros* fishing and of one big fish, in particular, being hauled in and killed, Rogerio plays in its entirety John Huston's emotional statement to the press on the day of Welles's death, which recounts Welles's difficulties in Hollywood and his greatness of spirit in confronting them, accompanied by Dori Cayimi's "The Jangada Came Home Alone," one of the songs Welles was thinking of using in "Four Men." The concluding montage of Welles and Brazil (which ends mysteriously on a shot of the Empire State Building) is accompanied by "Auld Lang Syne," in Brazilian. *Ave atque vale:* all the phantoms—so many phantoms—exorcised and laid to rest. I hope I'll have a chance to write at greater length about this perfect little film in the catalogue of the Locarno festival, where Marco and I plan to show it on a double bill with IT'S ALL TRUE this summer.

Which brings me to my other pet project, one that we've discussed many times: The Orson Welles Oral History Project. I think few would dispute that Welles is a large enough and important enough subject to merit his own oral history project, if an institution can be found to house it and money to fund it—it wouldn't take that much. A first step would be to assemble all the films, tapes, and recordings of interviews that have already been done, by Leaming, Brady, Higham, Bogdanovich, the authors of that two-volume book about Welles in Spain that you got in the mail, and anyone else who has written about Welles, or made a documentary: certainly Gary Graver's hilarious WORKING WITH ORSON WELLES, which conveys, as only Gary could, what it was like making THE OTHER SIDE OF THE WIND, and Ciro Giorgini's ROSABELLA, about Welles in Italy, with all their outtakes—not to mention ours. After that it would be time to fill in the gaps, by sending out an underpaid army of students with tape recorders to interview the surviving witnesses in Yugoslavia, Ireland, England, Argentina, etc. etc., before what happens to all the witnesses in MR. ARKADIN happens to them.

Then, at least, when a real biography of Welles is finally written, the author will have something besides newspaper accounts to base it on, and it will all be in one place. You know who I think should write that one—despite your avowed distaste for biography as a genre. In any case, we both agree that the job remains to be done, and that whoever does it is going to need all the help he can get.

As always,
Bill

June 13, 1994

Dear Bill,

It's good to have all your multifaceted thoughts about IT'S ALL TRUE, which makes your letter worth the long wait. I especially value what you have to say regarding the political implications of the film in the 1940s as well as the 1990s, because it seems that those implications have mainly eluded critics in both decades. As you well know, it wasn't until Robert Stam published "Orson Welles, Brazil, and the Power of Blackness" in the seventh issue of *Persistence of Vision* (1989), with corroborating essays by both Catherine and Susan Ryan, that it finally became clear, forty-odd years after the event, that part of what was rattling so many studio executives and Brazilian government officials alike about Welles's behavior in Rio was his particular interest in blacks. Maybe you're right that he wasn't a radical, but if IT'S ALL TRUE had been completed and released in the early 1940s, it still might have offered a radical precedent: three Latin American stories focusing on non-white heroes.

Of course the perils of embarking on such a transcultural and translingual project were as daunting in a way for you and your American collaborators as they were for Welles and his own (with Dick Wilson the common member of both teams): given all the divergent forces at play, ambiguities and misunderstandings were almost to be expected, which helps to account for why Welles himself in later years, for purposes of telling a "good yarn," was perfectly capable of misdescribing the death of Jacaré—not to mention inventing a nonexistent Brazilian voodoo sect in the opening footage of your documentary (a detail that I'm told has perturbed some Brazilian viewers), as well as paring away the urban trappings of Fortaleza to evoke a "natural" setting comparable to those in MOANA. (Flaherty, we know, was quite capable of making similar elisions and modifications.) The process of explaining unfamiliar material and adapting it to North American norms of understanding is not simply one of translation but one of acculturation, and every stage of this project has been subject to such dangers. For all the "universality" of the Man of La Mancha and Sancho Panza, I have little doubt that Welles's QUIXOTE is fraught with comparable contradictions—as is, for that matter, his multinational version of Kafka.

With or without these problems, I am nonetheless struck by the evidence offered by your documentary that IT'S ALL TRUE might well have been the most overtly Catholic of Welles's films—a discovery prompted in part by the revelation in Peter's introduction to *This Is Orson Welles* that Welles was raised as a Catholic, a basic fact missing from the biographies of Leaming, Higham, and Brady. (Let's hope that the Welles biographies in the works by Simon Callow and David Thomson—as well as Bart Whaley's book about Welles in relation to magic, which is still seeking a publisher—will know what to make of it.)[1] Consider the lovely blessing-of-the-animals scene glimpsed in your treatment of "Bonito," the periodic visits to churches made by the *jangadeiros* on their raft journey from Fortaleza to Rio, or the celebrations of Carnaval itself. It's truly discoveries of this kind that keep the Wellesian oeuvre in a perpetual state of becoming, where each new work or fragment thereof transforms our understanding of the rest.

On the other hand, even with an oeuvre as full of unexpected and still partly unexplored twists as that of Welles, we don't want to be guilty of our own form of idealism à la Flaherty by granting his career a volition it didn't always have. The charge of special pleading that you bring against the polemics we've been waging on behalf of Welles seems to me quite just in at least one important respect: that Welles was in some ways responsible for many of the disasters that plagued his career; that, indeed, as Higham concludes and Carringer reiterates, "he was the brilliant architect of his own downfall." Unfortunately, truths of this kind are never entirely disinterested even when they sound most reasonable, because behind them always lurk ideological as well as practical assumptions, acknowledged or otherwise: downfall, yes, but from what and to what? If we wish for a Wellesian ascension to power comparable to Spielberg's, what would we be giving up and settling for in the process? And if Welles's own intentionality is to serve as the ultimate criterion in gauging his own success or failure, where does that leave criticism, which thankfully left intentionality and its vagaries well behind once it decided that effects were more important than motives?

It seems to me that Welles's continuing force as an ideological disturbance in the cinematic apparatus—a force that went well beyond his own intentions, and that continues unabated long after his death, inflecting virtually every aspect of his work—can always be explained or rationalized as a series of strategic mistakes (or bad "career moves," as the current parlance has it). Let's list a few of them: the refusal (or inability) of a one-time mainstream artist to accept the status—including in some cases the benefits—of a marginal art house director; a conspira-

torial secrecy regarding many of his most personal projects, coupled
with a compulsive need to revise them, which often led him to tell in effect several disparate acquaintances and co-workers, sometimes on separate continents, "*You* are the only one I can trust," with predictably
chaotic posthumous consequences; a complete inability to handle
money, coupled with an incapacity to flatter or reassure the very finan-
ciers and producers he habitually depended upon; a passion for working on several projects at once, which often meant relegating several
films-in-progress to the back burner for years at a time; a failure to
package himself and his projects commercially in relation to what producers wanted . . . the list could be expanded indefinitely, and, of
course, has been.

What seems objectionable to me about the listing of such flaws is not
their falsity but the uses they're generally put to—parceling out blame
in order to reduce or deny the ideological disturbance, declaring Welles
sick in order to assign the apparatus a clean bill of health. From the vantage point of business, such an act obviously becomes necessary, but for
a historian or critic to add up these offenses merely implies a subsum-
ing of history and criticism under business interests—a process that is
already so dominant and triumphant in our culture that it scarcely
needs any assistance from a Higham or a Carringer, much less from you
or me.

This has a lot to do with why the notion of attempting yet another
Welles biography holds little attraction for me—much as I appreciate
your flattering confidence, which I don't happen to share. What's
needed at this stage, apart from further documentation of the work, is
social history, not biography—an account of the reception of Welles as a
mythological creature that continues to clog up most discourse about
him, the multiple ways in which he continues to become the site of
Oedipal fantasies, the "acting out" of mythomaniacs. In this respect,
André S. Labarthe's L'HOMME QUI A VU L'HOMME QUI A VU L'OURS,
known in English as THE BIG O—quite apart from its genuine interest as
an apotheosis of the mimetic principles of *Cinéastes de notre temps*, including their best and worst tendencies—is perhaps the only instance of
Wellesian "research" that fully bears witness to its own perversity and
partiality, so that exposing the deceptions of Henry Jaglom as Wellesian

heir apparent is deemed more important than challenging the deathbed lies of John Houseman about the authorship of the KANE script, simply because Labarthe/Szabo considers himself in competition with Jaglom but not with Houseman. Clearly, the Oedipal stakes are what matter in this sort of a game more than the facts themselves. To write a biography of Welles ultimately means to invite and submit to excesses of this kind, but to write a social history, assuming anyone could do it, would be to *place* these excesses, to try to understand them as mechanisms within larger ideological formations.

The Orson Welles Oral History Project that you outline holds more attractions for me; although there, too, I wonder if your aspirations might be a little utopian. To attempt such an endeavor would require moving beyond the capitalist and nationalist agendas that have regulated the handling of Welles's posthumous work so far, in one way or another, and it's not clear to me, things being what they are, how such a project could be financed *without* honoring those agendas, all of which tend to be at odds with honoring the integrity of the work in its own right.

There are exceptions, of course—scattered cinephiles across the globe who are still more interested in preserving the Welles legacy for its own sake than in using it as a brand name to promote other interests. Most recently, I was delighted to learn that Criterion is planning to release a laserdisc of the original 1952 version of OTHELLO that Welles showed in Cannes, bypassing both the 1955 version that he reedited for the U.S. and the highly debatable "restoration" of that version that was released in the U.S. to much uncritical fanfare in 1992, with postmodernist approximations of his original music and sound effects reworked in stereo, and compressions and expansions of the dialogue done in the interests of lip-sync—both signs of a blind faith in technology taking the place of research. When Criterion phoned to ask me to write liner notes for the 1952 version and mentioned that they'd be releasing THE LADY FROM SHANGHAI somewhat later, I told them about the phantom "alternative" version of that film that James Naremore recalls seeing at the Frankfurt Kommunales Kino in 1981 when he ordered a print to accompany his own lecture there—a version with some scenes or shots missing but other scenes containing shots he'd never seen before, subtitled in both French and German (which suggests a Swiss or perhaps a Luxembourgian print source)—most likely a version of the film comparable to the famous "Italian version" of FOOLISH WIVES written about by Rivette in *Cahiers du cinéma* no. 79, shipped out to a European location prior to its U.S. release. It's another piece of the SHANGHAI puzzle to go with Jim's superb account of the cutting continuity of the 155-minute rough cut in the second edition of his invaluable *The Magic World of Orson Welles*.

Indeed, if some European Welles fanatic could succeed in tracking down this alternative version of SHANGHAI, we'd have another instance of the transnational detective work that your dream of an Oral History Project envisages. There have been others: Ciro's two wonderful versions of TUTTA LA VERITÀ SU GREGORY ARKADIN for RAI were labors of love that paralleled my own ARKADIN research for the January–February 1992 *Film Comment*, which was paralleled in turn by Tim Lucas's independent research on the separate versions of ARKADIN carried out in *Video Watchdog* (an excellent scholarly "fanzine" in the U.S., mainly devoted to horror films) the same year. Ciro and I benefited a great deal from each other's labors, while Lucas worked in isolation from both of us, but all three of us failed to take account of all the Spanish documentation alluded to in Esteve Riambau's *Orson Welles: Una España Inmortal*, published in 1993 along with Juan Cobos's *Orson Welles: España Como Obsesión* by the Filmoteca Española—impressive-looking volumes that have already sent me to my Spanish-English dictionary to glean whatever discoveries I can make from them.

Therefore, an international repository for such material would obviously be a boon to all Welles scholars. But how could such a project ever get financed without business and/or national interests eventually overtaking and engulfing all the research? Consider the unhappy fate of QUIXOTE and all the competing agendas that assigned it that fate, including the off-screen narration intoned over the final freeze-frame of the English version of Jesus Franco's cut: "This film was written, produced, and directed by a man whose ashes, in accordance with his last wishes, [were] scattered on Spanish soil. His name was Orson Welles." Just as if he somehow intended the film to premiere at Expo 92 all along.

Many of these agendas, of course, can be traced directly back to
Welles. Even his decision to flee from Universal studios to Mexico to
start shooting the film when the editing of TOUCH OF EVIL encountered
some studio resistance can be labeled a strategic move with lasting consequences, effectively ending his Hollywood career as a director in the
name of independence. And much of what he wound up shooting in
Mexico—specifically a series of dialogues between himself and Patty
McCormack in a courtyard and later on a horse-drawn carriage, as well
as a subsequent scene in a movie theater featuring McCormack, Akim
Tamiroff (Panza), and Francisco Reiguera (Quixote)—he eventually decided to discard, as we know from Oja, with the intention of shooting
new material with his daughter Beatrice to replace it. That is why the
hasty posthumous version of the film edited by Franco for Expo 92 that
showed in Cannes the same year includes none of this material, nor
does the English version (which is scheduled to show at New York's
Museum of Modern Art in the fall). I assume that when Oja made her
agreement with Franco's Spanish producer, part of the agreement regarding a commercial version of the film was that none of this material
be used.

I was lucky enough to see this footage, or at least a large portion of
it—still in the possession of Mauro Bonanni, who worked with Welles
on the original editing—at an instructive Welles conference in Rome organized by Ciro in late October 1992, an event focusing on the same Italian collaborators of Welles who are interviewed by Ciro in his video
documentary ROSABELLA. (Franco and his collaborators were also invited, but failed to appear, and here again nationalist agendas sometimes threatened to overtake the proceedings, hovering around the
issue of whether the soul of Welles was "truly" Italian or "truly" Spanish.) Seeing the McCormack material from end to end, without a sense
of where it would be placed in the film proper—the courtyard and carriage footage with sound (mainly or exclusively direct, as I recall), the
fully edited theater sequence silent—I could only marvel at the resonance it might have had as a narrative framing device; and when it
came to the movie theater sequence, even without any sound, I felt privileged at being present at the one point in all the QUIXOTE material I've

seen when the comedy gives way not merely to pathos but to convulsive, unbearable tragedy.

Let me try to describe this sequence, as nearly as I can remember it. It's preceded in the courtyard and carriage scenes by Welles first telling McCormack about the story of Don Quixote and eventually by McCormack describing actual personal encounters of her own with Quixote and Panza (and at one point we actually see Panza appearing mysteriously in the courtyard as well, after Welles and McCormack have left the scene). Panza is then seen entering a crowded movie theater, finding himself a seat beside McCormack, and becoming enrapt in the movie. She hands him a lollipop, then patiently shows him how to remove the wrapper after he distractedly bites into it with the paper still on, unable to tear his eyes away from the screen. (As in the remainder of Welles's QUIXOTE, the childlike grubbiness and innate earthiness conveyed by Tamiroff are sublime.) The two of them watch the movie together, equally absorbed. Then they notice that Quixote is also watching the film from a few rows away, and taking what he sees on the screen—a scene of various women being crucified in what appears to be a conventional 50s peplum—very seriously. He gets up from his seat, strides toward the screen with his sword, and begins slashing away at the screen to free the movie damsel in distress from her movie persecutors.

Up to this point, the scene has been gently and genuinely comic, but now it turns cruel and harsh in a manner that seems peculiar to Cervantes: the audience begins to cheer Quixote on, boys in the balcony hoot with ecstatic derision, and the doleful knight continues to slash the screen to tatters, thrusting again and again until only a few pathetic strands in the fabric remain. Pandemonium has meanwhile broken out in the auditorium, most of the audience has stormed out, and yet the knight continues heedlessly in his task, stone-faced, relentlessly—in a scene so powerfully and painfully protracted that in some way I wanted to rush toward the larger screen exposing the knight's own futility, the screen showing Welles's DON QUIXOTE, and slash it to ribbons, too.

Research on Welles's QUIXOTE as a developing project still remains at such a primitive stage that I couldn't begin to judge the rightness or wrongness of this material in relation to the rest, much less explain what Welles intended to replace it with. I only know that it carries a raw, primordial force in its present state that is paralleled by only a few moments in the rest of Welles's work. Some of those few moments, to be sure, are in the Franco-edited version of QUIXOTE. But there, I'm sorry to say, they're often diluted and poorly served by their placement and by their poorly duped textures, both signs of unnatural haste. The English version of this cut is at least superior to the Spanish-dubbed version that premiered at Expo 92 and Cannes by virtue of having Welles's own voice narrating and dubbing both Quixote and Panza for roughly half of the film's running time; the remainder of the English voices seem to come from anyone the dubbing people could find to pull off the street—not that their task would have been easy under any circumstances. Worst of all is the misappropriation of footage from Welles's Italian TV documentary series in the mid-1960s, NELLA TERRA DI DON CHISCIOTTE. To my mind this TV series is a piece of honest if touristic hack-work, undertaken in order to finance work on QUIXOTE but by no stretch of the imagination a piece of QUIXOTE itself—which, alas, is exactly how Franco has treated it. Ironically and fatally, the gap left by the deleted McCormack material has been filled by the far more debatable material of Welles cruising around Spain in the back of a limousine, playing the celebrity big shot.

Of course the pressure to complete a feature in a few weeks or months, in time for the Expo 92 deadline, out of material that had occupied Welles for many decades, made the project doomed from the outset. This implies that the real work on QUIXOTE can only begin when scholars find their way to the Filmoteca Española in Madrid and begin to study all the many hours of QUIXOTE material housed there, and then—unless legal matters are finally resolved and all the footage is finally brought together—pay an additional visit to Bonanni in Rome to see the remaining footage. When I suggested to Bonanni in 1992 that perhaps, given Welles's penchant for revisions, there were not one but several QUIXOTES to choose from, he angrily replied that if Welles had truly decided to delete all the McCormack footage, he would have surely thrown it out (as, indeed, he did discard some of the earliest QUIXOTE footage he shot, back when it was still conceived of as a TV film produced by Frank Sinatra).

Given Welles's compulsive methods of secrecy and subterfuge regarding the shooting and editing of QUIXOTE (many of which are detailed by his former secretary Audrey Stainton in the Autumn 1988 *Sight and Sound*), I doubt that we'll ever know the whole story, but in this particular area of Welles scholarship, the work hasn't even begun. It's not even clear to me what written sources Franco and his collaborators had at their disposal for dubbing the silent portions of the footage in Spanish and English, and until such facts and others are made available, we can't even begin to evaluate the results—despite my provisional remarks here, based mainly on my memories of the edited sections, dubbed and silent, that Oja screened at New York University's Welles conference in 1988. There, at least, the marvelous moment of Sancho Panza looking directly at the camera in response to Welles's offscreen narration wasn't underlined by an ugly zoom, which I assume was added by Franco for unnecessary punctuation. But, of course, I can't be sure of this; with no documentation at my disposal, I can't absolutely prove that Welles didn't shoot another take that included that zoom, which Franco decided to retain.

We can, however, broach another issue about the etiquette of completing an unfinished film that applies equally to your version of IT'S ALL TRUE: namely, how does one edit material that Welles left unedited? Two antithetical approaches come to mind, both of which are found in separate portions of your film. One is to attempt to edit à la Welles, as Ed Marx has done with the blessing of the animals in "Bonito," which in this case means to make the images fleeting, rhythmic punctuations of the offscreen narration. (Especially in his 1940s and 1950s work, Welles's movies never linger over beauty; the pleasure of the images is almost always counteracted by a Calvinist form of abridgement and denial, rather like the extremely brief shot of the Italian partisans standing at the bar in Straub-Huillet's FROM THE CLOUD TO THE RESISTANCE. This is, in fact, true whether Welles is narrating off screen or not, and it theoretically means that, even if the AMBERSONS ball scene had remained uncut by RKO, it *still* would have left us with a sense of incompletion and regret at the end.)

The other solution, which Marx adheres to in most of the Fortaleza sequence—the part of your film without off-screen narration, although

Welles would certainly have narrated it himself—is the reverse approach: to linger over the images, allow the spectator to contemplate and fully digest what is there. To what end? To permit us to savor the material, even in its necessary incompleteness. From this standpoint, which is certainly defensible, I would have to withdraw my objection to an excessive use of close-ups, for what's at stake here isn't a Welles sequence but Welles footage—hardly the same thing. Yet the same defense could be theoretically made for the terminal dullness of Sancho Panza wandering endlessly through urban crowds in Franco's version of QUIXOTE—assuming, that is, that he, like Marx, was lingering over unedited material.

The point of all these qualms is that no solution is entirely adequate when it comes to completing uncompleted projects—a problem that Peter and I faced in editing *This Is Orson Welles* and that your team faced in editing "Four Men on a Raft." And one of the reasons for this necessary impasse corresponds, I'm sure, to why most of these projects were never completed within Welles's lifetime: because the artistic and commercial answers to the various questions posed by the material are never necessarily the same answers, and to opt for one solution often means to betray the interests of the other. (Could you believe that when I interviewed him in Paris for *Film Comment* back in 1972, Welles told me he was reluctant to release QUIXOTE right away because he didn't want it to "compete" with MAN OF LA MANCHA?) Caught between the conflicting identities of a mainstream entertainer (as he was in his TV appearances and in his turns as a "colorful" actor in the films of others) and of a private artist, with one foot firmly planted in each camp, Welles spent most of his life negotiating a contradiction that his chroniclers and archivists also have to face. And given the state of cinema in 1994, why should our task be any easier than his?

As ever,
Jonathan[2]

Notes

1. (March 1995): In Whaley's case, we don't have to wait for his finished book. (Callow's is scheduled for publication in England this month.) In a letter to me

234   ORSON WELLES IN THE U.S.

dated 7 November 1994 that includes his responses to the above, he expresses a good deal of skepticism about Welles's statement to Bogdanovich, noting that "Riambau (p. 17) writes that the Archbishop of Madrid approved the burial of Orson's ashes on Spanish soil in 1987 despite having satisfied himself that they weren't Catholic ashes." And in the same letter, Whaley reports that both Robert Wise and Betty Wilson "categorically denied" Endfield's allegation "that Jack Moss was disloyal to Welles in 1942." ("Both accepted Endfield's facts but reject his sinister conclusion.") He also questions whether Wise was responsible for the "overlit" restoration of KANE, noting that his role was only that of a consultant. (J. R.)

2. As a point of reference, the principal surviving Welles films that have not yet been released due to practical, legal, and/or financial difficulties are THE DEEP (a thriller shot off the Dalmatian coast between 1967 and 1969), THE MERCHANT OF VENICE (a 40-minute condensation of the Shakespeare play, completed circa 1970 but never shown after most of its soundtrack was stolen), and THE OTHER SIDE OF THE WIND (shot in Europe and the U.S. between 1970 and 1976). The rights to all three were willed by Welles to Oja Kodar.

—This exchange was originally commissioned by and written for *Trafic;* the first letter was published in issue no. 12 (Fall 1994), the latter two in issue no. 13 (Winter 1995), translated into French by Bernard Eisenschitz

The principal texts cited or alluded to in the above letters are as follows:

Bordwell, David, and Kristin Thompson. *Film Art: An Introduction,* 4th edition. New York: McGraw-Hill, 1993.
Carringer, Robert L. THE MAGNIFICENT AMBERSONS: *A Reconstruction.* Berkeley: University of California Press, 1993.
———. *The Making of* CITIZEN KANE. Berkeley: University of California Press, 1985.
Combs, Richard. "Burning Masterworks: From CITIZEN KANE to F FOR FAKE." *Film Comment,* January–February 1994.
Higham, Charles. *Orson Welles: The Rise and Fall of an American Genius.* New York: St. Martin's Press, 1985.
———. *The Films of Orson Welles.* Berkeley: University of California Press, 1970.
Kael, Pauline. "Raising KANE." In *The* CITIZEN KANE *Book.* Boston: Little, Brown, 1971.
Krohn, Bill. "The Class: Rencontre avec Nicholas Ray." *Cahiers du cinéma* no. 288, May 1978.
———. "Entretien avec Orson Welles." *Cahiers du cinéma* nos. 383–384, May 1986.
———. "La force de l'œuvre." *Orson Welles.* Paris: Editions de L'Etoile, 1986. (Note: this book also contains the previous and two following Krohn texts.)
———. "Les inachèves d'Orson Welles: L'héritage." *Cahiers du cinéma* no. 378, December 1985.

———. "IT'S ALL TRUE: A la récherche du film fantôme." *Cahiers du cinéma* no. 375, September 1985.
———. "Lettre d'un ami américain." *Trafic* no. 1, winter 1991.
Lucas, Tim. "The Cutting Room Floor." *Video Watchdog* no. 10, March–April 1992.
———. "MR. ARKADIN: The Research Continues." *Video Watchdog* no. 12, July–August 1992.
Mulvey, Laura. *CITIZEN KANE.* London: British Film Institute, 1992.
Naremore, James. *The Magic World of Orson Welles*, 2nd edition. Dallas: Southern Methodist University Press, 1989.
Riambau, Esteve. *Orson Welles: Una España Inmortal.* Published with Juan Cobos's *Orson Welles: España Como Obsesión.* Madrid: Filmoteca Española, 1993.
Rosenbaum, Jonathan. "The Invisible Orson Welles: A First Inventory." *Sight and Sound*, Summer 1986.
———. "OTHELLO Goes Hollywood." *Chicago Reader,* April 10, 1992. Reprinted in *Placing Movies: The Practice of Film Criticism.* Berkeley: University of California Press, 1995.
———. "The Seven ARKADINS." *Film Comment*, January–February 1992. Reprinted in *Movies as Politics.* Berkeley: University of California Press, 1997.
———. "The Voice and the Eye: Commentary on the HEART OF DARKNESS Script" and "Paris Journal." *Film Comment*, November–December 1972.
Stainton, Audrey. "DON QUIXOTE: Orson Welles' Secret." *Sight and Sound*, Autumn 1988.
Stam, Robert. "Orson Welles, Brazil, and the Power of Blackness." Published with related texts by Susan Ryan and Catherine Benamou. *Persistence of Vision*, no. 7, 1989.
Welles, Orson. *THE CRADLE WILL ROCK: An Original Screenplay.* Introduction by James Pepper; afterword by Jonathan Rosenbaum. Santa Barbara: Santa Teresa Press, 1994.
———. "Memo to Universal" (on TOUCH OF EVIL). Introduced by Jonathan Rosenbaum. *Film Quarterly* 46, no. 1, Fall 1992. (Also appeared in French in *Trafic* no. 4, Fall 1992.)
Welles, Orson, and Peter Bogdanovich. *This Is Orson Welles*, edited by Jonathan Rosenbaum. New York: HarperCollins, 1992. Audio edition: New York: Caedmon, 1992. English edition: London: HarperCollins, 1993. French edition *(Moi, Orson Welles):* Paris: Belfont, 1993. (See review by Bill Krohn in *Cahiers du cinéma* no. 470, July–August 1993, for errors in the French translation.) Italian edition *(Io, Orson Welles):* Milan: Baldini & Castoldi, 1993. German edition *(Hier spricht Orson Welles):* Berlin: Quadriga Verlag, 1994.
Welles, Orson, with Oja Kodar. *THE BIG BRASS RING: An Original Screenplay* (preface by James Pepper, afterword by Jonathan Rosenbaum), Santa Barbara: Santa Teresa Press, 1987. Italian edition *(La posta in gioco):* Genova: Costa & Nolan, 1989. English edition: London: Black Spring Press, 1991.

20

The Battle over Orson Welles

Biographies of Orson Welles reviewed in this article:

Orson Welles: The Road to Xanadu, by Simon Callow (New York: Viking, 1995). 640 pp.
Rosebud: The Story of Orson Welles, by David Thomson (New York: Alfred A. Knopf, 1996). 461 pp.
Orson Welles, revised and expanded edition, by Joseph McBride (New York: Da Capo, 1996). 243 pp.

Two prevailing and diametrically opposed attitudes seem to dictate the way most people currently think about Orson Welles. One attitude, predominantly American, sees his life and career chiefly in terms of failure and regards the key question to be why he never lived up to his promise—"his promise" almost invariably being tied up with the achievement of CITIZEN KANE. Broadly speaking, this position can be compared to that of the investigative reporter Thompson's editor in CITIZEN KANE, bent on finding a single formula for explaining a man's life. The other attitude— less monolithic and less tied to any particular nationality, or to the expectations aroused by any single work—views his life and career more sympathetically as well as inquisitively; this position corresponds more closely to Thompson's near the end of KANE when he says, "I don't think any word can explain a man's life."

The first attitude can be found in relatively undiluted form in six extended works by four authors—Charles Higham's *The Films of Orson Welles* (1970) and *Orson Welles: The Rise and Fall of an American Genius* (1985), Robert L. Carringer's *The Making of* CITIZEN KANE (1985; revised edition, 1996) and THE MAGNIFICENT AMBERSONS: *A Reconstruction* (1993), Pauline Kael's essay "Raising KANE" (1971—reprinted most recently in *For Keeps*, 1994), and David Thomson's recent biography *Rosebud: The Story of Orson Welles* (1996). A more diluted form of this attitude can be found in Simon Callow's *Orson Welles: The Road to Xanadu* (1995), the first volume of a projected two- or three-volume biography that basically ends with the release of CITIZEN KANE and the stage production of *Native Son*, the last two projects in which Welles collaborated with John Houseman.

The second attitude can be found in André Bazin's *Orson Welles: A Critical View* (1978), Jean-Pierre Berthomé and François Thomas's *CITIZEN KANE* (1992), Frank Brady's *Citizen Welles* (1989), Juan Cobos's *Orson Welles: España Como Obsesion* (1993), Peter Cowie's *The Cinema of Orson Welles* (1965; revised editions, 1973 and 1983), Barbara Leaming's *Orson Welles* (1985), Joseph McBride's *Orson Welles* (1972; revised edition, 1996), James Naremore's *The Magic World of Orson Welles* (1978; revised edition, 1989), Esteve Riambau's *Orson Welles: Una España Inmortal* (1993), and Orson Welles and Peter Bogdanovich's *This Is Orson Welles* (1992)—to offer an incomplete but fairly up-to-date list. (Laura Mulvey's interesting ideological and psychoanalytical reading of KANE in a 1992 BFI "Classic Film" monograph manages to absent itself from both of the positions outlined above.)

Though not all of the seven works representing the first attitude have received an equal amount of attention in the U.S., I think it would be fair to say that this still represents the most widely held mainstream position about Welles—the same position propounded in a recent documentary nominated for an Academy Award, *The Battle over* CITIZEN KANE. (By contrast, IT'S ALL TRUE: BASED ON AN UNFINISHED FILM BY ORSON WELLES, a 1993 documentary, represents the second position.) The usual corollary of this attitude is a reading of CITIZEN KANE as a Hollywood picture rather than the first feature of an independent filmmaker that happens to use certain Hollywood resources. Paradoxically, many of those who single out KANE as Welles's ultimate or only major achievement also routinely tend to support contemporary commercial filmmaking practices that would make such an achievement impossible and unthinkable today. For those, on the other hand, who tend to endorse Welles's moves toward freedom, diversity, and independence even when this necessitated moving outside the Hollywood mainstream, the jagged path of his career can't be charted according to any simple pattern of ascent or descent; there are peaks and valleys throughout. (For an artist who refused to repeat himself or turn his directorial talent into a commodity, this surely goes with the territory.) I should add that my preference for the ten books representing this second attitude is not a disinterested position; I translated and edited the first of these books and edited the last.

Another major distinction that can be made between these lists is that the first seven works all describe Welles as a deeply flawed, morally reprehensible human being and the last ten don't. Significantly, only one of the authors in the first list, Carringer, ever had any personal contact with Welles—unlike most of those in the second list, including Bazin, Bogdanovich, Brady, Cobos, Leaming, and McBride, and possibly others as well.

Does this mean that Welles was capable of charming the birds off the trees, hoodwinking all potential biographers and critics? Not necessarily. My own impression, the only time I ever met him, was that he was abnormally self-absorbed, yet so alert to this fact that he sought to compensate for it by being downright solicitous to whomever he was with—a disarming trait, but far from being a smokescreen. Yet such was his sense of privacy that I wonder if part of the moral censure of Higham, Callow, and Thomson might stem from their resentment at feeling closed out. (Provocatively, Phillip Lopate suggested in *Newsday* that Callow's book reads like the work of someone who expected he would have been sexually rejected by Welles—though Lopate perversely finds that Callow's peevish tone gives *The Road to Xanadu* more of an interesting edge than a more respectful and less personal approach would.)

Most of my own sense of what Welles was like derives from numerous conversations I've had over the years with Oja Kodar, Peter Bogdanovich, the late Richard Wilson, and Gary Graver, as well as briefer encounters with John Berry, George Fanto, the late Fletcher Markle, Patricia Medina,

Alessandro Tasca di Cuto, Ruth Warwick, and Beatrice Welles-Smith, among others. The composite picture I've gotten is far from complete, but it seldom gibes with the compulsive liar and shameless exploiter that emerges from Thomson's book and periodically turns up in Callow's. Some of this may arise from a temperamental difference in how we interpret the same data. Berry once described to me with relish his experience of holding up scenery outdoors for an entire morning during the shooting of a 1938 film intended as a prologue to the stage farce *Too Much Johnson.* When lunch arrived and Welles sat down to eat, Berry blurted out how hungry he was, whereupon Welles made a great show of offering him his own seat and plate. Berry was too intimidated to accept and went back to holding up the scenery.

The same anecdote is recounted in *Rosebud*—Thomson, who appears to have done virtually no original research, takes it from a Patrick McGilligan interview—but the resonance it takes on in this new setting is markedly different. Both versions of the story illustrate how adept Welles was at getting what he wanted from his employees, but when Berry told it to me, his overriding and unwavering affection for Welles was what mainly shined through (which makes this a typical and even archetypal Welles anecdote in my experience). In Thomson's account, thanks to the surrounding context, it registers as one more instance of Welles's hollow self-centeredness, another example of moral bankruptcy.

One lesson to be learned from this is how mythical and ideological a creature Welles remains, a site for the acting out of various fantasies. Critics and biographers of Franz Kafka don't waste much time worrying their heads or clucking their tongues about why Kafka "failed to live up to his promise," despite the fact that his own record of unfinished longer works—and his reluctance to make many of his shorter works available—is far worse than anything to be found in Welles. Curiously, even the most destructive Hollywood moguls, including those responsible for destroying the discarded Welles footage from THE MAGNIFICENT AMBERSONS, THE STRANGER, and THE LADY FROM SHANGHAI, have failed to elicit the sort of disapproval from writers that Higham and Thomson relentlessly heap on Welles.

The bad news about the recent Welles biographies by Callow and

Thomson is that they pretend to an authoritativeness about the man's inner nature and motivations that I doubt will be accepted by anyone who knew Welles intimately—or even by most of those like myself or Brady who encountered him only briefly and casually. Conscious or not, the agenda of both Callow and Thomson is to set certain ideological worries about Welles to rest rather than clarify what these worries represent, and exercising moral censure, puritanical or otherwise, is one of the most convenient methods available for carrying out this task. Another is the recourse of both biographers to a kind of spurious and, in Thomson's case, irresponsible word-spinning about Welles's inner life normally associated with fiction. In Callow's book, this resembles the way a Stanislavsky-inspired actor might prepare for a role; in Thomson's book, by his own admission, it often overlaps with the work undertaken by a novelist (although in this case, a rather self-indulgent and self-serving one). In both cases, this enterprise also calls to mind the efforts of certain British journalists to fill up a page with lively patter regardless of whether or not they have anything substantive to say. On this score, both Callow and Thomson are skillful writers whose skill often consists of creating smoke-screens. Although they both have functioned admirably in the past as critics, and their critical gifts never fully desert them here, the basic issue of whom they're writing about—not simply what he did and why—is never wholly engaged.

By contrast, one of the invaluable merits of McBride's modest critical study on Welles—originally published in 1972, and substantially revised and expanded for its second edition—derives from the fact that he worked for Welles as an actor on the still-unfinished THE OTHER SIDE OF THE WIND. This may make him more of a partisan, along with Berry, but it also gives his personal judgments some solid basis in experience. And in conscientiously updating the record on Welles's peripatetic career, he offers a balanced survey of the work that can be warmly recommended as a useful starting point for anyone wishing to delve into the subject. His four-page bibliography, apart from being mainly limited to English-language entries, succinctly sums up the current state of Welles studies—quite unlike Thomson's, which is nearly twice as long.

Although I think McBride underrates OTHELLO and THE TRIAL and overrates MACBETH and THE IMMORTAL STORY, such disagreements are secondary to the fact that he has plenty of valuable and interesting things to say about all four. (His brilliant observation that Hitchcock's THE WRONG MAN "could well serve as a step-by-step illustration of how to film the nightmarish aspect of Kafka's world" should perhaps be set alongside Noël Carroll's defense of THE TRIAL as a faithful literary adaptation, found in *Film Reader* no. 3, 1978.) And his lengthy chapters on CITIZEN KANE and THE MAGNIFICENT AMBERSONS, which take up almost a quarter of his text, manage to be both judicious and comprehensive.

■

As a writer, Simon Callow has two interlocking talents that make him especially well-suited to write about actors: a comprehensive understanding, through his own career as an actor, of what the craft of performance consists of, and a talent for performing on the page that might be regarded as an actorly form of writing. These gifts come together triumphantly in *Charles Laughton: A Difficult Actor* (1987), where Callow's complex empathy for his subject is apparent on every page. Consider the following comparison between Laughton and Laurence Olivier, which shows Callow's writing at its best:

> Olivier and Laughton . . . could hardly be said to be practicing the same art. Laughton the deep-sea diver who had to keep coming up for air, Olivier the surfer whose skill took him to places he never meant to go; they had the sea in common, but that was all.
>
> In SPARTACUS, the two modes can be seen side by side: Olivier . . . plays Crassus like a knife: it is an entirely linear performance with every point brilliantly made. His glacial patrician manner, his ruthless ambition, his strong desire for his handsome young slave, are all cleanly and sharply indicated, it is as if there were a thin black line drawn around the role. Laughton's Gracchus has no such boundaries, no such definition. It spreads, floats, expands, contracts. The whole massive expanse of flesh seems to be filled with mind— thoughts are conceived, born and die in different parts of that far-flung empire. Sedentary for the most part, Gracchus seethes with potential movement. He is a jelly that has escaped the mould; Olivier's (and Crassus's) sharp knife can gain no purchase on it.

The close identification that Callow clearly feels with Laughton—as an eloquent ham, as a homosexual, as a multifaceted and educated man of the theater—isn't matched by his troubled fascination with Welles, despite much valuable material in his new book about Welles's acting. If he identifies with anyone in *The Road to Xanadu*, this is John Houseman, whose positions about Welles he tends to adopt wholesale, even where there appears to be some room for debate. However reliable Houseman's memoirs may be on many Wellesian matters, my own research has repeatedly shown that he can't be trusted on the issue of Welles as a writer; Callow, however, not only trusts him on this matter but regards him as the final arbiter on the subject. This means that on such matters as the *War of the Worlds* radio broadcast and the KANE script, Callow goes overboard in denying Welles creative input, even when this means ignoring or minimizing much of the contrary evidence available.[1]

Though Callow's research into Welles's career has clearly been extensive—which pays off in particular when it comes to descriptions of the stage productions—the determination to be authoritative as well as judgmental about Welles's motives does not always have happy results. Stuart Klawans, in a dismissive review of *The Road to Xanadu* in *The Nation*, had many cogent points to make about its inadequacy in dealing with Welles's politics, noting in particular its failure to mention the Popular Front. (For a detailed consideration of Welles's leftist and liberal positions, Naremore's book—still the best critical study of Welles available in any language—remains the only extended and reliable source.)

Some of the books on Welles to have appeared are debatable (such as Callow's), and a few—such as the second books of Higham and Carringer—strike me as lamentable, but only Thomson's biography deserves to be called a disgrace. (For the record, however, it has by far better illustrations than the McBride or the Callow.) Much as the 1994 third edition of his *Biographical Dictionary of Film* owes much of its dubious prestige to its implicit denial that anything important happened in cinema over the previous decade,[2] *Rosebud* seems designed to give aid and comfort to amateur Welles sleuths who haven't bothered to keep up with Welles scholarship over the same period. (And judging from Janet Maslin's rave in *The New York Times Book Review*, it has already fully succeeded in that endeavor.) Thus the absence in the former book of any entries on Chantal Akerman, Hou Hsiao-hsien, Jon Jost, Abbas Kiarostami,

Mohsen Makhmalbaf, Sergei Paradjanov, Mark Rappaport, Râúl Ruiz, Béla Tarr, or Edward Yang—to cite only the first ten names that come to mind—is matched by Thomson's failure to acknowledge any of the important Welles film material that has come to light since his death (ranging from fragments to completed works), not to mention the second edition of James Naremore's *The Magic World of Orson Welles*, the extensive research on and re-evaluation of IT'S ALL TRUE carried out by Catherine Benamou and Robert Stam, or the recent French and Spanish books cited above. Admittedly, Thomson cites Stam and praises my own Welles chronology in *This Is Orson Welles* in his bibliography, but there's no evidence in his text that he's given much thought to either. To assert, as he does of IT'S ALL TRUE, "There was never a movie there, only an extravagant, self-destructive gesture"—a judgment quoted with approval by Maslin—one either has to refute the massive counter-evidence or pretend that it doesn't exist, and Thomson characteristically settles on the latter. (The same principle of outright denial underlines Maslin's claim that Welles "cavalierly [absented] himself from the studio's drastic re-editing of THE MAGNIFICENT AMBERSONS," an accurate paraphrase of Thomson at his worst.)

Both Callow and Thomson are disappointingly negligent when it comes to assessing Welles's radio work in any detail—a major subject that still awaits a critical chronicler—but only Thomson is so lazy in this regard that it leads him to make gross blunders about Welles's work as a whole. Thus *Horse Eats Hat*, one of his comedy stage productions, "reminds us on how very few occasions Orson Welles played anything strictly for laughs," a line that literally throws out dozens of radio shows. Similarly, we learn that "Nothing [of the voodoo *Macbeth*] remains but still photographs and memories"—an assertion leading to a bogus theory about Welles's attitude toward the production—which rules out the surviving newsreel footage of the play's ending (some of which can be seen in *The Battle over CITIZEN KANE*). Elsewhere, "Welles was inclined to give [*The Cradle Will Rock*] scant attention in his history of what he had done," which sounds fine until you consider that the most sustained piece of autobiography Welles ever wrote was a screenplay about that very production, cited in Thomson's bibliography.

The problem with such gaffes is that they're typical of Thomson's text rather than exceptional; *Rosebud* is bent on demonstrating that Welles was a horrible person, incapable of loving anyone but himself, and it rarely allows facts or contrary opinions to get in its way. If Callow is neglectful and perhaps simply naïve about Welles's politics, Thomson seems to go out of his way to misrepresent them: "Welles . . . always liked his revolutionaries to be sophisticated and well-heeled," he notes at one point, cavalierly ruling out, among others, Jacaré—the central, heroic, real-life radical in the central episode of IT'S ALL TRUE. But since he elsewhere characterizes the footage from this episode, dealing with Jacaré and other poor Brazilian fishermen, as "picturesque but inconsequential material," maybe it's Thomson and not Welles who likes—indeed, requires—revolutionaries to be "sophisticated and well-heeled," at least if they want to be considered consequential.

By the same token, Thomson tries to imply more than once that Welles's enthusiasm for jazz and samba and his affection for black people must add up to some form of racism: "There is sometimes a perilous proximity of old-fashioned racial stereotype and yearning sympathy," he notes on page 144—neglecting, of course, to say which times, which might require at least a smidgeon of research—so that by the time he gets around to Welles playing a black man in OTHELLO (on page 305), he can note that "There is no exploitation of that special racial-sexual paranoia that Welles must have encountered with the voodoo *Macbeth*, by being in Brazil and in talks with Lena Horne." "Must have"? Are we talking now about Welles's paranoia or Thomson's? If Thomson appears to be letting Welles off the hook in the second quote, the hook in question is plainly his own invention.

Clearly it's Thomson's lack of interest in IT'S ALL TRUE—a turning point in Welles's career as an independent as opposed to Hollywood filmmaker—that leads to his idiotic claim that the deleted first two reels of THE STRANGER, simply by virtue of being set in South America, is "surely . . . a reference to IT'S ALL TRUE." (A comparable lack of interest leads to the greatest single flaw in Carringer's book on AMBERSONS, a study so deep in political denial that it fails to mention the title IT'S ALL TRUE even once.)

Even if one faults him for laziness, one can readily excuse Thomson for such relatively common errors as his assertions that Welles's Shakespeare editions of the 30s "were only ever published by the Todd Press" (thereby ruling out Harper & Brothers' 1939 updated versions), that "eventually Welles would make a villain and a spoilsport out of" RKO studio chief George Schaefer (contradicted sharply by my own interview with Welles, who passionately defended him throughout our meeting as a "good guy"), that Welles wanted Agnes Moorehead to play Lady Macbeth, that Patricia Medina was already married to Joseph Cotten when she played in MR. ARKADIN (their marriage was six years afterward), that Charlton Heston was a conservative in the 50s, that Welles's last released documentary was called THE MAKING OF OTHELLO (and not FILMING OTHELLO), and that Welles "liked" Barbara Learning's biography (which he helped to promote but never read). Speaking personally, I can even forgive Thomson for chiding both Gore Vidal and me for praising THE BIG BRASS RING, an unrealized Welles script that I helped to get published and which he considers "as bad as anything Welles ever did or attempted." (For Thomson, this script—which I still regard as corrosive and brilliant—is "an OW shopping list" and "one more lame try at the thriller genre." Since Thomson's critique is the first indication I've come across that THE BIG BRASS RING has anything to do with "the thriller genre," this seems about as relevant as calling KANE a failed musical.)

What I find unforgivable about *Rosebud* is its often voiced desire to close down Welles research altogether, apparently motivated by the sentiment that since Welles clearly never delivered a second KANE to Thomson's local video store, there's no point in looking for anything else in his oeuvre, including unreleased work he's never seen. "Perhaps, one day, something called Welles's QUIXOTE will emerge," he writes at one point—clearly unaware that one already did emerge in Spain four years ago—and adds, "Yet I wonder if it should. . . . Its legend is tattered and complete enough. Actual screenings would be so deflating, so much less than the thought of existence," etc. It's another way of saying, "There was never a movie there." But having seen close to three hours of edited or re-edited QUIXOTE footage—some of it breathtaking, much of it major Welles—I would argue that however inadequate the two-hour Spanish and English versions cobbled together in 1992 might be, this QUIXOTE footage is considerably *more* exciting than the legend, and even some of the footage left out of the release version, which I've written about elsewhere (in *Persistence of Vision*, no. 11, 1995), has to be included among Welles's most powerful and lasting achievements.

Of course, this footage doesn't have the production values of KANE; it was shot in total independence, out of Welles's own pocket, which means its chance of making it to Thomson's video store even in its inadequate version is fairly unlikely. So Thomson, or any potential Welles scholar, has a hard choice to make: either to travel to the Filmoteca Española in Madrid to see most of the QUIXOTE footage (and to Rome, where QUIXOTE editor Mauro Bonnani possesses the rest), or to stay at home and spin theories about Welles's degradation based on what hasn't been seen. If Thomson had admitted such a choice exists, he might have at least tried to justify opting for the second course of action; he didn't and hasn't—opting instead, like most passive spectators, to let the video stores determine the Welles canon, for now and for the indefinite future.

And what about the almost-finished THE OTHER SIDE OF THE WIND, the feature that Welles most wanted to release when he was still alive, still kept unseen by legal and financial entanglements? Having seen most of this projected feature—calculated to confound all Welles fans whose measure of his achievement remains stuck in the 40s—I wonder what its complex and shocking reflections on machismo, homophobia, Hollywood, cinephilia, eroticism, and late-60s media, not to mention its kamikaze style, might do to someone of Thomson's tender sensibilities. Fortunately, we don't have to wait. "One day, it may be freed," he writes. "I hope not. THE OTHER SIDE OF THE WIND should stay beyond reach"—for reasons comparable to his arguments about why QUIXOTE should remain unseen (and why IT'S ALL TRUE should continue to be seen as an incomprehensible patchwork).

Perhaps Thomson should go further and argue for a retooling of the NEA, simply for the purpose of tracking down all remaining unreleased Welles footage and destroying it, thereby guaranteeing once and for all no future threats of disappointing his expectations or mocking his dashed Hollywood hopes. After all, we know in advance that whatever else THE OTHER SIDE OF THE WIND might be, it isn't another CITIZEN KANE. Come to think of it, that's what keeps Welles so interesting.

Notes

1. The definitive piece of scholarship on the authorship of KANE—and sadly one of the least well known—is Carringer's "The Scripts of CITIZEN KANE," originally published in *Critical Inquiry* 5 (1978): 369–400, and reprinted in both *Perspectives on CITIZEN KANE*, edited by Ronald Gottesman (New York: G. K. Hall, 1996), 141–171, and *Orson Welles's CITIZEN KANE: A Casebook*, edited by James Naremore (New York: Oxford University Press, 1994), 79–121. (2006)
2. Only slightly and inadequately amended in the expanded fourth edition. (2006)

—*Cineaste* 22, no. 3, 1996

21

TOUCH OF EVIL Retouched

The following—an account of my work as consultant for Universal Pictures on the re-editing of TOUCH OF EVIL *in 1997–98, based on a studio memo—is the only thing I've ever written for* Premiere. *I knew one of the editors, Anne Thompson, from her previous stint as assistant editor at* Film Comment, *and when I proposed this piece to her, she checked with other editors at the magazine and reported back that there was a lot of enthusiastic interest. When I asked her what approach I should take, she urged me to write a first-person account of my experience of the project from beginning to end, which yielded a first version. She reported back that I should interview Charlton Heston, Janet Leigh, and Walter Murch and integrate some of this material. After doing this, I was told that the editors felt that a first-person account made the piece too much about myself and that the readers of* Premiere *couldn't be expected to know anything about the film, so I should add a detailed plot summary without making the piece any longer. This second revision had to be cut further after the piece's layout was done, eliminating practically all of the interview material.*

When Peter Bogdanovich asked to reprint this article in the 1999 volume of The Best Movie Writing *that he edited, I sent him the expanded version printed below, but for reasons I've never understood, he opted for the skimpy published version instead.*

■

It all started with a book I was editing in the early 90s, *This Is Orson Welles*, by Orson Welles and Peter Bogdanovich—an extended interview interlaced with various documents about Welles's career. One of the most fascinating of these documents was an edited version of a 58-page memo written by Welles on December 5, 1957 after a single viewing of the studio rough cut of TOUCH OF EVIL, his last Hollywood picture. Addressed to Universal studio head Edward Muhl, the memo was a plea for certain changes in sound and editing in a cut that had been partially prepared in Welles's absence, and although some of Welles's suggestions were followed, many were not.

It was a rare glimpse into the strategies and motivations of a master filmmaker who usually preferred to keep silent about such matters. But *This Is Orson Welles* was already a hefty volume carved out of thousands of pages and 25 hours of audiotape, and the memo was one of the key treasures that HarperCollins obliged me to cut due to lack of space. Eager to get it published elsewhere, I sounded out several film magazines, all of whom passed on it except for two small-circulation quarterlies on separate continents—*Trafic* in France and *Film Quarterly* in the U.S.—who printed it, respectively, in their spring and fall issues in 1992. I was delighted when, two years later, the *Film Quarterly* version prompted Charlton Heston, the star of TOUCH OF EVIL, to write me a cordial letter about it.

The same year, I received a phone call from the cinematographer Alan Daviau, who was exploring the possibility of a deluxe laser disc edition of TOUCH OF EVIL and mentioned the memo as something that might be relevant to the project. He also put me in touch with producer Rick Schmidlin, who eventually inherited Daviau's project and then concocted a wild scheme out of it: to follow all the instructions in Welles's 1957 memo for the first time. Then, after many more calls, Rick secured the agreement of Universal Studios, flew to Chicago to engage me as a consultant, and acquired Walter Murch—the celebrated sound editor of THE GODFATHER, THE CONVERSATION, APOCALYPSE NOW, and THE ENGLISH PATIENT—to carry out the editing. Before long, the adventure was underway. (By happy coincidence, while some of this was happening, I was also persuading Da Capo Press to include the edited memo in the second edition of *This Is Orson Welles*, which came out last spring.)

During all this time I remained rooted in Chicago, joined umbilically by phone lines and mail routes to what Rick and Walter were doing in California—sending them various materials (articles, videos, radio shows) as stylistic reference points, putting Rick in touch with other Welles scholars, and meanwhile receiving the unedited copy of Welles's memo, certain elucidating studio documents, and Walter's rough cut on video once these became available. Apart from some brief stints as an extra for Robert Bresson and as a script consultant for Jacques Tati when I was living in Paris a quarter of a century ago, this was my first experience of working on a feature, and the first lesson I learned was that every decision made had multiple consequences.

At one point, Murch told me that it was like performing a skin graft using only skin from the same body, because none of the work entailed restoring lost footage; it was more a matter of different placements and configurations of existing shots, different uses of sound and music. Many of these changes were subtle, but virtually all of them had lasting reverberations that affected everything else—including the flow of the storytelling, the construction of mood and atmosphere, and the inflection of character and emotion.

It would be no exaggeration to say that no work of this kind has ever been done before—work that was neither a restoration nor a "director's cut" in any ordinary sense, but delicate revamping based on executing postproduction instructions that had been drafted 40 years earlier. Interpretation of Welles's requests was necessary, because no matter how straightforward they were, executing cuts and sound changes is never the same thing as describing them. And it was impossible as well as unthinkable to pursue what Welles might have wanted TOUCH OF EVIL to be in 1998. All we had to focus on was what Welles wanted in late 1957, which proved to be more than enough.

Originally released the following year in a 93-minute version that wasn't even shown to the press, TOUCH OF EVIL enjoyed a brief second life when the 108-minute preview version was discovered in the mid-70s, containing more of Welles's footage but also more footage shot by contract director Harry Keller during postproduction—a longer cut that has subsequently become the only one available (apart from the home video, which mixed parts of the two versions). Though the preview version has been erroneously labeled the "director's cut" in some sources, the fact that Welles was never able to finish or approve any cut during his lifetime makes the very existence of such a thing a hopeful fantasy—more useful as a marketing tool than as an accurate description. Because Welles's creative intentions were always in flux, predicated on what his existing options were at any given time, the most any posthumous cut can hope to achieve is an interpretation of what he wanted at one stage in that development.

■

Aptly labeled "film noir's epitaph" by Paul Schrader, TOUCH OF EVIL describes the dark events of one 24-hour period in a sleazy Mexican border town after a local businessman and his stripper girlfriend are blown apart by a time bomb planted in the trunk of their car. Though provisionally a mystery, the plot mainly focuses on the battle of wills between a Mexican cop named Vargas (Heston) who plays by the book and a crooked American cop named Quinlan (Welles) who plants evidence. The crime occurs within Quinlan's jurisdiction, and Vargas is around at the time only because he happens to be there on his honeymoon. But by the end of the story, Vargas's wife Susie (Janet Leigh), Quinlan's partner (Joseph Calleia), and a local gangster (Akim Tamiroff) and prostitute (Marlene Dietrich) are all sucked into the conflict, along with many others.

The opening shot, one of the most famous in Welles's career, is a dazzling crane shot that begins with the planting of the time bomb and ends several blocks away just before the explosion, taking in several other points of interest—including Heston and Leigh—en route. Included in the dense weave of the various paths taken by the camera, characters, vehicles, and extras, is an intricate crisscrossing pattern between the honeymoon couple on foot and the couple in the car as all four characters approach the border crossing and are checked through by a guard.

In all previous versions, this shot is accompanied by Henry Mancini's score—which almost subliminally picks up the time bomb's ticking in the bongos, generating a fair amount of *Peter Gunn*–like suspense—and overlaid by the film's credits, which divert part of one's attention from the unfolding events. In the new version, following Welles's specifications, there are no credits over this shot and the only music one hears comes from loudspeakers in front of the various clubs and a car radio. Though the suspense is lessened, the physical density, atmosphere, and many passing details are considerably heightened, altering one's sense of the picture from the outset.

"In retrospect and in hindsight," Murch said after completing his work, "the changes we made have made the film more consistent with itself. That's an odd thing for that film, because for all of its contradictions, it's been admitted into the gallery of one of the memorable films of the 20th century. And yet it was a hybrid of what Welles wanted and did and what the studio left unchanged. So people who know the film have accepted it with all the stylistic contradictions in it and have forgotten or forgiven those contradictions. Now that they're gone, in a sense it'll be a shock because those who know it have gotten used to it the other way. It's like when you jump on somebody else's bicycle: it just feels different, the way the pedals work and everything.

"Stylistically the film uses crosscutting between different parts of the story—particularly Susie in the motel, what Vargas is going through, and what Quinlan is going through. Yet the studio, in an attempt to clarify the film in the opening reel, eliminated the crosscutting that Welles had intended as being too confusing. So once the explosion happens, except for that brief glimpse of Susie in the street, they stuck with Vargas and Quinlan for a continuous five or six minutes, and then they went to Susie. That wasn't what Welles wanted and it's not true to the rest of the film, which depends on crosscutting as a stylistic support for the story.

"So what we've done in the first reel—which is tremendously important as an overture to the whole work—is use more crosscutting. It's better now because the opening reel is more like the rest of the film. That's certainly true of the removal of the Mancini music from the opening shot and substituting a montage of various source music cues, which is also what Welles wanted." Interestingly enough, this montage provides another kind of overture, strictly musical—an introduction to various elements in Mancini's score that recur later.

One of the consequences of using more crosscutting is a stronger sense of different things happening simultaneously in the same border town. In a few cases the soundtrack has become more densely layered (as in the use of a Mexican newscaster on a car radio), and sharpening some of the sound cues, as requested, removes occasional incongruities, such as the immediate departure of musicians with their instrument cases from a strip joint as soon as the music stops playing. A superfluous patch of dialogue between Heston and Leigh in a hotel lobby that Welles neither wrote nor directed and which throws both their characters slightly out of kilter has been removed. A few frames are pulled from a frightening close-up of a strangled corpse, making its impact more subliminal. And a rapid editing pattern in the climactic confrontation between Vargas and Quinlan that was only partially realized in the two previous versions has finally been brought closer to Welles's original design.

In many cases, when Welles didn't fully explain his motivations in the memo, understanding why he dictated a particular change came only gradually, once the shot or scene could be seen and heard the way he requested it. Cutting the pianola music halfway through Welles's first scene with Marlene Dietrich, for instance, made the whole second half of their dialogue play somewhat differently; lines that had previously teetered on the edge of camp mannerism suddenly came across as straight, and the whole scene ran more smoothly as a consequence. This in turn became part of Welles's overall plan to use less musical editorializing in the opening reels that also occasioned the use of on-screen (as opposed to off-screen) music during the opening crane shot.

Eventually a clearer understanding of his design for the film began to emerge—a design that included, among other things, a more fluid narrative, more opportunities for certain atmospheric elements to register, and even a stronger sense of Quinlan's partner Menzies (Joseph Calleia) switching his allegiances because of his moral principles rather than through any collapse in his willpower. The latter change came about through the removal of a single close-up of Menzies that Welles objected to in a scene with Vargas set in the Hall of Records; unfortunately, this deletion also meant losing a little bit of Vargas's dialogue in order to avoid a jarring mismatch in the editing, but the gain arguably more than made up for the loss.

As far as Schmidlin, Murch, and I were concerned, the point of making all these revisions wasn't to produce a "definitive" version that should necessarily replace or supersede all the previous ones. We simply wanted to see what happened when Welles's wishes were carried out—nothing more, but also nothing less. Not his "ultimate" or "final" wishes, which no one could ever know or even presume to hypothesize, but his wishes as expressed on paper on December 5, 1957, shortly before he left the project.

■

"I think what you guys have done is admirable and does a great deal to make the film available," Heston told me on the phone after seeing the revamped version. "What was most impressive to me was to have the whole soundtrack enhanced by the technology of the 90s. I'm really delighted with the work that's been done on a picture that was important to me."

Heston kept a diary for many years, and consequently in-depth accounts of the making of TOUCH OF EVIL can be found in two of his books, *The Actor's Life: Journals 1956–1976* and his more recent autobiography, *In the Arena.* Leigh also retains vivid memories of the experience, including the little-known fact that she broke her left arm shortly before she began work on the film while wrestling with character actor Jessie White on a TV drama called *Carriage from Britain:* "I had it set not at a right angle, which is normal, but halfway between a right angle and straight down, so I could drape a coat or purse or something like that over it." She recalls that Welles originally thought of having her play Susie Vargas with her arm cast visible, but then concluded, "That's too weird even for me: a bride on her honeymoon with a broken arm—I can't do that!" So her cast was either concealed or briefly removed (for scenes when she wore a nightie), and no one in the audience noticed.

Fortunately, Leigh's right hand was still free to write down lines of dialogue that she improvised at Welles's house during two weeks of rehearsals prior to shooting: "A lot of the interplay between the characters came from improvising during the rehearsals," she told me, and some of it came during filming as well, particularly her scenes with Tamiroff and Dennis Weaver (as a sexually deranged night clerk at the motel whose part barely existed in the original script). She remembers much of the shoot as a festive adventure: "I remember how the first night Marlene [Dietrich] worked, everybody had a bottle of champagne in their trailer. He did everything grandly; it was just a flair he had, and he didn't care if you drank it. I didn't happen to, but I'm sure he wouldn't have cared if I did."

For Leigh, the retouched TOUCH OF EVIL, which made her cry when she saw it, has "the original flavor more than the original released product did. Seeing it pure was wonderful; I was so thrilled that this genius is going to have a chance to show itself again."

—Published in a different and shorter
version in Premiere, September 1998

■

Afterword (2006): I must confess that when Rick Schmidlin first broached his idea for this project to me, I was pretty skeptical—both that Universal would ever go along with it and that the results would make it worth doing. Not only did he prove me wrong in both departments, but the re-edit went on to become a commercial and critical success, making it almost unique among Welles releases and rereleases. According to Rick, Universal originally struck 30 prints for the U.S. release, but eventually struck 40 more, and the film also fared quite well overseas.

My experience with Universal was mainly pleasant. Once Rick finally got the studio to greenlight the project and to agree not to interfere in creative decisions (both of which came about thanks to his shrewd strategy of acquiring the Oscar-winning Murch to work on the project and of requesting a modest budget—the latter in contrast to the costly recent restoration of VERTIGO *undertaken at the same studio, which had a mixed commercial as well as critical response), things proceeded fairly smoothly, though there were a few glitches along the way. One was that a complete version of the original memo was nowhere to be found, either in the studio files or in those that I acquired from Oja and Peter for my work on* This Is Orson Welles. *Fortunately, I remembered the two cordial letters sent to me by Heston when the edited version first appeared in* Film Quarterly, *one of which mentioned that he still had a copy of the original memo in his own files. But rather than allow Rick or myself to contact Heston directly about this, the studio set about doing this on its own, in an extremely circumspect and roundabout manner. (At the time, rumor had it that the request was finally made to Heston by none other than Lew Wasserman.) Then, once the full document was acquired, being allowed to view it was no simple matter. I first had to sign a statement declaring that I would agree not to even mention the existence of such a document to anyone outside the studio—a condition I reluctantly agreed to despite its evident absurdity insofar as I had already published and annotated most of this document five years earlier. But apart from a few oddities of this kind, my experience on the project up through its premiere was quite positive. Some critics I admire, such as Tom Gunning, prefer the original release version of* TOUCH OF EVIL, *ellipses and all, to any others—a preference that strikes me as legitimate—and it was never the intention of Rick, Walter, or myself for the version we worked on to supplant any of the others. The fact that it's been used that way by Universal is lamentable (I'm especially chagrined by the end of the film's entry in Leonard Maltin's* 1998 Movie & Video Guide—"*Beware* 95m. *version"—which implies that only one "correct" version can be tolerated, which unfortunately happens to be ours), though I suppose we should have predicted it. Our own ideal scenario would have been for our version, the original release version, and the "original" preview version (that is, the one I wrote about in chapter 6, before the studio combined elements of this with elements of the original release) to be released together in a DVD box set. We also thought that our opinion on this matter might have carried some weight with the studio, but in fact, once Rick failed in his bid to direct the "making of" documentary about our version for cable (which was assigned to a director who specialized in such documentaries), he and I fell out of contact with Universal. A plan of Rick's and mine to collaborate on a book about the film that would include the script, the entire memo, and many other production documents got as far as a contract with the University of California Press, but then got canceled once it became clear that Rick didn't feel comfortable with doing any of the writing.*

Then the release of the DVD of our version—which we played no role in preparing, though it contains the full text of the memo—got delayed several months once Beatrice Welles threatened the studio with legal action. Since I wasn't privy to any of the discussions that took place about this—apart from an early phone call from one of the lawyers hired by Universal—I can't comment on this in detail, except to note that another version of the same threat prevented the film at the last minute from premiering at Cannes (see chapter 22), and that I saw a letter from Beatrice to Janet Leigh apologizing about the contretemps at

Cannes after she saw our version. (For a more general piece about Beatrice Welles's many threatened lawsuits, including even an effort to claim ownership of the rights to CITIZEN KANE, see Geoffrey Macnab's article in the Guardian at http://film.guardian.co.uk/features/featurepages/0,4120,1031039,00.html.) To all appearances, an out-of-court settlement with Universal was reached. Then the DVD was released, and since by this time all of our communications with Universal had ceased, neither Rick nor I were sent a copy.

By far the biggest perk for me in working on this project was getting to spend time with Janet Leigh (1927–2004), after our initial and very cordial phone interview, both at Cannes (and on a day-long trip to Antibes and environs during that period) and in Toronto four months later. A rarity among the very few movie stars I've spent much time with, she was extremely unpretentious and plainspoken as well as uncommonly bright, and the fact that I'd already been smitten with her since the age of eight (when I saw her in ANGELS IN THE OUTFIELD, TWO TICKETS TO BROADWAY, and IT'S A BIG COUNTRY) only enhanced the overall experience. Her appreciation and understanding of both Welles and Alfred Hitchcock, moreover, seemed substantial.

22

Excerpt from "Problems of Access: On the Trail of Some Festival Films and Filmmakers"

(On TOUCH OF EVIL)

TOUCH OF EVIL (Cannes, Toronto, Ann Arbor, Torino, Rotterdam). The re-configuration of Welles's film based on forty-eight changes in sound and editing derived from a fifty-eight-page memo that he wrote to Universal studio head Edward Muhl in 1957 is scheduled to premiere in Cannes. But unfortunately this is planned to take place in the smallest auditorium in the Palais for a few hundred VIPs, most of them American. So I'm mainly glad when the spurious claims and legal threats of Welles's daughter Beatrice persuade Gilles Jacob—who doesn't have the time while directing the festival to check the facts of the matter—to cancel this screening, which would have entailed excluding most of the world press for the sake of American vanity.

As it turns out, the cancellation gives the film more publicity than it might have had otherwise, thanks mainly to the presence in Cannes of Janet Leigh, editor Walter Murch, picture restorer Bob O'Neil, and producer Rick Schmidlin. In fact, the task of convincing the woman in charge of foreign sales at Universal to show the film abroad has been an uphill battle from the start. Initially she rejected all offers from overseas festivals, and reportedly only after she attended Deauville and Venice did she arrive at the conclusion that people outside the United States might be interested in seeing this version—a good ex-ample of the fruits of contemporary American isolationism. (For the same reason, I suspect most Hollywood studios tend to avoid Cannes premieres because they don't feel they can gauge the commercial results in advance.)

So the world premiere of the film, which I don't attend, occurs in Telluride four months later, but I'm around for its second screening shortly afterward in Toronto, along with Leigh and Schmidlin. By this time, the press coverage on the new TOUCH OF EVIL has mainly been accurate as well as favorable, and it continues in this vein when the film opens domestically later in September.

In Ann Arbor in October, lecturing in a class taught by Welles scholar Catherine Benamou, I explain how the persistence of Schmidlin and the participation of Murch eventually allowed us to carry out Welles's instructions without interference, discovering in the process how pertinent and consequential most of these instructions were. (For instance, the removal of a single close-up of Joseph Calleia from the Hall of Records scene, requested by Welles for cosmetic reasons, actually transforms the character of Menzies from a weakling to a highly principled individual in the final section of the film.) I also illustrate with a video of Murch's rough cut the two changes I made in his editing decisions—the first one a correction of a simple error (restoring the sound of Sanchez being punched in the stomach by Quinlan during the long interrogation sequence), the second one a difference of opinion in which Schmidlin ultimately decided in my favor. (The request that Welles devoted the most space to in his memo was to cut the first scene between Leigh and Akim Tamiroff into two segments, cutting back to the scene of the explosion in between; Murch cut this scene into three segments with two cutaways to the explosion scene, and my objection, apart from the fact that Welles didn't request this, was that it played too smoothly, like the sort of mechanical crosscutting one finds nowadays in practically every TV cop show. As Welles noted in his memo, this scene "has—and was meant to have—a curious, rather inconclusive quality," but Murch's initial fragmentation prevented it from truly functioning *as* a scene.)

With Murch and Schmidlin in Torino, and then with Schmidlin in Rotterdam, we encounter more technical problems. At the first Torino screening, two of the middle reels get scrambled and then, to the audience's frustration, the film is screened to the end. (I'm told that one Italian journalist who stayed only for the beginning, as I did, rushed off to report in his paper the next day that the screening was a resounding success.) Then, in Rotterdam, the film fails to arrive in time for the first screening—scheduled in the largest auditorium at the Pathé (the largest and perhaps best-designed multiplex in Europe), with all the tickets sold—and attracts only a fraction of the same audience when it is subsequently shown twice. But the film has already acquired a Dutch distributor, and by this time Nanni Moretti, the director of DEAR DIARY and APRIL, has arranged to distribute it in Italy and other European distributors have picked it up, so such mishaps seem less serious than they might have otherwise. I'm more troubled by the fact that Rotterdam's catalogue and smaller program guide both describe it as a "director's cut," suggesting that all the efforts Schmidlin, Murch, Leigh, myself, and others have made to clarify that no such thing as a director's cut of TOUCH OF EVIL can ever exist haven't successfully crossed the Atlantic. Judging from the August video release of the preview version, it hadn't even crossed the Universal studio lot six months ago (I speak metaphorically, of course, because a studio's internal links nowadays are mainly by e-mail), so perhaps it's myopic to expect that a mainly accurate press coverage in the United States can be exported along with the film. But at least I can correct some of the misunderstandings when I'm interviewed by the festival's daily newspaper.

—Originally written for *Trafic,* no. 30 (Summer 1999);
published in English in chapter 9 of my *Movie Wars:
How Hollywood and the Media Limit What Films We Can
See* (Chicago: A Cappella, 2000)

23

Welles in the Lime Light

THE THIRD MAN

Ironically, the most successful and beloved movie Orson Welles was ever associated with—and the one that may have had the most significant effect on the remainder of his career—has not been one of his own. Admittedly, CITIZEN KANE has more prestige, but that's a relatively recent development; for the first quarter of a century after it was made, it was criticized as "uncinematic" in the few standard works of film history available, such as *The Liveliest Art* and *The Film Till Now*. Instead it was THE THIRD MAN (1950) that was most often cited with pleasure when Welles's name came up. "Didn't he direct that?" was something I used to hear a lot. Today I hear "Didn't he direct at least some of the scenes?"

From the testimony of everyone involved, including Welles, we know that he wrote one brief and highly memorable speech comparing Italy and Switzerland (which he once claimed he cribbed from an old Hungarian play) and rewrote a couple of his other lines in the same scene. But he didn't direct anything in the picture; the basics of his shooting and editing style, its music and meaning, are plainly absent. Yet old myths die hard, and some viewers persist in believing otherwise. Sometimes they also want to believe that he secretly directed portions of at least half of the other pictures he acted in. Similarly, some viewers persist in regarding this British movie set in postwar Vienna as American; it was even ranked 57th in the American Film Institute's "100 greatest American movies" poll last year [1998], though I've never known anyone outside the United States who harbored this colonialist fantasy.

Presumably people can sustain this fantasy because two of the three most important characters—the highly visible Holly Martins (Joseph Cotten) and the mainly invisible Harry Lime (Welles)—are American. Moreover, David O. Selznick, who also was American, plastered his name all over the movie, trimmed several shots and sequences for the American market, and even replaced producer-director Carol Reed's expository offscreen narration at the beginning with a slightly different narration delivered by Cotten. The original and better version released in Europe—what might be termed the Alexander Korda version—has recently been restored and is playing this week at the Music Box. This version, which has been available only in some video editions, has longer stretches during which the Austrian characters speak in German without subtitles as well as better pacing throughout.

Korda, the Hungarian-born British producer, played a much more active and creative role on the film than Selznick. He'd also developed many previous film projects for Welles to direct, though none of them ever came to fruition (including AROUND THE WORLD IN 80 DAYS, CYRANO DE BERGERAC, WAR AND PEACE, an American version of Pirandello's *Henry IV*, and two original scripts, V.I.P. and OPERATION CINDERELLA). But not even Korda qualifies as the movie's principal auteur. In fact, it's doubtful that the movie can be read in auteurist terms at all. Like GILDA and CHILDREN OF PARADISE, it's an anomaly whose special qualities come from a series of creative convergences rather than from a single dominant artistic sensibility—another reason people might fantasize that Welles directed parts of it.

THE THIRD MAN is wonderful entertainment, as it was designed to be, and there are certainly moments in it that deserve to be called artful as well as stylish; foremost among these are the first appearance of Welles, carefully plotted by Reed, and the final shot, which is 35 seconds longer in the Korda version and was conceived by Reed over the objections of Graham Greene, who scripted a more conventional happy and romantic ending (though he later admitted Reed was right). But even these virtues don't give it the art or style of Welles's own pictures; it has only superficial aspects of his art and style.

I'm also reluctant to call it anybody's masterpiece, because its virtues are so closely allied with its limitations. "Masterpiece" implies "master," and however accomplished Reed and Greene are in their roles, they arguably did a better job on the lesser-known THE FALLEN IDOL, a 1948 picture based on Greene's story "The Basement Room." To my taste, Reed's hokey but powerful ODD MAN OUT (1946), scripted by F. L. Green and R. C. Sherriff, and Greene's 1951 novel *The End of the Affair* are more deserving of the term masterpiece.

Perhaps the best account of the limitations of THE THIRD MAN can be found in Manny Farber's mixed review: "The movie's verve comes from the abstract use of a jangling zither and from squirting Orson Welles into the plot piecemeal with a tricky, facetious eyedropper. The charm, documentary skill, and playful cunning that fashioned this character make his Morse-code appearances almost as exciting visually as each new make-believe by Rembrandt in his self-portraits. . . . Reed's nervous, hesitant film is actually held together by the wires of its exhilarating zither, which sounds like a trio and hits one's consciousness like a cloudburst of sewing needles. Raining aggressive notes around the characters, it chastises them for being so inactive and fragmentary and gives the film the unity and movement the story lacks." Farber also faulted Greene for his snobbish handling of Cotten's character, more specifically his profession as a pulp writer, which Greene used largely for cheap laughs. (An alcoholic in love with Lime's former yet still loyal girlfriend Anna, Martins is depicted mainly as a weak character whose sense of decency, at least in contrast to Lime's, is partially and ironically perceived as a sign of weakness.)

Reed and Korda insisted on casting Welles as Lime—an American black marketer who sells diluted penicillin to Vienna hospitals—over Selznick's objections. Selznick became important only in the casting of Cotten (as Lime's best friend, summoned by Lime from the States) and Alida Valli (as Anna, a Czech refugee posing as an Austrian, betrayed by Lime to the Russians), both of whom he held under contract. Greene's original story was about the friendship between two Englishmen, but once they became two Americans, the picture began to echo the Wellesian theme of betrayed male friendship and certain related ideas from CITIZEN KANE—e.g., Cotten playing a writer and Welles playing a charming rogue of dubious morals who hires him.

To this Reed added the Wellesian visual motifs of shadows and tilted angles, though they don't function as dramatic and metaphysical markers but simply conjure up a mood and atmosphere: shadows equal mystery and skullduggery, tilted angles mean everything's slightly off-kilter. It's a loose strategy for depicting the rubble-strewn Vienna of that period, which had been sliced into American, British, Russian, and French zones with an international zone for the police at the center. Another strategy was hosing down the cobblestone streets and shooting most of the film at night to allow Robert Krasker's high-contrast cinematography to capitalize on all the murky ambience, and Greene's own background as a spy undoubtedly enhanced the sense of intrigue. Yet for all the art of Greene's storytelling, it wasn't until Reed added the solo zither music of Anton Karas—most of it recorded in Reed's house in London—that the picture acquired the "unity and movement" cited by Farber. This is why I find it easier to speak about artfulness and stylishness in this movie than about art and style; its pleasures are less those of a unified expression than those of several independent discourses merging in superficial harmony.

If the collective makers of THE THIRD MAN had a single precursor, it would have been Joseph Conrad, whose work considerably influenced both Welles and Greene. Welles's first film project, preceding KANE, was a contemporary adaptation of Conrad's "Heart of Darkness," a story built around the much-delayed appearance of its evil and ruthless but charismatic villain, Kurtz. And, as James Naremore points out in his recent book on film noir, there's a character named Kurtz in THE THIRD MAN. Greene's *The Heart of the Matter*, which preceded THE THIRD MAN by a year or so, was influenced in other ways by the same story. (Later in his career, Welles wrote unrealized scripts based on Conrad's *Lord Jim* and *Victory* and Greene's Conradian *The Honorary Consul*.)

THE THIRD MAN would have been inconceivable without *Heart of Darkness*, and when Welles the actor stepped into his villainous part, a character analogous to Conrad's Kurtz—the unscrupulous exploiter from abroad, putting in his first, brief appearance an hour into the film—he knew from his theater experience as well as from his first screenplay that less from an actor could add up to more in terms of public perception. He'd discovered that a great performance could dominate an entire film even if it consisted of only one terrific scene, one moment of standing hidden in a doorway, and a few stray shots of fleeing through the streets and sewers. As he put it to Peter Bogdanovich, "The old star actors never liked to come on until the end of the first act. *Mr. Wu* is a classic example—I've played it once myself. All the other actors boil around the stage for about an hour shrieking, 'What will happen when Mr. Wu arrives?' 'What is he like, this Mr. Wu?' and so on. Finally a great gong is beaten, and slowly over a Chinese bridge comes Mr. Wu himself in full mandarin robes. Peach Blossom (or whatever her name is) falls on her face and a lot of coolies yell, 'Mr. Wu!!!' The curtain comes down, the audience goes wild, and everyone says, 'Isn't that guy playing Mr. Wu a great actor!' That's a star part for you! What matters in that kind of role is not how many lines you have, but how few. What counts is how much the other characters talk about you. Such a star vehicle really is a vehicle. All you have to do is ride."

In these terms, Harry Lime became Welles's express train. For the first hour of THE THIRD MAN virtually nothing is discussed except Lime. When he finally turns up, he's played by Welles without any makeup or false hair (apparently for the only time in his career), giving the film a special and legendary status in his work as a whole. Yet his physical participation in the film was so brief and limited that assistant director Guy Hamilton served as his double for many of the shots in the sewer, and Reed's fingers were used when Lime's hands emerge from a sewer grate. At that point Welles had left Vienna and was off hustling money to complete his film version of OTHELLO; he had to settle for a flat acting fee for THE THIRD MAN rather than a percentage of the gross, which he much regretted later.

Although it wasn't his film, it was often remembered as his; consequently Harry Lime became part of his meal ticket—not so much his signature as his designated alias, which, metaphorically speaking, was useful when it came to cashing checks. In early 1951 he began playing Lime in a half-hour radio show recorded in London and occasionally Paris that had at least 39 episodes; at least a dozen were scripted by Welles, and a few may have been unofficially directed by him as well. This was by far the most extensive radio gig he'd had after abandoning American radio in the late 40s, and the series got some exposure in the U.S. when it was syndicated as *The Third Man: The Lives of Harry Lime*, though it's seldom spoken of today. Many of these shows have recently been revived on German radio; listening this past spring to several of them, I was struck by how consistently they traffic in the same world-weary depiction of postwar European dissolution projected by THE THIRD MAN, despite the wit and high spirits of the lead character. The Lime in these shows is more a hero than a villain—still a rogue but no longer evil (a quality typically reserved for scheming female characters and a few male crooks)—and the political bent of the shows is liberal, though less anti-American than most of Greene's work during the same period. In his little-known, progressive 1956 European TV series AROUND THE WORLD WITH ORSON WELLES, the third of six completed episodes was called "The Third Man in Vienna," and in the late 60s, when he was working on ORSON'S BAG, a never-completed TV special for CBS (currently being restored by the Munich Film Archives), he included a segment called "Spying in Vienna" that harks back directly to THE THIRD MAN. And not long before his death, in what may have been the best of his late scripts, THE BIG BRASS RING, he placed his own character, Menaker, on a Ferris wheel, just like Harry Lime in his best scene—though in this case the character's voyeuristic distance from others (a couple making love in a nearby flat) expressed pathos rather than chilling misanthropy (Lime's speech to Martins about the "dots" below). I'm told George Hickenlooper deleted this scene when he directed a substantially revised version of the script—a film scheduled to turn up on Showtime next month—which may be just as well considering how beautifully it's realized in the script.

Out of several of Welles's radio scripts for *The Adventures of Harry Lime* grew his screenplay for MR. ARKADIN (1955), with its own black-marketeering protagonist, set in a similar world of postwar European corruption and crime. (As if to acknowledge its source, ARKADIN literally restages one shot from THE THIRD MAN—a giant close-up of an eye behind a magnifying glass.) But here the Lime role is taken over by the completely uncharismatic Guy Van Stratten (Robert Arden), while Welles plays a Russian tycoon of mysterious origins.

I'm reminded of the process by which one of Welles's precursors, the great Erich von Stroheim, revised some of his own priorities early in his career. When his first feature, which he called THE PINNACLE, was retitled BLIND HUSBANDS without his consent or permission, he took out a full-page ad in a trade paper denouncing the head of Universal Pictures, Carl Laemmle, for the change. But after BLIND HUSBANDS cleaned up at the box office, he was quite happy to call his third feature, a spin-off of BLIND HUS-BANDS, FOOLISH WIVES; there's even some possibility that he briefly considered calling his adaptation of *McTeague*, by Frank Norris, GREEDY WIVES instead of GREED.

Welles—who hated the Harry Lime character too much to have been able to make him palatable in a movie of his own—was turned by Korda, Greene, and Reed into such a charming monster that most moviegoers have preferred to remember him that way: Welles without his customary self-critique, playing the guiltless profiteer. Moreover, because this is one of Greene's "entertainments," we're not shown any of the children in the Vienna hospital who've been treated with Lime's diluted penicillin—unlike Martins, who's taken there by a British officer (Trevor Howard) who correctly surmises that seeing the children will goad him into betraying his best friend. In other words, watered-down penicillin was actually sold on the Vienna black market during this period, but Greene was more interested in the effect of this on Martins than on the audience. "We had no desire to move people's political emotions," he wrote years later in his autobiography *Ways of Escape*. "We wanted to entertain them, to frighten them a little, even to make them laugh." (Greene's published novella *The Third Man* was written before that script and differs in several respects from the film, and as Greene notes, "The film in fact is better than the story because it is in this case the finished state of the story.")

Around the same time Greene was writing *The Third Man*, George Orwell was noting of this very Catholic writer that he seemed to share the Baudelairean notion that "there is something rather distingué in being damned," that "Hell is a sort of high-class nightclub." In some respects Herman Mankiewicz, Welles's cowriter on CITIZEN KANE, had a related talent for glorifying corruption, which is one reason Charles Foster Kane as a young idealist and Harry Lime as a somewhat older nihilist bear a certain resemblance to each other and seem to stand slightly apart from Welles's other characters. Perhaps it took a Mankiewicz or a Greene to

move Welles fully into the popular imagination and out of the more innocent view of innocence that characterized Welles's other work. In most
of Welles's roles over which he had some creative input, the self-criticism
tended to cancel out much of the charisma, yielding portraits that were
typically too troubled to be consumed in single gulps. Grinning and fe-
rocious Harry Lime may have been Lucifer, but he was also bite size—far
too easy to swallow.

—*Chicago Reader*, July 30, 1999. © *Chicago
Reader*, Inc. Reprinted with permission.

24

Orson Welles as Ideological Challenge

Nothing irritates one more with middlebrow morality than the
perpetual needling of great artists for not having been greater.
—Cyril Connolly

During my almost thirty years as a professional film critic, I've developed
something of a sideline—not so much by design as through a combination of passionate interest and particular opportunities—devoted to researching the work and career of Orson Welles. Though I wouldn't necessarily call him my favorite filmmaker, he remains the most fascinating
for me, both due to the sheer size of his talent, and the ideological force
of his work and his working methods. These continue to pose an awesome challenge to what I've been calling throughout this book [i.e., *Movie
Wars*] the media-industrial complex.

In more than one respect, these two traits are reverse sides of the same
coin. A major part of Welles's talent as a filmmaker consisted of his refusal
to repeat himself—a compulsion to keep moving creatively that consistently worked against his credentials as a "bankable" director, if only because banks rely on known quantities rather than on experiments. In industry parlance, a relatively bankable director—someone like Steven
Spielberg or James Cameron in the present era, Charlie Chaplin (for most
of his career, up through THE GREAT DICTATOR) in an earlier era—is someone who knows how to "deliver the goods," which doesn't necessarily
rule out experimentation but limits it to retooling certain tried-and-true
elements. On an art-house level, even Woody Allen remains relatively
bankable because no matter how much he experiments, most audiences
still have a pretty good idea of what "a Woody Allen movie" consists of.

Welles never came close to attaining this kind of public profile, and in terms of his ability to keep turning out movies that played to paying audiences, he paid dearly for this deficit. None of his pictures turned a profit on first release in this country with the sole exception of THE STRANGER, perhaps the least distinctive and adventurous item he directed—a film made in order to prove that he was bankable, and, because the commercial success even of that movie was only modest, it led to no sequels. In fact, the very notion of sequels of any kind remained anathema to Welles, and people who wonder why he couldn't or wouldn't turn out "another CITIZEN KANE"—including such unforgiving biographers as Charles Higham, Simon Callow, and David Thomson—tend to overlook not only the unique and complex set of circumstances that made his first feature possible but also the temperamental facets of his talent that made such a possibility unthinkable.

Comparing the respective film careers of Welles and Stanley Kubrick, it's interesting to consider that both started out in their early twenties, both died at the age of seventy, and both completed thirteen released features. Another significant parallel is that both wound up making all their completed films after the fifties in exile, which surely says something about the creative possibilities of American commercial filmmaking over the past four decades. But in other respects their careers proceeded in opposite directions: Welles entered the profession at the top regarding studio resources and wound up shooting all his last pictures on shoestrings and without studio backing; Kubrick began with shoestring budgets and wound up with full studio backing and apparently all the resources he needed.[1]

Even though the first of Kubrick's features, FEAR AND DESIRE (1952), has mainly been out of circulation for the past several years, the remainder of his work is sufficiently well known to make a recounting of his filmography unnecessary, but the same thing can't be said for all of Welles's completed features. The best known remain those released by Hollywood studios (CITIZEN KANE, THE MAGNIFICENT AMBERSONS, THE STRANGER, THE LADY FROM SHANGHAI, MACBETH, and TOUCH OF EVIL) and two independent features in the fifties that continue to circulate: OTHELLO and MR. ARKADIN. The remaining five, thanks to their independent financing and their checkered commercial careers, tend to be less known in the United States. In chronological order, these are THE TRIAL (an adaptation of the Franz Kafka novel, 1962), CHIMES AT MIDNIGHT (also known as FALSTAFF, adapting portions of all the Shakespeare plays featuring Falstaff, 1966— considered by many critics to be Welles's greatest feature), the hour-long THE IMMORTAL STORY (an adaptation of an Isak Dinesen story, in color, made for French television, 1968), and two rather different essay films: F FOR FAKE (about art forgery in general and art forger Elmyr de Hory, writer Clifford Irving, and Welles himself in particular, 1973) and FILM-ING OTHELLO (about the making of Welles's 1952 OTHELLO, his first completed independent feature, 1978).

The unexpected commercial success of the re-edited TOUCH OF EVIL in 1998 seems to have made Welles relatively "bankable" again, with the result that a good many other Welles or Welles-related projects have either just surfaced (such as movies entitled THE BIG BRASS RING, CRADLE WILL ROCK, and RKO #281) or are in the works (including possible restorations of Welles's THE OTHER SIDE OF THE WIND, THE MAGIC SHOW, THE DEEP/DEAD RECKONING, and ORSON'S BAG). Yet the ideological challenge posed by Welles's career remains as real and as operative as ever, because it continues to throw into question most of the working assumptions we have about the operations of the film industry.

I'm not claiming that this challenge was always or necessarily intentional. Though part of his ambition was to confound audience expectations and to shock or surprise, some of his unorthodox work habits were arrived at over the course of his unruly career rather than conceived as deliberate provocations. In order to summarize what these habits and practices consisted of, I've drawn up the following list and tried in each case to indicate the particular received ideas about filmmaking and film culture that they challenge (in some cases, these six topics overlap):

1. *Wells as an independent filmmaker.* His first and second features, CITIZEN KANE and THE MAGNIFICENT AMBERSONS, were studio releases, both made at and with the facilities of RKO, and this has led many recent commentators to regard Welles as an unsuccessful studio employee throughout his career rather than as an independent filmmaker, successful or other-

wise. Insofar as most film histories are written by industry apologists of one sort or another, this is an unexceptional conclusion, but not necessarily a correct one. To my mind, Welles always remained an independent who financed his own pictures whenever and however he could, and perhaps the only movie in his entire canon that qualifies as a Hollywood picture pure and simple, for better and for worse, is THE STRANGER. In many cases, one can easily separate his features into Hollywood productions (e.g., THE LADY FROM SHANGHAI, MACBETH) and independent productions (e.g., OTHELLO, F FOR FAKE), but the divisions aren't always so clear-cut: the unfinished IT'S ALL TRUE started out as a studio project and ended up as an independent project; according to Welles, ARKADIN in its release form was even more seriously mangled by its producer than any of his Hollywood films; THE TRIAL was largely financed by Alexander and Michael Salkind, some of whose productions (including SUPERMAN and THE THREE MUSKETEERS) can be loosely labeled as "Hollywood" or "studio" releases; and even a clearly independent effort like DON QUIXOTE started out as a TV project backed by Frank Sinatra.

Part of what made and continues to make CITIZEN KANE exceptional is that it was made with exceptional freedom and control *and* studio facilities, and this came about because Welles refused to sign a Hollywood contract to make pictures unless he had this control—and because he was formidable enough as a mainstream figure in the late thirties to demand it. People today tend to forget how much of an anomaly KANE was as a "Hollywood picture" when it was initially released in 1941; it took many decades of ideological spadework on the part of critics before it was perceived as a Hollywood classic, and paradoxically this achievement mainly came about through a demolition job—Pauline Kael's "Raising KANE"—that argued that, contrary to earlier claims that CITIZEN KANE was a "one-man show," made by Kael herself as well as many other critics, it was in fact a work that mainly owed its excellence to the creative screenwriting of Herman J. Mankiewicz, who was virtually the sole author of the script. This mainstream revisionist view was subsequently complemented by Robert L. Carringer's academic book *The Making of* CITIZEN KANE (Berkeley: University of California Press, 1985). Although Carringer thoroughly demolished Kael's claims about Mankiewicz's exclusive authorship of the script, he also argued more generally that KANE's greatness and singularity stemmed from its status as a collaborative venture, in which the roles played by cinematographer Gregg Toland, screenwriter Herman J. Mankiewicz, editorial supervisor John Houseman, and art director Perry Ferguson were pivotal. Left to his own devices, Carringer concluded, Welles was doomed to failure, and this accounted for KANE's preeminence over Welles's other films.

This is still a popular position, and there are plenty of arguments in favor of it—although most of them are rationalizations of Hollywood's industrial methods of turning out pictures. There's a lot at stake ideologically in classifying KANE as a Hollywood picture, as Kael and Carringer both do, because the moment one does, one arrives at a Platonic ideal of Hollywood practice that can be used—and generally *has* been used—as a way of dismissing the remainder of Welles's career as a filmmaker. Similarly, there's just as much at stake ideologically in classifying KANE, as I do, as an independent feature that uses Hollywood resources—which is not to deny the importance of collaborators (including actors as well as other participants) on KANE and other Welles movies, but rather to insist on the bottom line of who gets the final word on any production. Since everyone is in agreement that Welles had the final word on what went into CITIZEN KANE and that he had the full resources of a Hollywood studio on that picture, there is a certain amount of scholarly agreement between Carringer and myself about what the achievement of KANE consisted of. (There is no such scholarly agreement between both of us and Kael regarding the film's authorship; although her facts have been conclusively disproven by Carringer and others, Kael has opted to reprint "Raising KANE" without alteration, apology, or even acknowledgment of any counterpositions in the significantly titled *For Keeps*, her latest collection.) Where we start to differ is in what we take that achievement to mean. And once we combine the separate-but-overlapping arguments of Kael and Carringer—which in Kael's case also entails viewing KANE as the apotheosis of the Hollywood newspaper comedy—we wind up with a mainstream domestication of Welles's first feature. For roughly three decades after it was made, KANE remained a troubling anomaly in American film history, an unclassifiable object that was neither fish nor fowl. But once the domesticating arguments of Kael and Carringer took hold—the former in the mainstream, the latter in academia—the movie became

regarded as something much safer and more familiar, a Hollywood classic to stand alongside THE WIZARD OF OZ, CASABLANCA, BRINGING UP BABY,
and IT'S A WONDERFUL LIFE. (It's worth recalling that all four of the latter
movies were far from being "instant" classics either: THE WIZARD OF OZ
"tested" so poorly that M-G-M very nearly deleted "Over the Rainbow"
for making audiences too fidgety; CASABLANCA initially registered as
little more than a feel-good wartime entertainment; and both BRINGING UP
BABY and IT'S A WONDERFUL LIFE, like KANE, were outright flops at the box
office—assuming their current reputations many years later, after they
were revived repeatedly on TV.)

Revisionist film historian Douglas Gomery, who specializes in eco-
nomics, fundamentally agrees with my contention that Welles was an independent filmmaker throughout his career—and I hasten to add that he
arrived at this conclusion on his own, without any prompting from me.[2]
He argues that the simple notion that Welles was exploited by Hollywood
for the purposes of Hollywood has it backward: more generally, it was
Welles who exploited Hollywood for his own purposes. According to
Gomery's analysis, Hollywood of the thirties and forties was dominated
by four relatively strong major studios (Paramount, Fox, Metro, and
Warners), four major studios that were relatively weak (RKO, Columbia,
Universal, and United Artists), and a number of more marginal studios,
the strongest of which was Republic Pictures. Welles wound up making
films for the first three of the four weaker major studios, for Republic, and
for Sam Spiegel on THE STRANGER (released by RKO); he never worked for
any of the Big Four. In most cases, Gomery points out, Welles went over
budget and his films wound up losing money for the studios, all of which
contradicts the notion of him being exploited by Hollywood in general or
by the studios in particular.

So far, so good. Where I begin to part company with Gomery, as well
as with Carringer,[3] is in their uncritical acceptance of the business acumen
of those studios when they decided to tamper with Welles's work. Everyone is in agreement that CITIZEN KANE, which wasn't tampered with at
RKO, lost a certain amount of money, and that THE MAGNIFICENT AMBER-
SONS, which lost even more money, was substantially tampered with by
the same studio. Although neither Gomery nor Carringer conclude from

this that RKO would have been commercially justified in tampering with KANE—assuming that RKO's contact with Welles had allowed this—they both irrationally conclude that RKO was commercially justified in tampering with AMBERSONS, despite the fact that the resulting hybrid still lost the studio an enormous amount of money.

Obviously I can't prove that Welles's own version would have made more money, but I seriously doubt that they could prove the contrary. The only evidence they can summon up to support their view is the audience responses at the film's three test-marketing previews, and, as I hope this book [Movie Wars] has already demonstrated, this is tantamount to placing one's medical faith in a team of witch doctors. Both Gomery and Carringer accept without qualm the conclusion of studio executive George Schaefer that the first preview of AMBERSONS, when a version approximating Welles's own version was shown, was a "disaster." Certainly we have many eyewitness accounts that a significant portion of that audience was unsympathetic and even hostile—just as I'm sure we have evidence that members of the early preview audiences of THE WIZARD OF OZ started to squirm as soon as "Over the Rainbow" came on—but I'm not convinced that this constitutes any sort of conclusive evidence. I've seen most of the one hundred and twenty-five "comment cards" myself—fifty-three of which were positive, some of them outright raves ("a masterpiece with perfect photography, settings and acting," "the best picture I have ever seen")—and would conclude that declaring the preview a "disaster" on the basis of those cards is a highly subjective matter, very much dependent on what one is predisposed to look for. It all depends on whether the hostile responses definitively outweigh the favorable responses, and considering that the preview in question—held at the Fox Theater in Pomona, California on March 17, 1942—immediately followed a regular commercial screening of a Dorothy Lamour wartime musical, THE FLEET'S IN, one might easily conclude that an audience paying to see something like that might not have been exactly primed for an unusually long and depressing feature such as Welles's version of AMBERSONS.

Theoretically a preview of AMBERSONS that followed a commercial screening of HOW GREEN WAS MY VALLEY, released the previous year—even though this might have made for an unusually long program—

might have yielded seventy-two positive responses and fifty-three negative ones, a difference of only nineteen votes from what actually tran-
spired. Are Gomery and Carringer absolutely convinced that a minimum
of nineteen viewers at that preview couldn't have responded differently
if the studio had bothered to schedule the AMBERSONS preview after
something more appropriate? Or are they merely content to leave the
benefit of every doubt to RKO in this matter?

2. *Welles as an intellectual.* Starting around 1938, when at age twenty-three
Welles became a household name in the United States through the scandal of his *War of the Worlds* radio broadcast, the terms "genius" and "boy
genius" became attached to his name with increasing frequency, and they
clung to his public profile to varying degrees for the remainder of his life
and career. On the surface, these are terms of praise, but as Robert Sklar
has demonstrated at length in a brilliant essay,[4] they are just as clearly
terms of abuse—especially within the anti-intellectual context of American popular culture, where Welles came into prominence in the thirties
and forties. Moreover, the undertow of resentment behind these terms is
not merely a matter of after-the-fact interpretation. It becomes immediately apparent if one reads the three-part profile of Welles published in
the *Saturday Evening Post* in early 1940, if one listens to his radio appearances on popular comedy shows throughout the forties, or if one watches
"Lucy Meets Orson Welles," an episode of *I Love Lucy* broadcast in 1956.
Even the title and subtitles of the *Saturday Evening Post* profile coauthored
by Alva Johnson and Fred Smith spell out part of this undercurrent of hostility: "How to Raise a Child: The Education of Orson Welles, Who Didn't
Need It" (January 20), "How to Raise a Child: The Continuing Education
of Orson Welles, Who Didn't Need It" (January 27), and "How to Raise a
Child: The Disturbing Life—To Date—of Orson Welles" (February 3).

   Interestingly enough, Welles spoke favorably about these articles to
Peter Bogdanovich in 1969,[5] calling them accurate and implying that they
were sympathetic. (More precisely, he noted that the authors had worked
with him closely in preparing the profile, which raises the possibility that
Welles's own pronounced impulses toward self-criticism and self-
accusation were accurately reflected in the articles.) By the same token,

judging from the many appearances of Welles on comedy shows of the forties and fifties that I've heard and/or seen, he appears to be completely complicitous and comfortable with the extremely precocious, imperious, egomaniacal, and intimidating versions of himself comically presented and ridiculed on those programs. On July 19, 1946, he even presented an extended parody of his persona—"Adam Barneycastle," played by Fletcher Markle—on the Mercury Summer Theatre, explaining in his introduction that after hearing Markle's half-hour *Life with Adam* on Canadian radio, he couldn't resist importing it onto his own CBS radio show.

What are we to make of this apparent masochism on Welles's part, which seems to go well beyond "being a good sport" about the threatening figure he seemed to pose to the mass media? The negative aspects of this image hounded him for the remainder of his career, and continue to crop up even posthumously in works ranging from the Oscar-nominated documentary THE BATTLE OVER CITIZEN KANE (1995) and Tim Robbins's CRADLE WILL ROCK to Welles biographies by Charles Higham, Simon Callow, and David Thomson. Like most caricatures, this lampoon of Welles's personality had some basis in fact, even if it has tended to obscure other aspects of his character, often to ruinous effect. It points to fear as well as respect, intimidation as well as admiration, which was obviously part of the packaging he had to accept if he wanted to cut a figure in the mass media; and it must be admitted that Welles seemed to go along with this partial misrepresentation as a show-biz necessity. Unfortunately, this same distortion would interfere increasingly with public understanding of what he was up to as an artist, ultimately encouraging the same sort of mythology that mystifies most accounts of his more serious work today.

Welles's reputation as a "genius," which he eventually began to criticize in his late interviews, is not the same as his reputation as an intellectual, but the two images often overlap in the public imagination, especially in his case. Both are tied to his privileged upper-class background, though the usual unconscious taboos against discussions of class differences in American culture muddy the waters even further. This often leads to outright errors regarding Welles, such as David Thomson's assertion that he "always liked his revolutionaries to be sophisticated and well-heeled"—a premise that rules out, for starters, Jacaré, the central, heroic, real-life radical in the central episode of Welles's unfinished docu-drama feature about Latin America, IT'S ALL TRUE. But since Thomson elsewhere characterizes the footage from this episode, dealing with Jacaré and other poor Brazilian fishermen, as "picturesque but inconsequential material," one is forced to conclude that maybe it's Thomson and not Welles who likes—indeed, requires—revolutionaries to be "sophisticated and well-heeled," at least if they want to be considered consequential.[6]

The relation of culture to money is so fixed in the American popular imagination that it often becomes difficult to disentangle the two—a sit-uation much less prevalent in Europe, where, as Jim Jarmusch once pointed out to me in an interview, street cleaners in Rome are apt to dis-cuss Dante, Ariosto, and twentieth-century Italian poets, and "even guys who work in the street collecting garbage in Paris love nineteenth-century painting." Welles's intellectual activity often winds up imposing a lot of false assumptions about his politics, taking him to be an elitist rather than a populist—although in fact the reception of his work ran the gamut from popular (his theater and radio work in the thirties, his TV appearances) to elitist (most of his films from the forties onward, despite their populist intentions).

Welles has an interesting exchange on this issue with Bogdanovich in *This Is Orson Welles:*

PETER BOGDANOVICH: You once said that your tastes don't shock the middle-class American, they only shock the American intellectual. Do you think that's true?

ORSON WELLES: Yes.

PB: Why?

OW: Because I'm a complete maverick in the intellectual establishment. And they only like me more now because there's even less communication be-tween me and them. I've become kind of exotic, so they start to accept me. But basically I've always been completely at odds with the true intellectual establishment. I despise it, and they suspect and despise me. I am an intel-lectual, but I don't belong to that particular establishment.

PB: Well, it's true that America likes its artists and its entertainers to be either artists or entertainers, and they can't accept the combination of the two.

OW: Or any combination. They want one clear character. And they don't want you to be two things. That irritates and bewilders them.[7]

This final formulation expresses the problem in a nutshell. Welles was too much of a vulgar entertainer to endear himself to the intellectual establishment. But he was too much of an artist and intellectual to endear himself to the general public unless he mocked and derided his artistic temperament and intellectualism, thereby proving he wasn't on a higher level than his own audience and ratifying his own populism. (Significantly, to the best of my knowledge, this wasn't a form of self-disparagement he ever practiced in Europe, where it wasn't deemed necessary to establish his equity with the public.) To a large degree, straddling this contradiction is what his art and his life were all about.

3. *The taboo against financing one's own work.* I assume it's deemed acceptable for a low-budget experimental filmmaker to bankroll his or her own work, but for a "commercial" director to do so is anathema within the film industry, and Welles was never fully trusted or respected by that industry for doing so from the mid-forties on. This pattern started even before OTHELLO, when he purchased the material he had shot for IT'S ALL TRUE from RKO with the hopes of finishing the film independently, a project he never succeeded in realizing. As an overall principle, he did something similar in the thirties when he acted in commercial radio in order to surreptitiously siphon money into some of his otherwise government-financed theater productions during the WPA period, a practice he discusses in *This Is Orson Welles.* John Cassavetes, who also acted in commercial films in order to pay for his own independent features, suffered similarly in terms of overall commercial "credibility," which helps to explain why he and Welles admired each other. (In an early stage of his work on the unrealized THE BIG BRASS RING, a late script and project, Welles thought of casting Cassavetes and his wife, Gena Rowlands, as presidential candidate Blake Pellarin, the hero, and his wife, Diana.)

In the case of features that were largely financed out of Welles's own pocket, such as DON QUIXOTE and THE DEEP/DEAD RECKONING, Welles often insisted in interviews that when or if he finished and released these features was nobody's business but his own—an attitude that often met with resentment and/or incomprehension from his fans. This raises a good many intriguing and not easily resolvable questions about the implied social contract that exists between artist and audience, and one that is undoubtedly inflected by the relative power of the industry to deliver films to theaters and the relative powerlessness of most film artists to ensure that their own films get distributed.

In Welles's case, the poor critical receptions and poor business that greeted most of his releases, at least in the United States, made him understandably hesitant to risk whatever remained of his "bankability" by releasing any of his films prematurely, or at the wrong time; he was also handicapped throughout his career by being a terrible businessman and often made wrong guesses about the commercial viability of some of his projects. I'm told that he once turned down a relatively generous offer from Joseph Levine to distribute F FOR FAKE in the United States, an offer Levine made even though he had nodded off during a screening; convinced that his film would be a big moneymaker, Welles turned him down flat, only to accept a less lucrative offer years later in order to get any American distribution at all.

When I asked him about DON QUIXOTE in the early seventies, he replied that *Man of La Mancha* was currently being developed as a movie and he didn't want his own version to compete with it. This statement astonished me at the time, but after I reflected on all the abuse he received from the American press about the inferiority of his MACBETH to Laurence Olivier's HAMLET, I began to think his fears might have been justified. (When I asked him about THE DEEP, he insisted that it was the sort of melodrama that wouldn't date, and that he was more interested in releasing THE OTHER SIDE OF THE WIND first—although this eventually proved to be impossible for legal and financial reasons that are documented in Barbara Learning's Welles biography.)

4. *The unique forms of significant works.* It surely isn't accidental that we have only one completed version of CITIZEN KANE to evaluate. By contrast, we have at least two completed versions of Welles's MACBETH, three versions of his OTHELLO, and at least four versions apiece of his MR. ARKADIN and TOUCH OF EVIL, to provide only a short list. (There's also, for example, a separate version of THE LADY FROM SHANGHAI that has circulated in Germany containing some takes as well as shots that are different from those in the U.S. release version.)

The reasons for this confusing bounty are multiple, but all of them ul-timately stem from Welles's unorthodox practices as a filmmaker. When early audiences and critics complained about the Scottish accents and the length of the first version of MACBETH (which is incidentally the one prin-cipally available today), Welles obligingly had the film redubbed and deleted two reels' worth of material. (Most critics assume mistakenly that the only Hollywood film on which he had final cut was KANE; in fact, he also had final cut on both versions of MACBETH, even if the second version was done at the behest of Republic Pictures.) OTHELLO, on the other hand—Welles's first completed independent feature—was partially re-edited and redubbed at Welles's own initiative, between the time of its Cannes premiere and its belated U.S. release over three years later. Al-though you won't find this information in any of the "authoritative" books about Welles, French film scholar François Thomas has recently discovered that Welles redubbed Desdemona—played in the film by Suzanne Clothier, who shot her sequences in 1949 and 1950—with the voice of Gudrun Ure (later known as Ann Gaudrun), the actress who played Desdemona in his subsequent 1951 English stage production of the play, entailing a different interpretation of the same part. Over forty years later, long after Welles's death, the soundtrack of this second ver-sion was significantly altered—both sound effects and music were rere-corded in stereo, in the latter case without consulting composer Francesco Lavignino's written score, and the speed of the dialogue delivery was oc-casionally altered to improve the lip sync—in order to release the results as a so-called "restoration."[8]

Though it's theoretically possible to assign different evaluations to the separate versions of MACBETH and OTHELLO, critics have rarely bothered to carry out this work; in fact, most of them have been unaware that these separate versions exist. The fact that both versions of MACBETH and the first two versions of OTHELLO were all Welles's own handiwork means that we can't rank them in terms of authenticity (except to note that the second MACBETH wasn't instigated by him). We can't, for instance, argue that the European OTHELLO is "more Wellesian" or "truer to Welles's in-tentions" than the initial U.S. version, and consequently it becomes im-possible to speak of a "definitive" film version of Welles's OTHELLO.

The same principle was carried out more publicly by Jean-Marie Straub and Danièle Huillet—a European couple who make rigorous and beautiful avant-garde films that, in recent years, have rarely been screened in the United States—when they deliberately released four separate versions of their 1986 feature THE DEATH OF EMPEDOCLES, each employing separate takes of each shot, to correspond to the separate languages of each version: unsubtitled German, English subtitles, French subtitles, and Italian subtitles. Straub argued that this was done in order to challenge the notion of uniqueness that we habitually assign to individual films, and he certainly had a point, but Welles made the same point more off-handedly and surreptitiously three decades earlier when he refashioned his second OTHELLO without bothering to announce that he was doing so.

Why, one may ask, did Welles do this? Because he loved to work, one might surmise, and because for him all work was work-in-progress—both reasons helping to explain why he often wound up having to finance much of the work himself. To love the process of work to this degree evidently offends certain aspects of the Protestant work ethic. Judging from the jibes about Welles's obesity in his later years that often cropped up in his American obituaries—but not in most obituaries that appeared elsewhere in the world—Welles's reputation as a hedonist was often used against him to imply irrationally that all his production money went to pay for expensive meals; indeed, many people preferred to believe that the only reason he didn't make or finish or release more films was out of laziness and moral turpitude. (This is more or less the thesis of biographers Charles Higham, David Thomson, and, to a lesser extent, Simon Callow, none of whom ever met the man.)

Obviously the fact that Welles loved to make films—and often sacrificed his reputation as an actor by appearing in lots of TV commercials and bad movies in order to keep doing so—doesn't square with this hypothesis, except to imply that to some degree he wound up tarnishing part of his public profile in order to subsidize his art. The process by which a public figure became a private artist is obviously fraught with contradictions, but one should never forget that it was love of the art-making process itself that ultimately sabotaged Welles's commercial profile. And as the Chilean-French filmmaker and devoted Welles fan Râúl

Ruiz once said to me, in defense of Welles's reputation as a maker of unfinished films, "All films are unfinished—except, possibly, those of Bresson." Which leads us logically to

5. *Incompletion as an aesthetic factor.* Critics confronting Franz Kafka's
three novels have less of a problem with this—at least Kafka is rarely cas-
tigated as an artist to the degree that Welles is. Could this be because
money is involved more centrally with making movies than with writing
novels? It's also important to recognize that no two of Welles's unfinished
films remain unfinished for the same reason. This is the portion of
Welles's oeuvre that's most notoriously difficult to research, but on the
basis of what I've been able to glean over the years, Welles wanted and
made repeated efforts to finish both IT'S ALL TRUE and THE OTHER SIDE OF
THE WIND, came close to finishing DON QUIXOTE in at least one version in
the late fifties (according to former Welles secretary Audrey Stainton; see
her article, "Don Quixote: Orson Welles' Secret" in the Autumn 1988 *Sight
and Sound*) and eventually abandoned THE DEEP for personal as well as
commercial reasons.[9]

So much for incomplete works—which doesn't, of course, include features wrestled away from Welles's control and completed by others, such
as THE MAGNIFICENT AMBERSONS and MR. ARKADIN. But what about the incompleteness of Welles's oeuvre as a whole, an even more serious problem due to the unavailability of so many of his works, finished and unfinished alike? Some of these, like the films he made as integral parts of
stage productions in the thirties or the portions of features (THE MAGNIF-
ICENT AMBERSONS, THE STRANGER, THE LADY FROM SHANGHAI) deleted by
studios, are almost certainly lost for good. Some films, such as his first and
best TV pilot (THE FOUNTAIN OF YOUTH, 1956) and FILMING OTHELLO
(1979), remain unavailable simply because of "business reasons" (i.e., the
indifference of the copyright holder or legal obstacles, which often
amount to the same thing), with the result that most American viewers
are scarcely aware of their existence. Three extended TV series made by
Welles in Europe—ORSON WELLES'S SKETCH BOOK (six 15-minute episodes,
1955), AROUND THE WORLD WITH ORSON WELLES (five completed half-hour
episodes and one unfinished episode, 1955), and IN THE LAND OF DON
QUIXOTE (nine half-hour episodes, 1964)—survive but remain unavailable

in the United States. And most of the unfinished work has wound up in film archives—the Fortaleza footage of IT'S ALL TRUE at UCLA (although the footage that survives from that feature continues to be in peril until funds are found to preserve it), DON QUIXOTE and IN THE LAND OF DON QUIXOTE at the Filmoteca Española in Madrid, and, most recently, a varied collection of unfinished work (including THE DEEP, ORSON'S BAG, THE MAGIC SHOW, and THE DREAMERS) at the Munich Film Archive, which is still seeking ways of restoring and presenting it.

Without implying that all this material is equally important or interesting—I regard most of IN THE LAND OF DON QUIXOTE as amiable hackwork at best—I would argue that a significant part of it, judging from the portions that I've seen or sampled, substantially alters one's sense of Welles's oeuvre as a whole, extending its range and diversity while illuminating certain work that one already knows. This ultimately means that, fifteen years after his death, we are still years away from being able to grasp the breadth of Welles's film work, much less evaluate it.

6. *A confounding of the notion of art as commodity.* We're finally left with the problem of how to evaluate Welles's still-ungraspable oeuvre in relation to the international film market—an issue that is currently preoccupying a good many film executives as well as archivists considering the possibility of completing and/or releasing films by Welles that haven't yet been seen. Prior to the very successful commercial release of the reconfigured TOUCH OF EVIL, the prospects of getting any of these films out on the world market was beginning to look rather dim. (To date, Jesus Franco's lamentable version of Welles's DON QUIXOTE—hastily edited in order to premiere in a Spanish-language version at Spain's Expo 92, and subsequently completed in an English language version as well—has failed to find a U.S. distributor; to the best of my knowledge, it has only received a few scattered screenings in North America, most notably at New York's Museum of Modern Art.) Now that the commercial prospects are looking somewhat more favorable, numerous questions still remain—including how these "new" (or "old") works are to be represented.

"Welles's Lost Masterpiece" was the phrase used in ads for the significantly altered version of Welles's 1952 OTHELLO, released in 1992—although the film had never been lost at all; it had simply been out of distribution in the United States for many years. The new version, moreover, was billed as a "restoration," and this was how it was labeled by a good ninety-five-percent of the reviews in the press; in *The New York Times*, for instance, Vincent Canby called it "an expertly restored print that should help to rewrite cinema history." But as Michael Anderegg has pointed out,

> To term the project authorized by Beatrice Welles-Smith as a "restoration" is to make nonsense of the word. One cannot restore something by altering it in such a way that its final state is something new. To restore means, if it means anything, to bring back to some originary point—itself, of course, an extremely dubious concept. . . .
>
> If you find a Greek statue with a left arm missing, you might be able to restore it if (a) you can demonstrate, through internal and external evidence, that it once had a left arm and (b) you can discover some evidence of what the left arm looked like when it was still attached. If, however, the statue was meant to have no left arm (a statue, perhaps, of a one-armed man), or if the statue was never completed by the sculptor, or if, assuming the arm did once exist and had broken off, you have no evidence of what the missing arm had originally looked like, then adding an arm of your own design is not an act of restoration. You are, instead, making something new.[10]

According to Anderegg's subsequent analysis, the version of Welles's OTHELLO described as a "restoration" alters not only Welles's original sound design and Francesco Lavignino's score, but also reloops some of the dialogue with new actors, eliminates some words "so that a lip-synch could be achieved," and re-edits one sequence entirely. But of course the use of the term "restoration" in relation to movies has become so loose and imprecise in recent years that it characteristically gets employed every time a studio decides to strike a new print, add footage without consulting the original director, or, on a few rare occasions, rework an old movie with the original director's input (as in the rereleased BLADE RUNNER, which proved to be partly a restoration of Ridley Scott's original cut and partly a revision—including the insertion of a shot of a unicorn taken from Scott's LEGEND, a film made three years after BLADE RUNNER). Typically, the summer before Universal Pictures released the reedited version of TOUCH OF EVIL, it reissued on video the preview version of the film that had already been available since the seventies and mislabeled it not only a "restoration" but the "director's cut," which was even more ridiculous—adding insult to injury insofar as Universal had never allowed Welles to complete a final cut of his own in the first place, which in fact is what occasioned his fifty-eight-page memo to Universal studio head Edward Muhl.

Significantly in the early nineties when I originally tried to get an American film magazine interested in publishing roughly two-thirds of this memo, a document drafted in 1957, *Premiere* and *Film Comment* both turned me down flat; if memory serves, the former considered the document far too esoteric and the editor of the latter, who wasn't even interested in reading the text, felt that *Film Comment* had lately been concentrating too much on Welles.[11] For me, the document was fascinating and revealing because it delved so deeply into Welles's artistic motivations—something that he was rarely willing to comment about elsewhere, even in his book-length interview with Peter Bogdanovich—but this consideration cut no ice with either magazine. Then, seven years later, as soon as Universal Pictures had a version of TOUCH OF EVIL based on following the instructions of the memo, the same text suddenly became a hot item, and *Premiere* even wound up commissioning me to write a short article about the new version of the film. (The quarterly *Grand Street* also expressed a strong interest in printing excerpts from the memo until it discovered belatedly—not having grasped the fact earlier, through a misunderstanding—that excerpts were about to appear in the second edition of *This Is Orson Welles*.) The difference in attitudes was clear: in the early nineties, the text had no "currency" because it wasn't tied to any currently marketable item; by the late nineties, it had suddenly taken on a promotional value in relation to one of Universal's upcoming releases.

For more or less the same reason, a lengthy production report in the *Los Angeles Times* in 1998 on the upcoming release of George Hickenlooper's THE BIG BRASS RING, based on a much-revised version of Welles's 1982 script that had been revamped by film critic F. X. Feeney and Hickenlooper, went out of its way to disparage Welles's original script as something that needed to be updated and reworked in order to be relevant to a 1999 audience. The reporter gave no indication of having read the

Welles script in order to test this premise; the article was content to quote actor Nigel Hawthorne reading aloud from David Thomson's attack on the script in *Rosebud* in order to demonstrate that Welles's work clearly needed a polish. However ludicrous this assumption seemed to me at the time, I also realized it was typical of entertainment journalism. The fact that Hickenlooper's movie was shortly to become an item on the marketplace—while the limited [first] edition of Welles's screenplay, which had sold out its print run of one thousand copies shortly after its [American] publication in 1987, was no longer an item on the marketplace—was the only thing that mattered, and preemptive comparative evaluations of the two were relevant only insofar as they helped to promote the Hickenlooper feature. (In fact, Hickenlooper's film revised the original script so extensively that few traces of the original remained.)

■

The half-dozen forms of ideological challenge discussed above are by no means exhaustive when it comes to outlining the continuing provocation and interest of Welles's work. But I hope they adequately suggest the degree to which his work and the various problems it raises throw into relief many of the issues I've been discussing throughout this book [*Movie Wars*]. For generations to come, I suspect, Welles will remain the great example of the talented filmmaker whose work and practices deconstruct what academics, taking a cue from the late French theorist Christian Metz, are fond of calling "the cinematic apparatus." This is not necessarily because he wanted to carry out this particular project, but more precisely because his sense of being an artist as well as an entertainer was frequently tied to throwing monkey wrenches into our expectations—something that the best art and entertainment often do.

Notes

1. On the basis of this difference, one could argue that Kubrick succeeded in working within the system while retaining his independence on every picture except for SPARTACUS, while Welles retained his independence more sporadically and imperfectly, and ultimately at the price of working outside the system. Yet the price paid by Kubrick for his own success—a sense of paranoid

isolation that often seeped into his work, and finally no more completed features than Welles managed—can't be discounted either.

2. "Orson Welles and the Hollywood Industry," *Persistence of Vision* no. 7, 1989, 39–43.

3. "Oedipus in Indianapolis," in THE MAGNIFICENT AMBERSONS: *A Reconstruction* (Berkeley: University of California Press, 1993).

4. "Welles before Kane: The Discourse on a 'Boy Genius,' " *Persistence of Vision* no. 7, 1989: 63–72.

5. *This Is Orson Welles,* by Orson Welles and Peter Bogdanovich, edited by Jonathan Rosenbaum, 2nd ed. (New York: Da Capo Press, 1998), 358.

6. David Thomson, *Rosebud: The Story of Orson Welles* (New York: Alfred A. Knopf, 1996), 77, 237.

7. *This Is Orson Welles,* op. cit., 243–244.

8. In the cases of both MR. ARKADIN and TOUCH OF EVIL, Welles never had final cut on any version, so all of the existing versions represent different attempts to realize his intentions after the film slipped out of his control. (ARKADIN was taken away from him at a relatively early stage in the editing, TOUCH OF EVIL at a relatively late stage.) For a more detailed critique of the third version of OTHELLO—the only one readily available in the United States thanks to the pressures of Welles's youngest daughter, Beatrice, who maintains legal control of this film—see "OTHELLO Goes Hollywood" elsewhere in this volume and Michael Anderegg's excellent *Orson Welles, Shakespeare, and Popular Culture* (New York: Columbia University Press, 1999), 111–120.

9. One film commonly described as unfinished—Welles's forty-minute condensation of THE MERCHANT OF VENICE, his only Shakespeare film in color, designed in the late sixties to serve as the climax to a CBS TV special—was in fact fully edited, scored, and mixed, though most of it was spirited away by an Italian editor after a single private screening; one hopes that eventually the full version will see the light of day. Nine minutes of this film are currently held by the Munich Film Archive. Two other completed short films—CAMILLE, THE NAKED LADY, AND THE MUSKETEERS (1956) and VIVA L'ITALIA! (aka PORTRAIT OF GINA, circa 1958)—are unsold, half-hour TV pilots; the first of these is lost, though the second resurfaced three decades later, and was recently shown in its entirety on German TV. Needless to say, the list goes on. . . .

10. *Orson Welles, Shakespeare, and Popular Culture,* op. cit., 112.

11. More recently, *Film Comment* reviewed two dubious Welles-related films, CRADLE WILL ROCK and RKO #281, but refused to consider running any reports on restorations of unseen Welles films in Munich.

> —Chapter 10 of *Movie Wars: How Hollywood and the Media Limit What Films We See* (Chicago: A Cappella Books, 2000).

25

Orson Welles's Purloined Letter

F FOR FAKE

There were plenty of advantages to living in Paris in the early 1970s, especially if one was a movie buff with time on one's hands. The Parisian film world is relatively small, and simply being on the fringes of it afforded some exciting opportunities, even for a writer like myself who'd barely published. Leaving the Cinémathèque at the Palais de Chaillot one night, I was invited to be an extra in a Robert Bresson film that was being shot a few blocks away. And in early July 1972, while writing for *Film Comment* about Orson Welles's first Hollywood project, HEART OF DARKNESS, I learned Welles was in town and sent a letter to him at Antégor, the editing studio where he was working, asking a few simple questions—only to find myself getting a call from one of his assistants two days later: "Mr. Welles was wondering if you could have lunch with him today."

I met him at La Méditerranée—the same seafood restaurant that would figure prominently in the film he was editing—and when I began by expressing my amazement that he'd invited me, he cordially explained that this was because he didn't have time to answer my letter. The film he was working on was then called HOAX, and he said it had something to do with the art forger Elmyr de Hory and the recent scandal involving Clifford Irving and Howard Hughes. "A documentary?" "No, not a documentary—a new kind of film," he replied, though he didn't elaborate.

This sounds like a pompous boast, though like most of what he told me that afternoon about other matters, it's turned out to have been accurate.

He could have said "essay" or "essay film," which is what many are inclined to call F FOR FAKE nowadays. But on reflection this label is almost
as imprecise and as misleading as "documentary," despite the elements
of both essay and documentary (as well as fiction) employed in the mix.
Welles's subsequent FILMING OTHELLO (1978) clearly qualifies as an essay,
and this is plainly why Phillip Lopate, in his extensive examination of that
form,[1] prefers it—citing in particular its sincerity, which the earlier film
can't claim to the same degree. But by qualifying as Welles's most public
film *and* his most private—hiding in plain sight most of its inexhaustible
riches—this isn't a movie that can be judged by the kind of yardsticks that
we apply to most others.

When I wound up getting invited to an early private screening over a
year later, on October 15, 1973, the film was now being called FAKE. I was
summoned to Club 13—a chic establishment run by Claude Lelouch,
often used for industry screenings—by film historian and longtime Cinémathèque employee Lotte Eisner, whose response to the film was much
less favorable than mine. When I ventured, "This doesn't look much like
an Orson Welles film," she replied, "It isn't even a film." But neither of us
had a scrap of contextual information beyond what Welles had said to
me, and it wasn't until almost a decade later that he noted to Bill Krohn
in an interview that he deliberately avoided any shots that might be regarded as "typically Wellesian."[2] The following year, the *International
Herald Tribune* reported him saying, "In F FOR FAKE I said I was a charlatan and didn't mean it . . . because I didn't want to sound superior to
Elmyr, so I emphasized that I was a magician and called it a charlatan,
which isn't the same thing. And so I was faking even then. Everything
was a lie. There wasn't anything that wasn't."[3]

To complicate matters further, the film's production company sent me
a *fiche technique* a few days after the screening saying that the film's title
was QUESTION MARK, that it was codirected by Orson Welles and François
Reichenbach (presumably because of the outtakes of his documentary
about art forgery that were used), and written by Olga Palinkas (the real
name of Oja Kodar), and that its leading actors were Elmyr de Hory and
Clifford Irving (but not Welles). Clearly a "new kind of film" creates problems of definition and description for everyone, not merely critics, and by
the time the title mutated one last time into F FOR FAKE (an appellation

suggested by Kodar—who truthfully can also be credited with the story about her and Picasso, which Welles adapted), everyone was thoroughly confused. "For the time being," I concluded in *Film Comment* at the time, "I am content to call it THE NEW ORSON WELLES FILM, codirected by Irving and de Hory, written by Jorge Luis Borges, and produced by Howard Hughes. . . . As Welles remarks about Chartres, the most important thing is that it exists."[4]

■

It would be comforting to say my early appreciation of F FOR FAKE included an adequate understanding of just how subversive it was (and is). But leaving aside the critique of the art world and its commodification via "experts"—which is far more radical in its implications than CITIZEN KANE's critique of William Randolph Hearst—it's only been in recent years, with the rewind and stop-frame capacities of video, that the sheer effrontery of many of Welles's more important tricks can be recognized, making this film more DVD-friendly than any of his others. It's also taken some time for us to realize that his methodology in putting this film together gave him a kind of freedom with his materials that he never had before or since. For a filmmaker who often avowed that the art of cinema resided in editing, F FOR FAKE must have represented his most extended effort. According to Dominique Villain, who interviewed the film's chief editor, the editing took Welles a solid year, working seven days a week— a routine suspended only for the length of time that it took Michel Legrand to compose the score—and requiring the use of three separate editing rooms.[5]

   The key to Welles's fakery here, as it is throughout his work, is his audience's imagination and the active collaboration it performs—most often unknowingly—with his own designs, the kind of unconscious or semiconscious complicity that magicians and actors both rely on. ("A magician is just an actor . . . playing the part of a magician.") It's what enables us to accept Welles as Kodar's Hungarian grandfather and Kodar as Picasso in the final Orly sequence, when they're both dressed in black and moving about in the fog. And the key to this key can be found both literally and figuratively in the first words Welles speaks in the film—initially heard over darkness that gradually fades in to the window of a train compartment in a Paris station: "For my next experiment, ladies and gentle-men, I would appreciate the loan of any small personal object from your pocket—a key, a box of matches, a coin. . . ." This proves to be a literal key in the pocket of a little boy standing in for the rest of us. Welles promptly turns it into a coin, then back into a key inside the boy's pocket, mean-while offering us brief glimpses of and exchanges with Reichenbach's film crew, then Oja Kodar as she opens the train window. "As for the key," he concludes, "it was not symbolic of anything."

One sees his droll point, but I beg to differ. By virtue of being personal and pocketed, then taken away and eventually returned to its owner, the key is precisely symbolic of the viewer's creative investment and partici-pation solicited in Welles's "experiment" over the next 80-odd minutes. And distinguishing between what's public and private in these transac-tions, both for the viewer and for Welles, is much less easy than it sounds. A movie in which Welles can't resist showing off the beauty and sexiness of his mistress at a time when he's still married seems downright brazen, especially in contrast to the tact he shows in alluding to de Hory's homo-sexuality, yet he can't simply or invariably be accused of wearing his heart and libido on his sleeve. In some ways, the self-mocking braggado-cio—such as ordering a *steak au poivre* from the same waiter carrying off the remains of a gigantic lobster—becomes a kind of mask while his deep-est emotions and intentions are hidden away in his own pockets, just as firmly as our own private investments remain in ours. Those who decide that the exposés of various hoaxes (including those of de Hory, Irving, and Welles) are superficial and obvious may be overlooking the degree to which these very revelations are masking the perpetuation of various oth-ers, some of which are neither superficial nor obvious.

For an immediate example of this process, consider the word clusters in the title sequence that we're asked to read on the sides of film cans as the camera moves left from "a film by Orson Welles" to "WITH THE," then up in turn to "COLLABORATION," "OF CERTAIN," and "EXPERT," which sits alongside another can labeled "PRACTIONERS." Because we're so preoc-cupied with following the unorthodox direction of our reading imposed by the camera—proceeding from right to left and then from down to up—most of us are apt to read "practioners," a word existing in no dic-tionary, as "practitioners." And given how loaded, tainted, and double-sided the word "expert" is soon to become in this movie, it's possible to conclude that the real collaborators and "practioners"—the spectators of Welles's magic who collaborate with him by putting it into practice—are none other than ourselves. In other words, we know best and we know nothing.

Similarly, we should look very closely at what we're being shown in the early "Girl-Watching" sequence—perhaps the most intricately edited stretch in the film, especially in contrast to the more leisurely and conventionally edited late sequence devoted to Pablo Picasso's ogling of Kodar. (Both sequences incidentally feature a tune that Legrand calls "Orson's Theme," though Welles's placements of it suggest it might more fittingly be called "Oja's Theme.") If we freeze-frame in the right places towards the end of "Girl-Watching," we'll discover that a couple of full frontal long shots of "Oja Kodar" approaching us on a city street don't actually show Kodar at all but another woman (her sister Nina) of roughly the same size in the same dress. Given the whole sequence's elaborate peek-a-boo tactics—a mosaic of almost perpetual fragmentation—it stands to reason that two very brief shots pretending to reveal what many previous angles have concealed can readily fool us by hiding in full view, just like Edgar Allen Poe's "Purloined Letter."

■

As *Finnegans Wake* was for Joyce, F FOR FAKE is for Welles a playful repository of public history intertwined with private in-jokes as well as duplicitous meanings, an elaborate blend of sense and nonsense that carries us along regardless of what's actually being said. For someone whose public and private identities became so separate that they wound up operating routinely in separate households and sometimes on separate continents, exposure and concealment sometimes figured as reverse sides of the same coin, and Welles's desire to hide inside his own text here becomes a special kind of narcissism. When Welles made his never-released nine-minute F FOR FAKE trailer three years later, he even avoided having his name spoken or seen ("Modesty forbids")—except for when Gary Graver, his cinematographer and partial stand-in as host, prompts him with, "Ten seconds more, Orson."

For a filmmaker who studiously avoided repeating himself and sought always to remain a few steps ahead of his audience's expectations, thereby rejecting any obvious ways of commodifying his status as an auteur, Welles arguably found a way in F FOR FAKE to contextualize large portions of his career while undermining many cherished beliefs about authorship and the means by which "experts," "God's own gift to the fakers," validate such notions.

It's often been asserted that this film was his indirect response to Pauline Kael's "Raising KANE" and its (subsequently discredited) suggestion that practically all of CITIZEN KANE's screenplay was written by Herman J. Mankiewicz. It's worth adding, however, that his most direct and immediate response to Kael's screed was his masterful semiforgery of "The KANE Mutiny," a polemical article that deceptively ran in *Esquire* under Peter Bogdanovich's byline, included many quotations from Welles, and cogently responded to Kael's essay on a point-by-point basis—a remarkable display of Welles's gifts as a writer that paradoxically had to conceal this fact.[6]

If we abandon for a moment the unverifiable question of intentionality, there's little doubt that F FOR FAKE, for all its anti-auteurist ruses, abounds with subtle as well as obvious echoes of Welles's previous work. Catherine L. Benamou has noted the echoes of the fire consuming the Rosebud sled in the burning of a couple of forged canvases,[7] and one could also cite the way that various "conversations" manufactured through editing reproduce aspects of the community chatter about the Ambersons in THE MAGNIFICENT AMBERSONS, or the way a Gypsy-like fiddle, Welles's Slavic intonations, and all the frenetic plane-hopping calls to mind MR. ARKADIN. There's even a cuckoo clock thrown in at one point that summons up both ARKADIN and THE THIRD MAN. For all his regrets, this self-referentiality is one of the many elements that make F FOR FAKE the most celebratory of Welles's films. As he puts it while distant views of Chartres nearly replicate our first views of Kane's Xanadu: "Our songs will all be silenced—but what of it? Go on singing."

—Liner notes for Criterion DVD of F FOR FAKE, released 2005

Notes

1. "In Search of the Centaur: The Essay-Film," by Phillip Lopate, in *Totally, Tenderly, Tragically: Essays and Criticism from a Lifelong Love Affair with the Movies* (New York: Anchor Books, 1998).

2. Special Orson Welles issue, *Cahiers du cinéma*, hors série (1986).

3. Quoted by Mary Blume, *International Herald Tribune*, December 9, 1983.

4. "Paris Journal," by Jonathan Rosenbaum, *Film Comment*, January–February 1974.

5. *Le Montage au cinéma*, by Dominique Villain (Paris: Éditions Cahiers du Cinéma, 1991).

6. "The KANE Mutiny," by Peter Bogdanovich, *Esquire*, October 1972. Kodar alerted me to Welles's authorship of this essay in 1986. In "My Orson," Bogdanovich's introduction to the second edition of *This Is Orson Welles*, by Orson Welles and Peter Bogdanovich (New York: Da Capo Press, 1998), which I edited, he writes, "I did all the legwork, research, and interviews, and the byline carried only my name, but Orson had taken a strong hand in revising and rewriting. Why shouldn't he? He was fighting for his life." For a definitive refutation of Kael's thesis, see especially "The Scripts of CITIZEN KANE," by Robert Carringer, *Critical Inquiry* 5 (1978), reprinted in *Perspectives on "Citizen Kane,"* edited by Ronald Gottesman (New York: G. K. Hall & Co., 1996).

7. "The Artifice of Realism and the Lure of the 'Real' in Orson Welles's F FOR FAKE (1973) and Other T(r)eas(u)er(e)s," by Catherine L. Benamou, in *F Is for Phony*, edited by Alexandra Juhasz and Jesse Lerner (Minneapolis: University of Minnesota Press, 2006).

26

When Will—and How Can—We Finish Orson Welles's DON QUIXOTE?

This final chapter is a lecture delivered in Valencia, Spain, on November 17, 2005, at a conference, "Don Quixote and the Cinema," held at San Miguel de los Reyes, a convent built during the seventeenth century, making it roughly contemporary with Cervantes's novel. The same building was used as a prison during the Franco era and functions today as a municipal library, Biblioteca Valenciana. Given my virtually nonexistent grasp of spoken Spanish, I regretted that the event wasn't more international; as far as I know, my paper was the only one requiring the services of a translator. The only other non-Spanish participants in the three-day event were a French man and an Italian woman, both of whom seemed to be fluent in the language.

Thanks to the generosity of the conference's organizer, Carlos F. Heredero (the cowriter of ORSON WELLES EN EL PAÍS DE DON QUIJOTE, cited in my introduction to chapter 15, and an academic scholar and critic whose specialties include Spanish cinema and Wong Kar-wai), I was able to route my trip to Spain through Madrid before the conference and then briefly through Barcelona afterwards. In Madrid I made arrangements to spend three days at the Filmoteca Española looking at the QUIXOTE material mentioned in chapters 19 and 20, but I was severely disappointed to discover that the ten hours I'd arranged to see mainly consisted of material from the TV series NELLA TERRA DI DON CHISIOTTE and/or bits and pieces of what might be called the wreckage left by Jesus Franco's disposal of the other footage, not including anything shot in Mexico. I'm still unclear why none of the Mexico footage could be found there, though I did learn from José Maria Prado, director of the Filmoteca, that its negative material related to QUIXOTE *is held in Barcelona and the material kept over the years by Bonnani is now housed at Cinecittà.*

■

I'd like to dedicate these remarks to the memory of Henri Langlois, who in the early 1970s programmed Orson Welles's DON QUIXOTE as one of the first films to be shown at the New York Cinémathèque, which was never built.

When Orson Welles died in 1985, he left many of his films unfinished. Each one was unfinished in a different way and for somewhat different reasons, because, to the despair of anyone who has ever tried to market his work, no two Welles films are alike. Some of the unfinished ones aren't even regarded as such because people other than Welles finished them in some form; I'm thinking especially of THE MAGNIFICENT AMBERSONS and MR. ARKADIN. Some remain unfinished for reasons beyond his control— for legal and financial reasons (in the case of IT'S ALL TRUE and THE OTHER SIDE OF THE WIND) or for practical reasons (in the case of THE DEEP, where there's some evidence that he couldn't persuade Jeanne Moreau to dub her lines). He couldn't shoot more than a few fragments of THE DREAMERS or any of his KING LEAR or THE BIG BRASS RING or THE CRADLE WILL ROCK because he couldn't raise the money to do so. He shot most of a short film called THE MAGIC SHOW that he planned to incorporate into a larger work called ORSON WELLES SOLO, and he shot many other fragments of pieces for the same compilation.

His DON QUIXOTE is quite distinct from all of the above, for a number of reasons—apart from the fact that something calling itself the DON QUIXOTE of Orson Welles was finished by someone other than Welles, who did more to mutilate and distort Welles's material than anyone had ever done to THE MAGNIFICENT AMBERSONS or MR. ARKADIN, much less to THE STRANGER, THE LADY FROM SHANGHAI, or TOUCH OF EVIL. It remained an active project for almost the last three decades of Welles's life; it went through many versions and stages, and at least some of these versions may have come close to having been completed. The only time I met Welles, in July 1972, he maintained the film was by then virtually complete, needing only some additional sound work, including music. Maybe he was exaggerating, but maybe not. He also told me at the time with a grin, as he told many others, that whenever he did release the film he would call it WHEN WILL YOU FINISH DON QUIXOTE?—a title that's inspired my own here, because the question we used to ask Welles we now have to ask ourselves, in a different way: namely, when and how can we find closure? But maybe we should be asking ourselves, instead, *should* we find closure? For I would argue that, more than any other Welles project, DON QUIXOTE remained unfinished by choice—a choice that I will try to examine and to some extent defend.

■

There were at least four successive versions of the never-completed film: (1) Tests shot in Paris with Mischa Auer as Quixote and Akim Tamiroff as Sancho Panza. (2) Mexican footage with Patty McCormack, Tamiroff, and the substitution of Francisco Reiguera for Auer. (Unlike the various actresses cast as Desdemona in Welles's earlier OTHELLO, Reiguera remained his second and final Quixote.) (3) Footage shot in Italy and Spain, when Welles was still, at least initially, hoping to retain the McCormack footage by using a double for her (according to his Italy-based assistant Audrey Stainton). And (4) an essay film about Spain—specifically, about the paralysis of Spanish culture under Franco, and one that would raise the philosophical question of whether democracy would destroy the Man of La Mancha. I should add that the two versions on which Welles worked the longest were the second and third, while the first and fourth were more tentative and theoretical. My favorite is the second, and we know from Juan Luis Buñuel, who worked on it as assistant director, that Welles's inability to finish this version because of depleted funds left him in tears on his last day of shooting.

I regret to say that I've been limited in my research by my meager grasp of Spanish. On the whole my two most valuable research tools, apart from the various sections and versions of the film that I've seen over the years, have been Stainton's "DON QUIXOTE: Orson Welles' Secret" in the Autumn 1988 *Sight and Sound*—invaluable despite an error in her second sentence that "scraps" of QUIXOTE were shown in Rotterdam during the mid-80s—and the Spanish resources available to me in English, especially Esteve Riambau's "DON QUIXOTE: The Adventures and Misadventures of an Essay in Spain,"[1] as supplemented by some of Esteve's lectures in English and by the TV documentary he made with Carlos Rodríguez and Carlos F. Heredero, ORSON WELLES EN EL PAÍS DE DON QUIJOTE (2000).

A note about Jesus Franco's version. The disastrous misappropriation of footage from Welles's 1964 Italian TV documentary series NELLA TERRA DI DON CHISCIOTTE in Franco's edit of QUIXOTE essentially filled the gap left by the omitted McCormack material—which provided the film's original narrative framework but which, based on Oja Kodar's sense of Welles's subsequent plans for the film, she didn't allow Franco to use. Unfortunately, it appears that the few other Welles scholars who've written about his QUIXOTE in English have ignored this issue and assumed, like Franco, that IN THE LAND OF DON QUIXOTE and DON QUIXOTE belong together. Even Robert Stam in his *Literature through Film: Realism, Magic, and the Art of Adaptation* (Oxford: Blackwell Publishing, 2004)—who also erroneously assumes both that Oja was Welles's wife and that she worked on the film (thus eliding the production work and acting of Paola Mori)— makes this lamentable assumption and arrives at some debatable conclusions as a consequence. And the casual imprecisions and distortions in another recent book, by Clinton Heylin, suggests that we should expect to encounter much more confusion about what the film is and was in the foreseeable future.

In his Preface, Heylin first calls the 1992 Franco version a "documentary," to be grouped with the 1993 IT'S ALL TRUE: BASED ON AN UNFINISHED FILM BY ORSON WELLES and the 1995 ORSON WELLES: THE ONE-MAN BAND. One sentence later, he refers to it as a "partial 'reconstruction' . . . painstakingly put together by Jesus Franco."[2] Yet on the penultimate page of the same book, he writes, "Franco's film gives very little sense of the scope of Welles's vision, being little more than a random collection of sequences from the never-completed film."[3]

This third description I find fairly accurate, even though it flatly contradicts the first two, which also contradict each other. How can Franco's film be both a documentary and a reconstruction (even with the latter term modified by "partial" and placed between quotation marks), and both painstaking and random? And why, incidentally, does he give the running time as 76 minutes when it's 40 minutes longer? The problem isn't any ill will on Heylin's part, such as one finds in David Thomson's *Rosebud*, yet it shares with that book the task of having to fill in enormous gaps of knowledge with journalistic patter that pretends to wield some sort of authority about the subject, granting both it and us some unearned closure on the matter.

In Heylin's final chapter, a similar strain can be felt in the way he tries to argue that Welles's QUIXOTE was somehow meant to be the "Hispanic equivalent" of IT'S ALL TRUE—not only because "the bullfighting element" was carried over from the earlier documentary, "as Welles again sought to capture something Homeric in Latin culture," but also because "Welles struggled to formulate a method that he was prepared to pursue consistently"—a generality that may apply more to Heylin's struggles than to his. (An episode in AROUND THE WORLD WITH ORSON WELLES is also concerned with bullfighting, and by Heylin's logic this might make it both a remake of IT'S ALL TRUE and a prequel to DON QUIXOTE.) Then, after citing Welles's description of his QUIXOTE as an improvisation that would follow four weeks of rehearsals and would be "a silent film," he notes that "the idea was subsequently transposed to an altogether different film project, SACRED BEASTS." I assume he's thinking of Welles's pitch for THE SACRED BEASTS to potential investors in a Spanish bullring, briefly documented by the Maysles brothers in a short film in 1966. But he's surely wrong in suggesting that either film was meant to be silent simply because Welles once said that parts of QUIXOTE would be improvised in the spirit of Mack Sennett.[4]

Then, "In a subsequent reconfiguration Welles planned to place Don Quixote in modern Spain," when this was clearly part of the original configuration. Describing the sequence of Quixote in a movie theater "slashing [the screen] to shreds," which he admits he hasn't seen, Heylin then goes on to speculate that "This was presumably one of Welles's private little displays of piqué [I take it he means pique] at the critics who metaphorically slashed his work to shreds."[5] Such a far-fetched presumption can only trivialize what may be the greatest surviving scene in Welles's QUIXOTE—a scene that happens to be silent only because there's no dialogue and Welles apparently never added any sound effects.

A paragraph later, Heylin is misdescribing IN THE LAND OF DON QUIXOTE as a Spanish rather an Italian TV series, then proposing that this project only pointed to Welles's confusion about whether or not to make his QUIXOTE "one extended *essayage,* an IT'S ALL TRUE take two,"[6] without any clear grasp of such basics as the difference between this hack-work and the work on the feature Welles was subsidizing with it—a distinction that Franco also failed to honor—or the fact that Tamiroff could shoot in Spain while Reiguera, due to his anti-Franco past, couldn't. Finally, there's some muddle about McCormack and Welles speaking in the lobby (rather than in a patio) of a Mexican hotel, and this seemingly gets confused with or at least connected to another conversation between Welles and another hotel guest that was scripted in a 1943 postproduction treatment for IT'S ALL TRUE. But of course it's the last refuge of every Welles analyst who can't see a particular Welles film to try to make it seem like another Welles film, seen or unseen, when what's most important about it is obviously its uniqueness.

■

There are many references to Miguel de Cervantes's novel and its leading character throughout Welles's oeuvre, including portions that precede its existence as a film project. The earliest that comes to mind is the first scene between Michael O'Hara and Elsa Bannister in the rough cut of THE LADY FROM SHANGHAI (as James Naremore describes it from the cutting continuity) and the last is one of the few scenes that he managed to shoot for THE DREAMERS, but there are obviously quite a few others. More generally, we can make certain links between Quixote and Falstaff that relate to but also go beyond the fact that Cervantes and Shakespeare were contemporaries. For one thing, friendship is one of the key subjects in Welles's oeuvre—far more important and central than romantic love, I believe—and DON QUIXOTE and CHIMES AT MIDNIGHT are the two most important occasions in his work when friendship crosses class barriers. The other major examples that come to mind are all basically friendships within the same class—between Charles Foster Kane and Jed Leland in CITIZEN KANE, between Hank Quinlan and Pete Menzies in TOUCH OF EVIL, and, among the scripted but unrealized works, between Blake Pellarin and Kim Menaker in THE BIG BRASS RING, between Marc Blitzstein and Orson Welles in THE CRADLE WILL ROCK, and between Pellegrina and Marcus in THE DREAMERS. One should add that the betrayal of friendship is also a key subject in CITIZEN KANE, MACBETH, OTHELLO, TOUCH OF EVIL, and CHIMES AT MIDNIGHT, but not in QUIXOTE.

Nostalgia is one of the most powerful emotions in Welles's work, and it's generally expressed for two distinct historical periods—for the middle ages from the vantage point of the late 16th and early 17th centuries, which we find in CHIMES AT MIDNIGHT and DON QUIXOTE, and for the late 19th century from the vantage point of the 20th, which we find in CITIZEN KANE, THE MAGNIFICENT AMBERSONS, *Moby-Dick* (which Welles adapted in one of his major stage productions), and the tales of Isak Dinesen (which formed the basis for THE IMMORTAL STORY, THE DREAMERS, and many other Welles film projects). In Welles's version of *Quixote*, which has some resemblance to a western—a quintessentially mythical view of the 19th century from the vantage point of the 20th—one might say that it's the 20th century that winds up looking incongruous rather than the age of chivalry.

One further suggestion I'd like to make, a somewhat more debatable one, is that the most quixotic character in Welles's oeuvre apart from Quixote himself is not a fictional character but a real person, the art forger Elmyr de Hory in F FOR FAKE. Of course, one could argue that de Hory is a criminal while the Man of La Mancha is scrupulously honest, but I think this distinction is ultimately less important than the fact that both characters are dreamers who pretend to be other people and suffer as well as triumph as a consequence. (I should note here the cogent observation of Vladimir Nabokov, which he demonstrates at great length in his *Lectures on Don Quixote*, that, contrary to the way we usually view him, Quixote triumphs as often as he fails.) Welles views them both as generous and lovable innocents.

■

To understand Welles's filmic conception of Cervantes, it's worth citing the caveat of Esteve Riambau—that all four of the versions of QUIXOTE planned by Welles at one time or another were in fact essays of one sort or another. But I think we can add a few other eccentric constants to Welles's conception. One of the most curious absences to be found in all the projected versions is virtually all of the characters in the Cervantes novel, apart from Don Quixote, Sancho Panza, their respective horse and donkey, and some version of Dulcinea. We certainly see many crowds, all of them contemporary, of villagers as well as city folk, but hardly any individuals to speak of. I especially miss the curate, the barber, Quixote's housekeeper, and his niece.

There's a curious paradox at the heart of Cervantes's novel involving its two principal characters. In very different ways, they might be regarded as ineffectual fools: Quixote is well-educated, intelligent, thoughtful, and articulate, but also seriously delusional: Panza has a certain amount of practical intelligence and folk wisdom, but due to his lack of education is constantly tripping over his own language and expressing himself poorly. Yet as Harold Bloom points out, in what for me is one of the most profound things anyone has ever written about the novel, "We need to hold in mind as we read *Don Quixote* that we cannot condescend to the Knight and Sancho, since together they know more than we do." (It's very tempting to include both Cervantes and Welles in this "we.") Bloom continues, "The Knight and Sancho, as the great work closes, know exactly who they are, not so much by their adventures as through their marvelous conversations, be they quarrels or exchanges of insights."[7]

Welles is certainly attentive to both the profound self-knowledge of these characters and the wisdom that their combined foolishness yields. Yet it's questionable whether he maintains quite the same balance between these characters' strengths and weaknesses that Cervantes does. Part of this difference may be attributable to the casting. Akim Tamiroff qualifies in some ways as Welles's favorite actor as well as one of his best friends, whom he used in no less than four features, and his Sancho Panza is unquestionably Tamiroff's earthiest performance. It's important to add that his character's voice (like Reiguera's) isn't his own but Welles's, yet it does seem significant that, as Juan Luis Buñuel has pointed out, Welles "used a perfect Oxford accent for the voice of Don Quixote while giving Sancho Panza a particularly coarse American accent."[8] This corresponds to the aristocratic and populist strains in Welles's own personality, which all his films synthesize in various ways, while suggesting a fusion of American and European energies that seems far more fruitful than the Tower of Babel mixture of American and European accents heard in THE TRIAL. In both cases, of course, he's using English translations of novels written in other languages, but one could argue that Cervantes is far more amenable to this transformation than Kafka.

The correspondences we can trace between scenes shot by Welles and scenes in the novel are rarely precise. As nearly as I've been able to determine by comparing some lines of dialogue, Welles used a modified version of Samuel Putnam's English translation, but every scene has been substantially revised. When Paola Mori, Welles's third wife, appears briefly on a motorbike to quarrel with Quixote, she may be standing in for the six travelers with their servants in Part 1, Chapter 4—unless she's taking the place of the two shepherdesses or the several herdsmen who appear in Part 2, Chapter 58, which seems even less likely.

Problems of this kind in finding clear matches between Welles and Cervantes are frequent, although in some cases this may be because the original text hasn't been examined closely enough. A surprising number of commentators have described the brilliant sequence with McCormack, Reiguera, and Tamiroff in a movie theater, in which Quixote attacks the screen, as a scene derived somehow from Quixote's attack on several windmills in Part 1, Chapter 8, but surely this is unlikely. It seems to me that the attack of Quixote on the puppet theater on Part 2, Chapter 26 is closer to what Welles had in mind. But even if one accepts my hypothesis, precise correspondences between this scene in Cervantes and the responses to Quixote's behavior from McCormack's Dulcie and Tamiroff's Sancho Panza in the audience are nowhere to be found. One might argue, in fact, that this scene and others shot by Welles that we regard as major parts of the film might more accurately be described as improvisations based on themes by Cervantes than as adaptations in any normal sense of that term.

I'm now going to show you this sequence. The only context I can provide for it is that, in the other fragments of the Mexican footage that I've been able to see, this silent sequence is preceded by scenes with dialogue between McCormack and Welles. Initially they're seen seated at a table in a hotel patio, where he starts to tell her the story of the novel—with a skeptical interjection from the little girl's mother, who has previously insisted that these characters never existed, calling down from a balcony, and a strange appearance of Sancho sneaking into the patio after Welles and McCormack have left, as if to prove the mother wrong. Then Welles and McCormack are seen more briefly (and presumably much later) in a moving carriage, where she tells him that she took Sancho in a taxi to a movie theater, which leads one to surmise that the following sequence might have figured as a flashback, possibly with her narration. [*At this point I showed the sequence on video, from a copy originally recorded from late-night Italian TV.*]

■

The fetishism of DVD consumers towards excluded scenes as bonuses has recently yielded a not very good scene on a French DVD of THE TRIAL involving computers, with Katina Paxinou; the sound is missing, although one can look up the dialogue in the film's published script (unfortunately available only in French and in an English translation of that French, but not in the original English). In *This Is Orson Welles*, Welles maintains that he cut this scene only a day before the film opened, although Roberto Perpignani—who worked on the editing for many months as an assistant, although he received no screen credit for this work—told me in Locarno the summer before last that he never saw this scene once and that it must have been deleted early on.

The scene is clearly expendable, and one certainly can't object to it appearing as a DVD bonus—even though a more thoughtful presentation might have added subtitles with the dialogue to this silent version. But this unresolved question is worth stressing because it suggests that a good many of Welles's creative deliberations were in a continual state of flux, a situation that I believe was especially true of QUIXOTE. Positing therefore *any* version which "conforms to Welles's intentions" entails a necessary amount of both distortion and wishful thinking.

■

For those who remain confounded that Welles failed to arrange for a release of DON QUIXOTE after "virtually" completing at least one version of it, I should add that I find his motivations for this explicable and even, up to a point, defensible. Although I cherish much of the QUIXOTE material that I've seen (apart from the mainly egregious use of it in Jesus Franco's cut), I'm also convinced that the film would have been critically attacked had it come out in the early 70s, and the odds of it succeeding at the box office would have been virtually nil. So Welles would have had little to gain by releasing it—while continuing to tinker with it, as he did intermittently for the remainder of his life, obviously gave him a great deal of joy. (In many respects, it was his ultimate plaything.) I'm even persuaded, based on Stainton's article, that he actively took steps to prevent the film from being reassembled "correctly" after his death—which is perhaps less defensible (although he did legally own the film), but still understandable given Welles's often-voiced indifference to notions of artistic immortality. "Up to a point," he said to Kenneth Tynan in 1967, "I have to be successful in order to operate. But I think it's corrupting to care about success; and nothing could be more vulgar than to worry about posterity."⁹ And, as far as I can tell, his main methods to prevent DON QUIXOTE from being assembled correctly after his death included the coded and enigmatic slates he employed, described by Stainton, and, more generally, his practice of saying, in effect, to many different people at different times, "*You* are the only one I can trust."

Some people have reproached Oja Kodar for the way she disposed of QUIXOTE. My own feelings about the matter are conflicted. The best single presentation I've ever seen of material from the film was her own, at a Welles conference held at New York University in 1988, and without the benefit of the two screenings she gave of material that she selected herself, I wouldn't have the same basis to criticize what Franco did to much of this material a few years later. I also know that her motives for selling the film when she did several years afterwards had a lot to do with her personal priorities—above all, her desire to keep her Croatian parents alive during the war that was being fought at the time in Bosnia-Herzegovina, Croatia, and Yugoslavia.

■

Let me cite a particular theory I have about why Welles never finished any of his projected versions of DON QUIXOTE. I doubt that this could have been the only reason, but I do nonetheless consider it, for Welles, a compelling one: that he couldn't bear to face the prospect of Quixote's death at the end of the novel—the moment when the character renounces and abandons all his delusions, which is surely one of the most unbearable deaths in all of literature.

When will—and how can—we finish Orson Welles's DON QUIXOTE? Truthfully, we can't finish it, though we can certainly choose whether or not we want to be finished with it. I choose not to, because I think our imagination—which is at times difficult to distinguish from our capacity to become delusional—is always the most basic tool in Welles's bottomless bag of tricks, and I'd hate to put it out of work.

Notes

1. Included in the multilingual collection *The Unknown Orson Welles*, edited by Stefan Drössler (Filmmuseum München/Belleville Verlag, 2004), 71–76.
2. Clinton Heylin, *Despite the System: Orson Welles versus the Hollywood Studios* (Chicago: A Cappella, 2005), viii.
3. Ibid., 389.
4. Ibid., 333–334.
5. Ibid., 334.
6. Ibid.
7. Harold Bloom, "Introduction: Don Quixote, Sancho Panza, and Miguel de Cervantes Saavedra," to *Don Quixote* by Miguel de Cervantes, translated by Edith Grossman (New York: HarperCollins, 2005), xxiv.
8. Cited and paraphrased by Esteve Riambau in his essay in *The Unknown Orson Welles* (see note 1), 72.
9. *Orson Welles Interviews*, edited by Mark W. Estrin (Jackson: University Press of Mississippi, 2002), 145.

> —Paper delivered at Congreso Internacional, "El Cine y El Quijote," organized by Carlos F. Heredero in Valencia, Spain, November 17, 2005

Appendix

The Present State of the Welles Film Legacy

Providing a precise chronological sequence for films that Orson Welles worked on concurrently is often impossible, and some dates in his filmography remain only guesses, so the following checklist of films or videos he directed, whether or not they survive, in what state they survive, and their visibility as of late August 2006 is ordered only approximately. (Some of the running times given are also approximations, and I've periodically had to apply guesswork in other areas as well.) For the most part, works completed by Welles are listed in order of completion, and works not completed by Welles, some of which were completed by others, are listed in order of their shooting, release, or first public showing. (I have omitted films on which Welles did some uncredited direction, such as JOURNEY INTO FEAR, as well as some perfunctory film or video recordings of readings or recitations.) I haven't listed any of the commercial labels for the videos or DVDs, but this information is readily available via Internet searches. I've abbreviated ORSON WELLES: THE ONE-MAN BAND—a documentary listed at the end (see no. 38) that contains excerpts of several items—as OWTOMB.

Given the untidy and ever-changing state of Welles film studies (see introduction)—as well as certain ambiguities regarding what constitutes a film or video by Welles, which calls for some measure of selectivity—this checklist can't pretend to be exhaustive. Unless otherwise noted, films are in 35-millimeter and black and white, with sound.

1. HEARTS OF AGE (completed, 16mm, silent, 5 minutes, 1934). Codirected by William Vance, this piece of Wellesian juvenilia is an elaborate home movie shot one summer afternoon in and around the old firehouse in Woodstock, Illinois, during the Woodstock Summer Theatre Festival. Not widely seen until critic Joseph McBride discovered it in the 1960s. Widely available on film, VHS, and DVD. (See, for instance, "The Devil's Plaything: American Surrealism," volume 2 of *Unseen Cinema: Early American Avant-Garde Film 1894–1941*.)

2. In 1938, Welles filmed a two-part silent prelude to his stage farce *Too Much Johnson*, designed to replace cumbersome exposition, but the summer theater in Stony Creek, Connecticut (owned by William Castle), where the play premiered had an inadequate throw for film projection, making it impossible to show the film. Due to financial difficulties, the play never opened in New York, and the only copy of the film was lost in a fire at Welles's villa in Madrid (during Welles's absence) in August 1970.

3. In 1939, Welles filmed a much briefer prologue to his 20-minute condensation of William Archer's melodrama *The Green Goddess*, which Welles staged and performed on the RKO Vaudeville Circuit in July and August. His celebrated 1946 stage production of *Around the World in 80 Days*, presented in Boston, New Haven, Philadelphia, and New York, also included some filmed segments, and his 1950 stage production *The Blessed and the Damned*, presented in Paris, also included a brief segment of filmed rushes. All of these are lost, except for some fleeting fragments of the last, which have turned up on videos in the possession of a few collectors.

4. CITIZEN KANE (completed, 119 minutes, released 1941). Widely available on film, VHS, and DVD.

5. CITIZEN KANE TRAILER (completed, 4 minutes, 1941). Contains all new material; widely available as a DVD extra.

6. THE MAGNIFICENT AMBERSONS (unfinished). A 132-minute rough cut by Welles, which no longer exists, was completed in February 1942. A recut and partially reshot version was released in July 1942, and this version is widely available on film and VHS in the U.S., and on

DVD in France, Spain, and the U.K. The best way to grasp an approximation of Welles's rough cut is to read the cutting continuity in Robert L. Carringer's THE MAGNIFICENT AMBERSONS: *A Reconstruction* (Berkeley: University of California Press, 1993) and/or the shorter narrative summary included in Welles and Peter Bogdanovich's *This Is Orson Welles*, 2nd ed. (New York: Da Capo, 1998), both of which contain many illustrations, while listening to Bernard Herrmann's original and complete score, still available on CD.

7. IT'S ALL TRUE (unfinished). Shot in 1942 and essentially unedited by Welles, despite his many efforts to retain or recover the footage. A documentary about this project by Bill Krohn, Myron Meisel, and the late Richard Wilson that utilizes portions of the recovered footage, IT'S ALL TRUE: BASED ON AN UNFINISHED FILM BY ORSON WELLES, was released in 1993, and is widely available on film, VHS, and DVD. Some portions of the black-and-white and color footage (about 50,000 feet) have been preserved at the UCLA Film Archives, and some portions were thrown out or junked years ago by studio personnel. Still other portions that survive—about 130,000 feet—are in variable condition and will probably be lost if funds aren't raised to preserve them.

8. Magic act sequence in FOLLOW THE BOYS (completed, shot in 1943, released in 1944). Available on film and VHS.

9. THE STRANGER. Welles's own version of this 1946 feature, apparently completed, no longer exists; the studio's revised and cut version is widely available on film, VHS, and DVD, but mainly in poor public domain versions.

10. THE LADY FROM SHANGHAI. Shot between the fall of 1946 and early 1947, this film was 155 minutes in rough cut but only 86 minutes long when Columbia belatedly released it in late May 1948. The deleted 69 minutes were destroyed. (The late Richard Wilson, one of the two associate producers, once told me that his greatest single professional regret was not having preserved Welles's original funhouse sequence, which occurred towards the end of the picture.)

11. MACBETH. Shot over 23 days in the summer of 1947, though released only four months after THE LADY FROM SHANGHAI, this film survives

in two separate versions, both edited by Welles, running 107 minutes and 86 minutes respectively. The second version was edited at the request of Republic Pictures. The original and longer version is available in the U.S. on film, VHS, and DVD. The shorter version is available in an excellent three-disc DVD box set released in France that also includes the longer version, newsreel footage of the end of Welles's 1936 stage version presented in Harlem, and the 78-minute audio production with a Bernard Herrmann score done for 78 RPM records in 1940.

12.   OTHELLO. Made between 1949 and 1952. Like MACBETH, this film was edited at least twice by Welles, although in this case, since Welles retained full editorial control, this was entirely at his own initiative. The first version premiered at Cannes in May 1952; the second opened in the U.S. in September 1955. A "restoration" of the second version that resynchronized the dialogue, with a substantial revision and a complete rerecording of the sound effects and music (discussed at length in chapter 16), was released in 1992 and is the only version readily available today on film, VHS, and DVD. Unaltered editions of both versions can be found today only in archives (mainly overseas, but also in the Library of Congress) and in private collections.

13.   On August 30, 1950, Welles filmed two vignettes, by Oscar Wilde and Luigi Pirandello, from his touring stage presentation *An Evening with Orson Welles* in a studio outside Munich, but he was dissatisfied with the results and scrapped the footage.

14.   Although many alternative versions and supplementary materials are available in *The Complete* MR. ARKADIN aka CONFIDENTIAL REPORT, released in the spring of 2006, the title of this elaborate DVD box set is potentially misleading because Welles never completed any version of this film. (Whether or not this set can be considered "complete" in its incompleteness is a separate matter, but since I worked on it in several capacities, I'm not the best person to judge.) According to François Thomas's six-page, twelve-year chronology, included in the package, the film was shot entirely in 1954; however, the comment that the film was snatched out of Welles's hands in early 1955 seems oversimplified, given the mercurial relations be-

tween Welles and his producer (and onetime friend and mentor) Louis Dolivet—although the fact that Welles then lost control of the editing is irrefutable.

We also know that a version of CONFIDENTIAL REPORT opened in London in August 1955 and then went through further revisions (including loss of the flashback structure) before opening elsewhere in 1956, that a very different Spanish version called MR. ARKADIN opened in Madrid in November 1955, and that an "early, temporary version called MR ARKADIN (without the period)" opened in New York almost seven years later. The digital restorations on the American box set include the 1956 version of CONFIDENTIAL REPORT, some scenes from the Spanish version, the MR ARKADIN that opened in New York, and a new version edited by two archivists, Stefan Drössler and Claude Bertemes, drawing from and choosing between elements from all the available versions and materials. And apart from this collection, the surviving versions on film, VHS, and DVD are mainly inferior public domain versions, the 1956 CONFIDENTIAL REPORT, or the 1962 MR ARKADIN. (As of this writing, a print held in London's National Film Archive that may be one of the 1955 versions has apparently not yet been checked.)

15. In the spring of 1955, Welles presented six weekly 15-minute "talking-head" programs on BBC TV titled ORSON WELLES'S SKETCH BOOK, all of which survive on either 35mm or 16mm film. None is available commercially on VHS or DVD, though excerpts have turned up in several Welles documentaries (e.g., IT'S ALL TRUE: BASED ON AN UNFINISHED FILM BY ORSON WELLES).

16. Later the same year, Welles shot about 75 minutes of his celebrated London stage production *Moby Dick—Rehearsed* at the Hackney Empire and Scala theaters in London (with the same cast in both settings), with plans to sell it to the American TV show *Omnibus*, but stopped filming when he found the results unsatisfactory. Rumors have persisted about this footage possibly still existing somewhere (I once received a long distance phone call from Christopher Lee, one of the cast members, about it), but in recent years I have encountered no evidence of it having survived.

17. Around this time, Welles planned another TV series for British commercial television and possible American syndication, AROUND THE WORLD WITH ORSON WELLES, produced by Louis Dolivet. The shot material was used in seven separate episodes, all shown in Europe (though none were shown in the U.S.), six of which survive. (It is not yet clear which of these, if any, were edited by Welles.) The seventh, called THE THIRD MAN IN VIENNA, originally survived in a single print that was reportedly borrowed by the late Maurice Bessy and never returned. The remaining six—THE BASQUE COUNTRIES, LE PELOTE BASQUE (which recycles some material from the preceding), ST.-GERMAIN-DES-PRES, THE QUEEN'S PENSIONERS, BULLFIGHTING IN SPAIN (with Kenneth Tynan), and THE DOMINICI AFFAIR (unfinished)—are currently available in the U.S. on two DVDs and two videos: AROUND THE WORLD WITH ORSON WELLES (134 minutes) and THE DOMINICI AFFAIR (52 minutes); the latter is a documentary by Christophe Cognet that includes a restoration of the materials Welles shot as well as some speculation about what he intended to add. (There is some evidence that French censorship may have played a part in his abandoning this episode.)

18. Three half-hour TV pilots are known to have been shot and completed by Welles in the middle to late 50s, two of which survive. The one that appears not to have survived, made with the $5,000 Welles received for appearing on *I Love Lucy* in 1956, was CAMILLE, THE NAKED LADY, AND THE MUSKETEERS, about the Dumas family; Welles's friend and sometime collaborator Fletcher Markle (1921–1991), one of the few people who saw it, wrote me a letter about it in 1987 that I quote from on pages 534–535 of *This Is Orson Welles*. The most ambitious of these pilots, THE FOUNTAIN OF YOUTH (1958), which I'm far from alone in considering a major Welles work, was produced by Desilu and has allegedly remained commercially unavailable due to rights issues, though others have suggested that the studio personnel involved simply can't be bothered with clearing those rights. It has been shown on 35mm or 16mm at various Welles tributes and conferences. The third, known variously as POR-TRAIT OF GINA and VIVA ITALIA!, was shot in Italy, and after it was re-

jected by American television (accounts differ as to whether ABC or CBS sponsored it), Welles left the only copy behind in his hotel room at the Ritz in Paris. Almost 30 years later, in 1986, the film was discovered in a lost and found department, excerpted on French TV, and then shown at the Venice film festival, at which time Gina Lollobrigida placed a legal injunction on the film to prevent further showings—although it was subsequently shown at least once again on German TV. Its current whereabouts and legal status are unknown to me.

19. Technically, TOUCH OF EVIL (1958) qualifies as another unfinished film completed by the studio after Welles was taken off the project, although in this case he was removed from the editing and other postproduction work at a relatively late stage. As with ARKADIN, several versions survive—most notably the original 93-minute release version; a 108-minute preview cut that Universal rediscovered in the mid-70s, which then supplanted the shorter version; and a 112-minute re-edited and remixed version (1998) produced by Rick Schmidlin and edited by Walter Murch, on which I served as consultant—erroneously described as a director's cut, though based on a lengthy memo written by Welles to Universal in 1958. Lamentably, Universal has chosen to make this the only version that's commercially available today, although it was the hope of Schmidlin, Murch, and myself that all three versions could be released in a single box set.

20. During the run of the Dublin stage version of *Chimes at Midnight* in early 1960, Welles filmed a solo reading of *Moby Dick—Rehearsed* followed by a question and answer session with the audience, in 16mm. Only 18 minutes of the discussion have survived with sound, and in 2002, the Munich Film Archives restored this segment as ORSON WELLES ON STAGE IN DUBLIN.

21. THE TRIAL (1962, 119 minutes) was Welles's first completed feature after OTHELLO on which he had final cut. Since this film fell into public domain, many copies available on video and DVD have been incomplete and unreliable in terms of quality, although apparently complete copies are still available in the U.S. and elsewhere.

22. In 1964, in order to raise money for DON QUIXOTE and continue shooting portions of the film with Akim Tamiroff in Spain, Welles shot an eight-episode miniseries for Italian TV called NELLA TERRA DI DON CHISCIOTTE, consisting basically of touristic home movies featuring himself, his wife Paola Mori, and his daughter Beatrice traveling through Spain. Seven of the episodes, each lasting about 25 minutes, aired on RAI in late 1964 and early 1965. The version edited by Welles had no narration, but the version that aired added one in Italian that Welles had nothing to do with. A restoration of the original series is currently in the works, to appear on Italian DVDs.

23. Welles also had final cut on CHIMES AT MIDNIGHT (1966, 119 minutes), which was also made in Spain. Rights issues have made this film hard to see in the U.S. in recent years, but imported DVDs aren't difficult to find on the Internet.

24. THE IMMORTAL STORY (1968, 58 minutes). Welles's first completed color film is another title that's been scarce in the U.S. and somewhat easier to see in Europe. The only DVD version I'm aware of at present is Italian and includes both the English and French versions, but not Welles's final cut of either.

25. ORSON'S BAG (unfinished, 1968–1973). A color TV special of many parts, portions of which were shot in 35mm and 16mm, and some of which have been restored by the Munich Film Archives in recent years, despite their missing parts. It appears that ORSON WELLES' LONDON (29 minutes, five sequences, excerpted in OWTOMB) was finished at one point, but portions of the soundtrack were lost in the early 70s; ORSON WELLES' VIENNA (8 minutes, excerpted in OWTOMB), also known as SPYING IN VIENNA, is unfinished; a 40-minute condensation of THE MERCHANT OF VENICE (1969, also excerpted in OWTOMB) was completed, but the soundtrack of two of the three reels was stolen in Rome, and has not been recovered. In the early 70s, Welles also filmed various takes of his performance of the most famous of Shylock's monologues in outdoor locations—excerpted in OWTOMB and held by the Munich Film Archives.

26. ORSON WELLES' MOBY DICK. The posthumous title given by the Munich Film Archives to its 2000 restoration of 22 minutes of color

16mm footage of Welles, under watery, speckled lighting, reciting various passages from his own play *Moby Dick—Rehearsed*, shot by Gary Graver in France. A few excerpts are in OWTOMB.

27. THE DEEP (unfinished, 1967–1973). This adaptation of Charles Williams's *Dead Calm*, a thriller set on two boats and filmed in color near the Dalmatian coast of former Yugoslavia, was conceived of as a commercial project. However, Welles was apparently forced to abandon the project after he had difficulty in getting Jeanne Moreau to postdub her dialogue. (A more scaled-down adaptation of the novel, DEAD CALM, directed by Phillip Noyce from a Terry Hayes script, with Nicole Kidman, Sam Neill, and Billy Zane, was released in 1989.) It appears that most of the Welles film was edited at one point, but the rough cut was lost, possibly due in part to unpaid lab bills (a recurring problem with some of Welles's long-range projects), and the restoration of what remains by the Munich Film Archives, including some portions with "live" dialogue (recorded as a guide for future dubbing) and some portions that remain silent, remains a patchy work in progress. (A 17-minute sampler was put together in 2001.) Probably the most interesting unsolved mystery in the footage is what appears to be several dream sequences, with no clear indications of where or how Welles intended to use them. A trailer that Welles prepared for the film at one point is included on OWTOMB.

28. F FOR FAKE (completed, color, 88 minutes). Apparently finished in 1972, this film didn't premiere until September 1974 at the New York and San Sebastian film festivals, over two years before it opened commercially in the U.S. People who regard this as Welles's "last" completed feature are obviously, for some reason, exempting the 16mm FILMING OTHELLO, which was completed seven years later. Neither a documentary nor a fiction film in any pure sense (see chapter 25), this film, to the best of my knowledge, is one of the four features on which Welles had final cut that have never been issued in another version. (The other three are CITIZEN KANE, CHIMES AT MIDNIGHT, and FILMING OTHELLO.)

29. F FOR FAKE TRAILER (completed, 9 minutes, 1976). Made over a two-and-a-half-week period in December 1976, in anticipation of the U.S.

release of F FOR FAKE, and consisting almost entirely of new material, this trailer was rejected by the U.S. distributor, who refused to process it. It survives today only in work print form, and possibly only in black and white video. (It can be found in this form in OWTOMB and on the American DVD box set of F FOR FAKE.)

30. A CONVERSATION WITH ROGER HILL, HORTENSE HILL, AND ORSON WELLES (shot in 16mm color, approximately 60 minutes). As part of a projected film, ORSON WELLES SOLO, developed over several years, Welles got Gary Graver to shoot an extended conversation between himself, his mentor Roger Hill, and Hill's wife, Hortense, in June 1978. (Welles is only heard, but the elderly couple are seen.) This material is held by the Munich Film Archives on film and video and by Todd Tarbox, the Hills's grandson, on video.

31. THE ORSON WELLES SHOW (completed, 74 minutes, color video, 1978). A pilot for a TV variety show featuring Welles with Burt Reynolds; Jim Henson, Frank Oz, and the Muppets; Lynn Redgrave; Patrick Terrail; Angie Dickinson; and Roger Hill. This material was carefully rehearsed—though designed to look spontaneous—and submitted to Greg Garrison and probably other producers, but never sold or aired. The Munich Film Archives holds a copy.

32. FILMING OTHELLO (completed, 84 minutes, 16mm, color, 1979). Made for West German television, this documentary about the making of Welles's OTHELLO has remained unavailable in the U.S.—the U.S. rights are held by Oja Kodar—due to legal threats by Beatrice Welles, who retains the world rights of OTHELLO (see no. 12).

33. FILMING THE TRIAL (1981, shot but unedited, color, 16mm). Welles planned a documentary about making THE TRIAL—a companion piece to FILMING OTHELLO (see no. 32) that got no further than filming an 82-minute discussion with an American audience in Los Angeles. A few excerpts are included in OWTOMB.

34. DON QUIXOTE (unfinished). This project's earliest known stage was color tests shot in Paris with Mischa Auer and Akim Tamiroff in 1955, financed by Louis Dolivet. The latest stage I'm aware of is Welles's mentioning to Bill Krohn in a phone interview (February 18 and 19, 1982) his plans to return to Spain "sometime in the next

couple of years," to finish QUIXOTE as an essay film. In 1972, he told me the film was virtually finished apart from some sound work, and his former assistant Audrey Stainton in the Autumn 1988 issue of *Sight and Sound* has suggested that this might have been true. My own hypothesis is that the film was made and unmade several times according to different plans (see chapter 26), and that the most disastrous unmaking, by far—not just of QUIXOTE, but of any Welles film to date—is in fact the only version of DON QUIXOTE that's commercially available and purports to be finished—namely, the version hurriedly edited by Jesus Franco in time for Spain's Expo 92. This version is currently available from various sources on film, video, and DVD (although it thankfully hasn't been commercially released in the U.S.). An atrocity on every level, this film draws indiscriminately from NELLA TERRA DI DON CHISCIOTTE as if that and QUIXOTE were indistinguishable, mixes Welles's own dubbed voice with the voices of many others enlisted by Franco to play the same characters, and alters shots by Welles with added zooms and clumsy mattes while using what appear to be poor copies throughout, meanwhile omitting all the material with Patty McCormack.

Legal disputes are still being waged over this film—especially involving the McCormack footage and other materials said to probably be the best available in terms of both visual quality and Welles's editing— held by Welles's former editor Mauro Bonnani in Rome. A contract was reportedly signed in 2005 for Bonnani to prepare a version of this material for the Venice International film festival, and the reasons for Bonnani's nondelivery so far remain obscure. (He speaks only Italian, and it appears that his statements to the press are infrequent.) Spending some time looking at the QUIXOTE material held by the Filmoteca in Madrid, I lamentably found little more than the wreckage left by Franco, although I've been told that the original negatives of this material are housed in Barcelona and reportedly remain intact. A few scenes, mainly silent and roughly edited, are held by the Cinémathèque Française.

35.   THE DREAMERS (unfinished; material mainly in color). One of Welles's most cherished late projects, worked on between 1978 and

1985, this is adapted from two Isak Dinesen stories. The Munich Film Archive restored and put together a 24-minute film from the available material in 2002; several excerpts are also available on OWTOMB (see no. 38).

36. THE MAGIC SHOW (incomplete, 35mm and 16mm, color and black and white material, 1969–1985). Shot piecemeal in Atlanta, Los Angeles, and Orvilliers (France), this mixture of a history of stage magic, farce, and various stage presentations of magic (all performed without camera tricks) featuring Welles and young magician Abb Dickson was a project Welles intended at times to integrate with ORSON WELLES SOLO (see no. 30). Welles shot and edited over half an hour of material for a film that was reportedly meant to be about twice as long. Most of this material is held by the Munich Film Archives, which put together a 27-minute compilation in 2000 that it has since expanded; other portions and some script elements are held by Dickson. Excerpts are included in OWTOMB (see no. 38).

37. THE OTHER SIDE OF THE WIND. The unseen Welles feature with the most complicated legal history, this project was shot in the U.S. and France between 1970 and 1976 and partially edited. Reportedly all but a handful of shots were filmed, but accounts of how much of the footage was edited by Welles differ. The film's producer, Dominique Antoine, maintains having once seen a two-hour rough cut, but Oja Kodar (who coauthored the script, appears in the film, thought up the film's title, as she did for F FOR FAKE, and even designed and directed one sequence in the film) and Gary Graver, the cinematographer, have claimed more recently that only 40 minutes were fully edited by Welles. Various attempts have been made over the past few years to produce a final version of the film for the cable channel Showtime, but Kodar, to whom Welles willed most of the rights, has been unwilling as coauthor to risk losing final cut and has said that all contracts offered to her so far have allowed for that possibility. (Postscript: As this book was going to press, this obstacle has apparently been overcome.)

38. ORSON WELLES: THE ONE-MAN BAND. This 1995 documentary "made possible by Oja Kodar," written by Vassili Silovic and Roland Zag,

and directed by Silovic, is most readily available in the American F FOR FAKE DVD box set. An alternate version that includes clips from Welles's better-known films (such as CITIZEN KANE and THE LADY FROM SHANGHAI) and reduces the clips from lesser-known films was prepared and hosted by Peter Bogdanovich for American cable television.

Index

323

Text:	10/14 Palatino
Display:	Palatino; Runic
Compositor:	Binghamton Valley Composition, LLC
Printer and Binder:	Maple-Vail Manufacturing Group